The
HIDDEN PLACES
of
YORKSHIRE

Edited by
David Gerrard

ii

Published by:
Travel Publishing Ltd
7a Apollo House, Calleva Park
Aldermaston, Berks, RG7 8TN

ISBN 1-902-00742-5
© Travel Publishing Ltd

First Published:	1990	Fourth Edition:	1998
Second Edition:	1993	Fifth Edition:	2000
Third Edition:	1995		

Regional Titles in the Hidden Places Series:

Cambridgeshire & Lincolnshire	Channel Islands
Cheshire	Chilterns
Cornwall	Derbyshire
Devon	Dorset, Hants & Isle of Wight
Essex	Gloucestershire & Wiltshire
Heart of England	Hereford, Worcs & Shropshire
Highlands & Islands	Kent
Lake District & Cumbria	Lancashire
Norfolk	Northeast Yorkshire
Northumberland & Durham	North Wales
Nottinghamshire	Potteries
Somerset	South Wales
Suffolk	Surrey
Sussex	Thames Valley
Warwickshire & W Midlands	Yorkshire

National Titles in the Hidden Places Series:

England	Ireland
Scotland	Wales

Printing by: Ashford Press, Gosport
Maps by: © MAPS IN MINUTES ™ (2000)
Line Drawings: Sarah Bird
Editor: David Gerrard
Cover Design: Lines & Words, Aldermaston
Cover Photographs: River Swale from Richmond Castle; Whitby Harbour, Abbey and
St Mary's Church; Abbeydale Industrial Hamlet, Sheffield.
© Britain on View/Stockwave.

FOREWORD

The Hidden Places series is a collection of easy to use travel guides taking you, in this instance, on a relaxed but informative tour of Yorkshire. Yorkshire is the largest and most scenically diverse county in England. In the northwest are the picturesque Dales with the varied scenery of peat moorland, green pastureland and scattered woods intersected by the numerous streams and rivers. To the northeast are the imposing Yorkshire Moors, the rich agricultural Vale of York, the chalky hills of the Wolds and the dramatic storm-tossed coastline. To the south are the industrial and commercial cities and towns which have made such a major contribution to our industrial and cultural heritage.

Our books contain a wealth of interesting information on the history, the countryside, the towns and villages and the more established places of interest in the county. But they also promote the more secluded and little known visitor attractions and places to stay, eat and drink many of which are easy to miss unless you know exactly where you are going.

We include hotels, inns, restaurants, public houses, teashops, various types of accommodation, historic houses, museums, gardens, garden centres, craft centres and many other attractions throughout Yorkshire, all of which are comprehensively indexed. Most places have an attractive line drawing and are cross-referenced to coloured maps found at the rear of the book. We do not award merit marks or rankings but concentrate on describing the more interesting, unusual or unique features of each place with the aim of making the reader's stay in the local area an enjoyable and stimulating experience.

Whether you are visiting the area for business or pleasure or in fact are living in the county we do hope that you enjoy reading and using this book. We are always interested in what readers think of places covered (or not covered) in our guides so please do not hesitate to use the reader reaction forms provided to give us your considered comments. We also welcome any general comments which will help us improve the guides themselves. Finally if you are planning to visit any other corner of the British Isles we would like to refer you to the list of other *Hidden Places* titles to be found at the rear of the book.

CONTENTS

1 North York Moors, Heritage Coast & Vale of Pickering

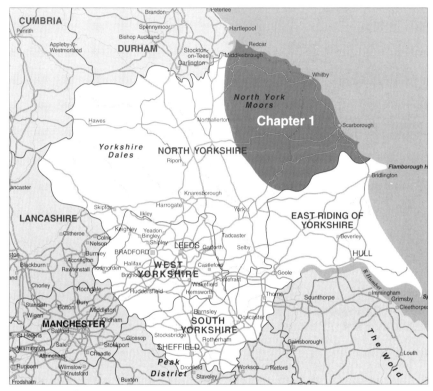

© MAPS IN MINUTES ™ (1998)

THE NORTH YORK MOORS

Some forty miles across and about twenty miles deep, the North York Moors encompass a remarkable diversity of scenery. There are great rolling swathes of moorland rising to 1400ft above sea level, stark and inhospitable in winter, still wild and romantic in summer, and softened only in early Autumn when they are mantled by a purple haze of flowering heather. Almost one fifth of the area is woodland, most of it managed by Forest Enterprise which has established many picnic sites and forest drives. Settlements are few and far between: indeed, there may have been more people living here in the Bronze Age (1500-500 BC) than there are now to judge by the more than 3000 'howes', or burial mounds, that have been discovered. (The climate was much warmer and drier then).

Also scattered across these uplands is a remarkable collection of medieval stone crosses. There are more than thirty of them and one, the **Lilla Cross,** is reckoned to be the oldest Christian monument in northern England. It commemorates the warrior Lilla who in AD626 died protecting his King, Edwin, from an assassin's dagger. Most of them have names - such as Fat Betty which has a stumpy base surmounted by the top of a wheelhead cross. Perhaps the finest of these monuments is **Ralph Cross**, high on Westerdale Moor. It stands nine feet tall at almost precisely the geographical centre of the moors and has been adopted by the North York Moors National Park as its emblem.

Wild as they look, the moors are actually cultivated land, or perhaps managed by fire is the better term. Each year, gamekeepers burn off patches of the old heather in carefully limited areas called 'swiddens' or 'swizzens'. The new growth that soon appears is a crucial resource for the red grouse which live only in heather moorland, eat little else but heather and find these young green shoots particularly appetising. The older heather that remains provides the birds with protective cover during their nesting season.

Gisborough Priory, Guisborough

Just as the Yorkshire Dales have large areas of moorland, so the North York Moors have many dales - Eskdale, Ryedale, Farndale, more than a hundred of them in all. They cut deep into the great upland tracts and are as picturesque, soft and pastoral as anywhere in Yorkshire. To the west lies the mighty bulk of the Cleveland Hills; to the east the rugged cliffs of the Heritage Coast. This is marvellously unspoilt countryside, a happy state of affairs that has come about as a result of the Moors being designated a National Park in 1952, a status which severely restricts any development that would adversely affect either its natural or man-made beauty.

Two spectacularly scenic railways wind their way through this enchanting landscape. Both of them provide a satisfying and environmentally friendly way of exploring this comparatively 'undiscovered' area, anciently known as 'Blackamor'. The Middlesbrough to Whitby route, called the **Esk Valley Line**, runs from west to east following the course of the river Esk and passing through a succession of delightful villages. The vintage steam locomotives of the **North York Moors Railway** start at Pickering and run northwards for 18 miles through Newtondale to join the Esk Valley Line at Grosmont. The dramatic route through this glacial channel was originally engineered by George Stephenson himself. During the season, the Moors Railway runs special Pullman Dining Coaches for either dinner or Sunday lunch - a memorable experience. A very popular excursion is to take the train to Newtondale Halt and then follow one of the waymarked walks that range from easy trails to longer walks for the more adventurous. Alternatively, the Forestry Commission's **Newtondale Forest Drive** takes motorists through some splendidly rugged scenery.

ESKDALE

Eskdale is the largest, and one of the loveliest, of the dales within the National Park. It is unusual in that it runs east-west, the Esk being the only moorland river that doesn't find its way to the Humber. Instead, the river winds tortuously through the dale to join the sea beneath the picturesque cliffs at Whitby. Along the way, many smaller dales branch off to the north and south - Fryup, Danby, Glaisdale - while even narrower ones can only be explored on foot. The Esk is famed for its salmon fishing, but permits are required. These can be obtained from the local branches of the National Rivers Authority. Walkers will appreciate the **Esk Valley Walk**, a group of ten linking walks which traverse the length of the valley.

DANBY
MAP 3 REF J3

10½ miles W of Whitby off the A171

A visit to **The Moors Centre** at Danby Lodge provides an excellent introduction to the North York Moors National Park. The Centre is housed in a former shooting lodge and set in 13 acres of riverside, meadow, woodland, formal gardens and picnic areas. Visitors can either wander on their own along the waymarked woodland walks and nature trails or join one of the frequent guided walks. Inside the Lodge various exhibits interpret the natural and local history of the moors, there's a bookshop stocked with a wide range of books, maps and guides, and a Tea Room serving refreshments.

Downstream from The Moors Centre is a narrow medieval packhorse bridge, one of three to be found in Eskdale. This one is known as **Duck Bridge** but the name has nothing to do with aquatic birds. It was originally called Castle Bridge but re-named after an 18th century benefactor, George Duck, a wealthy mason who paid for the bridge to be repaired. To the south of Duck Bridge are the remains of **Danby Castle**, now a private farmhouse and not open to the public. Built in the 14th century, and originally much larger, it was once the home of Catherine Parr, the sixth wife of Henry VIII. In Elizabethan times, the justices met here and the Danby Court Leet and Baron, which administers the common land and rights of way over the 11,000 acres of the Danby Estate, still meets here every year in the throne room. One of the court's responsibilities is issuing licences for the gathering of sphagnum moss, a material once used for stuffing mattresses but now more commonly required for flower arranging.

CASTLETON
MAP 3 REF J3

10 miles W of Whitby off the A171

Spread across the hillside above the River Esk, Castleton is a charming village which at one time was the largest settlement in Eskdale. It still has a weekly market and a station on the scenic **Esk Valley railway** that runs between Whitby and Middlesbrough. Its amber-coloured **Church of St Michael and St George** was built in memory of the men who fell in World War I and inside there is some fine work by Robert Thompson, the famous "Mouseman of Kilburn". The benches, organ screen and panelling at each side of the altar all bear his distinctive 'signature' of a crouching mouse.

LEALHOLM
Map 3 ref J3

9 miles W of Whitby off the A171

From The Moors Centre at Danby a scenic minor road winds along the Esk Valley and brings you to the attractive village of Lealholm, its houses clustering around a 250 year old bridge over the Esk. A short walk leads to some picturesque stepping stones across the river. A much-travelled foreign journalist remarked, "Elsewhere, you have to go in search of beautiful views; here, they come and offer themselves to be looked at". On one of the stone houses, now a tea room and restaurant, a carved inscription reads "Loyal Order of Ancient Shepherds" together with the date 1873 in Roman numerals. The Loyal Order ran their lodge on the lines of a men-only London club but their annual procession through the village and the subsequent festivities were one of the highlights of the autumn. In recent years, Lealholm has become very popular with naturalists who come to study the wealth of trees, ferns, flowers and rare plants in the deep, dramatic ravine known as **Crunkley Gill**. Sadly, the ravine is privately owned and not open to the public.

GLAISDALE
Map 3 ref J4

8 miles W of Whitby off the A171

From Lealholm a country lane leads to Glaisdale, another picturesque village set at the foot of a narrow dale beside the River Esk with **Arncliffe Woods** a short walk away. The ancient stone bridge here was built around 1620 by Thomas Ferris, Mayor of Hull. As an impoverished young man he had lived in Glaisdale and fell in love with Agnes Richardson, the squire's daughter. To see Agnes, he had to wade or swim across the river and he swore that if he prospered in life he would build a bridge here. Fortunately, he joined a ship which sailed against the Spanish Armada and captured a galleon laden with gold. Tom returned

Beggar's Bridge, Glaisdale

to Glaisdale a rich man, married Agnes and later honoured his promise by building what has always been called the **Beggar's Bridge**.

Surrounded by magnificent open moorland, **Postgate Farm** is a small working sheep farm situated just over a mile from Glaisdale village and offering top quality farmhouse bed and breakfast. Parts of the lovely old farmhouse, a Grade II listed building, date back to the 1600s and the interior contains many olde worlde features such as a vintage salt box by the fire and a witch post dated 1664. The house and farm have been in John and

Mary Thompson's family for more than 300 years. Today, the guest facilities they provide in this delightful house which enjoys a 4-diamond Tourist Board rating include a private sitting room with TV, a dining room and a small private kitchen suitable for making up picnics, hot drinks and snacks. Visitors also have the use of a microwave oven and a fridge/freezer and there's a separate games room with a snooker/pool table, table tennis, and darts board. The sleeping accommodation at Postgate Farm comprises 1 large double

Postgate Farm, Glaisdale, Whitby, North Yorkshire YO21 2PZ Tel/Fax: 01947 897353 e-mail: j-m.thompson.bandb@talk21.com

room with en suite shower; another large double with en suite shower and bath and a four-poster bed; and a twin room with en suite bath. Tea and coffee-making facilities are provided and in each bedroom there's a TV, hair dryer and radio/alarm clock. Also available at the farm is a self-catering studio flat sleeping 2 people.

EGTON BRIDGE

7 miles SW of Whitby off the A171

MAP 3 REF K3

This little village tucked around a bend in the River Esk plays host each year to the famous **Gooseberry Show.** Established in 1800, the show is held on the first Tuesday in August. It attracts entrants from all over the world who bring prize specimens in an attempt to beat the current record of 2.18oz. for a single berry. The village is dominated by the massive **Church of St Hedda** built in 1866. It has a dazzling roof painted blue with gold stars and the altar incorporates some distinguished Belgian terracotta work. Appropriately, St Hedda's is a Roman Catholic church since it was at Egton Bridge that the martyr Nicholas Postgate was born in 1596. He was ordained as a priest in France but returned to the moors to minister to those still loyal to the outlawed Catholic faith. He travelled disguised as a jobbing gardener and eluded capture for many years but was finally betrayed for a reward of £20. He was 81 years old when he was hung, drawn and quartered at York. A sad story to be associated with such a delightful village.

Situated on the bank of the River Esk, the **Horse Shoe Hotel** is a charming, well kept village inn dating back to the 18th century and offering a fine range of ales, food and accommodation. The proprietors of this free house are Sue and Tim Boulton who have created a really homely and welcoming atmosphere in this very well presented hostelry. Immediately striking is its neatness and old world style. Good quality home cooked food is available either from the bar snack menu or in the dining room where traditional English dishes are served as well as more exotic cuisine. The menus are complemented by an excellent wine list. The Horse Shoe is a popular venue so it's a good idea to book ahead for weekend meals. In good weather, you can enjoy your meal in the delightful beer garden beside a stream where you can relax and watch the ducks and geese busying themselves with their daily tasks. If your favourite pastime is fishing, that too can be arranged. Bed and breakfast accommodation is also available here - and what a lovely place to stay. There

**Horse Shoe Hotel, Egton Bridge, Whitby,
North Yorkshire YO21 1XE Tel: 01947 895245**

are 6 guest bedrooms, some with en suite facilities and all of them attractively furnished and decorated.

EGTON

6 miles SW of Whitby off the A171

Map 3 ref K3

Surrounded by the unspoilt countryside of Esk Dale, **Flushing Meadow** offers quality bed and breakfast accommodation in an attractive modern house, the home of Stella and Trevor Johnson. They have 3 guest rooms, one en suite double, and a twin and single which share a bathroom, all of them enjoying lovely views. Guests at Flushing Meadow have the use of a TV lounge which, like the rest of the house, is non-smoking. A full English breakfast is included in the tariff and although evening meals are not available, Stella and Trevor can direct you to one of the many good eating places in the neighbourhood. The name "Flushing Meadow", incidentally, is very ancient and is found

**Flushing Meadow, Egton, Whitby,
North Yorkshire YO21 1UA Tel: 01947 895395
e-mail: flushing_meadow_egton@yahoo.co.uk**

on old maps of the area. It denotes small pieces of lush pasture where the tups graze before being put in with the ewes for the purpose of mating. The rich grass was said to raise fertility levels!

CENTRAL MOORS

The area around Goathland provides some of the wildest scenery in the National Park. Murk Mire Moor, Black Rigg, Howl Moor - the very names conjure up the rigours of these upland tracts where heather reigns supreme. Even those who know the moors well treat its sudden mists and savage storms with respect. The historian of the area, Joseph Ford, recollected hearing as a child of an itinerant trader who travelled the moorland paths selling bottle corks to farmers' wives. During one particularly severe winter it was re-marked that he had not paid his usual calls. The following autumn a skeleton was found on Wintergill Moor: the unfortunate victim was only "identified by the scattered bottle corks lying nearby". As Ford noted, "the story was not unusual".

It's a very different picture in the narrow dales that cleave their way down to the rivers. The sheltered villages here are as pretty as any in the better known western dales.

GOATHLAND   MAP 3 REF K4
8 miles SW of Whitby off the A169

Goathland today is perhaps best known as 'Aidensfield' - the main location for the television series "Heartbeat". This attractive village 500ft up on the moors, where old stone houses are scattered ran-

Goathland Station, Goathland

houses are scattered ran-domly around spacious sheep-groomed greens, was popular long before televi-sion. Earlier visitors mostly came in order to see **Mallyan Spout**, a 70ft high waterfall locked into a cres-cent of rocks and trees. They were also interested in Goathland's rugged church and the odd memorial in its graveyard to William Jefferson and his wife. The couple died in 1923 within a few days of each other, at the ages of 80 and 79, and chose to have their final resting place marked by an enormous anchor.

In the award-winning **Goathland Exhibition Centre** you'll find a full ex-planation of the curious tradition of the **Plough Stots Service**, performed at Goathland every January. It's an ancient ritual for greeting the new year which originated with the Norsemen who settled here more than a thousand years ago. "Stots" is the Scandinavian word for the bullocks which would drag a plough through the village, followed by dancers brandishing 30-inch swords. This pagan rite is still faithfully observed but with the difference that nowadays Goathland's young men have replaced the "stots" in the plough harness. The Exhibition Centre can also provide you with information about the many walks in the area and guide you to one of the oldest thoroughfares in the country, **Wade's Way.** If you believe the legend, it was built by a giant of that name, but it is actually a remarkably well-preserved stretch of Roman road.

Just outside Goathland, **Whitfield House Hotel** is a family-run hotel that has been in the same family for 20 years. Occupying a scenic and peaceful position, this handsome hotel was once a farmhouse, and dates back to 1650. It has been a hotel since 1907. Much of its original character and charm
has been retained,
and the atmos-
phere is homely
and relaxing. This
welcoming estab-
lishment boasts 9
individually-styled
guest bedrooms, all
en suite. Varying in
size from single to
family rooms, each
is comfortable and
attractive. There is
also a lovely guests'
lounge and distinc-

**Whitfield House Hotel, Darnholm, Goathland,
North Yorkshire YO22 5LA Tel: 01947 896215**

tive lounge bar in which to relax. The standard of service is high and the full English breakfasts and table d'hote and a la carte menus offer the very best in country cooking and make use of the freshest local produce. A hotel for all seasons, it is open all year round, with special out of season breaks (November to March) available.

BECK HOLE

7 miles SW of Whitby off the A169

Map 3 ref K4

A mile or so up the dale from Goathland is the pretty little hamlet of Beck Hole. When the North Yorkshire Moors Railway was constructed in the 1830s, (designed by no less an engineer than George Stephenson himself), the trains were made up of stage coaches placed on top of simple bogies and pulled by horses. At Beck Hole, however, there was a 1 in 15 incline up to Goathland so the carriages had to be hauled by a complicated system of ropes and water-filled tanks. (Charles Dickens was an early passenger on this route and wrote a hair-raising description of his journey). The precipitous incline caused many accidents so, in 1865, a "Deviation Line" was blasted through solid rock. The gradient is still one of the steepest in the country at 1 in 49, but it opened up this route to steam trains. The original 1 in 15 incline is now a footpath, so modern walkers will understand the effort needed to get themselves to the summit, let alone a fully laden carriage.

Every year, this little village plays host to the **World Quoits Championship**. The game, which appears to have originated in Eskdale, involves throwing a small iron hoop over an iron pin set about 25 feet away. Appropriately enough, one of the houses on the green has a quoit serving as a door knocker. On the hillside, a mile or so to the west of Beck Hole, is the curiously-named **Randy Mere**, the last place in England where leeches were gathered commercially. An elderly resident of Goathland in 1945 recalled how as a young man he had waded into the lake and emerged in minutes with the slug-like creatures firmly attached to his skin. For those interested, the leeches are still there.

LOCKTON
4 miles NE of Pickering on the A169

MAP 3 REF K5

About 3 miles north of Lockton, the **Hole of Horcum** is a huge natural amphitheatre which, so the story goes, was scooped out of Levisham Moor by the giant Wade and is now a popular centre for hang gliders. Lockton village itself is set high above a deep ravine and here you'll find the famous **Fox & Rabbit Inn**, set back from the main Pickering to Whitby road and enjoying grand views over the North York Moors. Howard Roberts and his son Greg took over this Free House in July 1999 and have built on the inn's excellent reputation for quality food. Greg is a qualified chef and his menus offer a varied choice of traditional dishes, available at lunchtimes and evenings every day. The restau-

Fox & Rabbit Inn, Lockton, Pickering, North Yorkshire YO18 7NQ
Tel: 01751 460213

rant seats 60 people but such is its popularity it's a good idea to make a booking if you are visiting during the season, especially if you want to sample Greg's superb Sunday roast. Howard, a former chairman of Newbridge Rugby Union Club, is a genial host and the wide range of well-kept ales he stocks includes Camerons Creamy, Banks, John Smiths, 2 draught lagers and cider. If you are anywhere in the North York Moors area, the Fox & Rabbit is well worth making a lengthy detour to visit.

APPLETON-LE-MOORS
5 miles NW of Pickering off the A170

MAP 3 REF J5

Located just inside the southern boundary of the Moors National Park, Appleton-le-Moors is noted for its fine church whose tower and spire provide a landmark for miles around. It was built in Victorian times to a design by J. L. Pearson, the architect of Truro Cathedral, and it has the same Gothic style as the Cornish cathedral.

Applegarth stands on the main street of this picturesque village and has been owned by Mrs Wilson's family since the 1880s. It was first let as self-catering accommodation in

1982 and some of the guests who stayed that season still return year after year. Applegarth has two bedrooms, (1 double and 1 single), and the comfortably furnished, well equipped house feels like a real home from home. Outside, there's a lovely, long garden and orchard, a soothing place to settle down on a fine afternoon with a good book. Mrs Wilson lives next door at Rose Cottage and is always on hand to give any assistance you might require.

Bookings through Mrs A. Wilson, Rose Cottage, Appleton-le-Moors, York, North Yorkshire YO62 6TF Tel: 01751 417588

Everything you could possibly need is included in the tariff apart from bed linen, towels and electricity, which is charged by meter reading. Appleton-le-Moors is ideally located for exploring the North York Moors, while historic Castle Howard and the popular seaside resort of Scarborough are both just a short drive away.

HUTTON-LE-HOLE   MAP 3 REF J5
10 miles NW of Pickering off the A170

Long regarded as one of Yorkshire's prettiest villages, Hutton-le-Hole has a character all of its own. "It is all up and down" wrote Arthur Mee, visiting half a century ago, "with a hurrying stream winding among houses scattered here and there, standing at all angles". Fifty years on, little has changed.

Facing the green is the **Ryedale Folk Museum**, an imaginative celebration of 4,000 years of life in North Yorkshire. Amongst the thirteen historic buildings is a complete Elizabethan Manor House rescued from nearby Harome and reconstructed here; a medieval crofter's cottage with a thatched, hipped roof, peat fire and garth; and the old village Shop and Post Office fitted out as it would have looked just after Elizabeth II's Coronation in 1953. Other exhibits include workshops of traditional crafts such as tinsmiths, coopers and wheelwrights, and an Edward-

Ryedale Folk Museum. Hutton-le-Hole

ian photographic studio. The National Park has an Information Centre here and throughout the year there are special events such as a Rare Breeds Day and re-enactments of Civil War battles by the Sealed Knot.

Anyone interested in unusual churches should make the short trip from Hutton-le-Hole to **St Mary's Church, Lastingham**, about three miles to the east. The building of a monastery here in the 7th century was recorded by no less an authority than the Venerable Bede who visited Lastingham not long after it was completed. That monastery was rebuilt in 1078 with a massively impressive crypt that is still in place - a claustrophobic space with heavy Norman arches rising from squat round pillars. The church above is equally atmospheric, lit only by a small window at one end.

GILLAMOOR

MAP 3 REF J5

10 miles NW of Pickering off the A170

This pleasant little village is well worth a visit to see its very rare, and very elegant four-faced sundial erected in 1800 and to enjoy the famous **Surprise View**. This is a ravishing panoramic vista of Farndale with the River Dove flowing through the valley far below and white dusty roads climbing the hillside to the heather-covered moors beyond.

Also of interest is the village church which was once the church at Bransdale about six miles away. In the late 1700s, Bransdale Church was in good repair but little used; Gillamoor's was dilapidated but the villagers wanted a place of worship. This was achieved by appointing a single stonemason, James Smith, to remove Bransdale church stone by stone and re-erect it at Gillamoor.

FADMOOR

MAP 3 REF I5

11 miles NW of Pickering off the A170

The tiny village of Fadmoor lies right on the National Park boundary and about 1½ miles north is **Mount Pleasant**, a truly Hidden Place. It's a delightful early 18th century house set back approximately half a mile from the road amongst fields and open moorland, surrounded by picturesque gardens and with a lawn tennis court for relaxation. Bed & breakfast visitors receive a warm and friendly welcome from Mary and Dennis Clarke for whom this delightful house is home. They have just 2 guest bedrooms, both overlooking the lovely garden and both with its own bathroom. The rooms sleep up to 5 people, making Mount Pleasant an ideal place for families: - they can book both rooms and have the "run

Mount Pleasant, Fadmoor, Kirkbymoorside, York YO62 7JJ
Tel: 01751 431579 e-mail: mary@rudland59.freeserve.co.uk
website: www.rudland59.freeserve.co.uk

of the place". The house has a charming atmosphere, with original beams still in place and antique furniture adding to the sense of stepping back in time. Guests have their own dining room and a separate lounge with a roaring log fire - a popular place after a winter's day out on the moors. Evening meals are available if required and the Clarkes have a brochure and menu to send out on request. Mount Pleasant is close to Farndale, the famous "Dale of Daffodils", and Yorkshire's Heritage Coast, the family fun park and zoo, Flamingo Land, and historic houses such as Castle Howard and Duncombe Park are all within easy reach.

CHURCH HOUSES   MAP 3 REF I4
14 miles N of Pickering off the A170

A few miles north of Hutton-le-Hole, the moorland road comes to Lowna set beside the River Dove in one of the Moors most famous beauty spots, **Farndale.** In spring, some six miles of the river banks are smothered in thousands of wild daffodils, a short-stemmed variety whose colours shade from a pale buttercup yellow to a rich orange-gold. According to local tradition, the bulbs were cultivated by monks who used the petals in their medical concoctions. Yorkshire folk often refer to daffodils as Lenten Lilies because of the time of year in which they bloom. The flowers, once mercilessly plundered by visitors, are now protected by law and 2,000 acres of Farndale are designated as a local nature reserve.

Hidden away in Upper Farndale you'll find a superb old country inn with all the charm, character and tradition you could wish for. **Feversham Arms** is set in picturesque surroundings in what is locally known as "Daffodil Valley" because of the stunning display of thousands of flowers each year. This delightful pub has been owned and personally run by Frances for the past eleven years and provides its guests the very best in comfort and hospitality. Offering a well stocked bar, this free house serves cask-brewed ale as well as stout and lager. Fine food prepared by Heather the cook is always available, with bar meals served every lunchtime and evening, and you will wish to enjoy the tra-

**Feversham Arms, Church Houses, Farndale,
North Yorkshire YO6 6LF Tel: 01751 433206**

ditional Yorkshire Sunday Lunch served in the à la carte restaurant. Wake up to superb views of the Farndale countryside from your bedroom window before sitting down and enjoying a full Yorkshire English breakfast in the stone walled and oak beamed dining room. All of the three individually styled and decorated bedrooms have a colour television and tea and coffee making facilities, and comprise of one en suite double, another double and a single.

ROSEDALE ABBEY

MAP 3 REF J4

11 miles NW of Pickering off the A170

To the east of Farndale is another lovely dale, Rosedale, a nine-mile-long steep-sided valley through which runs the River Seven. The largest settlement in the dale is Rosedale Abbey which takes its name from the small nunnery founded here in 1158. Nothing of the old Abbey has survived although some of its stones were recycled to build the village houses. A peaceful village now, Rosedale was once crowded with workers employed in iron-ore mines on the moors. It was said that, such was the shortage of lodgings during the 1870s, "the beds were never cold" as workers from different shifts took turns to sleep in them. The great chimney of the smelting furnace was once a striking landmark on the summit of the moor, but in 1972 it was found to be unsafe and demolished. Its former presence is still recalled at Chimney Bank where a steep and twisting road, with gradients of 1 in 3, leads up to the moor. High on these moors stands **Ralph Cross**, nine feet tall and one of more than thirty such stone crosses dotted across the moors. It was erected in medieval times as a waymark for travellers and when the North York Moors National Park was established in 1952, the Park authorities adopted Ralph Cross as its emblem.

BLAKEY RIDGE

MAP 3 REF J4

15 miles NW of Pickering off the A170

Hidden away in the heart of the moors, **High Blakey House** enjoys stunning panoramic views over the beautiful vale of Rosedale. Apart from the famous Lion Inn just across the road, there are no other houses in sight - a wonderfully quiet and peaceful place to stay for bed and breakfast. There has been a house or cottage on this site for many hundreds of years but the present building is an attractive modern property of stone walls and red pantiled roofs. High Blakey's owners, Roy and Kath Atherton, bought the house early in 1999, carried out an extensive refurbishment, and now offer top quality B&B accommodation in 3 beautifully furnished and decorated rooms. Some of the furniture was actually made by Roy, an accomplished carpenter and interior decorator.

High Blakey House, Blakey Ridge, nr Kirkbymoorside, North Yorkshire YO62 7LQ Tel/Fax: 01751 417186

A generous breakfast is included in the tariff and although the Athertons do not provide an evening meal, guests only have to step across the road to the Lion Inn. By the time you read this, Roy and Kath hope to have a small tea room up and running here, another good reason for seeking out this quite outstanding location.

THE HERITAGE COAST

Between Saltburn and Filey lies some of the most striking coastal scenery in the country. Along this stretch of the Heritage Coast you'll find the highest cliffs in the country, a shoreline fretted with rocky coves, golden with miles of sandy beaches, a scattering of picture postcard fishing villages, and, at its heart, the historic port of Whitby dramatically set around the mouth of the River Esk.

This glorious seaboard was designated as a Heritage Coast in 1979 in recognition of its beauty and its long history. From its small ports, fishermen have for centuries sailed out in their distinctive cobles to harvest the sea; from Whitby, sturdy whaling ships set off on their dangerous and now, thankfully, abandoned trade. It was at Whitby that one of England's greatest mariners, Captain Cook, learnt his seafaring skills and it was from here that he departed in the tiny bark, *Endeavour*, a mere 370 tons, on his astonishing journeys of exploration.

Further down the coast are the popular resorts of Scarborough, (where visitors were frolicking naked in the sea as early as 1735), and Filey, both of them offering long stretches of sandy beach and a huge variety of holiday entertainments.

SALTBURN-BY-THE-SEA
MAP 3 REF I2

10 miles E of Middlesbrough on the A174

The charming seaside resort of Saltburn lies at the northern end of the Heritage Coast. It was custom-built in Victorian times and designed for affluent middle-class visitors - so much so that in the early years excursion trains were barred from calling there. Created in the 1860s by the Quaker entrepreneur Henry Pease, Saltburn is set on a cliff high above a long sandy beach. To transport visitors from the elegant little town to the promenade and pier below, an ingenious water-balanced **Tramway** was constructed. It is still in use, the oldest such tramway to have survived in Britain. Saltburn's Victorian heritage is celebrated in mid-August each year with a full programme of events, many of them with the participants clad in appropriate costume. It seems appropriate, too, that such an olde-worlde town should be well-known for its many shops selling antiques and collectables.

Saltburn's genteel image in Victorian times was a far cry from its notoriety in the late 18th century when it was one of the north east's busiest centres for smuggling. The "King of the Smugglers", John Andrew, had his base here and during a long and profitable career was never apprehended. His story, and that of his partners in villainy, is colourfully re-

Inclined Tramway, Saltburn

called at **The Saltburn Smugglers Heritage Centre** near the Ship Inn of which Andrew was landlord. From the sea front, a miniature railway will take you to the splendid **Italian Gardens** - another Victorian contribution to the town. Here you can take tea on the lawn and explore the **Woodlands Centre** set between the formal pleasure gardens and the wild natural woodlands beyond.

STAITHES
Map 3 ref J2
7 miles SE of Saltburn-by-the-Sea off the A174

Visitors to this much-photographed fishing port leave their cars at the park in the modern village at the top of the cliff and then walk down the steep road to the old wharf. Take care - one of these narrow, stepped alleys is called **Slippery Hill**, for reasons that can become painfully clear. The old stone chapels and rather austere houses testify to the days

Staithes Harbour

when Staithes was a stronghold of Methodism.

The little port is proud of its associations with Captain James Cook. He came here, not as a famous mariner, but as a 17 year old assistant in Mr William Sanderson's haberdashery shop. James didn't stay long, leaving in 1746 to begin his naval apprenticeship in Whitby with Thomas Scottowe, a friend of Sanderson.

Staithes is still a working port with one of the few fleets in England still catching crabs and lobsters. Moored in the harbour and along the river are the fishermen's distinctive boats. Known as cobles, they have an ancestry that goes back to Viking times. Nearby is a small sandy beach, popular with families (and artists), and a rocky shoreline extending north and south pitted with thousands of rock pools hiding starfish and anemones. The rocks here are also rich in fossils and you may even find ingots of 'fools gold' - actually iron pyrites and virtually worthless. A little further up the coast rises Boulby cliff, at 666ft (202m) the highest point on the east coast of England.

RUNSWICK BAY
Map 3 ref K3
9 miles NW of Whitby, off the A174

A little further down the coast, Runswick Bay is another picturesque fishing village with attractive cottages clinging to the steep sides of the cliff. This perilous position proved disastrous in 1682 when the cliff face collapsed and the whole of Runswick, with the exception of a single cottage, tumbled into the sea. A disaster fund was set up and a new village established.

At Runswick, as in most of Yorkshire's remote communities, superstition was once widespread. Even at the beginning of the 20th century, many still believed in witches and almost everyone would avert their gaze or cross the road to avoid someone afflicted with the "Evil Eye". The Revd Cooper, Vicar of Filey, visited the village at the turn of the century and came across a "perfectly horrible superstition". Apparently, it was considered unlucky to save a drowning man. The Vicar was told of "men nearly dragged ashore, and then, by the advice of the elders, abandoned to their fate lest ill-fortune should result from saving them".

GOLDSBOROUGH
Map 3 ref K3

5 miles NE of Whitby off the A174

Just outside this small village are the remains of one of 5 signal stations built by the Romans in the 4th century when Saxon pirates were continually raiding the coastal towns. The stations were all built to a similar design with a timber or stone watchtower surrounded by a wide ditch.

In Goldsborough itself, the charming stone building that houses **The Fox & Hounds** dates back more than 400 years. It's an inviting place with its beamed ceilings, real open fire and spectacular views. Visitors are offered a warm welcome from mine hosts, Robin and Steph. The inn is gaining an excellent reputation for its hand-pulled beers, first class food and comfortable accommodation. Food is available at lunchtimes and evenings every day except Wednesday lunchtimes in the winter. You can eat throughout the inn or in the non-smoking dining room and, on fair-weather days, in the attractive beer garden where there's also a secure children's area. Children are also welcome in the family room inside. Real Ale lovers will be pleased to

The Fox & Hounds, Goldsborough, Whitby, North Yorkshire YO21 3RX Tel: 01947 893372

find at least two of them always on tap and if your preference is for the grape, wine is available by the glass or bottle. If you are planning to stay in this scenic area, The Fox & Hounds has two quality guest rooms, both doubles with an extra fold-up bed if required. And if you are a keen walker, the Cleveland Way is just a field and a half away! Walking weekends are available and for details of overnight camping, please phone.

LYTHE
Map 3 ref K3

4 miles NW of Whitby off the A174

Perched on a hill top, Lythe is a small cluster of houses with a sturdy little church which is well worth a visit. Just south of the village is **Mulgrave Castle**, hereditary home of the Marquis of Normanby. The Castle grounds, which are open to the public, contain the ruins of Foss Castle built shortly after the Norman Conquest. Charles Dickens once spent a holiday at Mulgrave Castle and "danced on its lawns in ecstasy at its beauty". It's not known whether the great author witnessed the ancient custom of "Firing the Stiddy".

This celebrates notable events in the Normanby family and begins with dragging the anvil from the blacksmith's shop, upturning it, and placing a charge of gunpowder on its base. A fearless villager then approaches with a 20ft long metal bar, its tip red hot, and detonates the powder.

In the 1850s, Mulgrave Castle was leased by an exiled Indian Maharajah, Duleep Singh. He enjoyed going hawking on the moors in full oriental dress and the story is often told of how he had the first road between Sandsend and Whitby constructed because his elephants disliked walking along the beach. Much as one would like to believe this tale, no one has yet proved it to be true.

The Red Lion, situated on the top of the steep Lythe Bank, has been run for the last few years by Gill and John Wood: John is a local man, well-known and regarded in the area. In such a wonderful position, the inn itself also looks a picture, with a profusion of hanging baskets, window boxes and patio tubs full of colour surrounding the entrance.

**The Red Lion, High Street, Lythe,
North Yorkshire YO21 3RT Tel: 01947 893300**

The interior of the Red Lion lives up to the expectation of its exterior: well-decorated and furnished and full of character and charm. As well as having an excellent reputation for serving good ales, Gill and John have also made the inn a popular place to come to for delicious, home-cooked food. Most importantly though, this is a friendly pub where no one is a stranger for long and, with three comfortable en suite guest bedrooms available, it is a superb place to take a short break.

SANDSEND   MAP 3 REF K3
2 miles NW of Whitby on the A174

From Runswick Bay, the A174 drops down the notoriously steep Lythe Bank to Sandsend, a pretty village that grew up alongside the Mulgrave Beck as it runs into the sea at 'sands end', - the northern tip of the long sandy beach that stretches some two and a half miles from here to Whitby. The Romans had a cement works nearby, later generations mined the surrounding hills for the elusive jet stone and for alum, and the Victorians built a scenic railway along the coast. The railway track was dismantled in the 1950s but sections of the route now form part of the **Sandsend Trail**, a pleasant and leisurely two and a half hour walk around the village which is made particularly interesting if you follow it with the National Park's booklet describing the route.

WHITBY   MAP 3 REF K3
20 miles NW of Scarborough on the A171

From Sandsend, the A174 skirts the shore and then passes between open fields and a breezy cliff-top Golf Course before entering one of North Yorkshire's most historic and attractive towns. Whitby is famed as one of the earliest and most important centres of Christianity in England; as Captain James Cook's home port, and as the place where, according to Bram Stoker's famous novel, Count Dracula in the form of a wolf loped ashore from a crewless ship that had drifted into the harbour. The classic 1931 film version of the story, starring Bela Lugosi, was filmed in the original locations at Whitby and there were several reports of holidaymakers being startled by coming across the Count, cloaked and fanged, as he rested between takes.

High on the cliff that towers above the old town stand the imposing and romantic ruins of **Whitby Abbey**. In AD664, many of the most eminent prelates of the Christian Church were summoned here to attend the Synod of Whitby. They were charged with settling once and for all a festering dispute that had riven Christendom for generations: the precise date on which Easter should be celebrated. The complicated formula they devised to solve this problem is still in use today.

A short walk from the Abbey is **St Mary's Church**, a unique building "not unlike a house outside and very much like a ship inside". Indeed, the fascinating interior with its clutter of box-pews, iron pillars and long galleries was reput-

Whitby Abbey

edly fashioned by Whitby seamen during the course of the 18th century. The three-decker pulpit is from the same period; the huge ear trumpets for a rector's deaf wife were put in place about fifty years later. St Mary's stands atop the cliff: the old town clusters around the harbour mouth far below. Linking them are the famous 199 steps that wind up the hillside: many a churchgoer or visitor has been grateful for the frequent seats thoughtfully provided along the way.

The old port of Whitby developed on the slim shelf of land that runs along the east bank of the River Esk, an intricate muddle of narrow, cobbled streets and shoulder-width alleys. Grape Lane is typical, a cramped little street where ancient houses lean wearily against each other. Young James Cook lived here during his apprenticeship: the handsome house in Grape Lane where he lodged is now the **Captain Cook Memorial Museum.**

By the early 19th century, old Whitby was full to bursting and a new town began to burgeon on the west bank of the River Esk. The new Whitby, or "West Cliff", was carefully planned with the nascent industry of tourism in mind. There was a quayside walk or

Captain Cook's Endeavour

"promenade", a bandstand, luxury hotels, and a Royal Crescent of upmarket dwellings reminiscent of Buxton or Cheltenham but with the added advantage of enjoying a sea air universally acknowledged as "invariably beneficial to the health of the most injured constitution".

In a dominating position on West Cliff, a bronze statue of Captain Cook gazes out over the harbour he knew so well and nearby the huge jawbone of a whale, raised as an arch, recalls those other great Whitby seafarers, the whalers. Between 1753 and 1833, Whitby was the capital of the whaling industry, bringing home 2761 whales in 80 years. Much of that success was due to the skills of the great whaling captains William Scoresby and his son, also named William. The elder William was celebrated for his great daring and navigational skills, as well as for the invention of the crow's nest, or masthead lookout. His son was driven by a restless, enquiring mind and occupied himself with various experiments during the long days at sea in the icy Arctic waters. He is most noted for his discoveries of the forms of snow crystals and the invention of the "Greenland" magnet which made ships' compasses more reliable. The whaling industry is now, thankfully, long dead, but fortunately the fishing industry is not, as many of Whitby's restaurants bear witness, being famous for their seafood menus.

Whitby Glass in the ancient Sandgate part of Whitby is a distinguished glassware studio that is home to the world-famous "Whitby Lucky Duck". The studio was founded

in 1957 by Peter Rantell. Today it is owned and personally run by Dorothy Clegg, twice former Mayor of Scarborough. Visitors are welcome to call in at the 400-year-old building to observe the skilled craftsmen as they draw, bend and fashion coloured glass into the intricately shaped "lucky duck" talismans synonymous with Whitby. These have been exported to places as far away as Mexico and Japan , with their al-

Whitby Glass Ltd, 9 Sandgate, Whitby, North Yorkshire
YO22 4DB Tel: 01947 603553

leged influence over their owners' fortunes succeeding in bringing about, among other beneficence, financial windfalls and the ending of a drought in southern France. Recently featured on The Holiday Programme, this interesting and impressive studio is well worth a visit. Many visitors leave with their own memento of Whitby and the exquisite handiwork of its gifted craftsmen.

One of the best is **The Magpie Café**, a welcoming and distinguished eatery occupying a splendid position on Whitby's bustling quayside, The building dates back to the 18th

century and was once home to the Scoresby whaling family. It was then used as a shipping office for many years before opening as a café in the 1930s. More like a first-class restaurant than your average café, it has been recommended by Egon Ronay and has featured in the *Good Food Guide*. In the same family since 1954, the present owners Alison and Ian have gained a well-earned reputation for the quality of the food and service. The house speciality is fresh locally-caught fish and seafood - many aver that they serve the best fish and chips in the area. The varied menu has something for everyone, from salads and vegetarian meals to traditional and more innovative dishes. The selection of desserts is truly impressive and definitely worth saving room for! The furnishings are comfortable and the ambience warm and welcoming. The upper level commands magnificent views. Open daily from early February to mid-January, the opening hours vary according to season but are generally 11.30am to 9pm.

The Magpie Café, 14 Pier Road, Whitby,
North Yorkshire YO21 3PU
Tel: 01947 602058 Fax: 01947 601801
e-mail: ian@magpiecafe.co.uk
website: www.magpiecafe.co.uk

One of Whitby's unique attractions is **The Sutcliffe Gallery** in Flowergate. The Gallery celebrates the great photographer Frank Meadow Sutcliffe who was born in Whitby in 1853. His studies of local people, places and events powerfully evoke the Whitby of late-Victorian and Edwardian times in photographs that are both beautifully composed and technically immaculate. Few visitors to the Gallery can resist the temptation to purchase at least one of the nostalgic prints on sale.

Another popular souvenir of the town is jet stone, a lustrous black stone which enjoyed an enormous vogue in Victorian times. After the death of Prince Albert, jewellery in jet was the only ornament the Queen would allow herself to wear. The Court and the middle classes naturally followed her example and for several decades Whitby prospered greatly from the trade in jet. By 1914, workable deposits of the stone were virtually ex-

**The Europa Hotel, 20 Hudson Street,
Whitby, North Yorkshire YO21 3EP
Tel/Fax: 01947 602251**

hausted and a new generation shunned its gloomy association with death. Recent years have seen a revival of interest in the glossy stone and several shops have extensive displays of jet ornaments and jewellery.

Ideally positioned on the West Cliff, just minutes from the town centre, **The Europa Hotel** is an elegant Victorian residence built in 1881. This intimate family-run hotel has a stylish Lounge Bar and a licensed à la carte restaurant offering excellent home made cuisine in a friendly atmosphere. There's a cosy first floor lounge and library, and the en suite bedrooms are furnished in pleasing co-ordinating schemes. All nine bedrooms are well-equipped with colour television, hospitality tray, clock radio alarm, shaver point, central heating and hair dryer. The hotel is well known for its outstanding value-for-money evening meals, available every day except Sunday. There's a good choice of appetising dishes with a Warm Mixed Pepper Salad amongst the starters; steaks or poached Whitby cod with a prawn sauce among the main dishes; and a delicious home made Crumble of the Day leading the choice of desserts. The hotel is licensed and offers a sensibly-priced selection of wines by the bottle, large or small glass, as well as a range of Irish coffees. Your hosts, Anne and Michael Craven-Moulder, will do everything they possibly can to make your stay as relaxing and enjoyable as possible.

ROBIN HOOD'S BAY
5 miles SE of Whitby off the A171

Map 3 ref L3

Artists never tire of painting this "Clovelly of the North", a picturesque huddle of red-roofed houses clinging to the steep face of the cliff. Bay Town, as locals call the village, was a thriving fishing port throughout the 18th and 19th centuries. By 1920 however there were only two fishing families left in the Bay, mainly because the harbour was so dilapidated, and the industry died out. Today, small boats are once again harvesting the prolific crab grounds that lie along this stretch of the coast.

Because of the natural isolation of the bay, smuggling was quite as important as fishing to the local economy. The houses and inns in the Bay were said to have connecting cellars and cupboards, and it was claimed that "a bale of silk could pass from the bottom of the village to the top without seeing daylight". These were the days too when press gangs from the Royal Navy were active in the area since recruits with a knowledge of the sea were highly prized. Apparently, these mariners were also highly prized by local women: they smartly despatched the press gangs by means of pans and rolling pins.

Shipwrecks in the Bay were frequent, with many a mighty vessel tossed onto its reefs by North Sea storms. On one memorable occasion in the winter of 1881, a large brig called the Visitor was driven onto the rocks. The seas were too rough for the lifeboat at Whitby to be launched there so it was dragged eight miles through the snow and let down the cliffside by ropes. Six men were rescued. The same wild seas threatened the village itself, every storm eroding a little more of the chalk cliff to which it clings. Fortunately, Robin Hood's Bay is now protected by a sturdy sea wall.

Robin Hood's Bay

The most extraordinary building in Robin Hood's Bay is undoubtedly **Fyling Hall Pigsty**. It was built in the 1880s by Squire Barry of Fyling Hall in the classical style although the pillars supporting the portico are of wood rather than marble. Here the Squire's two favourite pigs could enjoy plenty of space and a superb view over the Bay. The building is now managed by the Landmark Trust who rent it out to holidaymakers.

FYLINGTHORPE

MAP 3 REF K4

5 miles SE of Whitby on the B1447

Standing at the heart of this quiet little village less than a mile from Robin Hood's Bay, **The Fylingdales Inn** has thrived under the management of Rita and Terry Milsom who took over here in late 1998. Before that, Rita had worked at the inn for some 15 years.

Built in 1905 as a private house, Fylingdales became an inn in 1955 and nowadays offers customers top quality food and drink. Meals are available every day all year round, from noon until 2pm, and again from 6.30pm to 9pm. There are 5 or more special main courses each day and customers can enjoy their meal in the lovely conservatory. At least 4 Real Ales are always on tap and other attrac-

The Fylingdales Inn, Thorpe Lane, Fylingthorpe, Whitby, North Yorkshire YO22 4TH Tel: 01947 880433

tions of this lively hostelry include a quiz night on Tuesdays and entertainment on Saturday evenings. Pool players, incidentally, might like to test their skills on the circular pool table! Outside, there's an attractive beer garden with a childrens' play area and a large car park. If you are looking for a place to stay in this gloriously scenic part of North Yorkshire, the inn has 2 guest rooms to let - 1 double room with private bathroom and w.c. and 1 family room which is en suite.

RAVENSCAR
Map 3 ref L4

10 miles N of Scarborough off the A171

The coastline around Ravenscar is particularly dramatic and, fortunately, most of it is under the protection of the National Trust. There are some splendid cliff-top walks and outstanding views across Robin Hood's Bay. **Smugglers Rock Country House** is a handsome stone built Georgian house which also enjoys panoramic views of the surrounding National Park and the sea. Offering a choice of either bed & breakfast or self-catering accommodation this former coaching inn stands on the old coach road between Whitby

Smugglers Rock Country House, Ravenscar, Scarborough,
North Yorkshire YO13 0ER Tel: 01723 870044
e-mail: info@smugglersrock.co.uk website: www.smugglersrock.co.uk

and Scarborough, (now a quiet country lane leading to the beach). The house has links with the smugglers who once flourished in this area. There is still, in the east wall above the cellar, a 9 inch by 3 inch window from which the smugglers would watch out for the constabulary and then shine a light when it was safe to bring up contraband through tunnels from the beach.

Bed & breakfast guests at Smugglers Rock stay in the main house where there are 8 en suite, well-equipped bedrooms. Guests have the use of a beautiful, spacious open beamed lounge, a separate "olde-worlde" breakfast room, and a recreation room with pool table, table football and numerous other games. The spacious garden can also be used at any time. Each of the two self-catering cottages at Smugglers Rock sleep 4 people in comfortable 2-bedroomed accommodation and is available on a weekly basis throughout the year and also on a Short Break basis in low season.

About 3 miles south of Ravenscar, at Staintondale, are two very different animal centres. At the **Staintondale Shire Horse Farm** visitors can enjoy a 'hands-on' experience with these noble creatures, watch a video of the horses working and follow a scenic route around the area. Cart rides are also usually available. There's also a café, souvenir shop, picnic area and a play area with a variety of small farm animals to entertain the children. At nearby **Wellington Lodge Llamas** a variety of treks on llama-back is on offer, ranging from a 3 or 4 hour journey to a whole day with a 3-course meal included in the price. The llamas have many years of trekking experience and are sure-footed and friendly. They carry heavy loads of food, drink, stools and extra clothing leaving the rider free to admire the splendid surroundings. All treks must be pre-booked - for more details call 01723 871234..

CLOUGHTON   MAP 3 REF L4
4 miles N of Scarborough on the A171

Cloughton village lies less than a mile from the coast and the rocky inlet of **Cloughton Wyke**. Here, in 1932, a huge whale was cast, or threw itself, ashore. Press photographers and postcard publishers rushed to the scene and paid the smallest local children they could find to pose beside the stranded Leviathan. For a while, Cloughton village was busy with a steady stream of sightseers. Their numbers quickly diminished as the six tons of blubber began to rot. In Cloughton itself, residents came to dread an east wind: it reached them only after washing over the vast hulk lying on the rocks. It's surely the worst thing that has ever happened to this pleasant little village, set around a sharp kink in the A171, where the breezes now - depending on the direction of the wind - either bring a fresh tang of ozone from the sea or a soft perfume of heather from the moors.

The Falcon Inn, a former farmhouse dating back to the late 18th century which stands just off the main Scarborough to Whitby coastal road, offers some of the most spectacular views in the whole of the North Yorkshire coastal region. "Mine hosts" David and Wendy Kemp, have many years of experience in the licensed trade and The Falcon is

**The Falcon Inn, Whitby Road, Cloughton, nr Scarborough,
North Yorkshire YO13 0DY   Tel: 01723 870717**

regarded as one of the best inns in the area. There are two Real Ales on offer in the attractive bar, and the stylish restaurant - housed in the old stables - serves delicious, freshly prepared dishes that draw people from far and wide. Food is available every lunchtime and evening. In the tradition of all good inns, The Falcon also offers comfortable and welcoming overnight accommodation in six en suite bedrooms. Housed in the old cowsheds, the bedrooms are well-appointed and, staying a little longer, guests can take advantage of the extensive grounds in which the inn is set and also wander around the attractive woodland walk.

SCARBOROUGH

MAP 5 REF L5

20 miles SE of Whitby on the A165

With its two splendid bays and dramatic cliff-top castle, Scarborough was targeted by the early railway tycoons as the natural candidate for Yorkshire's first seaside resort. The railway arrived in 1846, followed by the construction of luxury hotels, elegant promenades and spacious gardens, all of which confirmed the town's claim to the title *"Queen of Watering Places"*. The *"quality"*, people like the eccentric Earls of Londesborough, established palatial summer residences here, and an excellent train service brought countless thousands of 'excursionists' from the industrial cities of the West Riding.

Even before the advent of the railway, Scarborough had been well-known to a select few. They travelled to what was then a remote little town to sample the spring water discovered by Mrs Tomyzin Farrer in 1626 and popularised in a book published by a certain Dr Wittie who named the site Scarborough Spaw. Anne Brontë came here in the hope that the spa town's invigorating air would improve her health, a hope that was not fulfilled. She died at the age of 29 and her grave lies in St Mary's churchyard at the foot of the castle. **Scarborough Castle** itself can be precisely dated to the decade between 1158 and 1168 and surviving records show that construction costs totalled £650. The castle was built on the site of a Roman fort and signal station and its gaunt remains stand high on Castle Rock Headland, dominating the two sweeping bays. The spectacular ruins often provide a splendid backdrop for staged battles commemorating the invasions of the Danes, Saxons and the later incursions of Napoleon's troops. The surrounding cliffs are also well worth exploring, just follow the final part of the famous Cleveland Way.

If you happen to be visiting the resort on Shrove Tuesday, be prepared for the unusual sight of respectable citizens exercising their ancient right to skip along the highways. This unexpected traffic hazard is now mostly confined to the area around Foreshore Road. Another tradition maintained by local people around this time is the sounding of the Pancake Bell, a custom started by the wives of the town to alert their menfolk in the fields and in the harbour that they were about to begin cooking the pancakes.

As befits such a long-established resort, Scarborough offers a vast variety of entertainment. If you tire of the two sandy beaches, there's **Peasholm Park** to explore with its glorious gardens and regular events, amongst them the unique sea battle in miniature on the lake. Or you could seek out the intellectual attractions of the **Rotunda Museum** on Vernon Road, *"the finest Georgian museum in Britain"*, which includes amongst its exhibits a genuine ducking stool for 'witches'; the art collections at the **Scarborough Art Gallery**; or the futuristic world of holograms at **Corrigans Arcade** on Foreshore Road. **The Stephen Joseph Theatre in the Round** is well-known for staging the premiere performances of comedies written by its resident director, the prolific playwright Alan Ayckbourn. And at Scalby Mills, on the northern edge of the town, **Sea-Life** offers the chance of close encounters with a huge variety of marine creatures from shrimps to sharks, octopi to eels.

Also worth visiting is the **Wood End Museum of Natural History** on The Crescent, once the home of the eccentric Sitwell family. There are permanent displays of their books and photographs, as well as changing exhibitions of local wildlife. The double-storeyed conservatory and the aquarium here are particularly interesting.

CAYTON

MAP 5 REF L5

3 miles S of Scarborough on the B1261

Cayton is one of only 31 "Thankful Villages" in England. They were so named after the First World War because all of their men came back safely from that horrific conflict. Cayton had all the more reason to be grateful since 43 of its men returned - more than to any other of the Thankful Villages.

Back in 1884 William Lazenby opened his stained glass works in Bradford. His skills were passed on to his sons and his grandsons and today his great granddaughter, Valerie Green, carries on the family tradition at the **Stained Glass Centre** in the countryside between Scarborough and Filey. Valerie and her team produce new stained glass and leaded lights for churches, hotels, restaurants, public houses and homes throughout the country. The showroom at the Stained Glass Centre is an Aladdin's Cave of lampshades,

Stained Glass Centre, Killerby Lane, Cayton, Scarborough, North Yorkshire YO11 3TP
Tel: 01723 581236 Fax: 01723 585465

mirrors and gifts, as well as window panels. An exhibition of stained glass in the Studio charts the history of the art and craft from medieval times and visitors can watch lampshades and windows being made. Round off your visit by sampling the delicious home baking and light refreshments available in the Garden Tea Room. If you are planning to stay in this lovely area, Valerie and her husband Simon will be pleased to welcome you for bed and breakfast at Killerby Cottage Farm, a delightful farmhouse with many attractive features just over a mile from beautiful Cayton Bay.

FILEY

MAP 5 REF M5

7 miles S of Scarborough off the A165

With its six mile crescent of safe, sandy beach, Filey was one of the first Yorkshire resorts to benefit from the early 19th century craze for sea bathing. Filey's popularity continued throughout Victorian times but the little town always prided itself on being rather more select than its brasher neighbour just up the coast, Scarborough. Inevitably, modern times have brought the usual scattering of amusement arcades, fast food outlets and, from 1939 to 1983, a Butlin's Holiday Camp capable of accommodating 10,000 visitors. But Filey has suffered less than most seaside towns and with its many public parks and gardens still retains a winning, rather genteel atmosphere.

Until the Local Government reforms of 1974, the boundary between the East and North Ridings cut right through Filey. The town lay in the East Riding, the parish church and graveyard in the North. This curious arrangement gave rise to some typically pawky Yorkshire humour. If, as a resident of Filey town, you admitted that you were feeling

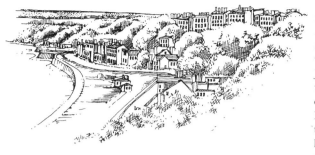

Filey Bay

poorly, the response might well be *"Aye, then tha'll straightly be off t'North Riding"* - in other words, the graveyard. Just to the north of the town, the rocky promontory known as **Filey Brigg** strikes out into the sea, a massive mile-long breakwater protecting the town from the worst of the North Sea's winter storms. From the Brigg, there are grand views southwards along the six-mile-long bay to the cliffs that rise up to Flamborough Head and Scarborough Castle. Despite the fact that there is no harbour at Filey, it was once quite a busy fishing port and one can still occasionally see a few cobles - direct descendants of the Viking longships that arrived here more than a millennium ago - beached on the slipways. Filey's parish church, the oldest parts of which date back to the 12th century, is appropriately dedicated to St Oswald, patron saint of fishermen, and the Fishermen's Window here commemorates men from the town who died at sea. At the **Filey Folk Museum**, housed in a lovely old building dating back to 1696, you can explore the town's long history, while the **Edwardian Festival**, held every June, re-creates the pleasures of an earlier, more innocent age.

The Brigg - one of Filey's former cinema's - was converted some years ago into an interesting mix of shops and eating-places. Amongst them is **Edwin's Cafe** which is situated at the front of Patrick Corrigan's amusement arcade. The cafe offers a good selection of food and drink in a friendly, informal atmosphere. It is run by Yvonne and Steve Ports who share the cooking. In addition to the regular menu, there's always a daily special - on Friday's, it's a delicious plate of fish and chips. The All Day Breakfast is very popular but you can be sure of finding something on the menu to suit your taste. Family's large and small from far and wide are always welcome at Edwin's. there is also a no-smoking area.

Edwin's Café, Unit 5, The Brigg, Station Avenue, Filey, Yorkshire YO14 9AR Tel: 01723 514664

The cafe is open from 5am to 6pm (9pm on Friday and Saturday evening) during the summer season but remains open throughout the year, except for Christmas day, Boxing day and New Year's day. Edwin's is in a convenient location in the town centre which also makes it a popular place to stop and put your feet up whilst you're out and about doing the shopping for the week ahead.

HUNMANBY   MAP 5 REF M6
3 miles SW of Filey between the A165 and A1039

Here's a question worthy of Trivial Pursuits: "On which vehicle was the wing mirror first used?". Your answer is almost certainly wrong unless you know about the grave of a 1st century British charioteer uncovered at Hunmanby in 1907. Along with his bones, those of his horses, and fragments of the chariot wheels was a rectangular strip of shiny metal: archaeologists are convinced that this was fixed to the side of the chariot as a mirror so that the driver could see the competitors behind him. Another curiosity in Hunmanby is the village lock-up with two cells and tiny windows designed for human miscreants, and next to it a circular stone pinfold intended for straying cattle.

In this typically quaint North Yorkshire village, a good pint and excellent food can be relished at **The White Swan.** Standing opposite the parish church, it is thought that the building was originally a farm, later became a courtroom, then a coaching inn before finally settling down as a public house. The restaurant at the back of the pub used to be the courtroom for the Manor of Hunmanby, though the only orders issued these days are for the delicious food served there. In the summer months, lunches are served in the non-smoking restaurant, otherwise the White Swan is open for dinner between 7pm and 9pm, whilst bar meals are served throughout the day.

The White Swan, 1 Church Hill, Hunmanby, Scarborough, North Yorkshire YO14 0JU Tel: 01723 890232

The pub itself is open all day, 7 days a week, and offers a wide choice of ales, including real ales. If you are planning to stay in this scenic area, the White Swan has five en suite bedrooms - 2 doubles, 1 twin and 2 single, and there are special rates for longer stays. Alan and Dorothy have been hosts here for the past six years and will make you welcome. Various entertainments such as quiz nights and live bands are a regular feature.

THE VALE OF PICKERING

Not all that long ago, the Vale of Pickering was the Lake of Pickering, an immense stretch of water far larger than any English lake today, about 32 miles long and four to eight miles wide. As the Ice Age retreated, the waters gradually drained away leaving a low-lying plain of good arable soil based on Kimmeridge clay. Much of it remained marshy however and at Star Carr, near Seamer, archaeologists have uncovered a late Stone Age lake community, dating back some 7,500 years, where the houses were built on stilts above the water. Sadly, the remains of this fascinating excavation lie on private land and are not open to the public. It is only in comparatively recent times that the Vale has been properly drained, which explains why most of the towns and villages lie around its edge in a rough kind of horseshoe formation.

For much of its length, the Vale is watered by the River Derwent, which was also powerfully affected by the changes that occurred during the Ice Age. Originally it entered the sea near Scarborough but an Ice Age glacier blocked that outlet. The Derwent still flows to within a mile and a half of Scarborough, but now turns abruptly and makes a 90-mile detour through the vale and then southwards to join the River Ouse near Howden.

The main traffic artery through the vale is the Thirsk to Scarborough road, the A170, which in summer peak periods can become very congested. But you only have to turn off this busy thoroughfare to find yourself in quiet country lanes leading to sleepy market towns and unspoilt villages. To the north rise the intricate folds of the North York Moors: to the south, the Yorkshire Wolds roll gently away towards Beverley, Hull and the River Humber. Our exploration of the vale begins at the eastern end of this broad, low-lying corridor, at East Ayton near Scarborough, and follows it westwards to the lower slopes of the Hambleton Hills.

HACKNESS
MAP 4 REF L5
4 miles NW of Scarborough off the A170 or A171

For generations the **Forge Valley** has attracted sightseers - especially in autumn when the steep wooded banks of the ravine present a dazzling display of colours. There are several splendid walks along this lovely two mile stretch of the River Derwent, a valley which takes its name from the ancient iron workings of which today not a trace remains.

Situated at the head of the picturesque Forge Valley **The Everley Country Hotel** enjoys a wonderfully peaceful location, ideal for exploring the North York Moors National Park and the Heritage Coast. Once the property of the local landowner, Lord Derwent, this handsome building with a datestone of 1754 has been owned and run by Jill and

Richard Taylor since 1983. Visitors can enjoy Jill's cooking at lunchtimes (noon until 2pm) and evenings (7pm to 9pm) - a good choice of hearty bar meals or assorted sandwiches, with a separate children's menu also available. The ambience is relaxed and you can eat in any of the lounge bars. (Please note that no food is available on Sunday evenings or Mondays all day). Children are welcome at the Everley and at the rear of the hotel the spacious gar-

The Everley Country Hotel, Hackness, Scarborough, North Yorkshire YO13 0BT Tel: 01723 882202

den has a play area where they can let off steam. This is a delightful place to stay and the excellent accommodation comprises 4 guest rooms, 3 of them en suite, and all attractively furnished and decorated. Definitely the kind of place where you will want to linger.

EAST AYTON   MAP 4 REF L5
4 miles W of Scarborough, on the A170

Victorian visitors to Scarborough, occasionally tiring of its urban attractions, welcomed excursions to beauty spots such as the **Forge Valley** near East Ayton. Aeons ago, a sharp-edged glacier excavated the valley; then centuries of natural growth softened its hills, clothed them with overarching trees and, quite by chance, created one of the loveliest woodland walks in England. For a steady walker, going say 4 miles an hour, the round trip walk from East Ayton to the old forge from which the valley derives its name - along one side of the river returning on the other, takes about 2½ hours. A short diversion will lead you to the ruins of **Ayton Castle** at the edge of the road near the junction of the A170 and B1261. Dating from around 1400, this is one of the most southerly of the hundreds of pele towers built in those turbulent times as a protection against invading Scottish marauders. In more peaceful days, many of these towers had a more comfortable mansion added but their defensive origins are still clearly recognisable.

BROMPTON-BY-SAWDON   MAP 4 REF K5
8 miles W of Scarborough on the A170

It was in the medieval church of this small village, on an autumn day in 1802, that William Wordsworth was married to Mary Hutchinson whose family lived at nearby Gallows Hill Farm. *A perfect woman*, he wrote of Mary, *nobly planned / To warn, to comfort, and command; / And yet a spirit still, and bright / With something of an angelic light*. Wydale Hall (private) was the home of the Squire of Brompton, Sir George Cayley (1773-1857), a pioneer aviator who achieved successful flights with small gliders although it was his coachman who was actually dragooned into being the pilot. Sir George is also credited with inventing the caterpillar tractor.

With its white-painted walls and large cartwheel sign, the **Brompton Forge Restaurant** looks very inviting and the interior is just as pleasing - old beams and stone walls, crisp white tablecloths and subdued lighting, vintage blacksmith's tools displayed on one

**Brompton Forge Restaurant, Brompton-by-Sawdon, nr Scarborough
North Yorkshire YO13 9DP Tel: 01723 859409**

of the walls. The prime attraction though is the food - quality cuisine prepared by the Forge's owners Kirsty and Paul Mills - both of them professional chefs. Their menu changes regularly but always offers a good choice of dishes. At lunchtime (noon until 2pm), for example, you may well find home-cured salmon with a lemon and crushed peppercorn dressing and a herb salad amongst the starters; Medallions of pork fillet in a sweet cider cream as a main course. The dinner menu, available between 6.30pm and 9.30pm, is equally appetising. Half portions are available for children and the well-chosen wine list sensibly includes a selection of wines by the half-bottle. The Forge is non-smoking, except in the comfortable bar area, and open for lunch and dinner every day except Sunday evenings and all day on Monday.

EBBERSTON
MAP 4 REF K5
10 miles W of Scarborough on the A170

About a mile to the west of Ebberston, in the early 18th century, Mr William Thompson, MP for Scarborough, built for himself what is possibly the smallest stately home in England, **Ebberston Hall.** From the front, the house appears to be just one storey high, with a pillared doorway approached by a grand flight of stone steps flanked by a moderately sized room on each side. In fact, behind this modest front, there's also an extensive basement - 'deceptively spacious' as the estate agents say. If you would like to visit Ebberston Hall, please remember that it is open to visitors only by appointment.

Set in exceptional gardens and grounds of 5 acres, **The Lodge** is a charming Georgian country house overlooking the Vale of Pickering and beyond to the Yorkshire Wolds. Audrey and Robert Clement have been welcoming bed and breakfast visitors to their

The Lodge, Ebberston, Scarborough, North Yorkshire YO13 9PA
Tel/Fax: 01723 850001

lovely home since 1996. Guests have the use of a relaxing sitting room with direct access to the gardens and equipped with colour TV, books and brochures. The Lodge is non-smoking and offers comfortable, centrally heated modern facilities in an old world setting with 3 twin-bedded rooms (one with vanity basin), all provided with tea/coffee making facilities, colour television, and guests' private bathrooms. The nearby inn serves good food and there are many eating establishments in the neighbourhood to suit all tastes. The Lodge's location makes it an ideal centre for exploring the beauties of the North York Moors National Park and the lovely Heritage Coast, both of them within easy reach.

THORNTON-LE-DALE

MAP 4 REF K5

14 miles W of Scarborough, on the A170

As long ago as 1907, a *Yorkshire Post* poll of its readers acclaimed Thornton-le-Dale as the most beautiful village in Yorkshire. Despite stiff competition for that title, most visitors find themselves in agreement. If further proof were needed, just off the A170 near the parish church of All Saints you'll find one of the most photographed houses in Britain, appearing regularly on chocolate boxes, jigsaws and calendars. The North York Moors National Park actually creates a special loop in its boundary to include this picture-postcard village which, somewhat confusingly, is also frequently shown on maps as 'Thornton Dale'.

In Turkish *"cherafey"* means "Enjoy our hospitality", so it's a very appropriate name for **The Cherafey Bistro**, Ann King's friendly and intimate restaurant which boasts a well-stocked bar, an interesting wine list and serves what many consider to be the finest food in the area. The imaginative menu ranges from traditional favourites such as Rack of Lamb and steaks, ("David" is the 10oz version; "Goliath" a mighty 20oz serving), to appetising treats such as Chicken Anise. Ann has visited Turkey many times so it's not surprising to find a main course called "Turkish Delight" on the menu - a peasant dish of best quality meat, peppers and various Turkish spices, cooked and served in the pan, and eaten with bread. The bar even stocks a Turkish beer to go with it! The menu also offers a choice of light meals, including Provencettes - hot grilled sandwiches in an authentic ciabatta baguette. In good weather, guests can enjoy their meal outside on the patio overlooking the continental style terraced gardens. The Cherafey Bistro

The Cherafey Bistro, Whitbygate,
Thornton-le-Dale, Pickering,
North Yorkshire YO18 7RY Tel: 01751 474732

bills itself as "Thornton-le-Dale's Best Kept Secret" but the quality cuisine and delightful surroundings ensure that it won't remain secret for much longer. (Please note: the Bistro is closed on Mondays).

About 3 miles north of Thornton-le-Dale, the Dalby Visitor Centre is the starting point for the **Dalby Forest Drive**, a 9-mile circuit through what was once the royal hunting Forest of Pickering. The Visitor Centre can provide plentiful details of the various facilities available - waymarked walks, picnic/barbecue sites, children's play areas, an orienteering course and wildlife observation hide, and much more.

PICKERING

Map 4 ref J5

17 miles W of Scarborough on the A170

This busy little town developed around the important crossroads where the Malton to Whitby, and the Thirsk to Scarborough roads intersect. It's the largest of the four market towns in Ryedale and possibly the oldest, claiming to date from 270 BC when (so it's said) it was founded by a King of the Brigantes called Peredurus. William the Conqueror's attempts to dominate the area are recalled by Pickering's ruined castle, and the many inns and posting houses reflect the town's prosperity during the stage coach era. Lying at the heart of the fertile Vale of Pickering, the town's reputation was originally based on its famous pigs and horses. Vast quantities of pork were transported across the moors to Whitby, salted and used as shipboard rations. The famous Cleveland Bay horses, with their jet-black manes and tails, were extensively bred in the area. (In Eskdale, a little further north, they still are). These sweet-natured, sturdy and tireless animals have always been in great demand. During the 19th century, their equable temperament made them ideal for pulling Hansom cabs and street-cars, and nowadays they are often seen in more dignified events such as State Processions.

Overlooking the Market Place the **Bay Horse Inn** is a charming old hostelry dating back to the early 1600s. Amongst the inn's earliest customers was Oliver Cromwell whose troops were billeted here in 1640 during the Civil War. In those days, the Bay Horse had its own brew house, an in-house facility which it maintained until 1813. Today, its well-kept beers include Tetleys, a fortnightly guest ale and many other quality beers and lagers. The inn's front bar has an inviting olde worlde atmosphere with its low beams and open fires. Another bar to the rear is popular with younger people who gather here to enjoy good music, especially at weekends. Mine hosts, Susan and Colin, also provide some excellent home cooking with bar lunches available Monday to Saturday, and an upstairs restaurant which is still served by a "dummy waiter" - a service lift for food from the kitchen down below. Especially popular is the first class Carvery, available on Sundays from noon until 4pm (3pm in winter), which offers a choice of two succulent roasts and no fewer than 12 different vegetables.

Bay Horse Inn, Market Place, Pickering, North Yorkshire YO18 7AA Tel: 01751 472526

The parish church of **St Peter and St Paul** is well worth visiting for its remarkable 15th century murals. During the glum days of Puritanism, these lively paintings were denounced as idolatrous and plastered over. They stayed forgotten for some two hundred years but were rediscovered when the church was being restored in 1851. Unfortunately, the vicar at that time shared the Puritans' sentiments and, despite opposition from his parishioners and even from his bishop, had them smothered again under whitewash. A more liberal successor to the Vicar had the murals restored once again in 1878 and they now give one a vivid idea of how cheerful, colourful and entertaining many English churches were before the unforgivable vandalism of the Puritan years. These superb paintings, sharp, vigorous and well-observed, happily embrace scenes from the Bible, old legends and actual history: a real insight into the medieval mind that had no difficulty in accepting both the story of St George slaying the dragon and the martyrdom of St Thomas à Becket as equally real, and inspiring, events.

Also not to be missed in Pickering is the **Beck Isle Museum** housed in a gracious Regency mansion. Its 27 display areas are crammed with a *"magnificent assortment of items curious, mysterious, marvellous and commonplace from the last 200 years"*. There are intriguing re-creations of typical Victorian domestic rooms, shops, workshops and even a pub. The comprehensive collection of photographs by Sydney Smith presents a remarkable picture of the Ryedale area as it was more than half a century ago. The exhibition is made even more interesting by its acquisition of the very cameras and other photographic equipment used by Sydney Smith.

Virtually the only detached house in the old part of tree-lined Eastgate, **Heathcote House** still boasts many of its original early Victorian features including a beautiful mahogany staircase, large panelled doors (weighing about 40 kilos each) to the lounge and dining room, and arched marble fireplaces - though there is full central heating too! Comfort is the priority in the bedrooms. Each has a colour TV, hostess tray, hairdryer, radio alarm and all have en suite facilities. Joan and Rod Lovejoy, whose lovely home this is, believe their guests deserve nothing less than a freshly cooked, hearty English breakfast and are happy to cater for individual preferences. Dinner is strictly for connoisseurs of succulent, flavoursome home cooking. Local produce is used when available and everything is prepared and cooked in either traditional style or with imaginative variations. Dinner can be complemented, if you wish, with your choice from the wine list. After dinner, or indeed

Heathcote House, 100 Eastgate, Pickering,
North Yorkshire YO18 7DW   Tel/Fax: 01751 476991
e-mail: joanlovejoy@lineone.com

at any time, why not relax in the lounge where an open log fire burns on chilly evenings. There's a wide selection of books, magazines and local papers, along with visitor information to help you plan your day.

If you catch a whiff of sulphurous smoke, then you must be close to the station. Pickering is the southern terminus of the **North York Moors Railway** and here you can board a steam-drawn train for an 18-mile journey along one of the oldest and most dramatically scenic railways in the country. And at the **Pickering Trout Lake** you can hire a rod and tackle and attempt to beat the record for the largest fish caught here - it currently stands at a mighty 25lb 4oz (11.45 kg).

KIRBY MISPERTON
Map 4 ref J5

5 miles S of Pickering, off the A169

A few miles south of Pickering, the 375 acres of wooded parkland surrounding Kirby Misperton Hall provide an attractive setting for **Flamingo Land,** a Zoo and Fun Park that is home to more than 1,000 birds, animals and reptiles. Beyond doubt, the most spectacular sight is that of the flock of pink flamingos gathered around the lake fringed with willow trees. With more than one hundred different attractions, including a fun fair, an adventure playground and a real working farm, this is an ideal venue for families with young children.

WRELTON
Map 4 ref J5

3 miles NW of Pickering off the A170

The eight charming old properties that make up **Beech Farm Cottages** effectively create their own little hamlet. An 18th century house and outbuildings have been sympathetically converted into these superb self-catering cottages, each one varying in size and character. They surround a south facing courtyard opening onto fields and range from "Fat Hen", which sleeps 2 people, up to the Farmhouse, or "Shepherd's Lodge", which can sleep 9 or 10 people. Throughout their renovation, care was taken to retain many of the original features - huge old timbers, beamed ceilings, local stone and mellow brick blend skilfully with all the modern appliances such as double glazing and coal effect gas fires. Comfortable armchairs and sofas dominate the spacious living rooms

**Beech Farm Cottages, Main Street, Wrelton, Pickering
North Yorkshire YO18 8PG Tel: 01751 476612
Fax: 01757 475032 e-mail: massara@compuserve.com**

and the bright and airy kitchens have been individually designed, luxuriously fitted and professionally equipped. Guests at Beech Farm Cottages have the use of an indoor swimming pool, jacuzzi and coin-operated sauna, a laundry with coin-operated washing machine and tumble dryer, and a paddock with barbecue and games area. The outstanding quality of Beech Farm Cottages is reflected in the awards they have won, amongst them the English Tourist Board's prestigious "Self-catering Holiday of the Year" award. Uniquely for the area, the Board has also rated all the cottages "de luxe". Amongst the many compliments recorded in the Visitors' Books is one that reads *Even better than expected, a five star holiday!*".

SINNINGTON
Map 4 ref J5

5 miles W of Pickering off the A170

At Sinnington the River Seven leaves the moors and the valley of Rosedale for the more open country of the Vale. It passes through this tiny village, running alongside a broad green in the centre of which is a graceful old packhorse bridge. At one time this medieval bridge must have served a useful purpose but the old watercourse that ran beneath it is now dry.

KIRKBYMOORSIDE
Map 4 ref J5

7 miles W of Pickering on the A170

Set quietly off the main road, this agreeable market town of fine Georgian houses, narrow twisting lanes and cobbled market place, straggles up the hillside. Where the town ends, the moors begin. One of the 17th century's most reviled politicians ended his life here in what is now Buckingham House but was then part of the adjoining King Head's Hotel. George Villiers, 2nd Duke of Buckingham, was a favourite of Charles II and had come to the town to hunt in the nearby Forest of Pickering. He was thrown from his horse and badly injured. Taken to the King's Head he died later that day. An entry in the parish register notes the date with an entry for 1687 that reads *April 17th George Viluas: Lord Dooke of Bookingham.*

HELMSLEY
Map 4 ref I5

13 miles W of Pickering on the A170

One of North Yorkshire's most popular and attractive towns, Helmsley lies on the banks of the River Rye at the edge of the North York Moors National Park. The spacious market square is typical of the area but the Gothic memorial to the 2nd Earl of Feversham that stands there is not. This astonishingly ornate construction was designed by Sir Giles Gilbert Scott and looks like a smaller version of his famous memorial to Sir Walter Scott in Edinburgh.

The Earls of Feversham lived at **Duncombe Park** whose extensive grounds sweep up to within a few yards of the Market Place. Most of the original mansion, designed by Vanbrugh, was gutted by a disastrous fire in 1879: only the north wing remained habitable and that in its turn was ruined by a second fire in 1895. The Fevershams lavished a fortune on rebuilding the grand old house, largely to the original design, but the financial burden eventually forced them to lease the house and grounds as a preparatory school for girls. Happily, the Feversham were able to return to their ancestral home in 1985 and the beautifully restored house and lovely grounds are now open to the public.

Helmsley Castle

Before they were ennobled, the Fevershams' family name was Duncombe and it was Sir Thomas Duncombe, a wealthy London goldsmith, who established the family seat here when he bought **Helmsley Castle** (English Heritage) and its estate in 1687. Founded in the early 1100s, seriously knocked about during the Civil War, the castle was in a dilapidated state but its previous owner, the Duke of Buckingham, had continued to live there in some squalor and discomfort. Sir Thomas quickly decided to build a more suitable residence nearby, abandoning the ruins to lovers of the romantic and picturesque.

The creator of Cuisine Eclairée, Elaine Lemm is already something of a legend in the world of fine cuisine so a visit to **Lemm's**, overlooking the market square, is strongly recommended. A former art student at Leeds, Elaine discovered her passion for cooking when she moved to France in 1987. Three years later she opened a school in the Dordogne to teach the *French (!)* classical cooking. *Sacré bleu!* Today, Elaine organises cookery schools all over the world, but Lemm's in Helmsley is the first full time restaurant serving Cuisine Eclairée. During the day, Lemm's is a stylish café bar; in the evenings from Wednesday to Saturday it becomes an elegant bistro where the menu changes in accordance with Elaine's enthusiasms. A typical menu might offer 4 starters, (potted ginger and lime shrimp with paprika cream, perhaps amongst them), 3 main courses (swordfish filled with prosciutto, pecorino cheese & garlic, possibly), a vegetarian option, and a choice of 4 wonderful home made desserts. Lovers of good cooking will be delighted to know that they can also stay here overnight, with a choice of 3 attractive guest rooms available, (1 family, 1 twin, 1 double).

**Lemm's, 19 Bridge Street, Helmsley,
North Yorkshire YO62 5BG
Tel: 01439 771555 Fax: 01439 771515
e-mail: cuisine_eclairee@compuserve.com**

Church Farm Holidays, based in Helmsley, offer a superb selection of well-equipped, smartly furnished accommodation. Each of the apartments, and the cottage, has been newly-built, using tradi-tional local stone, and all of them have been de-signed to form a quiet courtyard. The self-cater-ing accommodation ranges from a flat for two people to a cottage which can sleep up to five, and there's also a flat that sleeps six people.

Church Farm itself has been home to the Otterburn family for gen-erations. It is no longer a working farm - Christine and Richard Otterburn now run a thriving home made ice cream business called **The Ryeburn Ice Cream Parlour** from

**Church Farm Holidays and Ryeburn Ice Cream Parlour,
Church Farm, Cleveland Way, Helmsley,
North Yorkshire YO62 5AE Tel: 01439 770331**

buildings which have been carefully and sympathetically converted. It's well worth pop-ping in here to spoil yourself with one of the many award-winning concoctions. All the ice cream and other products, including fudge, are made in the factory and are on sale here. David, the ice cream maker, has won more than 30 diplomas for his ice cream. There's also a café selling refresh-ments and tasty snacks.

Just to the west of Helmsley rise the indescribably beautiful remains of **Rievaulx Abbey** (English Herit-age), standing amongst wooded hills beside the River Rye - *"the most beau-tiful monastic site in Europe"*. JMW Turner was enchanted by this idyl-lic landscape; Dorothy Wordsworth, *"spellbound"*. Founded in 1131, it was the first Cistercian abbey in Yorkshire and, with some 700 people - monks, lay brothers, servants -eventually liv-ing within its walls, became one of the largest. Like Kirkham Abbey a few years earlier, Rievaulx was en-dowed by Walter l'Espec, Lord of Helmsley, still mourning the loss of his only son in a riding accident. The Abbey was soon a major landowner in the county, earning a healthy in-

Rievaulx Abbey

come from farming - at one time owning more than 14,000 sheep. The Abbey also had its own fishery at Teesmouth, and iron-ore mines at Bilsdale and near Wakefield.

Looking down on the extensive remains of the Abbey is **Rievaulx Terrace** (National Trust), a breathtaking example of landscape gardening completed in 1758. The cunningly contrived avenues draw your eyes to incomparable views of the Abbey itself, to vistas along the Rye Valley and to the rolling contours of the hills beyond. At each end of the terrace is a classical temple, one of which is elaborately furnished and decorated as a dining room.

MUSCOATES
MAP 4 REF J5

7 miles SW of Pickering off the A170

Nunnington Hall (National Trust), a mile or so to the west of Muscoates, is a late 17th century manor house set beside the River Rye with a picturesque packhorse bridge within its grounds. Inside, there is a magnificent panelled hall, fine tapestries and china, and the famous Carlisle collection of miniature rooms exquisitely furnished in different period styles to one eighth life size.

HOVINGHAM
MAP 4 REF J6

10 miles SW of Pickering on the B1257

"Hall, church and village gather round like a happy family" wrote Arthur Mee describing Hovingham some 60 years ago. Today the idyllic scene remains unspoilt, a lovely place boasting no fewer than three village greens. Overlooking one of them is an elegant Victorian school, still in use and boasting a lovely oriel window.

Nearby **Hovingham Hall**, an imposing Georgian mansion, was built in 1760 for Sir Thomas Worsley, Surveyor General to George III, and almost exactly two hundred years later, on June 8th 1961, his descendant Katherine Worsley returned here for a royal reception following her marriage to the Duke of Kent. The Worsley family still live at the Hall so it is only open to visitors by arrangement, but you can see its unusual entrance which leads directly off the village green. The huge archway opens, not as you would expect, into a drive leading to the Hall but to a vast riding school and stables.

MALTON
MAP 4 REF J6

8 miles S of Pickering off the A169/B1257

Malton has been the historic centre of Ryedale ever since the Romans came. They built a large fort and called it "Derventio" after the river Derwent beside which it stands. For many years, archaeologists were puzzled by the large scale of the fort, a mystery resolved in 1970 when a building dedication was uncovered which revealed that the fort housed a cavalry regiment, the Ala Picentiana, - the extra space was needed to accommodate their horses. Many relics from the site, showing the sophisticated life-styles of the Roman centurions and civilians, can be seen in the **Malton Museum,** along with items from the Iron Age settlement that preceded the Roman garrison.

The River Derwent was vitally important to Malton. The river rises in the moors near Scarborough, then runs inland through the Vale of Pickering bringing an essential element for what was once a major industry in Malton - brewing. In the 19th century, there were nine breweries here, now only the Malton Brewery Company survives. It operates in a converted stable block behind Suddabys Crown Hotel in Wheelgate and welcomes visitors, but telephone them first on 01653 697580. Old Malton is located just to the north of the **Roman Fort**, an interesting and historic area on the edge of open countryside. Nearby villages such as Settrington and their secluded country lanes are home to many famous racehorse stables: if you are up and about early enough you will see the horses out on their daily exercises. In the centre of Old Malton stands a beautiful fragment of **St Mary's Priory**, incorporating a particularly fine Norman doorway. The Priory was built around 1155 by the only monastic order in Christendom to have originated entirely in England - the Gilbertines. The order was founded in 1148 by a Lincolnshire parish priest, St Gilbert of Sempringham. Parts of the parish church are quite as old as the Priory but one of its most interesting features is relatively modern, the work of the "Mouseman of Kilburn", Robert Thompson. A gifted woodcarver and furniture maker, Thompson 'signed' all his pieces with a discreetly placed carving of a mouse. There's one on the stout oak door of the church and, inside, the stalls are carved elaborately with all manner of wondrous beasts and historical and mythical scenes.

A mile or so north of Old Malton is **Eden Camp**, a theme museum dedicated to re-creating the dramatic experiences of ordinary people living through World War II. This unique museum is housed in the huts of a genuine prisoner of war camp, built in 1942. Sound, lighting effects, smells, even smoke generators are deployed to make you feel that you are actually there, taking part. Visitors can find out what it was like to live through an air raid, to be a prisoner of war or a sailor in a U-boat under attack. Amongst the many other exhibits are displays on Fashion in the 40s, Children at War, and even one on Rationing. In 1941, one discovers, the cheese ration was down to 1oz (28 grams) a week! Right next door to Eden Camp is **Eden Farm Insight,** a working farm with a fascinating collection of old farm machinery and implements, (including a very old horse wheel), lots of animals, a blacksmith's and a wheelwright's shop, as well as a choice of farm walks, all clearly signposted and with useful information boards. The Farm also offers a café, gift shop, and a picnic and play area.

RYTON   MAP 4 REF J6
3 miles N of Malton off the A169

About a mile north of Eden Camp Insight, the tiny village of Ryton is hidden away in peaceful countryside near the River Rye, an ideal spot for a restful and relaxing holiday. And at **Swan's Nest Cottage** on Abbott's Farm you'll find the perfect self-catering accom-

**Swan's Nest Cottage, Abbotts Farmhouse, Ryton, nr Malton,
North Yorkshire YO17 6SA Tel: 01653 694970**

modation in a charming cottage which dates back to 1810. It was erected then as an outbuilding for the farm but has been thoroughly renovated and modernised and now provides excellent accommodation for up to 5 people in the two cosy bedrooms. Everything, apart from electricity which is paid for by a coin meter, is included in the tariff - even the logs for the open fire. Children are welcome and the cottage is available by the week, or for shorter periods out of season. The owners, Mike and Yvonne Dickinson, live in the nearby farmhouse and will do everything they can to make your stay as pleasant and comfortable as possible.

LOW MARISHES
MAP 4 REF K5

5 miles NE of Malton off the A169

This tiny hamlet appears on few maps but it's well worth seeking out in order to visit **The School House Inn**, an attractive whitewashed house with a large conservatory at one end. When Geoff and Helen Thompson, both of them Yorkshire born and bred, bought the pub in the summer of 1999 it had been closed for several months but they have revived its fortunes and the inn now offers quality food and ale in wonderfully traditional

**The School House Inn, Low Marishes, nr Malton,
North Yorkshire YO17 6RJ Tel: 01653 668247**

surroundings. Pewter tankards and beer mugs hang from the dark old beams, along with gleaming copper, lucky horseshoes - and even a concertina! The menu is written up on the blackboard above the fireplace and the tasty dishes are available every lunchtime from 11.30am until 2pm (or later if required) and again from early evening up to 9.30pm. Children are welcome and you can enjoy your food either in the bar, the dining room or the conservatory. If you happen to be visiting on a Monday evening, feel free to join in the regular quiz. Incidentally, the inn was never a schoolroom but takes its name from the old schoolroom in the grounds which closed in 1917.

SCAGGLETHORPE
MAP 4 REF K6

2 miles E of Malton off the A64

Nobody knows how or why **The Ham & Cheese Inn** acquired its unusual name but it is known that the inn is the only hostelry in the country with this distinctive title. Situated just off the A64, the inn dates back to 1907 and since the summer of 1999 has been in the capable hands of Steve and Diane Shier, aided by their son Luke. Steve is a fully qualified, professional chef who trained and worked in top class London hotels before running hotels, inns and even a golf club in Wales. Steve's outstanding cuisine is available every day from noon until 3pm, again from 6.30pm until 10pm, and such is the inn's reputation for good food it's definitely wise to book ahead.

The Ham & Cheese Inn, Scagglethorpe, nr Malton, North Yorkshire YO17 8DY   Tel: 01944 758249

Look out in particular for Steve's fish dishes, a speciality of the house served with his own special sauces. Luke tends the cellar and bar where you'll find at least three Real Ales and a wide choice of other quality beverages.

EAST HESLERTON
Map 4 ref K6

7 miles NE of Malton on the A64

This little village is distinguished by one of the many churches gifted by Sir Tatton Sykes of Sledmere House in the mid-1800s. Designed in 13th century style the church has a fine west portico, a vaulted chancel and an iron screen of very fine workmanship. The north tower has an octagonal belfry and spire, and statues of the four Latin Doctors (Ambrose, Augustine, Gregory and Jerome) originally sculpted for Bristol Cathedral.

Conveniently located alongside the A64 Malton to Scarborough road, **The Snooty Fox** has something for just about everybody. Bruce Price bought the pub in the autumn of

The Snooty Fox, East Heslerton, nr Malton, North Yorkshire YO17 8EN Tel: 01944 710554

1999 after it had fallen on hard times and have transformed it into a lively inn serving good food and real ales. A free house, The Snooty Fox is open all day, every day, and serves quality food every day from noon until 9.30pm. The inn also offers both bed & breakfast and self-catering in attractive chalet-style accommodation. If you are touring with a caravan or camping, you can also stay here at the Motel on the site of a former aerodrome, the very one where the famous aviator, Amy Johnson, learned to fly. The 4-acre site has electric hook-ups and fishing is available nearby. Yet another attraction is the recently created Duckworld, home to several rare breeds of duck. The Snooty Fox is centrally located with the North York Moors, the Heritage Coast and the Wolds all within easy reach, and the historic city of York about a 25 mile drive away.

CASTLE HOWARD   Map 4 ref J6
5 miles SW of Malton off the A64

Lying in the folds of the Howardian Hills about 5 miles southwest of Malton stands one of the most glorious stately homes in Britain, **Castle Howard.** Well known to television

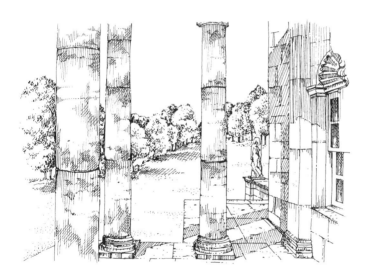

viewers as the Brideshead of *Brideshead Revisited*, Castle Howard has astonished visitors ever since it was completed in the early 1700s. Even that world-weary 18th century socialite Horace Walpole was stirred to enthusiasm: *"Nobody had informed me"* he wrote *"that at one view I*

Castle Howard

should see a palace, a town, a fortified city, temples on high places, ...the noblest lawn in the world fenced by half the horizon and a mausoleum that would tempt one to be buried alive: in short, I have seen gigantic places before, but never a sublime one". Perhaps the most astonishing fact of all concerns the architect of Castle Howard, Sir John Vanbrugh. Vanbrugh had been a soldier and a playwright but until he began this sublime building had never yet overseen the placing of one block of masonry on another.

Yet another attraction at Castle Howard is **Jorvik Glass**, housed in the handsome 18th century stable yard. Established in March 1995 by Angela Henderson when the Costume Gallery here was closed, Jorvik Glass offers a beautifully crafted range of functional and decorative glassware, all of it manufactured on the premises. Amongst the exquisite items available in the gift shop are perfume bottles, paper-weights, jewellery, wine glasses and decanters, vases and bowls, and attractive animal figurines. In the adjoining hot glass studio visitors can watch at close quarters the traditional techniques of glassblowing, a difficult skill whose history has been traced back to Syria in the 1st century BC. The individually hand made glassware created at Jorvik Glass is supplied to numerous gift shops, galleries and department stores, and a mail order catalogue is also available. The Studio also undertakes commissions, corporate incentive work and repairs. Open every day of the week between March and December, from 10am until 6pm, Jorvik Glass should definitely not be missed.

Adjoining the parkland of the Castle Howard estate, the tranquil ambience of **High Gaterley Farm** with its magnificent views over the Howardian Hills and surrounding countryside makes it a perfect location for a peaceful and relaxing stay. The attractive old farmhouse, part late 18th century, part early 19th, is the home of Sandie and Peter Turner - warm and welcoming hosts who, in addition to the quality breakfast included in the tariff, will be happy to provide an

Jorvik Glass, The Stable Yard,
Castle Howard, York YO60 7DA
Tel: 01653 648555

evening meal on request. Special diets can be catered for by arrangement. The non-smoking house is centrally heated (although the comfortable residents lounge also has a log fire), and the delightful guest rooms are either en suite or have washbasins, charmingly furnished and equipped with TV and tea/coffee facilities. There's an attractive garden for

High Gaterley Farm, nr Castle Howard, York YO60 7HT Tel: 01653 694636
e-mail: relax@highgaterley.com website: www.highgaterley.com

fairweather days and even though tucked away in the depths of the countryside, High Gaterley is within easy reach of the coast, moors, wolds and the City of York and have one of Yorkshire's premier attractions, Castle Howard, virtually on its doorstep.

WELBURN MAP 4 REF J6

6 miles SW of Malton off the A64

A grand tree-lined avenue, four miles long, leads to Castle Howard. Near the southern end of this impressive approach is the village of Welburn where you'll find **Cherry Tree Cottage**. Enjoying open and uninterrupted views of the Howardian Hills and close to Castle Howard, this is a delightful place to stay on either a bed & breakfast or self-catering basis. Bed and breakfast guests stay in the main house, the home of Paul and Jane Cade who

have been welcoming visitors here since 1991. For those who prefer self-catering, the adjacent cottage has 2 bedrooms and is traditionally furnished with some antiques, paintings and prints. In the living room there's a nice "Victorian style" open fireplace which can be lit for your arrival if you wish. The cottage is available all year round and the tariff includes linen and electricity. If you grow tired of cooking breakfast, you can have it in the main house and

Cherry Tree Cottage, 1 Holmes Crescent, Welburn, York, North Yorkshire YO60 7EJ Tel: 01653 618678

evening meals are also available. Welburn is ideally situated for both young and old alike, convenient for the East Coast, the North York Moors, Flamingo Land Theme Park and Eden Camp War Museum. You could take the steam train from Pickering into *Heartbeat* country or drive the few miles to York and its manifold attractions.

Two miles south of Welburn, in a lovely, peaceful setting beside the River Derwent, stand the remains of **Kirkham Priory**. According to legend, the priory was founded in 1125 by Walter l'Espec after his only son was thrown from his horse and killed at this very spot. (A few years later, Walter was to found another great abbey at Rievaulx). Visitors to Kirkham pass through a noble, exquisitely decorated gatehouse but one of the most memorable sights at the Priory, perhaps because it is so unexpected, is the sumptuous lavatorium in the ruined cloister. Here the monks washed their hands at two bays with lavishly moulded arches supported by slender pillars, each bay adorned with tracery.

2 The City of York and Central Yorkshire

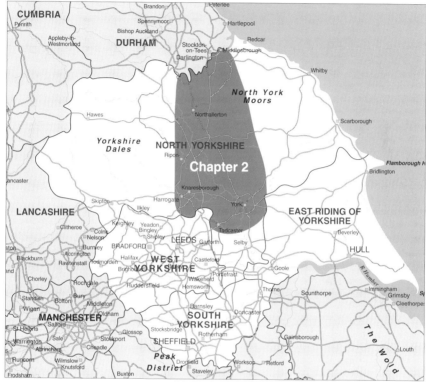

YORK

"The history of York is the history of England" said the Duke of York, later to become George VI. A bold claim but well justified. For almost two thousand years the city has been at the centre of great events and, better than any other city in England, it has pre-served the evidence of its glorious past. One of the grandest cityscapes in the country opens up as you walk along the old city walls towards **York Minster,** a sublime expression of medieval faith.

The Minster stands on the site of an even older building, the headquarters of the Roman legions. The Imperial troops arrived here in AD71 when the governor, Quintus Petilius Cerealis, chose this strategic position astride the Rivers Ouse and Foss as his base for a campaign against the pesky tribe of the Brigantes. The settlement was named Eboracum. From this garrison, Hadrian directed the construction of his great wall and a

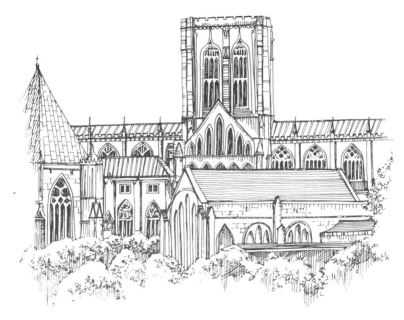

York Minster, York

later general, Constantine, was proclaimed Emperor here. The legions finally left the city around AD410, but the evidence of their three and a half centuries of occupation is manifest all around York in buildings like the **Multangular Tower,** in rich artefacts treasured in the city's museums and even in a pub: at the **Roman Bath Inn** you can see the remains of steam baths used by the garrison residents.

Little is known of York during the Dark Ages but by the 8th century the city had been colonised by the Anglo-Saxons, who named it Eoferwic, and it was already an important Christian and academic centre. The Vikings put an end to that when they invaded in the 9th century and changed the name once again, this time to Jorvik. The story of York during those years of Danish rule is imaginatively told in the many displays at the **Jorvik Centre**.

After the Norman Conquest, the city suffered badly during the Harrowing of the North when William the Conqueror mounted a brutal campaign against his rebellious northern subjects. Vast tracts of Yorkshire and Northumberland were laid waste and some historians reckon that it took more a hundred years for the area to recover from this wholesale devastation.

In later Norman times, however, York entered one of its most glorious periods. The Minster, the largest Gothic church in England, was begun around 1230 and the work was on such a scale that it would not be completed until two and a half centuries later. Its stained glass windows - there are more than a hundred of them - cast a celestial light over the many treasures within. A guided tour of the Great Tower gives dizzying views across the city; a visit to the crypt reveals some of the relics from the Roman fortress that stood here nearly 2000 years ago.

This superb building has survived seemingly unscathed from three major fires. The first occurred in 1829 and was started by a madman, Jonathan Martin. Believing that God wanted him to destroy the church, he started a fire using prayer and hymn books. The fire was not discovered until the following morning by which time the east end of the Minster had been severely damaged. The second blaze, in 1840, was caused by a workman leaving a candle burning. As a result of his carelessness, the central part of the nave was destroyed. The most recent conflagration was in July 1984, shortly after a controversial Bishop of Durham had been installed. Some attributed the fire to God's wrath at the Bishop's appointment; the more prosaic view was that it had been caused by lightning. The subsequent restoration has allowed modern masons and craftsmen to demonstrate that they possess skills just as impressive as those of their medieval forebears.

If you are planning to stay in this beautiful and historic city, **Barbican House** is strongly recommended. It enjoys an ideal situation overlooking the famous medieval city

walls and is just a 10-minute stroll from all the city centre attractions. This small and friendly bed & breakfast establishment is owned and managed by Michael and Juliet Morgan. Michael, whose home town is York and Juliet, a native of California, will ensure a warm Yorkshire welcome. Their house is a Victorian residence of individual charm and character which has been sympathetically restored, retaining many of its lovely original features to provide delightful accommodation. Guests enjoy a full English breakfast in the attractive dining room, with a fresh fruit platter, yoghurt, scones and American blueberry muffins also available. Barbican House is a mere 100 yards from the splendid Barbican Leisure Centre with its pool and many quality concerts and functions,

Barbican House, 20 Barbican Road, York YO10 5AA
Tel: 01904 627617 Fax: 01904 647140
e-mail: barbican@thenet.co.uk
website: http://www.thenet.co.uk/~barbican/

and some of the best and most reasonable restaurants and pubs in town are also just a short walk away. You could leave your car idle in the Morgans' floodlit car park for the whole of your stay!

The network of medieval streets around the Minster is one of the city's major delights. Narrow lanes are criss-crossed by even narrower footpaths - ginnels, snickets or 'snickelways', which have survived as public rights of way despite being built over, above and around. Narrowest of all the snickelways is Pope's Head Alley, more than 100ft long but only 31 inches wide. The alley was also known as Introduction Lane - if you wanted to know someone better, you simply timed your walk along it so as to meet the other party half-way. Whip-ma-Whop-ma-Gate, allegedly, is where felons used to be "whipped and whopped". Probably most famous of these ancient streets is **The Shambles**. Its name comes from 'Fleshammels', the street of butchers and slaughter houses. The houses here were deliberately built to keep the street out of direct sunlight, thus protecting the carcasses which were hung outside the houses on hooks. Many of the hooks are still in place.

During these years, York was the second largest city in England and it was then that the town walls and their 'bars', or gates, were built. The trade guilds were also at their most powerful and in Fossgate one of them built the lovely black and white timbered **Merchant Adventurers Hall**. The Merchant Adventurers controlled the lucrative trade in all "goods bought and sold foreign" and they spared no expense in building their Great Hall where they conducted their affairs beneath a complex timbered roof displaying many colourful banners of York's medieval guilds. To this period too belong the **York Mystery Plays**, first performed in 1397 and subsequently every four years.

During Tudor times, York's importance steadily declined but re-emerged in the 18th century as a fashionable social centre. Many elegant Georgian houses, of which **Fairfax House** in Castlegate is perhaps the most splendid, were built at this time and they add another attractive architectural dimension to the city.

The following century saw York take on a completely different rôle as the hub of the railway system in the north. At the heart of this transformation was the charismatic entrepreneur George Hudson, founder of what became the Great Northern Railway, part visionary, part crook. His wheeler-dealing eventually led to his disgrace but even then the citizens of York twice elected him as Lord Mayor and he still has a pub named after him. It was thanks to Hudson that York's magnificent railway station, with its great curving roof of glass, was built, a tourist attraction in its own right. Nearby, in Leeman Street, is the **National Railway Museum**, the largest of its kind in the world. This fascinating exhibition covers some two hundred years of railway history, from Stephenson's *Rocket* to the Channel Tunnel. Amongst the thousands of exhibits demonstrating the technical and social impact of the 'Iron Horse' are Gresley's record-breaking locomotive, *Mallard,* Queen Victoria's royal carriage, and displays demonstrating the workings of the railway system. There's an extensive library and reading room (booking advised), and the 'Brief Encounter' restaurant is themed on the classic movie.

Another aspect of railway history is on view at the **York Model Railway**, next door to the station, which has almost one third of a mile of track and up to 14 trains running at any one time. Machinery of a very different kind is on display at the **Museum of Automata**. Automata are "man made objects that imitate the movement of living things through a mechanism that is concealed, so as to make them appear to move spontaneously". The museum traces the history of automata, from the simple articulated figurines of ancient civilisations, through to displays of modern robotics: the Automata Shop sells contemporary pieces, music boxes, mechanical toys and craft kits suitable for all ages.

In Coppergate is the **Jorvik Centre**, a fairly recent innovation celebrating a 1000-year-old story. Visitors

Jorvik Centre

step aboard a time-car for a journey through representations of real-life Viking Age Britain. You pass through a bustling market thronged with Danes bartering for chickens, corn and other provisions and wares, penetrate dark smoky houses, cross a busy wharf where goods transported along the rivers Ouse and Foss are being off-loaded. The experience comes complete with authentic sounds and even smells and for children in particular is both fun and educational.

In a beautifully restored church close to the Shambles is the **Archaeological Research Centre** (ARC), an award-winning hands-on exploration of archaeology for visitors of all ages. Here you can meet practising archaeologists who will demonstrate how to sort and identify genuine finds or to try out ancient crafts. For the more technically minded, there's a series of interactive computer displays which illustrate how modern technology helps to discover and interpret the past. Fascinating.

Very popular with those who have an interest in the more macabre aspects of York's long history is the **Original Ghostwalk of York** which starts at the King's Arms pub on Ouse Bridge and sets off at 8pm every evening. At the last count, York was reckoned to have some 140 resident ghosts within its walls - on this guided walk you visit some of their haunts and hear dark tales, grim accounts of murder, torture, and intrigue. Prepare to have your blood chilled.

It's impossible here to list all York's museums, galleries and fine buildings, but you will find a wealth of additional information at the Tourist Information Centre close to one of the historic old gateways to the city, **Bootham Bar**.

THE VALE OF YORK

The Vale, or Plain as it's sometimes called, is rich, agricultural land that stretches some 60 miles northwards from York almost to the Tees. Although flat itself, there are almost always hills in view: the Hambleton and Cleveland Hills to the east, the Dales and the Pennines to the west. In between lies this fertile corridor of rich farmland and low-lying meadows, a vast plain bisected by the Great North Road linking London and Edinburgh. For most of its life, the Great North Road has been a rocky, pot-holed and swampy obstacle course. The best stretches, by far, were those where it ran along the meticulously engineered course the Romans had built centuries earlier. It took more than eighteen hundred years for the English to realise themselves the importance of constructing viable, all-weather roads. We were, one might say, slow learners. We begin our survey in the south of the vale - the locations mentioned here are all within a few miles of York itself.

STAMFORD BRIDGE   MAP 4 REF J7
6 miles NE of York on the A166

Everyone knows that 1066 was the year of the Battle of Hastings but, just a few days before that battle, King Harold had clashed at Stamford Bridge with his half-brother Tostig and Hardrada, King of Norway who between them had mustered some 60,000 men. On a rise near the corn mill is a stone commemorating the event with an inscription in English and Danish. Up until 1878, a Sunday in September was designated 'Spear Day Feast' in commemoration of the battle. On this day, boat-shaped pies were made bearing the impression of the fatal spear, in memory of the Saxon soldier in his boat who slew the single

Norseman defending the wooden bridge. Harold's troops were triumphant but immediately after this victory they marched southwards to Hastings and a much more famous defeat.

Occupying a pleasant riverside location, **The Cottage Guest House & Waterside Tea Rooms** provides quality accommodation as well as first class food in its characterful tea shop and restaurant. In good weather, tea room customers can enjoy their refreshments in the garden leading down to the River Derwent or sample Carol Todd's wholesome cuisine in the tea room itself. The menu includes an All Day Breakfast, omelettes, salads, jacket potatoes, ploughman's and sandwiches with cream teas and fresh cream cakes also available. Carol also

The Cottage Guest House & Waterside Tea Rooms, 6-8 The Square, Stamford Bridge, nr York YO41 1AF
Tel: 01759 371115 Fax: 01759 373662

runs "Creative Cuisine" which provides outside catering for any occasion. The large old house, dating back to 1760, has 6 guest rooms of various sizes and styles, one of them boasting a four-poster bed and a grand view over the river. Some of the rooms are non-smoking, children are welcome, but pets cannot be accommodated. Both the guest house and the tea room are open throughout the year with food available from 10am to 6pm in summer, 10am to 5pm in winter.

Located a couple of miles southeast of Stamford Bridge, **High Catton Grange** offers a choice of bed and breakfast or self-catering accommodation in a wonderfully peaceful rural area. The Grange, which stands within a 300-acre mixed arable farm, is the home of Tom and Sheila Foster who has been providing quality B&B here since 1984. Bed and

High Catton Grange, Stamford Bridge, York YO41 1EP
Tel/Fax: 01759 371374

breakfast guests stay in the main farmhouse where there are 2 double rooms, one en suite, one with its own bathroom, and both of them qualifying for a Tourist Board 4-diamond rating. For those who prefer self-catering, there is accommodation for up to 4 people (plus a cot) in the attractively converted former stable/gig-shed/hayloft which dates back to the 18th century. This charming property has a 4 Keys Commended rating and one of its many attractive features is a secluded patio where you can enjoy those (hopefully) balmy summer days. Everything you are likely to need is provided and the property is available all year round, for weekly lets during the summer and for shorter breaks also at other times.

FLAXTON

MAP 4 REF J7

8 miles NE of York off the A64

Located about halfway between the city of York and the grandeur of Castle Howard, the picturesque village of Flaxton is best known for its outstanding pub, **The Blacksmiths Arms**. This ancient hostelry has been at the heart of village life for more than 250 years, a long history witnessed by the characterful old beams and real fires. Owned since 1995 by Jeff and Alison Jordan, the inn serves quality food every evening and at Sunday lunch-time (bookings advisable for Sunday lunch). There's a separate non-smoking dining room or you can enjoy your meal in either of the bars. The well-kept ales on offer include

Timothy Taylor Landlord, as well as guest ales, and if you're here on a Monday evening feel free to join in the regular Quiz Night. Flaxton is a peaceful place to choose as a base for exploring the area and the Blacksmiths Arms has two self-catering

The Blacksmiths Arms, Flaxton, York YO60 7RJ
Tel: 01904 468210

cottages available from March to the end of October. They have been ingeniously converted from former barns and each sleeps up to four people. If the cottages are not occupied, the Jordans will happily let them on a bed & breakfast basis.

WESTOW

MAP 4 REF J6

12 miles NE of York off the A64

This quiet backwater near the River Derwent and close to Howsham Woods is well worth seeking out in order to pay a visit to, or stay at, **The Blacksmiths Arms Inn**. A listed building dating back some 250 years, the inn was indeed a blacksmith's-cum-hostelry in

The Blacksmiths Arms Inn, Westow, nr York YO60 7NE
Tel: 01653 618365 / 618343 Fax: 01653 618365 Mobile: 0421 858910

the days when that combination of businesses was quite usual. Today, David and Suzanne Greenwood confine themselves to providing good food, quality ales and top of the range bed & breakfast accommodation. The appetising traditional home cooking on offer is prepared by Suzanne and chef Jackie. Bar meals and are available at lunchtime and again in the evenings along with full meals, except on Monday and Tuesday lunchtimes (unless the Monday is a Bank Holiday). Bed and breakfast guests stay in the beautifully converted former stables where there are 6 en suite bedrooms, including one disabled suite, all of them well furnished and thoughtfully equipped. Please note that a non-smoking policy is requested in the bedrooms. The inn is conveniently located for visiting many of Yorkshire's major attractions - the magnificent Castle Howard is just a few miles distant, the Yorkshire Wolds roll away to the southeast, and the City of York itself is only a short drive away.

ACOMB   MAP 4 REF 17
On the western edge of York off the B1224

Once a separate village, Acomb has been absorbed into Greater York but still preserves much of its village character. **The Sun Inn**, situated opposite the village green, dates back to the early 1800s when it was a coaching inn and teams of horses were kept here so that they could be changed on the carriage's way to York - now only a ten minute car journey away. The main bar has an interesting array of pictures of Matt Busby and some of the great Manchester United players as well as well-known jockeys. In the

The Sun Inn, 35 The Green, Acomb,
North Yorkshire YO26 5LL Tel: 01904 798500

lounge there is a rather fine collection of teapots and other items of crockery on display. The Sun Inn serves a limited range of bar snacks and an excellent choice of fine ales, including John Smiths and three other cask ales. Expertly run by landlady Maureen Yoward with the help of her manager Phil, this is a true English pub and, as such, guests can be sure of a warm welcome. Traditional pub games such as darts and dominoes are played here and there is also a quiz every Sunday evening which is open to all.

NEWTON ON OUSE
8 miles NW of York off the A19

MAP 4 REF H7

Hailed by the *Yorkshire Evening Press* as the Community Pub of the Year 1996, the **Blacksmiths Arms** stands across the road from the parish church in this picturesque village

beside the River Ouse. To the south stretches the extensive parkland of Beningbrough Hall and there are lovely riverside walks in both directions. Glenn and Lesley Mimms have been here since 1990 and their welcoming personalities have made the Blacksmiths Arms the centre of village life. This atmospheric pub with its real fires and lots of local memorabilia is noted for the quality of the cuisine on offer. It's prepared by an Italian chef which explains why there's a choice of no fewer than 40 varieties of pizza! Meals are available

Blacksmiths Arms, Cherry Tree Avenue, Newton on Ouse, York YO30 2BN Tel: 01347 848249

every evening from 5.30pm until 10pm and on Sundays a Roast Lunch is served from noon until 2.30pm. The inn has a pleasant front garden with picnic tables and as we go to press plans are under way to add four guest rooms, all of which will be en suite.

About a mile to the south of Newton on Ouse is **Beningbrough Hall** (National Trust), a baroque masterpiece from the early 18th century with 7 acres of gardens, wilderness play area, pike ponds and scenic walks. There's also a fully operational Victorian laundry which graphically demonstrates the drudgery of a 19th century washing day. A major attraction here is the permanent exhibition of more than one hundred portraits on loan from the National Portrait Gallery. Other exhibitions are often held at the Hall - for these there is usually an additional charge.

LINTON-ON-OUSE
8 miles NW of York off the A19

MAP 4 REF H7

If you are caravanning or camping in North Yorkshire, **Linton Lock Leisureways** offers a charming and secluded site at Linton Lock on the River Ouse. Open from March 1st to October 31st, this picturesque site can accommodate up to 16 touring caravans and 20 tents. Visitors will find all modern amenities available on site - electric hook-ups, toilet and shower facilities, and an excellent licensed restaurant and café, The bar is open every evening from 7pm and additionally on Saturday and Sunday from 9am until 4pm. The restaurant serves an outstanding Sunday lunch

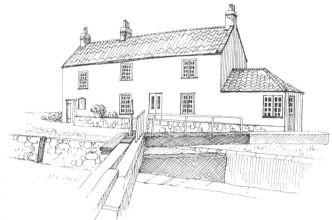

Linton Lock Leisureways, Lock House, Linton-on-Ouse, York YO6 2AZ Tel/Fax: 01347 848486

for which booking is strongly recommended. Whatever your particular interests, Linton Lock provides an excellent base. The River Ouse provides some of the finest fishing in Yorkshire and day tickets are available for one the 16 pegs. You'll also find facilities for boating and golfing. The historic city of York is just 8 miles away, and also within easy reach are some of the country's grandest stately homes and the beauty of the Yorkshire countryside.

ALNE   MAP 4 REF H6

11 miles NW of York off the A19

It's well worth making the short detour from the A19 to this secluded and attractive little village set beside the River Kyle in order to sample the food, drink and relaxing atmosphere to be found at **The Blue Bell Inn.** Owned and run by Jayne and Trevor Porter, this

former farmhouse is a hostelry maintaining the best traditions of English country pubs. You'll find a choice of at least 3 real ales in summer, with a weekly guest ale, a good selection of wines, and an appetising menu which offers all the traditional favourites along with some delicious Thai dishes. Jayne, who is in charge of the kitchen, wanted something a

The Blue Bell Inn, Main Street, Alne, York, YO61 1RR Tel: 01347 838331

little bit different on the menu so she taught herself Thai cuisine, and very good it is too. Meals can be enjoyed either in the restaurant with its low beamed ceiling and open fire, or in the cosy bar. Food is available at lunchtimes, (noon to 2pm, Wednesday to Sunday, and on Bank Holiday Mondays), and in the evenings, Tuesday to Saturday, from 5.30pm to 9.30pm. Every other Wednesday, there's a pub quiz in which everyone is welcome to join in.

STILLINGTON

MAP 4 REF I6

10 miles N of York on the B1363

In 1758, one of the great works of English literature almost perished in the fireplace of **Stillington Hall**. The parson of Coxwold had been invited to dinner and when the meal ended was asked to read from a book he had just completed. The guests had all wined and dined well and were soon dozing off. Incensed by their inattention the parson threw the pages of his manuscript onto the fire. Fortunately his host, the Squire of Stillington, rescued them from the flames and Laurence Sterne's immortal *Tristram Shandy* was saved for posterity.

Located in the heart of this sizeable village and well known for its quality food, ale and hospitality, the **White Bear Inn** is an attractive white-painted tavern whose history stretches back to the 18th century when it was a staging post and stables for coaches. A free

house, owned and run by Philip and Susan Robinson, the White Bear offers a good selection of fine ales, including J. Smiths, Tetleys and Black Sheep, and an extensive choice of excellent food. Susan is the cook and her comprehensive menu, which includes such dishes as game in season, is inscribed on a large blackboard over the vintage iron fireplace. Apart from Sunday evenings, food is available every lunchtime (12 noon until 2pm) and evening (5.30pm to 9pm). Spe-

The White Bear Inn, Main Street, Stillington, York YO61 IJU Tel: 01347 810338

cial "meal deals" are on offer every weekday lunchtime, and weekday evenings up until 7.30pm. As we go to press, plans are under way to provide accommodation at the White Bear and this may well be available by the time you read this.

EASINGWOLD

MAP 2 REF H6

12 miles NW of York off the A19

This agreeable market town was once surrounded by the Forest of Galtres, a vast hunting preserve of Norman kings. It lies at the foot of the Howardian Hills, an Area of Outstanding Natural Beauty covering 77 acres of woods, farmland and historic parkland. Easingwold's prosperity dates back to the 18th century when it flourished as a major stage coach post - at that period the town could offer a choice of some 26 public houses and inns. Until the recent construction of a bypass the old town was clogged with traffic but it is now a pleasure again to wander around the market place with its impressive **Market Cross** and, nearby, the outline of the old bull-baiting ring set in the cobbles. Easingwold used to enjoy the distinction of having its own private railway, a two and a half mile stretch of track along which it took all of ten minutes to reach the main east coast line at

Market Cross, Easingwold

Alne. Older residents fondly remember the ancient, tall-chimneyed steam locomotive that plied this route until its deeply regretted closure to passenger traffic in 1948.

A little to the south of Easingwold, on the B1363, is **Sutton Park**, a noble early 18th century mansion, built in 1730 by Thomas Atkinson and containing some fine examples of Sheraton and Chippendale furniture, and much-admired decorative plasterwork by the Italian maestro in this craft, Cortese. The ubiquitous 'Capability' Brown designed the lovely gardens and parkland in which you'll find a Georgian ice-house, well-signposted woodland walks and a nature trail. There's also a gift shop and a cafe.

HUSTHWAITE

MAP 2 REF H6

8 miles SE of Thirsk off the A19

Old stone houses mingle with mellow Victorian and Edwardian brick and overlooking the village green where three lanes meet the Church of St Nicholas still retains its original Norman doorway. Just outside the village, on the road to Coxwold, there's a stunning view across to the Hambleton Hills and the **White Horse of Kilburn**.

COXWOLD

MAP 2 REF I6

9 miles SE of Thirsk off the A19 or A170

Coxwold enjoys a particularly lovely setting in the narrow valley that runs between the Hambleton and Howardian Hills. At the western end of the village stands the 500 year old **Shandy Hall**, home of Laurence Sterne, vicar of Coxwold in the 1760s. Sterne was the author of *Tristram Shandy*, that wonderfully bizarre novel which opened a vein of English surreal comedy leading directly to The Goons and the Monty Python team. The architecture of the Hall, Tudor in origin, includes some appropriately eccentric features - strangely-shaped balustrades on the wooden staircases, a Heath Robinson kind of contraption in the bedroom powder-closet by which Sterne could draw up pails of water for his ablutions, and a tiny, eye-shaped window in the huge chimney stack opening from the study to the right of the entrance. A more conventional attraction is the priceless collection of Sterne's books and manuscripts.

The Revd Sterne much preferred the cosmopolitan diversions of London to the rustic pleasures of his Yorkshire parish and rarely officiated at the imposing church nearby with its striking octagonal tower, three-decker pulpit and Fauconberg family tombs. A curiosity here is a floor brass in the nave recording the death of Sir John Manston in 1464. A space was left for his wife Elizabeth's name to be added at a later date. The space is still blank. Outside, against the wall of the nave, is Sterne's original tombstone, moved here from London's Bayswater when the churchyard there was deconsecrated in 1969.

Just to the south of Coxwold is **Newburgh Priory**, founded in 1145 as an Augustinian monastery and now a mostly Georgian country house with fine interiors and a beautiful water garden. Since 1538, the Priory has been the home of the Fauconberg family. An old tradition asserts that Oliver Cromwell's body is interred here. Cromwell's daughter, Mary, was married to Lord Fauconberg and when Charles II had her father's corpse hanged at Tyburn and his head struck off, Lady Fauconberg claimed the decapitated body, brought it to Newburgh and, it is said, buried the remains under the floorboards of an attic room. The supposed tomb has never been opened, the Fauconbergs even resisting a royal appeal from Edward VII when, as Prince of Wales, he was a guest at the

Newburgh Priory, nr Coxwold

Priory. The house, which is still the home of the Earls of Fauconberg, and its extensive grounds are open to the public during the spring and summer months.

From Coxwold, follow the minor road northeastwards towards Ampleforth. After about 2 miles, you will see the lovely, cream-coloured ruins of **Byland Abbey.** The Cistercians began building their vast compound in 1177 and it grew to become the largest Cistercian church in Britain. Much of the damage to its fabric was caused by Scottish soldiers after the Battle of Byland in 1322. The English king, Edward II had been staying at the Abbey but fled after his defeat, abandoning vital stores and priceless treasures. In a frenzy of looting, the Scots made off with everything the king had left and ransacked the Abbey for good measure. The ruined west front of the Abbey, although only the lower arc of its great rose window is still in place, gives a vivid impression of how glorious this building once was.

AMPLEFORTH
MAP 2 REF I5

10 miles SE of Thirsk off the A170

Set on the southern slopes of the Hambleton Hills, Ampleforth is perhaps best known for its Roman Catholic public school, **Ampleforth College**, established by the Benedictine community that came here in 1809, fleeing from persecution in post-revolutionary France. The monks built an austere-looking Abbey in the Romanesque style amongst whose treasures are an altar stone rescued from Byland Abbey and finely crafted woodwork by the 'Mouseman of Kilburn', Robert Thompson.

OLDSTEAD
MAP 2 REF H5

6 miles E of Thirsk off the A170

Overlooking rolling meadows and woodland, the **Black Swan Inn** presents a pleasing picture with its bow windows and stone walls. It was built in the 1700s to serve the cattle drovers on their way from the North Yorkshire moors to the Vale of York and although it has been extended and modernised over the years visitors will be pleased to see that all the character and atmosphere of a country tavern have been retained, with lots of exposed stonework and flagged floors. Mine hosts Ian and Joy Skinner extend a warm

Black Swan Inn, Oldstead, nr Coxwold, York YO61 4BL
Tel: 01347 868387

welcome, providing a good range of ales, (including 2 real ales), and an excellent choice of food. Joy is the cook and her menu changes daily, offering a selection of at least 15 main courses. Food is available every lunchtime and evening except Monday lunchtimes. If you are planning to stay in this lovely area, the Black Swan has 6 en suite ground floor rooms, (4 double, 2 twins), in attractive chalet-style accommodation. Children and pets are welcome - both in the accommodation and in the bar.

A mile or so to the west of Oldstead, a minor road off the A170, signposted to **Kilburn**, leads to the famous **White Horse** inspired by the prehistoric White Horse hill-carving at Uffingham in Berkshire. John Hodgson, Kilburn's village schoolmaster, enthused his pupils and villagers into creating this splendid folly in 1857. It is 314ft long and 228ft high and visible from as far away as Harrogate and Otley. Unlike its prehistoric predecessor in Berkshire, where the chalk hillside keeps it naturally white, Kilburn's 'White' horse is scraped from grey limestone which needs to be regularly groomed with lime-washing and a liberal spreading of chalk chippings.

Just beyond the White Horse is Kilburn village, the home of one of the most famous of modern Yorkshire craftsmen, Robert Thompson - the **"Mouseman of Kilburn"**. Robert's father was a carpenter but he apprenticed his son to an engineer. At the age of 20 however, inspired by seeing the medieval wood carvings in Ripon Cathedral, Robert returned to Kilburn and begged his father to train him as a carpenter. An early commission from Ampleforth Abbey to carve a cross settled his destiny: from then until his death in 1955 Robert's beautifully crafted ecclesiastical and domestic furniture was in constant demand. His work can be seen in more than seven hundred churches, including Westminster Abbey and York Minster. Each piece bears his 'signature' - a tiny carved mouse placed in some inconspicuous corner of the work. According to a family story, Robert adopted this symbol when one of his assistants happened to use the phrase "as poor as a church mouse". (Signing one's work wasn't an entirely new tradition: the 17th century wood-carver Grinling Gibbons' personal stamp was a pod of peas). Robert Thompson's two grandsons have continued his work and their grandfather's former home is now both a memorial to his genius and a showroom for their own creations.

SUTTON-UNDER-WHITESTONECLIFF
MAP 2 REF H5
4 miles E of Thirsk on the A170

Boasting the longest place name in England, Sutton is more famous for the precipitous cliff that towers above it, **Sutton Bank**. For one of the grandest landscape views in England, go to the top of Sutton Bank and look across the vast expanse of the Vale of York to the Pennine hills far away to the west. James Herriot called it the *"finest view in England"*. He knew this area well since his large veterinary practice covered the farms from here right over to the Dales. A continuation of the Cleveland Hills, the Hambleton Hills themselves lead into the Howardian Hills: together they form the mighty southwest flank of the North York Moors.

There's a National Park Information Centre at the summit of Sutton Bank and a well-marked Nature Trail leads steeply down to, and around, **Lake Gormire**, an Ice Age lake trapped here by a landslip. Gormire is one of Yorkshire's only two natural lakes, the other being Semerwater in Wensleydale. Gormire is set in a large basin with no river running from it: any overflow disappears down a 'swallow hole' and emerges beneath White Mare Cliffs.

Sutton Bank used to be a graveyard for caravans because of its steep (1 in 3) climb and sharp bends. On one July Saturday in 1977, some thirty vehicles broke down on the ascent and five breakdown vehicles spent all day retrieving them. Caravans are now banned from this route. Sutton Bank may be tough on cars but its sheer-sided cliffs create powerful thermals making this a favoured spot for gliders and bright-winged hang-gliders.

BOLTBY
MAP 2 REF H5
6 miles NE of Thirsk, off the A170

Boltby is an engaging village tucked away at the foot of the Hambleton Hills, close to where the oddly-named **Gurt of Beck** tumbles down the hillside and, depending on how much rain has fallen on the moors, passes either under or over a little humpback bridge.

On the plain below is **Nevison House**, reputed to be the home of the 17th century highwayman, William Nevison, 'Swift Nick' as Charles II dubbed him. Some historians claim that it was Swift Nick, not Dick Turpin, who made the legendary ride on Black Bess from London to York to establish an alibi.

THIRSK
Map 2 ref H5
23 miles NW of York off the A19

Thirsk has become famous as the home of veterinary surgeon Alf Wight, better known as James Herriot, author of *All Creatures Great and Small*, who died in 1995. In his immensely popular books, Thirsk is clearly recognisable as 'Darrowby'. The Easter of 1999 saw the opening in Thirsk of a £1.4m tribute to the celebrated vet. **The World of James Herriot** is housed in the original surgery in Kirkgate and offers visitors a trip back in time to the 1940s, exploring the life and times of the world's most famous country vet. There's also the opportunity to take part in a TV production, and a 'Visible Farm' exhibit where you can explore farm animals inside and out!

Just across the road from the surgery is the birthplace of another famous son of Thirsk. The building is now the town's museum and tourist office and a plaque outside records that Thomas Lord was born here in 1755: thirty years later he was to create the famous cricket ground in Marylebone that took his name. A more recent celebrity whose home is in Thirsk is Bill Foggitt, renowned for his weather forecasts based on precise observations of nature.

This pleasant small town of mellow brick houses has a sprawling Market Place and a magnificent 15th

James Herriot's Surgery, Thirsk

century **St Mary's Church** which is generally regarded as the finest parish church in North Yorkshire. It was here that the real life 'James Herriot' married his wife, Helen. Cod Beck, a tributary of the River Swale, wanders through the town, providing some delightful - and well-signposted riverside walks.

Thirsk appeared in the Domesday Book not long after William the Conqueror had granted the Manor of Thirsk to one of his barons, Robert de Mowbray. The Mowbrays became a powerful family in the area, a fact reflected in the naming of the area to the north and west of Thirsk as the Vale of Mowbray. In the early 1100s the family received permission to hold a market at Thirsk but then blotted their copybook by rebelling against Henry II in 1173. The rebellion failed and their castle at Thirsk was burnt to the ground. Not a trace of it remains. The market however is still thriving, held twice-weekly on Mondays and Saturdays. An old market by-law used to stipulate that no butcher be allowed to kill a bull for sale in the market until the beast had been baited by the town dogs. That by-law was abandoned in the early 1800s and the bull-ring to which the animal was tethered has also disappeared.

Located only 2 minutes walk from the town centre and James Herriot's veterinary surgery, **Fourways Guest House** began life as a Victorian public house, a fact which explains its unusually spacious proportions. Fourways is now the home of Sharon and David Barker who provide a warm welcome to their bed and breakfast guests. Sharon is

Fourways Guest House, Town End, Thirsk, North Yorkshire YO7 1PY
Tel: 01845 522601 Fax: 01845 522131

an experienced cook so breakfast here is definitely special, with vegetarian and special diets catered for. Evening meals are also available, if booked in advance, with licensed beverages available or, if you prefer an evening out, the Barkers can recommend good eating places in the town. Fourways has 10 guest bedrooms of varying sizes, most of them en suite, some on the ground floor, and offering the option of smoking or non smoking rooms. Guests have the use of a comfortable residents' lounge and there's ample parking. With Thirsk's many attractions virtually on the doorstep and the North York Moors within easy reach, Fourways provides an ideal holiday base.

On the edge of town, the **Trees to Treske Visitor Centre** is an imaginative exhibition exploring how trees grow, the character of different woods and examples of the cabinet maker's craft. Nearby is Thirsk Racecourse, known to devotees of the turf as the 'Country Racecourse'. There are around 12 race meetings each year, all well attended by visitors keen to experience this intrinsic feature of Yorkshire life. Travelling through the areas between the Dales and the North York Moors, one is constantly reminded of the great tradition of horse-breeding that the county is famous for. The tradition runs deep: - even the long flat straight stretch of main railway line between York and Darlington is known as the 'racecourse'.

SOWERBY

MAP 2 REF H5

1 mile S of Thirsk on the B1448

Georgian houses stand beneath a majestic avenue of lime trees, an old packhorse bridge crosses Cod Beck, footpaths lead across fields and alongside the quiet stream, and Millgate Gardens provides a peaceful refuge. Located in the heart of this charming village, **The George Hotel** was built as a substantial private residence in the early 1800s and only became a public house in 1947. Almost exactly half a century later The George was taken over by Tony Watson, a local man who carried out extensive renovations and added a 64-cover restaurant and function room which offers good food in a pleasant, friendly atmosphere. The George's head chef, Suzie Jones, trained at Scarborough University and specialises in good quality home cooked food which ranges from home made Chilli through a delicious Haddock and Prawn Mornay to a hearty 10oz Sirloin Steak. For lighter appetites there's a good choice of snacks, including a Yorkshire Pudding sandwich,

The George Hotel, 57 Front Street, Sowerby, Thirsk, North Yorkshire YO7 1JF Tel: 01845 522085

salads and open sandwiches. Such is the restaurant's popularity, you'd be well-advised to book on weekend evenings, although you can also eat in the bar. The George is a free house and Tony prides himself on maintaining the reputation of its well known cask ales. Lovers of real ale are well provided for and, for those who prefer the grape, there's a good selection of sensibly priced wines.

Animal lovers have a treat in store for them when they stay for bed and breakfast at **Long Acre**, the home of Rose and John Dawson. The 2 acres of grounds to the rear of the Dawsons' house are a kind of Noah's Ark annexe, inhabited by a wonderful array of animals ranging from rescue owls to sheep, along with chickens, ducks, dogs and cats, all lovingly cared for by Rose and John. Bed and breakfast guests are also pampered, with spacious, attractively decorated and furnished bedrooms, complimentary tea on arrival, and a delicious breakfast prepared by Rose who is a gifted cook. You'd be well advised to take advantage of the optional evening meal since only fresh local produce is used, including fresh vegetables from the

Long Acre, 86a Topcliffe Road, Sowerby, Thirsk, North Yorkshire YO7 1RY Tel: 01845 522360

Dawsons'own garden in season, and the best of cuts from the local butcher. Vegetarians and vegans can also be catered for. Long Acre is an easy walk from the town centre and the spectacular scenery of the North York Moors is just a short drive away.

SION HILL

MAP 2 REF G5

4 miles NW of Thirsk off the A167

Sion Hill Hall, about four miles northwest of Thirsk, is celebrated as the 'last of the great country houses'. Its light, airy and well-proportioned rooms, all facing south, are typical of the work of the celebrated Yorkshire architect, Walter Brierley - the 'Lutyens of the North'. He completed the building in 1913 for Percy Stancliffe and his wife Ethel, the wealthy daughter of a whisky distiller. The rooms haven't altered one bit since they were built, but the furniture and furnishings certainly have. In 1962, the Hall was bought by Herbert Mawer, a compulsive but highly discerning collector of antiques. During the twenty years he lived at Sion Hill, Herbert continued to add to what was already probably the best collection of Georgian, Victorian and Edwardian artefacts in the north of England. Furniture, paintings, porcelain, clocks (all working), ephemera, crowd the twenty richly furnished rooms and make Sion Hill a delight to visit. A recent addition to the many sumptuous displays is a charming exhibition of dolls from the early 1900s.

In the Hall's Victorian Walled Garden is another major visitor attraction - **Falconry U.K.'s Bird of Prey and Conservation Centre.** More than eighty birds from 34 different species have their home here: owls, hawks, falcons, buzzards, vultures and eagles from all around the world. At regular intervals throughout the day these fierce-eyed, sharp-beaked predators behave in a remarkably docile and co-operative way as they take part in fascinating flying demonstrations.

NORTHALLERTON

MAP 2 REF G4

9 miles NW of Thirsk on the A165/A684

The county town of North Yorkshire, Northallerton has the broad High Street, almost half a mile long, typical of the county's market towns. In stage coach days the town was an important stop on the route from Newcastle to London and several old coaching inns still stand along the High Street. The most ancient is **The Old Fleece**, a favoured drinking haunt of Charles Dickens during his several visits to the town. It's a truly Dickensian place with great oak beams and a charming olde-worlde atmosphere. The Old Fleece recalls the great days of the stage coach which came to an abrupt end with the arrival of the railway. One day in 1847, a coach called the Wellington made the whole of the 290 mile journey from Newcastle to London, via Northallerton, completely empty. The era of this romantic - if uncomfortable and extremely expensive - mode of transport was over.

Northallerton has many old buildings of interest, including an ancient **Grammar School** whose history goes back to at least 1322. The school was rebuilt in 1776 at the northern end of the High Street - a building that is now a solicitors' office. By the end of the 19th century the school had *"no great reputation"* and by 1902 only thirteen pupils were registered. Things went from bad to worse the next year when the headmaster was convicted of being drunk and disorderly. Fortunately the school, now Northallerton College and in new buildings, has recovered its reputation for academic excellence.

The town also boasts a grand medieval church, a 15th century almshouse and, of more recent provenance, a majestic County Hall built in 1906 and designed by the famous

Yorkshire architect Walter Brierley. The oldest private house in Northallerton is Porch House which bears a carved inscription with the date '1584'. According to tradition, Charles I came here as a guest in 1640 and returned seven years later as a prisoner.

Back in the 1700s Northallerton had its own racecourse and the nearby hostelry was known as the Horse and Jockey, a busy place servicing the Posting Carriages, providing stabling for the horses and accommodation for the travellers. The racecourse has gone and the inn, rebuilt in 1901, is now the **Station Hotel**, located just a few yards from the town station. It's a beautiful period building with wonderful architecture both inside and outside. The main bar was completely refurbished by the hotel's new owner, Brian Simpson, in November 1999, retaining the colours and designs of the Edwardian period and such features as the open fireplace. The lounge bar is a smaller meeting area and just off the main hall is a function room where the Folk Club play every week and which is available for events of every kind. The bar is open every day from noon to 3pm,

The Station Hotel, 2 Boroughbridge Road, Northallerton, North Yorkshire DL7 8AN   Tel: 01609 772053

and from 7pm until 11pm, with tasty bar meals available between noon and 2.30pm and again from 7pm until 8.30pm. If you're planning to stay in the area, this splendid old building also has 12 guest rooms, including a family room.

Two miles north of the town, a stone obelisk beside the A167 commemorates the **Battle of the Standard**, fought here in 1138. It was one of the countless conflicts fought between the English and the Scots, and also one of the bloodiest with more than 12,000 of the Scots, led by King David, perishing under a rain of English arrows. The battle took its name from the unusual standard raised by the English: the mast of a ship mounted on a wagon and, crowning its top, a pyx containing the consecrated Host.

APPLETON WISKE
Map 2 ref G4
6 miles NE of Northallerton off the A167 or A19

In this peaceful little village with its broad main street, is a hostelry which must be unique amongst traditional Yorkshire inns - **The Lord Nelson**. Where else would you find a menu offering more than 50 authentic Thai dishes, created by a genuine Thai cook? This exotic and tasty food can be enjoyed either in the pub's inviting restaurant or as a takeaway. The Lord Nelson has a long history that stretches back to the late 1700s. During the 19th century, farmers gathered here each Quarter Day to pay their rents to the Lord of

The Lord Nelson, Front Street, Appleton Wiske, North Yorkshire DL6 2AD Tel: 01609 881351

the Manor and the inn is still a popular meeting place for the surrounding farming community. Mine hosts at this delightful old inn are Phil and Liz Dinsdale who, in addition to Thai food, offer their customers a good choice of well kept quality ales, and a superb traditional Yorkshire Sunday lunch. Food is available Thursday to Saturday evenings from 7pm until 10pm; on Sundays from 12 noon until 3pm; and at lunchtime on Bank Holiday Mondays. Booking a table is strongly advised. There's always a lively atmosphere at the Lord Nelson, especially on Tuesday evenings when everyone is welcome to take part in the pub quiz which starts at 8.30pm.

OSMOTHERLEY   Map 2 ref H4
6 miles NE of Northallerton off the A19

Long distance walkers will be familiar with this attractive moorland village since it is the western starting point for the **Lyke Wake Walk**, which winds for more than 40 miles over the moors to Ravenscar on the coast. At the centre of the village is a heavily carved cross and, next to it, a low stone table which was probably once a market stall and also served John Wesley as a pulpit.

Overlooking the village green of this picturesque little place, the row of handsome stone cottages that now forms the **Queen Catherine Hotel** dates back to the early 1700s.

Queen Catherine Hotel, 7 West End, Osmotherley, Northallerton, North Yorkshire DL6 3AG Tel: 01609 883209

Alan Woof and his son Robert arrived here early in 1998 and speedily established the inn's reputation for good food, well kept ales and a welcoming atmosphere. The hospitality business was something of a new departure for Alan, who is a former Ferry Captain, but he certainly runs a happy ship here. Robert already had almost a decade's experience in catering and his skills are evident in the appetising menus available every lunchtime and evening. (Best to book ahead if you want to enjoy Sunday lunch in the restaurant, by the way). There's a good choice of ales on offer, amongst them the local Hambleton brew. If you are planning to stay in this lovely area, the hotel has 5 quality guest bedrooms, all of them en suite and attractively furnished and decorated.

About a mile northeast of the village, **Mount Grace Priory** (English Heritage & National Trust) is quite unique amongst Yorkshire's ecclesiastical treasures. The 14th century building set in tranquil surroundings was bought in 1904 by Sir Lothian Bell who decided to rebuild one of the well-preserved cells, a violation of the building's 'integrity' that would provoke howls of outrage from purists if it were proposed today. When English Heritage inherited the Carthusian Priory, however, it decided to go still further by reconstructing other outbuildings and filling them with replica furniture and artefacts to create a vivid impression of what life was like in a 14th century monastic house. The Carthusians were an upper class order whose members dedicated themselves to solitude - even their meals were served through an angled hatch so they would not see the servant who brought them. Most visitors find themselves fascinated by Mount Grace's sanitary arrangements which were ingeniously designed to take full advantage of a nearby spring and the sloping site on which the Priory is built.

GREAT AYTON
Map 2 ref I3

6 miles SE of Middlesbrough on the A173

This appealing village, set around the River Leven, is an essential stopping point for anyone following the Captain Cook Country Tour, a 70 mile circular trip taking in all the major locations associated with the great seafarer. Cook's family moved to Great Ayton when he was eight years old and he attended the little school which is now the **Captain Cook Schoolroom Museum.** Here you will find a fascinating re-creation of the village in which he spent some of his most formative years. The house in which the Cook family lived is sadly no longer here. In 1934 it was transported to Australia brick by brick, together with the climbing plants that covered them, and re-erected in Fitzroy Park, Melbourne. A cairn of stones is all that remains to mark the site.

The Monaghan family have run **The Royal Oak Hotel** at Great Ayton since 1978. This 18th-century rural hostelry is at the heart of the village. Original features include the beamed ceilings and welcoming log fires, and

The Royal Oak Hotel, Great Ayton, North Yorkshire TS9 6BW Tel: 01642 722361 Fax: 01642 724047

add to the charm and character of this traditional inn. The lively public bar is popular with visitors and locals alike. Good ales on tap include Theakstons Old Peculiar, Theakstons XB and Directors, along with keg ales, lager, cider and a good range of wines and spirits. The accommodation comprises five comfortable en suite guest bedrooms available (three doubles, one twin and one single). The quality restaurant has earned a well-deserved reputation for great food and service. The comprehensive menu includes traditional and more innovative favourites such as grilled farm trout, lamb and onion balti, vegetable enchilada and cold poached salmon and tiger prawn salad vinaigrette. Booking advised for non-residents. Food is served all day Monday to Saturday, and from noon-9.30 on Sundays.

Originally the village dairy for over 30 years, the **Park Square Coffee Shop** stands just a couple of hundred yards from the Captain Cook Schoolroom Museum. The

building dates back to the early 1900s when it was a row of 3 cottages, but it is now a popular eating place with lots of character and charm. "We don't serve fast food" says the owner Jeanette Alderson, "we serve fresh food as quickly as we can!". Both Jeanette and her daughter Jeanne share in the cooking, offering a wholesome menu that includes a home made soup of the day, scones and tea-cakes baked fresh every day, hot or cold sandwiches, spicy enchiladas, and a variety of delicious puddings, cakes and pastries. A generous English breakfast is available all day, the daily specials list offers a choice of main courses and on Sundays there's a traditional lunchtime roast. In good weather, you can enjoy your refreshments on the secluded patio to the rear of the shop. Jeanne has some 20 years experience in catering and is happy to provide outside catering. Please note that Park Square Coffee Shop is closed on Mondays and Tuesdays (except Bank Holidays), and open from 10am until 5pm all other days.

Park Square Coffee Shop,
5 Park Square, Great Ayton,
North Yorkshire TS9 6BP
Tel: 01642 722646

A much more impressive monument on Easby Moor above the village is the 60ft obelisk to Cook's memory erected by Robert Campion, a Whitby banker, in 1827. It can only be reached by a steepish climb on foot but it is well worth making the effort: from the base of the monument there are stupendous views over the Moors, the Vale of Mowbray and across to the oddly shaped hill called **Roseberry Topping**. The loftiest of the Cleveland Hills and sometimes called the Matterhorn of Yorkshire, Roseberry's summit towers 1000ft above Great Ayton.

STOKESLEY

Map 2 ref H3

6 miles S of Middlesbrough on the A172

This pleasing market town lies beneath the northern edge of the moors, its peace only troubled on market day which has taken place here every Friday since its charter was granted in 1223. There are rows of elegant Georgian and Regency houses reached by little bridges over the River Leven which flows through the town, and an old water wheel which marks the entrance to the town. In the Middle Ages, Stokesley was owned by the Balliol family, one of whose scions is remembered as the founder of the Oxford college of that name.

GREAT BROUGHTON

Map 2 ref I3

8 miles SE of Middlesbrough on the B1257

Located about ¾ mile outside the village, **Red Hall** is a striking Queen Anne-style house parts of which date back to 1695. This elegant and impressive house stands in 3 acres of its own land with a lovely walled garden to the rear and splendid views in all directions. Red Hall is the home of Carol Ann and Nathan Richmond who have been welcoming guests here since 1995. They take extremely good care of their visitors, happy to ferry you

Red Hall, Ingleby Road, Great Broughton, North Yorkshire TS9 7ET
Tel: 01642 712300 Fax: 01642 714023

to the station or airport, for instance, order a daily newspaper for you, or wash and dry any articles of laundry. Carol Ann is an excellent cook and in addition to either an English or Continental breakfast, (served in the walled garden when weather permits), will provide a superb dinner or light supper at any time you wish by prior arrangement. Red Hall is fully licensed to sell alcoholic beverages and a wine list is also available. The guest bedrooms in this beautifully decorated, non-smoking house are attractively appointed, with one of them boasting a sumptuous 19th century antique bed.

INGLEBY GREENHOW

Map 2 ref I3

8 miles SE of Middlesbrough off the B1257

Located on the very edge of the National Park, Ingleby Greenhow enjoys a favoured position, protected from east winds by the great mass of Ingleby Moor. The beckside church looks small and unimposing from the outside, but inside there is a wealth of rugged Norman arches and pillars, the stonework carved with fanciful figures of grotesque men and animals.

WEST OF YORK

LONG MARSTON
MAP 7 REF H8

6 miles W of York off the B1224

Lying on the edge of the Vale of York and sheltered by a hill, this village is an ancient agricultural community. However, in July 1644, the peace of this tranquil village was shattered by the battle of Marston Moor, one of the most important encounters of the Civil War and one which the Royalists lost. The night before the battle, Oliver Cromwell and his chief officers stayed at **Long Marston Hall** and the bedroom they used is still called The Cromwell Room.

Each year the anniversary of the battle is commemorated by the members of the Sealed Knot and, it is said, that the ghosts of those who fell in battle haunt the site. Certainly, local farmers still, occasionally, unearth cannonballs from the battle when they are out ploughing the fields.

Less than 100 years later, Long Marston Hall saw the birth, in 1707, of the mother of General James Wolfe, the famous English soldier who scaled the Heights of Abraham to relieve the siege of Quebec.

TADCASTER
MAP 7 REF H8

9 miles SW of York off the A64

The lovely magnesian limestone used in so many fine Yorkshire churches came from the quarries established here in Roman times. Their name for Tadcaster was simply 'Calcaria' - limestone. By 1341, however brewing had become the town's major industry, using water from river Wharfe. Three major breweries are still based in Tadcaster: John Smiths whose bitter is the best selling ale in Britain, Samuel Smiths (established in 1758 and the oldest in Yorkshire), and the Tower Brewery, owned by Bass Charringtons. The distinctive brewery buildings dominate the town's skyline and provide the basis of its prosperity. Guided tours of the breweries are available by prior booking.

Also worth visiting is **The Ark**, the oldest building in Tadcaster dating back to the 1490s. During its long history, The Ark has served as a meeting place, a post office, an inn, a butcher's shop, and a museum. It now houses the Town Council offices and is open to the public in office hours. This appealing half-timbered building takes its name from the two carved heads on the first floor beams. They are thought to represent Noah and his wife, hence the name. Tadcaster also offers some attractive riverside walks, one of which takes you across the **'Virgin Viaduct'** over the River Wharfe. Built in 1849 by the great railway entrepreneur George Hudson, the viaduct was intended to be part of a direct line from Leeds to York. Before the tracks were laid however Hudson was convicted of fraud on a stupendous scale and this route was never completed.

If you enjoy good food with an Italian flavour the place to make for in Tadcaster is **Guys Bistro** in the town's main street. Gaetano and Maria Vicari have been here since

1985 and have built up a reputation for providing great food served with a smile in a friendly ambience. Daughters Francesca and Domenica add to the charm of this popular eating place where it's definitely advisable to book for Friday and Saturday evenings. Italian favourites such as home made lasagne, spaghetti, pasta dishes and pizzas all feature on the menu, naturally, but you'll also find steak dishes, a wonderful home made steak and mushroom pie, and a good choice of snacks and light meals amongst the 35 dishes on offer. No wonder Guys received a rave review from the *Yorkshire Evening Press* eating out section in 1999. The bistro was completely refurbished in September 1999 and its eye-catching interior is very stylish and appealing. Guys is open Monday to Saturday from 8.30am to 9.30pm, closed on Sundays.

About 4 miles southwest of Tadcaster is **Hazelwood Castle**, now owned by the Carmelite Friars who use it as a retreat and conference centre. But for more than eight centuries it was the home of the Vavasour family who built it with the lovely white limestone from their quarry at Thevesdale - the same quarry that provided the stone for York Minster and King's College Chapel, Cambridge. The well-maintained gardens and nature trail are open every afternoon, (tea room and shop open on Sundays only), and guided tours of the Castle with its superb Great Hall and 13th century Chapel, can be arranged by telephoning 01937 832738.

Guys Bistro, 28 Bridge Street, Tadcaster, North Yorkshire LS24 9AL Tel: 01937 833529

BOSTON SPA

Map 7 ref H8

10 miles SW of York on the A659

Set beside the broad-flowing River Wharfe, this attractive little town enjoyed many years of prosperity after a Mr John Shires discovered a mineral spring here in 1744. There's a pleasant riverside walk which can be continued along the track of a dismantled railway as far as Tadcaster in one direction, Wetherby in the other. The town's impressive 19th century church is notable for stately tower and the 36 stone angels supporting the nave and aisles.

With its whitewashed walls, cherry-red door and colourful window boxes **The Royal Hotel** looks very inviting indeed. Built in 1768 and converted to a coaching inn in 1771 to serve travellers on the Great North Road, the Royal has had a long history of dispensing hospitality to both wayfarers and locals alike. Recently refurbished, the hotel provides guests with all the convenience and comfort of home, and the friendly and efficient service makes the Royal a place you will want to return to again and again. Food is taken seriously here. "Harts" is a light, airy modern restaurant serving a well-balanced à la carte menu complemented by daily specials reflecting seasonal and locally available produce. The varied menu ranges from starters such as the ever-popular Harts Fish Cakes, to main courses like Braised Wild Boar, to a tempting selection of superb home made desserts. The

The Royal Hotel, 182 High Street, Boston Spa, Wetherby LS23 6BT
Tel: 01937 842142 Fax: 01937 541036 e-mail: www.royalhotel-bostonspa.com

Royal has 13 guest rooms, (12 of them en suite; 1 with its own private bathroom), two friendly bars, and a function room ideal for all kinds of private parties and business conferences.

WETHERBY

MAP 7 REF H8

10 miles W of York on the A661

Situated on the Great North Road, at a point midway between Edinburgh and London, Wetherby was renowned for its coaching inns, of which the two most famous were The Angel and The Swan & Talbot. It is rumoured that serving positions at these inns were considered so lucrative that employees had to pay for the privilege of employment in them! The town fortunately has remained unspoilt and has a quaint appearance with a central market place that was first granted to the Knights Templar. Many of the houses in the town are Georgian, Regency, or early Victorian. Apart from its shops, galleries, old pubs, and cafés, there is also a popular racecourse nearby. Another feature is the renowned 18th century bridge with a long weir which once provided power for Wetherby's corn mill and possibly dates from medieval times.

The Brunswick Hotel, High Street,
Wetherby LS22 4LT Tel: 01937 582008

Located on the main street of this attractive market town, **The Brunswick Hotel** has changed little in its outside appearance since 1824 when, as The Devonshire Arms, it was described as "a substantial stone house" in a Bill of Sale. At that time Wetherby's cattle market was held to the rear of the inn so the Brunswick provided ample stabling for the farmers and good accommodation for those who thought it wiser not to travel home after a hard day's sheep-selling and supping. The hotel has 8 comfortable guest rooms, ranging from family rooms to a single. The Brunswick is also well known for its excellent pub food which is available every day from noon until 2pm. The menu presents a good choice, supplemented by at least 4 daily specials. Landlords Gillian Knowles and Steven Simpson offer quality ales from John Smiths and on Thursday, Friday and Saturday evenings they host a lively disco from 8pm. They also lay on live entertainment about once a month - just call in for details.

SPOFFORTH
6 miles SE of Harrogate on the A661

MAP 7 REF G8

This ancient village, situated on the tiny River Crimple, is home to the splendid Palladian mansion, **Stockeld Park**, built between 1758 and 1763 by Paine. Containing some excellent furniture and a fine picture collection, the house is surrounded by extensive parkland which offers garden walks. Though privately owned, the house is open by appointment.

    Spofforth Castle is another place of note, an historic building whose sight stirs the imagination, despite its ruined state. The powerful Percy family originally built the castle here in the 16th century to replace the manor house which had been repeatedly laid to waste. The castle itself is now a crumbling ruin after it too was destroyed during the Civil War. Among the many events which took place here it is said to have been the birthplace of Harry Hotspur. The ruins are now in the care of English Heritage.

GOLDSBOROUGH
2 miles E of Knaresborough off the A59

MAP 7 REF G7

This rather special village was an estate village since the time of the Norman Conquest until the 1950s when it was sold by the Earl of Harewood to pay enormous death duties. The charming 12th century **Church of St Mary** has some interesting features including a Norman doorhead and an effigy of a knight. It is also a *'green man church'* and the image of the Celtic god of fertility, with his oak-leafed head, is well hidden on one of the many Goldsborough family tombs. In 1859, whilst the church was being restored, a lead casket was discovered containing Viking jewellery and coins. In the 1920s, Mary, the daughter of George V and Queen Mary, lived here after her marriage and her eldest son, George, was christened in the church.

KNARESBOROUGH
4 miles E of Harrogate on the A59

MAP 7 REF G7

This ancient town of pantiled cottages and Georgian houses is precariously balanced on a hillside by the River Nidd. A stately railway viaduct, 90ft high and 338ft long, completed in 1851, spans the gorge There are many unusual and attractive features in the town, amongst them a maze of steep stepped narrow streets leading down to the river and numerous alleyways. In addition to boating on the river, there are many enjoyable riverside walks.

    The town is dominated by the ruins of **Knaresborough Castle**, built high on a crag overlooking the River Nidd by Serlo de Burgh, who had fought alongside William the

Conqueror at Hastings. Throughout the Middle Ages, the castle was a favourite with the court and it was to Knaresborough that the murderers of Thomas à Becket fled in 1170. Queen Philippa, wife of Edward III, also enjoyed staying at Knaresborough and she and her family spent many summers here. However, following the Civil War, when the town and its castle had remained loyal to the king, Cromwell ordered its destruction.

Also in the town is the **Old Courthouse Museum** which tells the history of the town and houses a rare Tudor Courtroom. The nearby **Bebra Gardens** are named after Knaresborough's twin town in Germany and its attractive flower beds are complemented by luxurious lawns and a paddling pool. In the High Street, visitors should also keep an eye out for **Ye Oldest Chymists' Shoppe** in England which dates back to 1720. For the last century and more, it's been owned by the Pickles family which manufactures some forty lotions, ointments and creams. Amongst their potions are *'Fiery Jack'*, a rubbing ointment, *'Snowfire'* for chapped hands, and *Snufflebabe Vapour Rub*.

Knaresborough

However, Knaresborough is probably best known for **Mother Shipton's Cave**, the birthplace of the famous prophetess, and for its Petrifying Well which provides a constant source of curiosity to the visitor. The effects that the well's lime rich water has on objects are truly amazing and an array of paraphernalia, from old boots to bunches of grapes, are on view - seemingly turned to stone. It is little wonder that these were considered magical properties by the superstitious over the centuries or that the well was associated with witchcraft and various other interesting tales.

The foremost tale concerns Mother Shipton, who was said to have been born in the cavern situated by the well on 6th July 1488 and who has the reputation of being England's most famous fortune-teller. The story says that she was born in the midst of a terrible storm and was soon found to have a strange ability to see the future. As she grew older her prophetic visions became more widely known and feared throughout England. However, the most singular feature about Mother Shipton has to be that she died peacefully in her bed, as opposed to being burnt at the stake as most witches were at that time.

She had been threatened with burning by, amongst others, Cardinal Wolsey, when she had warned him on a visit to York that he might see the city again but never enter. True to her prediction Wolsey never did enter York, for he was arrested on a charge of treason at Cawood. Among her many other prophesies she reputedly foretold the invasion and defeat of the Spanish Armada in 1588 and Samuel Pepys recorded that it was Mother Shipton who prophesied the disastrous Great Fire of London in 1666.

Whilst in Knaresborough, it is well worth taking the opportunity to visit the **House in the Rock** hewn out of solid rock by Thomas Hill, an eccentric weaver, between 1770 and 1786. It was Hill's son who renamed the house Fort Montagu and flew a flag and fired a gun salute on special occasions. On the banks of the River Nidd there is also the infamous **St Robert's Cave** which is an ancient hermitage. Robert was the son of a mayor of York who, at the time of his death in 1218, was so beloved that the people of Knaresborough would not allow the monks of Fountains Abbey to bury him. Instead they kept his bones and finally interred him in a place near the altar in the **Chapel of Our Lady of the Crag**. It is guarded by the statue of a larger than life-size figure of a knight in the act of drawing a sword.

In the tradition of this town's reputation for exceptional and odd characters is *"Blind Jack of Knaresborough"*. Jack Metcalfe was born in 1717 and lost his sight at the age of six, but went on the achieve fame as a roadmaker. He was a remarkable person who never allowed his blindness to bar him from any normal activities - he rode, climbed trees, swam, and was often employed to guide travellers through the wild Forest of Knaresborough. He was a talented fiddle player and one of his more roguish exploits was his elopement with Dolly Benson, the daughter of the innkeeper of the Royal Oak in Harrogate, on the night before she was due to marry another man. His most memorable achievement however, was the laying of roads over the surrounding bogs and marshes which he achieved by laying a foundation of bundles of heather, a feat which had never been done before.

Just a short walk from the town centre, the **George & Dragon Inn** is a sturdy Georgian building which has been dispensing hospitality since the mid-1700s. It has the typical bow windows of the period and inside there's lots of atmosphere as befits such an ancient hostelry. A free house, the George & Dragon is owned and run by Philip Clegg who, after working here as a barman for several years, bought the inn in 1998 and now offers a wide range of quality ales including real ales such as Black Sheep, Tetleys and John Smith's Smooth. Sunday evening is a good time to drop in for a pint since there's a free quiz with a gallon of ale for the winners. The inn has 4 guest bedrooms, (2 family, 1 twin and 1 single), some with their own showers, and overnight guests will find a generous breakfast awaiting them in the morning. Open all day on Saturday and

George & Dragon Inn, 9 Briggate, Knaresborough, North Yorkshire HG5 8BQ Tel: 01423 862792

Sunday, the George & Dragon is closed on Mondays (except Bank Holidays), and from 5pm on weekdays.

Tucked away in a quiet corner of the town, close to the railway station, **The Mitre Hotel** is a venerable old building with a warm and inviting ambience. The owners, Dawn and Eric Eades, are very experienced in the hospitality business and since their arrival here in the summer of 1999 have made the hotel a popular venue for both locals and visitors. During the season, the hotel bar is open all day, with bar meals available at

The Mitre Hotel, 4 Station Road, Knaresborough, North Yorkshire HG5 9AA
Tel: 01423 863589

lunchtimes and a splendid traditional roast dinner served from noon until 3pm on Sundays. On Market Days, (Wednesdays), the Eades also offer a special value-for-money "Market Lunch". Real ale lovers will find at least two quality ales on tap. The Mitre has 5 guest bedrooms, (3 twins, 1 double & 1 single), all of them en suite and attractively furnished and decorated. Overnight guests are served a hearty breakfast and, as we go to press, Dawn and Eric are finalising plans for creating a traditional tea room within the hotel which will offer quality teas, coffees, sandwiches and fancy cakes.

Another of Knaresborough's attractive amenities is **Conyngham Hall**, a majestic old house enclosed within a loop of the River Nidd. Once the home of Lord Macintosh, the Halifax toffee magnate, the Hall itself is not open to the public but its landscaped grounds, stretching down to the river, are and provide tennis, putting and other activities.

Enjoying a prime location within a walled garden in the grounds of the Hall, **Henshaw's Arts and Crafts Centre** offers unique opportunities for people with disabilities to gain vocational training and work experience in a variety of artistic and commercial disciplines. The Centre provides a range of 10 craft workshops where clients learn practical skills in areas that extend from pottery to paper-making, weaving to woodwork, horticulture to music & drama. The Centre is open to the public and organises an interesting programme of exhibitions, workshops and performing arts events. The public facilities include a fashionable Café Gallery which not only displays fine arts for sale, but can also be hired for private functions, from business lunches to wedding celebrations.

Outside, there are 2 magnificent courtyards. One features imaginative planting, with a living willow tunnel and a lovely Japanese garden. The second is a magical place, dominated by an extraordinary wooden storyteller's throne, carved by the renowned sculptor Colin Wilborn. Seated on this wonderful throne, guest storytellers such as Roger McGough will keep groups of children enthralled.

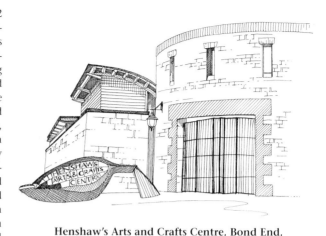

Henshaw's Arts and Crafts Centre, Bond End, Knaresborough, North Yorkshire HG5 9AL Tel: 01423 541888 Fax: 01423 541889 web site: www.knaresborough.co.uk/charities/henshaws

Just outside Knaresborough and situated at Moorland Nurseries is **Polly's Pantry**, a charming coffee shop owned and personally run by Denise Newby. Since opening in 1994 Denise and her very capable and friendly colleagues Anne, Sheila, Ivy and daughter Sophie, have made this one of the best places to eat in the area. All the delicious food here is home made. Anne is in charge of the baking and the display counter is full of wonderful-looking (and tasting) quiches, tarts, cakes, scones and biscuits - even home baked bread. Really, Polly's Pantry is much more than just a coffee shop. From the menu which is supplemented by a list of daily specials it is possible to put together a magnificent feast fit for a king. Cosy and attractive, the no-smoking Pantry comprises two different rooms and both are furnished with comfortable chairs. This is an ideal place to take a well-

Polly's Pantry, Moorland Nurseries, Forest Moor Road, Knaresborough, North Yorkshire HG5 8JY Tel: 01423 869964

earned break after looking round the nursery. Polly's Pantry is closed on Mondays, except for Bank Holidays, and open on other days from 10am until 5pm (4.30pm on Sundays).

A mile or so to the south of Knaresborough, **Plumpton Rocks** provide an ideal picnic spot. There's an idyllic lake surrounded by dramatic millstone grit rocks and woodland paths that were laid out in the 18th century. It has been declared a garden of special historic interest by English Heritage and is open every weekend and daily during July and August.

HARROGATE
MAP 7 REF G7

13 miles N of Leeds on the A61/A59

One of England's most attractive towns and a frequent winner of Britain in Bloom, Harrogate features acres of gardens that offer an array of colour throughout the year, open spaces, and broad tree-lined boulevards. However, until the 17th century Harrogate - or *'Haregate'* as it was then called - was just a collection of cottages close to the thriving market town of Knaresborough. It was William Slingsby, of Bilton Hall near Knaresborough, who, whilst out walking his dog, discovered a spring bubbling up out of the rock that was to found the fortunes of the town. Tasting the waters, Slingsby found them to be similar to those he had tasted at the fashionable wells of Spaw, in Belgium. Expert opinion was sought and, in 1596, Dr Timothy Bright confirmed the spring to be a chalybeate well and the waters to have medicinal powers - curing a wide variety of illness and ailments from gout to vertigo.

Slingsby's well became known as **Tewit Well**, after the local name for peewits, and it can still be seen today, covered by a dome on pillars. Other wells were also found in the area, St John's Well in 1631 and the **Old Sulphur Well** which went on to become the most famous of Harrogate's springs. Though this spring had been known, locally, for years it was not until 1656 that this sulphurous smelling well, nicknamed the "Stinking Spaw", began to attract attention.

During the mid-17th century bathing in the heated sulphurous waters became fashionable as well as a cure for various ailments and lodging houses were built around the sulphur well in Low Harrogate. Bathing took place in the evening and, each morning, the patients would drink a glass of the water with their breakfasts. The cupola seen over the well was erected in 1804.

In order to serve the growing number of people arriving at Harrogate seeking a cure for their ailments the Queen's Head Hotel was built and it is probably the oldest inn here as it dates from before 1687. When stagecoaches began to arrive in the 18th century the inn moved with the times and it became the first at the spa to serve the needs of the coaches.

By the late 1700s it was one of the largest hotels in the fast growing town and, though the hotel changed its name to the Queen's Hotel in 1828 and underwent extensive renovation and remodelling in the mid-19th century, it did not survive the decline of the spa and, in 1951, it became the offices for the Regional Hospital Board. Many other hotels were built including the Crown Inn, next to the Old Sulphur Well, which too became a coaching inn in 1772 and hosted a visit by Lord Byron in 1806. However, one of the town's most famous hotels, The Majestic, a turn of the century red brick building, does survive and it was the place where Elgar stayed whilst visiting Harrogate.

The **Royal Pump Room Museum** was built in 1842 to enclose the Old Sulphur Well and this major watering place for spa visitors has been painstakingly restored to illustrate all the aspects of Harrogate's history. Beneath the building the sulphur water still rises to the surface and can be sampled.

There will be few Harrogate residents who have not heard of Betty Lupton, the almost legendary *'Queen of the Wells'* who, for over 50 years, dispensed the spa waters, dishing out cupfuls to paying visitors, who were then encouraged to walk off the dubious effects of the medicine by taking a trip around the Bogs Fields, known today as **Valley Gardens**. She conducted her business in the ostentatiously named **Royal Baths Assembly Rooms** which, in their hey-day, were full of rich visitors sampling the waters. Today, the buildings have been restored to house the Turkish Baths where visitors can enjoy a sauna and solarium, and are

Royal Bath Assembly Rooms, Harrogate

open to the public daily. The **Mercer Art Gallery** is housed in the oldest of the town's surviving spa buildings, originally built in 1806. The 'Promenade Room' has been restored to its former glory and displays a superb collection of fine art.

By the late 18th century Harrogate had become one of Europe's most fashionable spa towns and it was not only serving the needs of those with acute and chronic ailments but also members of *'good society'*. Fuelled by competition from spa towns abroad, Harrogate sought to provide not only medical care for the sick but also to appeal to the needs of the fashionable. In 1858, Charles Dickens visited the town and described it as *'the queerest place, with the strangest people in it leading the oddest lives of dancing, newspaper reading, and table d'hôte.'* Though its status as a spa town has declined, it is still a fashionable place, a sought after conference location, home of the annual Northern Antiques Fair, and a town with much to offer the visitor.

As well as a spa, Harrogate developed into a centre for shopping for the well-to-do and the many old fashioned shops are typified by **Montpellier Parade**, a crescent of shops surrounded by trees and flowerbeds. Another attractive aspect of the town is **The Stray**, which is unique to Harrogate and virtually encircles the town centre. The 200 acres of open space are protected by ancient law to ensure that the residents of, and visitors to, the town always have access for sports, events, and walking. The spacious lawns are at their most picturesque during the spring when edged with crocus and daffodils. Originally part of the Forest of Knaresborough the land was, fortunately, not enclosed under the 1770 Act of Parliament. The large gritstone pillar, beside The Stray, marks the boundary of the Leeds and Ripon turnpike. On The Stray stands the Commemorative Oak Tree, planted in 1902 by Samson Fox to commemorate the ox roasting that took place here as part of the celebrations for Queen Victoria's Jubilee in 1887 and the end of the Boer War in 1902.

Located on the edge of the famous Stray, **Eton House** offers excellent bed and breakfast accommodation in a warm and friendly atmosphere. Dating back to 1877, Eton House is a fine example of a Victorian town house on the grand scale. It's the home of Janet Wyatt who has been welcoming bed & breakfast visitors here for some years. Guests will find spacious, comfortable rooms, some en suite and all with television and tea/coffee-making facilities. There is a large visitors' lounge with colour TV which pro-

Eton House, 3 Eton Terrace, on Knaresborough Road, Harrogate HG2 7SU
Tel/Fax: 01423 886850

vides a welcoming room in which to relax. A full English breakfast is served in the dining room which, for the comfort of all guests, is non-smoking. Vegetarians are fully catered for. Eton House is just 5 minutes drive from the Harrogate Conference Centre, the town centre with its elegant shops, bars and restaurants, and is also within easy reach of such attractions as the Valley Gardens, Harlow Carr Botanical Gardens and Harewood House. It's also ideal as a base for exploring the glorious Yorkshire Dales.

Perhaps the most well known tale associated with Harrogate is the disappearance of Agatha Christie in 1926. In a set of circumstances reminiscent of one of her novels, Agatha went missing in the December of that year, possibly as a result of marital difficulties. Her crashed car was discovered near a chalk pit near her home but the novelist was nowhere to be found and one of the largest police manhunts was put into operation. Agatha had, in fact, travelled to Harrogate, after abandoning her car, and booked into the Old Swan Hotel under the name of her husband's mistress, Theresa Neele. After 10 days she was spotted and her husband came to collect her, putting her disappearance down to loss of memory. However, this did not dispel rumours that the marriage was in trouble or that the surprising event was nothing more than a publicity stunt. Whatever the truth, two years later the couple divorced and Colonel Christie married his long-time mistress Theresa. One of Harrogate's major visitor attractions is **Harlow Carr Botanical Gardens**, just over a mile from the town centre. Established in 1948 by the Northern Horticultural Society and now covering some 68 acres, the gardens feature all manner of plants in a wide variety of landscapes which allows members of the public to see how they perform in the unsympathetic conditions of northern England. The society, as well as having their study centre here, has also opened a fascinating **Museum of Gardening**.

BECKWITHSHAW
MAP 7 REF G7

2 miles SW of Harrogate on the B6161

This village, as its name suggests, was once bounded by a stream and woodland though, sadly, most of the trees are now gone. Once part of the great Forest of Knaresborough, a local legend tells how John O'Gaunt promised John Haverah, a cripple, as much land as he could hop around between sunrise and sunset. By throwing his crutch the last few yards, just as the sun was setting, John Haverah managed to secure himself 7 square miles, the remainder of which is today called Haverah Park.

Only a mile or so from Harlow Carr Gardens and offering first class self-catering accommodation, **The Old Mistal** is an outstanding barn conversion which has been designed with great flair, featuring beams in most rooms and enjoying attractive views. The furnishings and fittings are of the highest standard and The Old Mistal's owner, Christine Williams, ensures that the house is always immaculately presented for her guests. There's quality pine furniture and Laura Ashley soft furnishings throughout, colour TVs in both the sitting room and master bedroom, and arriving guests are provided with a "Welcome Pack" of essentials (milk, eggs, etc.) together with samples of toiletries. The Old Mistal has 3 bedrooms, sleeping a total of 5 people, a sitting room with French windows opening

The Old Mistal, Bluecoat Farm, Howhill Road, Beckwithshaw, Harrogate, North Yorkshire HG3 1QJ Tel: 01423 561385

onto the patio and garden, and a well-equipped kitchen/dining area with a stable door overlooking the garden. All linen, towels, heating and electricity are included in the rental, and other amenities include washer/dryer facilities and cot, if required, a payphone and ample parking. For the comfort of other guests, The Old Mistal is a no-smoking house and pets cannot be accommodated.

RIPON
MAP 2 REF G6

11 miles N of Harrogate on the A61

This attractive cathedral city, on the banks of the Rivers Ure, Skell, and Laver, dates from the 7th century when Alfrich, King of Northumbria granted an area of land here, surrounding a new monastery, to the Church. Later that century, in 672, St Wilfrid built a church on the high ground between the three rivers but, at the time of the demise of the

Northern Kingdom in the mid-10th century, the monastery and church were destroyed, though the Saxon crypt survives to this day. By the time of the Norman Conquest, Ripon was a prosperous agricultural settlement under ecclesiastical rule and it was at this time that a second St Wilfrid's Church was erected on the site of the Saxon building. On Christmas Day 1132, monks from York worshipped here whilst they were making a journey to found Fountains Abbey and, traditionally, the people of Ripon follow this ancient route on Boxing Day.

Ripon Cathedral

A striking survival of the Saxon cathedral is the 1300-year-old Crypt. At its northeast corner is a narrow passage known as The Needle. According to the 17th century antiquary Thomas Fuller, women whose chastity was suspect were made to pass through it. If they were unable to do so, their reputations were irretrievably tarnished. *"They pricked their credits"* Fuller wrote *"who could not thread the Needle"*.

The Crypt is all that remains of St Wilfrid's church but the magnificent **Cathedral of St Peter and St Wilfrid**, which now stands on the site, is certainly well worth visiting. Begun in the mid-12th century by Archbishop Roger of York, it was originally designed as a simple cruciform church; the west front was added in the mid-13th century and the east choir in 1286. Rebuilding work was begun in the 16th century but the disruption of the Dissolution of the Monasteries caused the work to be abandoned and it was only the intervention of James I in the early 1600s, that saved the building from ruin. Then established as a collegiate church, the diocese of Ripon was formed in 1836 and the church made a cathedral. Often referred to as the Cathedral of the Dales, the building, though one of the tallest cathedrals in England, is also the smallest.

Throughout the Middle Ages, the town prospered: its market charter had been granted by King Alfred in the 9th century and, at one time, Ripon produced more woollen cloth than Halifax and Leeds. The collapse of the woollen industry saw a rise in spur manufacture in_the 16th century and their fame was such that Ripon spurs were referred to in the old proverb: *"As true steel as a Ripon rowel"*. As well as having three rivers, Ripon also had a canal. Built between 1767 and 1773 to improve the navigation of the River Ure: John Smeaton, builder of the Eddystone Lighthouse, was the designer. However, by 1820 the company running the canal had fallen into debt and it was little used after that time.

Fortunately for today's visitor, the Industrial Revolution, and all its associated implications, by-passed Ripon and it was not until the early 20th century that the town flourished, though briefly, as a spa. However, many ancient customs and festivals have survived down the centuries and perhaps the most famous is the sounding of the *"Wakeman's Horn"* each night at 9pm in the market place. Dating back to the 9th century, the Wakeman was originally appointed to patrol the town after the nightly curfew had been blown and, in many ways, this was the first form of security patrol. The Wakeman was selected each year from the town's 12 aldermen and those choosing not to take office were fined heavily. Today, this old custom is revived in the Mayor-making Ceremony when the elected mayor shows great reluctance to take office and hides from his colleagues.

As might be expected, any walk around this ancient town reveals, in its buildings, its interesting and varied past. The heart of the town is the **Market Place** and here stands a tall obelisk which was erected in 1702 to replace the market cross. Restored in 1781, at its summit are a horn and a rowel spur, symbolizing Ripon's crafts and customs. Situated at the edge of the square are the 14th century **Wakeman's House** and the attractive **Georgian Town Hall**.

The Spa Baths building, opened in 1905 by the Princess of Battenberg, is a reminder of Ripon's attempt to become a fashionable spa resort. With no spring of its own, the town had to pipe in sulphur mineral water from Aldfield near Fountains Abbey. However, the scheme failed, though the baths building, which now houses the city's swimming pool, is a fine example of art nouveau architecture and the **Spa Gardens** are still a pleasant place for a stroll.

Near to the cathedral is Ripon's old Courthouse that was built in 1830 on the site of an earlier 17th century Common Hall, used for the Quarter Sessions and the Court Military. Adjacent to this fine Georgian courthouse is a Tudor building that was part of the Archbishop of York's summer palace.

Also not far from the cathedral is the House of Correction, built in 1686 which served as the local prison between 1816 and 1878 and then became the police station until the late 1950s. This austere building is now home to the **Ripon Prison and Police Museum**, established in 1984, which depicts the history of the police force as well as giving visitors a real insight into the life of a prisoner in Victorian times. Almost as unfortunate as those prisoners were the inmates of **Ripon Workhouse**, the city's newest museum. The restored vagrants' wards of 1877 provide a chilling insight into the treatment of paupers in Yorkshire workhouses and the displays include a 'Victorian Hard Times Gallery'.

Finally, horse racing at Ripon dates back to 1713 and the present course opened in 1900. Meetings are held between April and August and the course is widely regarded as one of the most beautiful in the country.

WATH

3 miles N of Ripon off the A1

MAP 2 REF G6

The stately home of **Norton Conyers** has been owned by the Graham family since 1624 though, undoubtedly, the house's main claim to fame is the visit made by Charlotte Brontë. During her stay here the novelist heard the story of Mad Mary, supposedly a Lady Graham. Apparently Lady Graham had been locked up in an attic room, now tantalisingly inaccessible to the public, and Charlotte eventually based the character of Mrs Rochester in her novel *Jane Eyre* on the unfortunate woman. Visitors to the hall will also see the famous painting of Sir Bellingham Graham on his bay horse, as Master of the Quorn hunt. It is rumoured that ownership of the painting was once decided on the throwing of a pair of dice. Other family pictures, furniture and costumes are on display and there's a lovely 18th century walled garden within the grounds.

NORTH STAINLEY
MAP 2 REF G6

3 miles N of Ripon on the A6108

Just over 100 years ago, in 1895, excavations in a field just outside the village revealed the site of a Roman villa called Castle Dykes though all that can be seen now are the grassed outlines of the foundations and the moat. However, the discovery does prove that there has been a settlement here for many centuries. The monks of Fountains Abbey also knew North Stainley. Slenningford Grange is thought to have been one of their many properties and a fishpond, dating from medieval times, is still in existence.

Just to the south of the village lies the **Lightwater Valley Theme Park** set in 175 acres of scenic grounds. The Park boasts 'Ultimate' - the biggest roller coaster in the world, (authenticated by the *Guinness Book of Records*), the Rat Ride, Falls of Terror, and the Viper to name just a few and there are also plenty of more appropriate activities for younger children. Also within the grounds is Lightwater Village (free) which offers a wide variety of retail and factory shops, a garden centre, restaurant and coffee shop.

STUDLEY ROGER
MAP 2 REF G6

1 mile SW of Ripon off the B6265

The magnificent **Studley Royal Gardens** were created in the early 18th century before they were merged with nearby Fountains Abbey in 1768. Started by John Aislabie, the

disgraced Chancellor of the Exchequer and founder of the South Sea Company that spectacularly burst its bubble in 1720, the landscaping took some 14 years. It then took a further 10 years to complete the construction of the buildings and follies found within the gardens. With a network of paths and the River Skell flowing through the grounds, it is well worth exploring these superb gardens.

A National Trust property, like the adjoining gardens, **Fountains Abbey** is the pride of all the ecclesiastical ruins in Yorkshire and the only World Heritage Site in Yorkshire. The abbey was one of the wealthiest of the Cistercian houses and its remains are the most complete of any

Fountains Abbey

Cistercian abbey in Britain. Founded in 1132, with the help of Archbishop Thurstan of York, the first buildings housed just 12 monks of the order and, over the centuries its size increased, even spreading across the River Skell itself. The abbey reached its peak in the 15th century with the grandiose designs of Abbot Marmaduke Huby, whose beautiful tower still stands as a reminder of just how rich and powerful Fountains became. In fact, the abbey was run on such businesslike lines that, at its height, as well as owning extensive lands throughout Yorkshire, it had an income of about a thousand pounds a year, then a very substantial sum indeed.

It is commonly thought that one of the abbey's friars, renowned for his strength and skill as an archer, challenged Robin Hood to a sword fight. Forced to concede, the friar joined the Merry Men of Sherwood and became known as Friar Tuck. The Dissolution hit the abbey as it did all the powerful religious houses. The abbot was hanged, the monks scattered, and its treasures taken off or destroyed. The stonework, however, was left largely intact, possibly due to its remote location. In 1579, Sir Stephen Proctor pulled down some outbuildings, in order to construct **Fountains Hall**, a magnificent Elizabethan mansion which still stands in the abbey's grounds and part of which is open to the public.

ALDFIELD
MAP 2 REF F6

3 miles W of Ripon off the B6265

Just across the road from the entrance to the Studley Royal Estate and Fountains Abbey, **Mallard Grange** is a wonderfully rambling 16th century farmhouse which oozes character and charm. The house enjoys a glorious rural setting, surrounded by a 450-acre working farm extending over picturesque countryside. There's been a building on this site since at least 1355 and the present building is the home of Maggie and Charles Johnson whose family have farmed Mallard Grange since the 1930s. The Johnsons offer superb

Mallard Grange, Aldfield, nr Fountains Abbey, Ripon,
North Yorkshire HG4 3BE Tel: 01765 620242

quality bed and breakfast accommodation, with spacious rooms furnished with care and some lovely antique pieces plus lots of peace and quiet! There are 2 guest rooms in the main farmhouse and 2 more in the recently converted former blacksmith's shop and stable right next door. All are en suite and equipped with remote control colour TV, hair dryer, beverage tray and lots of extra country comforts. At breakfast time there's an extensive choice complemented by home made preserves, and although evening meals are not available, the Johnsons can recommend some excellent restaurants and country pubs in the locality.

BOROUGHBRIDGE

MAP 2 REF G6

7 miles SE of Ripon on the B6265

This attractive and historic town dates from the reign of William the Conqueror though it was once on a main thoroughfare used by both the Celts of Brigantia and, later, the Romans. The bridge over the River Ure, from which the village takes its name, was built in 1562 and it formed part of an important road link between Edinburgh and London. Busy throughout the coaching days with traffic passing from the West Riding of Yorkshire to the North, Boroughbridge has now returned to its former unassuming role of a small wayside town now bypassed by the A1(M) which takes most of the 21st century traffic from its streets.

The great **Devil's Arrows**, three massive Bronze Age monoliths, stand like guardians close to the new road and form Yorkshire's most famous ancient monument: thought to date from about 2000 BC, the tallest is 30ft high. The monoliths stand in a line running north-south and are

Devil's Arrows, Boroughbridge

fashioned from millstone grit which has been seriously fluted by weathering. A local legend, however, attributes the great stones to the Devil suggesting that they were, actually, crossbow bolts that he fired at nearby Aldborough which, at the time, was a Christian settlement.

SKELTON

MAP 2 REF G6

3 miles W of Boroughbridge off the B6265

This charming little village has some surviving cottages, dating from 1540, which are built from small handmade bricks with pantiled roofs. A ferry used to cross the River Ure, at this point, to Bishop Monkton and, in 1869, it was the scene of a notorious hunting accident. Members of the York and Ainsty Hunt boarded the ferry in order to follow a fox that had swum across the river. Half way across the horses panicked, capsizing the boat, and the boatman, along with five hunt members, were drowned.

Hidden away just to the south of the village is one of the area's finest stately homes, **Newby Hall**. Built in the 18th century and designed by Robert Adam, much of the house is open to the public including the splendid Billiard Room with its fine portrait of Frederick Grantham Vyner; an ancestor of the family which has lived here from the mid-19th century, Frederick was murdered by Greek bandits after being kidnapped. The house, though is perhaps most famous for its superb tapestries and there is also a fine collection of Chippendale furniture.

It is, though, the award winning **Newby Hall Gardens** that draw most people to the house. Extensive and well designed, it was the present owner's father who transformed a 9-hole golf course into the 25 acres of award-winning gardens that offer something for everyone whatever the time of year. Also found here is a wonderful Woodland Discovery Walk, a miniature railway, plenty of other attractions specially designed for children, a Plant Stall, Shop and Restaurant.

ALDBOROUGH   MAP 2 REF H6
1 mile E of Boroughbridge off the B6265

The ancient Roman town of Isurium Brigantum, or Aldborough, as it is known today, was once the home of the 9th Legion, who wrested it from the Celtic Brigantian tribe. The modern day focal point of the village is the tall maypole on the village green, around which traditional dances take place each May. At one end of the green is a raised platform which is all that remains of the Old Court House and it bears an inscription recalling that up to 150 years ago the election of members of Parliament was announced here. Below are some well-preserved stocks that are, in fact, only replicas of the originals. The **Aldborough Roman Museum** houses relics of the town's past. This was once a thriving Roman city of vital strategic importance and near the museum are some of the original walls and tessellated pavements of that city.

The **Church of St Andrew** was built in 1330 on the site of a Norman church that was burnt down by the Scots in 1318. This in turn had been built on the site of an ancient Temple of Mercury. Modern archaeologists no doubt reel in horror at the thought that parts of the present church were built with stones from the Temple's walls. One ancient relic that is still preserved in the church's grounds is an Anglo-Saxon sundial known as the Ulph Stone.

3 The East Riding and North Humberside

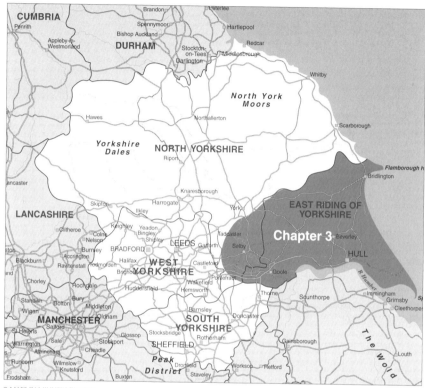

© MAPS IN MINUTES ™ (1998)

BRIDLINGTON & THE WOLDS

"Fold upon fold of encircling hills, piled rich and golden" - such was the author Winifred Holtby's fond memory of the Wolds landscape. She was born in 1898 in Rudston on the northern edge of the Wolds, a village dominated by the prehistoric **Rudston Monolith.** This colossal block of stone, a daunting symbol of some misty pagan belief, stands challengingly close to Rudston's Christian parish church. Twenty-five feet (7.6m) high, it is the tallest standing stone in Britain. Winifred Holtby left the village and became a leading figure in London literary circles, editor of the influential magazine *Time and Tide*, but in her own books it was those *"rich and golden"* hills that still enthralled her. In her most successful novel, *South Riding*, the fictional Riding is unmistakably recognisable as the Wolds amongst whose gently rolling acres she had spent her childhood.

The Wolds are a great crescent of chalk hills that sweep round from the coast near Flamborough Head to the outskirts of Hull. There were settlers here some 10,000 years ago - but never very many. In the early 1700s, Daniel Defoe described the area as *"very thin of towns and people"* and also noted the *"great number of sheep"*. Little has changed: the Wolds remain an unspoilt tract of scattered farmsteads and somnolent villages with one of the lowest population densities in the country. Artists remark on the striking quality of the light and air, and on the long views that open up, perhaps across undulating hills to the twin towers of Beverley Minster or to the great towers of the Minster at York. The Wolds never rise above 800ft but the open landscape makes them particularly vulnerable to winter snowstorms: children may be marooned in their schools, the dipping and twisting country roads can be blocked for weeks at a time.

BRIDLINGTON
MAP 5 REF M6

18 miles SW of Scarborough on the A165

Bridlington lies at the northern tip of the crescent of hills that form the Wolds. The old town lies a mile inland from the bustling seaside resort with its manifold visitor amusements and attractions that has been understandably popular since early Victorian times. The attractions of a vast, ten mile stretch of sandy beach distract most visitors from the less obvious beauties of **Bridlington Priory** in the old town. The Priory was once one of the wealthiest in England but it was ruthlessly pillaged during the Reformation. Externally it is somewhat unprepossessing, but step inside and the majestic 13th century nave is unforgettably impressive. A corner of the Priory churchyard recalls one of the most tragic days in the town's history. During a fearsome gale in January 1871, a whole fleet of ships foundered along the coast. Bridlington's lifeboat was launched but within minutes it was *"smashed to matchwood"*: most of its crew perished. Twenty bodies were washed ashore and later buried in the Priory churchyard: it was estimated that ten times as many souls found only a watery grave. This awesome tragedy is still recalled each year with a solemn service of remembrance when the lifeboat is drawn through the town.

Queen Henrietta Maria's visit to Bridlington was not as tragic, but it was certainly quite exciting. In February 1643, she landed here from a Dutch ship laden with arms and aid for her beleaguered husband, Charles I. Parliamentary naval vessels were in hot pursuit and having failed to capture their quarry, bombarded the town. Their cannonballs actually hit the Queen's lodging. Henrietta was forced to take cover in a ditch where, as she reported in a letter to her husband, *"the balls sang merrily over our heads, and a sergeant was killed not 20 paces from me"*. At this point Her Majesty deemed it prudent to retreat to the safety of Boynton Hall, three miles inland and well beyond the range of the Parliamentary cannon.

These stirring events, and many others in the long history of Bridlington and its people, are vividly brought to life with the help of evocative old paintings, photographs and artefacts in the **Bayle Museum**. Quite apart from its fascinating exhibits the museum is well worth visiting for its setting inside the old gatehouse to the town, built around 1390.

A more recent attraction, opened at Easter 1999, is **Beside the Seaside**, an all-weather venue where visitors can take a promenade through Bridlington's heyday as a resort, sampling the sights, sounds and characters of a seaside town. Film shows and period amusements such as antique coin-in-the-slot games and a Punch & Judy Show, displays reconstructing a 1950s boarding house as well as the town's maritime history - the museum provides a satisfying experience for both the nostalgic and those with a general curiosity about the town's past.

On the northern outskirts of Bridlington is **Sewerby Hall**, a monumental mansion built on the cusp of the Queen Anne and early Georgian years, between 1714 and 1720. Set in 50 acres of garden and parkland, (where there's also a small zoo), the house was first opened to the public in 1936 by Amy Johnson, the dashing, Yorkshire-born pilot who had captured the public imagination by her daring solo flights to South Africa and Australia. The Museum here houses some fascinating memorabilia of Amy's pioneering feats along with displays of motor vehicles, archaeological finds and some remarkable paintings amongst which is perhaps the most famous portrait of Queen Henrietta Maria, wife of Charles I. Queen Henrietta loved this romantic image of herself as a young, carefree woman, but during the dark days of the Civil War she felt compelled to sell it to raise funds for the doomed Royalist cause which ended with her husband's execution. After passing through several hands, this haunting portrait of a queen touched by tragedy found its last resting place at Sewerby Hall.

Close by is **Bondville Miniature Village**, one of the finest model villages in the country. The display includes more than 1000 hand-made and painted characters, over 200 individual and unique villages, and carefully crafted scenes of everyday life, all set in a beautifully landscaped 1-acre site. The Village is naturally popular with children who are fascinated by features such as the steam train crossing the tiny river and passing the harbour with its fishing boats and cruisers.

FLAMBOROUGH

MAP 5 REF N6

5 miles NE of Bridlington on the B1255.

At **Flamborough Head**, sea and land are locked in an unremitting battle. At the North Landing, huge, foam-spumed waves roll in between gigantic cliffs, slowly but remorselessly washing away the shoreline. Paradoxically, the outcome of this elemental conflict is to produce one of the most picturesque locations on the Yorkshire coast, much visited and much photographed.

Victorian travel writers loved Flamborough. Not just because of its dramatic scenery, but what about the people! They were so clannish and believed in such strange superstitions! No boat would ever set sail on a Sunday, wool could not be wound in lamplight, anyone who mentioned a hare or pig while baiting the fishing lines was inviting doom. No fisherman would leave harbour unless he was wearing a navy-blue jersey, knitted by his wife in a cable, diamond mesh peculiar to the village and still worn today. Every year the villagers would slash their way through Flamborough in a sword-dancing frenzy introduced here in the 8th century by the Vikings. Eventually, local fishermen grew weary of this primitive role so although the sword dance still takes place it is now performed by boys from the primary school, accoutred in white trousers, red caps and the traditional navy-blue jerseys.

Flamborough's parish church contains two particularly interesting monuments. One is the tomb of Sir Marmaduke Constable which shows him with his chest cut open to reveal his heart being devoured by a toad. The knight's death in 1518 had been caused, the story goes, by his swallowing the toad which had been drowsing in Sir Marmaduke's lunchtime pint of ale, apparently. The creature then devoured his heart. The other notable monument is a statue of St Oswald, patron saint of fishermen. This fishing connection is renewed every year, on the second Sunday in October, by a service dedicated to the

Harvest of the Sea, when the area's seafarers gather together in a church decorated with crab pots and fishing nets.

Flamborough Head's first, and England's oldest surviving **lighthouse,** is the octagonal chalk tower on the landward side of the present lighthouse. Built in 1674, its beacon was a basket of burning coal. The lighthouse that is still in use was built in 1806. Originally signalling four white flashes,

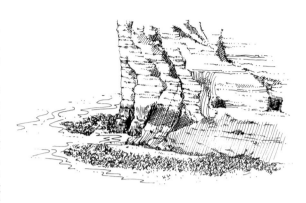

Flamborough Head

developments over the years have included a fog horn in 1859 and in more recent years, a signal of radio bleeps. Until it was automated in 1995, it was the last manned lighthouse on the east coast.

Just to the north of Flamborough is **Danes Dyke,** a huge rampart four miles long designed to cut off the headland from hostile invaders. The Danes had nothing to do with it, the dyke was in place long before they arrived. Sometime during the Bronze or Stone Age, early Britons constructed this extraordinary defensive ditch. A mile and a quarter of its southern length is open to the public as a Nature Trail.

BEMPTON
3 miles N of Bridlington on the B1229

Map 5 ref M6

Bempton Cliffs, 400ft high, mark the northernmost tip of the great belt of chalk that runs diagonally across England from the Isle of Wight to Flamborough Head. The sheer cliffs at Bempton provide an ideal nesting place for huge colonies of fulmars, guillemots, puffins and Britain's largest seabird, the gannet, with a wingspan 6ft wide. In Victorian times, a popular holiday sport was to shoot the birds from boats. Above them, crowds gathered to watch gangs of 'climmers' make a hair-raising descent by rope down the cliffs to gather the birds' eggs. Most were sold for food, but many went to egg collectors. The climmers also massacred kittiwakes in their thousands: kittiwake feathers were highly prized as accessories for hats and for stuffing mattresses. The first Bird Protection Act of 1869 was specifically designed to protect the kittiwakes at Bempton: a ban on collecting eggs here didn't come into force until 1954. Bempton Cliffs are now an RSPB bird sanctuary, a refuge during the April to August breeding season for more than 200,000 seabirds making this the largest colony in Britain.

BARMSTON
6 miles S of Bridlington off the A165

Map 5 ref M7

The road leading from Barmston village to the sands is just over half a mile long: in Viking times it stretched twice as far. The whole of this coast is being eroded at an average rate of three inches every year, and as much as three feet a year in the most vulnerable locations. Fortunately, that still leaves plenty of time to visit Barmston's village pub before it too tumbles into the sea.

Situated opposite the village pond, **The Black Bull** was built some 60 years ago on the site of an older pub and it's very much at the centre of village life. Lively and fun, this is the place people gather to relax and enjoy the long summer evenings. There always seems

to be something going on at The Black Bull. Friday night is Quiz Night, with a gallon of beer for the winners, and singers entertain the drinkers on Saturday nights and on Bank Holidays. As well as serving excellent ales to the customers, mine host Julie Colgan also offers delicious home cooked dishes that

The Black Bull, Barmston, East Yorkshire, YO25 8PG
Tel: 01262 468244

are sure to satisfy even the hungriest of customers. For those customers with caravans, there is occasional accommodation on a self-catering site and those interested should ring for details. Open all day during the season, The Black Bull is closed between the end of October and Whitsun on Monday and Wednesday lunchtimes. This is a very popular place, so it's always a good idea to book a table during the weekend, especially for Sunday lunch. Coach parties are welcome by arrangement.

FOSTON ON THE WOLDS   MAP 5 REF M7
7 miles SW of Bridlington off the A165

If you can't tell a Gloucester Old Spot from a Saddleback, or a Belted Galloway from a Belgian Blue, then take a trip to **Cruckley Animal Farm** where all will become clear. This working farm supports many different varieties of cattle, sheep, pigs, poultry and horses. Some of the animals are endangered species - Greyfaced Dartmoor and Whitefaced Woodland Sheep, for example, and the farm also tends all seven breeds of rare British pigs. The farm has been approved by the Rare Breeds Survival Trust since 1994 and is the only farm in East Yorkshire to achieve this accolade. Enormously popular with children, this 60-acre working farm is home to more than fifty varieties of farm animals. There are daily milking demonstrations, seasonal events such as sheep-clipping and harvesting, and a children's paddock with hand-reared small animals where the undoubted star is Cecil the Vietnamese pot-bellied pig. Cruckley Farm is open daily from the end of April until early October and is clearly signposted.

In the village itself, the place to seek out is **The Plough Inn**. As you might expect of a hostelry which dates back to the early 1700s, the Plough has plenty of character - low beams, lots of exposed brickwork, real fires, a vintage bread oven built into the wall and a fascinating collection of local memorabilia. The Plough is owned and run by Adrienne

The Plough Inn, Foston on the Wolds, Driffield, East Yorkshire YO25 8BJ
Tel: 01262 488303

and Richard Greenbank, former teachers who bought the inn in the summer of 1999 and have enhanced its reputation for good food and for well-kept ales which always include one or two guest beers. During the season, an excellent choice of meals is available every lunchtime and evening, (but please note that in winter the inn is closed at lunchtime, Monday to Thursday). At the time of writing, Adrienne and Richard are planning to provide quality accommodation at the inn which should be in place by the time you read this. And if you happen to be travelling with a caravan, there's a site with standings for up to 5 tourers to the rear of the inn's large car park.

BEEFORD
Map 5 ref M7

8 miles SW of Bridlington on the A165

In this small village, strung out along a main street stretching for a mile or more, you'll find **The Tiger Inn** pub and restaurant, a lovely old English inn which maintains the tradition of sending the traveller on his or her way after excellent refreshment. Your hosts are Martin and Teresa Gill who took over here in 1996. Martin is the third generation of the Gill family to become a publican so he certainly knows how to pull a good pint. The food at The Tiger is also excellent - a good choice of bar meals and sandwiches, tasty starters like Kiwi Mussels served in sizzling garlic butter, and main courses such as Butter-

The Tiger Inn, Main Street, Beeford, Driffield, East Yorkshire YO25 8AS
Tel: 01262 488733

fly Chicken or a hearty mixed grill. There's also a splendid home cooked Roast of the Day, served seven days a week and all day Sunday. In the evening, the menu also offers steaks, Somerset Pork, Catalan Chicken and Halibut Versailles. Popular with locals and visitors alike, the children's outdoor play area and the extensive, secluded beer garden make The Tiger an ideal hostelry for all the family.

CARNABY
MAP 5 REF M6

4 miles SW of Bridlington on the A166

Leaving Bridlington on the A166 will shortly bring you to **John Bull - World of Rock** which has become a premier tourist attraction in this part of East Yorkshire and really is a great day out. Whether you are young or old, you will be fascinated as you discover the history and delights of rock making. The older generation will particularly revel in the smell of the old-fashioned way of making toffee and the interesting bygone displays. Animation and taped conversation accompany you as you explore the establishment which is described as a total sensory experience. You can even try your hand at making a personalised stick of rock.

BURTON AGNES
MAP 5 REF M7

6 miles SW of Bridlington on the A166

The overwhelming attraction in this unspoilt village is the sublime Elizabethan mansion, Burton Agnes Hall, but visitors should not ignore **Burton Agnes Manor House** (English Heritage), a rare example of a Norman house: a building of great historical importance but burdened with a grimly functional architecture, almost 800 years old, that chills one's soul. As Lloyd Grossman might say, "How could anyone live in a house like this?".

    Burton Agnes Hall is much more appealing: an outstanding Elizabethan house, built between 1598 and 1610 and little altered, Burton Agnes is particularly famous for its

splendid Jacobean gatehouse, wondrously decorated ceilings and overmantels carved in oak, plaster and alabaster. It also has a valuable collection of paintings and furniture from between the 17th and 19th centuries - including a portrait of Oliver Cromwell "warts and all" - and a large collection of Impressionist paintings. The gardens are extensive with over 2,000 plants, a maze and giant board games in the Coloured

Burton Agnes Hall, Burton Agnes, Driffield, East Yorkshire, YO25 0ND
Tel: 01262 490324 Fax: 01262 490513

Gardens. Other visitor facilities include a new ice cream parlour, a dried-flower and herb shop, a children's animal corner, and an artists' studio. A very popular addition is the plant sales where numerous uncommon varieties can be obtained. "The Impressionist

Cafe", open throughout the Hall's season, seats 64 inside and, in good weather, 56 outside. Non-smoking, but licensed and offering only the very best in home cooking. The scones are particularly delicious. An interesting day out for all the family.

KILHAM
Map 5 ref L7
8 miles W of Bridlington off the A614

This sizeable village standing on an old Roman road is dominated by the unusually spacious parish church, a medieval building incorporating fragments of an earlier Norman church. Just across the road from All Saints' Church, **The Star Inn** is well known locally

for its excellent food and for its delightful olde-worlde atmosphere. The inn dates back to the late 1600s and has lots of character and warmth. The stylish restaurant to the rear has some fine old beams and a real log fire adds to the appeal. Food is served every lunchtime from noon until 2pm (2.30pm on Sundays), and on Wednesday to Sunday evenings from 7pm until 9.30pm (9pm on Sundays). There is an All Day Menu covering a wide range of high quality, home cooked food and, at weekends, there is a Special Menu on Friday and Saturday evenings and traditional

The Star Inn, Church Street, Kilham, nr Driffield, East Yorkshire YO25 4RG Tel: 01262 420619

roasts on a Sunday lunchtime. Wherever possible, the Star Inn's owners, Jo and Greg Frend use fresh produce from local suppliers and, to the best of their knowledge, there are no GM foodstuffs in any of their dishes. The restaurant's popularity is such that it's advisable to book for Friday and Saturday evenings.

NAFFERTON
Map 5 ref L7
10 miles SW of Bridlington off the A614

Dating back to the early 1800s, **The Cross Keys Inn** is an appealing traditional hostelry offering both good food and comfortable accommodation. Your hosts at this welcoming Free House are Susan and Christopher who bought the inn in 1996 and quickly established a reputation for serving quality ales and wholesome meals. During the season, food is available every lunchtime and evening (except Mondays, unless it's a Bank Holiday) and at weekends during the winter. The delightful restaurant is full of character but as it seats only 30, bookings are strongly recommended at weekends. On Sunday evenings in the summer the inn hosts a Quiz Night and on Fridays during the season there's live

The Cross Keys Inn, 1 North Street, Nafferton, Driffield , East Yorkshire YO25 4JW Tel: 01377 254261

entertainment from 9pm. Nafferton's location, close to the coast and on the edge of the Wolds, makes this an ideal place to stay: the Cross Keys has 4 comfortable guest rooms to let - 1 double, 1 twin and 2 singles, all at very reasonable rates.

GREAT DRIFFIELD

MAP 5 REF L7

13 miles SW of Bridlington on the A166

Located on the edge of the Wolds, Great Driffield is a busy little market town at the heart of an important corn growing area. A cattle market is held here every Thursday; a general market on both Thursday and Saturday, and the annual agricultural show has been going strong since 1854. **All Saints Parish Church**, dating back to the 12th century has one of the highest towers in the county and some lovely stained glass windows portraying local nobility.

Great Driffield was once the capital of the Saxon Kingdom of Dear, a vast domain extending over the whole of Northumbria and Yorkshire. It was a King of Dear who, for administrative convenience, divided the southern part of his realm into three parts, 'thriddings', a word which gradually evolved into the famous "Ridings" of Yorkshire.

The Railway Hotel, 5 Middle Street South, Great Driffield, East Yorkshire YO25 6PT Tel: 01377 252839

Conveniently located across the road from Driffield's railway station, **The Railway Hotel** naturally has lots of railway paintings and memorabilia scattered around the walls. The building is believed to date back to the arrival of the railway in the mid-1800s and it has considerable charm. Hilary and Roger Brayshaw took over here in the summer of 1999 and have already earned a reputation for the quality of the food on offer. Menus change weekly and they present diners with a huge choice, supplemented by daily specials. Meals are served from 11.30am to 2.45pm, and from 5pm until 7.45pm every day except Sunday evening. Please note too that there's a limited menu on Monday lunchtime and evening, and at Tuesday lunchtime. Children are welcome, with high chairs provided and a boxful of toys to keep them entertained. Outside, there's a spacious garden and if you're travelling with a caravan there are standings available in the grounds - but do book ahead.

Driffield has expanded westwards to meet up with its smaller neighbour, **Little Driffield**. A tablet in the church here claims that, in the Saxon monastery that stood on this site, Aldred, King of Northumbria was buried in AD 705 after being wounded in a battle against the Danes.

KIRKBURN
MAP 5 REF L7

2 miles SW of Driffield on the A614

The architectural guru Nikolaus Pevsner considered **St Mary's Church** in Kirkburn to be one of the two best Norman parish churches in the East Riding. Dating from 1119, the church has an unusual tower staircase, a richly carved and decorated Victorian screen, and a spectacular early Norman font covered with carved symbolic figures.

Another building of interest in the village is **The Queens Head**, a former coaching inn dating back to the early 1700s. This delightful traditional hostelry is run by Phil and Sue Walker who arrived here early in 1999 and quickly established an excellent reputation for serving quality Real Ales (including Black Sheep, Tetley's, and John Smiths) and good home-cooked food. Sue is in charge of the kitchen and the ever-changing menu offers a good choice of traditional and modern - starters, main courses (including vegetarian options), and sweets. Food is served in the dining room (booking advisable), the bar or, in good weather, on the attractive patio area outside. Food is available at lunchtime (from noon until 2pm) and in the evening from 6pm. Children are welcome and there is a garden area where they can play. Phil and Sue have a pro-

The Queens Head, Kirkburn, nr Driffield, East Yorkshire YO25 9DU Tel: 01377 229261

gramme of improvements for the Queens Head, some of which will be in place by the summer of 2000. Access to the inn's large car park is from either the A614 or from the main street of the village.

SLEDMERE
MAP 4 REF K6
7 miles NW of Driffield on the B1252

About 8 miles north of Kirkburn is **Sledmere House**, a noble Georgian mansion built by the Sykes family in the 1750s when this area was still a wilderness infested with packs of marauding wolves. Inside, there is fine furniture by Chippendale and Sheraton, and decorated plasterwork by Joseph Rose. The copy of a naked, and well-endowed, Apollo Belvedere in the landing alcove must have caused many a maidenly blush in Victorian times, and the Turkish Room - inspired by the Sultan's salon in Istanbul's Valideh Mosque - is a dazzling example of oriental opulence.

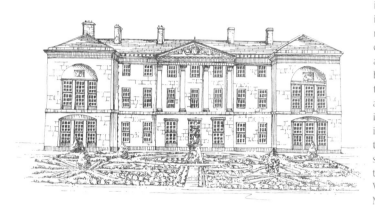

Sledmere House

Outside, the gardens and the 220 acres of parkland were landscaped, of course, by 'Capability' Brown.

The Sykes family set a shining example to other landowners in the Wolds by agricultural improvements that transformed a *"blank and barren tract of land"* into one of the most productive and best cultivated districts in the county. They founded the famous Sledmere Stud, and the second Sir Tatton Sykes spent nearly two million pounds on building and restoring churches in the area. Sledmere House itself was ravaged by fire in 1911. Sir Tatton was enjoying his favourite lunchtime dessert of rice pudding when a servant rushed in with news of the fire and urged him to leave the house. "First, I must finish my pudding, finish my pudding" he declared, and did so. An armchair was set up for him on the lawn and Sir Tatton, then eighty-five years old, "followed the progress of the conflagration" as the household staff laboured to rescue the house's many treasures. After the fire, Sledmere was quickly restored and the Sykes family is still in residence. The house is open to the public and music lovers should make sure they visit between 2 and 4pm when the enormous pipe organ is being played.

Across the road from Sledmere House are two remarkable, elaborately detailed, monuments. The **Eleanor Cross** - modelled on those set up by Edward I in memory of his Queen, was erected by Sir Tatton Sykes in 1900; the **Waggoners Memorial** designed by Sir Mark Sykes, commemorates the 1000-strong company of men he raised from the Wolds during World War I. Their knowledge of horses was invaluable in their role as members of the Army Service Corps. The finely-carved monument is like a 'storyboard', its panels depicting the Waggoners' varied duties during the war.

WEST LUTTON
MAP 4 REF K6

11 miles NW of Driffield off the A64 or B1253

West Lutton church is yet another of the many repaired or restored by Sir Tatton Sykes in this corner of the East Riding. It stands overlooking the village green and pond, its lych gate reached by a tiny bridge.

Standing across from the village church, there has been a **Three Tuns Inn** in this picturesque village for generations but the present inn is actually the Coach House of the original. It was converted to a pub in 1922 but the atmos-
phere inside is everything you would expect from a traditional village inn with some interesting old photographs of West Lutton. Your host is Stephen Swaffield and the quality ales he has on offer include Tetleys and John Smiths, and if you are feeling peck-

**The Three Tuns Inn, West Lutton, Malton,
North Yorkshire YO17 8TA Tel: 01944 738200**

ish, freshly made sandwiches are available at lunchtime, but please note that the Three Tuns is closed Tuesday to Thursday lunchtimes unless by prior arrangement for walking parties, etc. Places of interest in the neighbourhood include the grand Georgian mansion, Sledmere House, and its attractive estate village, the deserted medieval village at Wharram Percy, while just a short drive will bring you to either Bridlington and Filey or the peaceful open spaces of the Yorkshire Wolds.

A few miles to the southwest of West Lutton, a minor road off the B1248 leads to one of the most haunting sights in the county - the deserted medieval village of **Wharram Percy**. There had been a settlement here for some 5,000 years but by the late 1400s the village stood abandoned. For a while the church continued to serve the surrounding hamlets but in time, that too became a ruin. The manor house of the Percy family who gave the village its name, peasant houses dating back to the 13th century, a corn mill, a cemetery complete with exposed skeletons - these sad memorials of a once thriving community stand windswept and desolate. Until fairly recently it was assumed that the villagers had been driven from their homes by the plague but scholars are now certain that the cause was simple economics: the lords of the manor, the Percys, turned their lands from labour-intensive crop cultivation to sheep farming which needed only a handful of shepherds. Unable to find work, the villagers drifted elsewhere.

HUGGATE
MAP 4 REF K7

10 miles W of Great Driffield off the A166

Huggate is tucked away deep in the heart of the Wolds with two long distance walks, the **Minster Way** and the **Wolds Way**, skirting it to the north and south. The village clusters around a large green with a well which is claimed to be the deepest in England.

Hidden gems are few and far between, but one that is waiting to be discovered is the **Wolds Inn** at Huggate. Surrounded by breathtaking countryside, this inn - the highest on the Wolds - offers the visitor excellent facilities for which country inns are renowned. The atmosphere that has been created by owners Peter and Patricia, along with their daughter Jane and son-in-law John, is unique and unbeatable. On entering the Wolds Inn there is a characterful lounge bar and dining area to one side and a public bar on the other. The

interior features exposed wooden beams and pan-elled walls throughout and the bar includes pew-style seats. Voted Restaurant of the Year (Best Pub) 1996 by the Hull Daily Mail, the meals served here are delicious with a good selec-tion of traditional tasty dishes on

The Wolds Inn, Huggate, York YO4 2YH
Tel: 01377 288217 e-mail: huggate@woldsinn.freeserve.co.uk

offer. As well as the excellent food, behind the bar is an array of well-kept real ales and the pub is recommended by CAMRA. The warm welcome and friendly hospitality extends to the four comfortable en suite guest bedrooms that provide the opportunity for a longer stay in this relaxing establishment. The Wolds Inn is closed all day Monday, except Bank Holidays, and it is essential to book at weekends if you wish to eat. With many pleasant walks in the area, the pub is popular with walkers and ramblers. This is an outstanding establishment with great hosts and an even better atmosphere. Somewhat off the beaten track, the inn can be found to the south of the main A166 mid-way between York and Driffield. Once found, however, the Wolds Inn will be hard to forget.

The pretty village of **Warter**, about 4 miles south of Huggate, is where the "oldest horserace in the world" has its winning post. The post is inscribed with the date 1519, the year in which the **Kipling Cotes Derby** was first run. This demanding steeple chase which passes through several parishes is still held annually on the third Thursday in March.

POCKLINGTON   Map 4 ref K8
10 miles E of York off the A1079

Set amidst rich agricultural land with the Wolds rising to the east, Pocklington is a lively market town with an unusual layout of twisting alleys running off the market place. Its splendid church, mostly 15th century but with fragments of an earlier Norman building, certainly justifies its title as the Cathedral of the Wolds (although strictly speaking Pocklington is just outside the Wolds). William Wilberforce went to the old grammar school here and, a more dubious claim to fame, the last burning of a witch in England took place in Pocklington. Founded in Anglo-Saxon times by 'Pocela's people', by the time the Domesday Book was compiled Pocklington was recorded as one of the only two boroughs in the East Riding. A market followed in the 13th century, but it was the building in 1815 of a canal linking the town to the River Ouse, and the later arrival of the railway, that set the seal on the town's prosperity.

A popular and unusual attraction in Pocklington is the **Penny Arcadia** housed in the Ritz Cinema in the market place. "Not so much a museum as a fun palace" it contains a wonderful collection of penny-in-the-slot amusement machines ranging from "What the Butler Saw" to fortune telling and pinball machines.

The people of Pocklington have good reason to be grateful to Major P.M. Stewart who, on his death in 1962, bequeathed **Burnby Hall and Gardens** to the town. The eight acres of gardens are world-famous for the rare collection of water-lilies planted in the two large lakes. There are some fifty varieties and in the main flowering season from July to early September they present a dazzling spectacle. The Major and his wife had travelled extensively before settling down at Burnby and there's a small museum in the Hall displaying his collection of sporting trophies.

Waterloo Lane is a narrow little snicket running off Pocklington's market square and it should definitely be tracked down since this is where you'll find **Peter Ward's Coffee House & Tea Rooms**. Peter learned all about quality tea rooms when he started his working life in the kitchens of the famous "Betty's" in York. He bought the distinctive premises in Waterloo Lane in 1997 determined to create somewhere that would offer value for money without compromising on standards and service. He has succeeded completely. Opening after a comprehensive refurbishment, the non-smoking Coffee House is attractively furnished and decorated, with fresh flowers on each of the tables. In addition to top quality teas and coffees, the menu lists a good range of appetising snacks and light meals -Welsh Rarebit with bacon, scrambled

Peter Ward's Coffee House & Tea Rooms,
6-8 Waterloo Lane, Pocklington,
York YO42 2AG Tel: 01759 304868

eggs with smoked salmon, for example, as well as traditional Yorkshire Cream Teas. Once you've sampled the fare on offer, this is the kind of place you'll return to again and again.

A few miles to the south of Pocklington is **Londesborough Park**, a 400 acre estate which was once owned by the legendary railway entrepreneur, George Hudson. He had the York to Market Weighton railway diverted here so that he could build himself a comfortable private station. The railway has now disappeared but part of its route is included in the popular long distance footpath, the Wolds Way.

About 8 miles west of Pocklington, on the B1228 near Elvington, is the **Yorkshire Air Museum**. A memorial to the Allied Air Forces who flew from the area in World War II, the museum celebrates the history of aviation in Yorkshire and Humberside. Housed in the original wartime buildings, the museum has recreated the authentic atmosphere of the 1940s. Aircraft on display include a rebuilt Halifax and Mosquito, and one of the last surviving Lightnings.

SHIPTONTHORPE
Map 4 ref K8

2 miles NW of Market Weighton on the A1079

For a true taste of Yorkshire hospitality, a visit to **The Ship Inn** is strongly recommended. Your hosts, Ann and Roger, arrived here in early 1999 and completely refurbished the 150-year-old inn, laying down new wooden floors and lining the walls with half-panelling. Real Ale lovers will feel at home here since there are 3 regular ales on offer (John

Smiths, Tetley and Black Sheep), along with a guest ale during the summer months. Ann is in charge of the kitchen and offers a comprehensive menu along with daily specials. Food is available every day from noon until 2.30pm, again from 5pm until 8pm and if you want to eat in the dining room bookings are advisable. As we go to press, Ann and Roger are finalising plans for providing accommodation at The Ship Inn so by the time you

The Ship Inn, 30 York Road, Shiptonthorpe,
East Yorkshire YO43 3PG   Tel: 01430 872006

read this you should be able to stay at this attractive old inn within easy reach of York, the coast and the Wolds.

GOODMANHAM
Map 4 ref K8

2 miles NE of Market Weighton off the A614 or A1079

Goodmanham is always mentioned in accounts of early Christianity in northern England. During Saxon times, according to the Venerable Bede, there was a pagan temple at Goodmanham. In 627AD its priest, Coifu, was converted to the Christian faith and with his own hands destroyed the heathen shrine. Coifu's conversion so impressed Edwin, King of Northumbria, that he also was baptised and made Christianity the official religion of his kingdom. Other versions of the story attribute King Edwin's conversion to a different cause. They say he was hopelessly enamoured of the beautiful Princess Aethelburh, daughter of the King of Kent. Aethelburh, however, was a Christian and she refused to marry Edwin until he too had adopted her faith.

MARKET WEIGHTON
MAP 4 REF K8

16 miles SW of Driffield on the A614/A1069

Market Weighton is a busy little town where mellow 18th century houses cluster around an early Norman church. Buried somewhere in the churchyard is William Bradley who was born at Market Weighton in 1787 and grew up to become the tallest man in England. He stood 7 feet 8 inches high and weighed 27 stones. William made a fortune by travelling the country and placing himself on display. He was even received at Court by George III who, taking a fancy to the giant, gave him a huge gold watch to wear across his chest.

SOUTH DALTON
MAP 4 REF L8

6 miles NW of Beverley off the B1248

The most prominent church in East Yorkshire, **St Mary's Church** has a soaring spire more than 200ft high, an unmistakable landmark for miles around. Built in 1861 by Lord Beaumont Hotham, the church was designed by the famous Victorian architect J.L. Pearson and the elaborate internal and external decorations are well worth looking at.

   Standing at the centre of this tiny hamlet in the heart of the Wolds **The Pipe and Glass** looks very inviting with its whitewashed walls and pantiled roof. The interior is just as appealing - old beams, wooden floors, a real fire and lots of decorative bygones all contribute to the charm. The Pipe and Glass is a family-run business with owners James and Valerie Weatherhead assisted by their daughter Helen. The inn has a pleasant separate restaurant serving excellent food every lunchtime and evening, and to the rear of the restaurant there's a function room looking out over a pretty garden which boasts a grand old yew

**The Pipe and Glass, West End, South Dalton, Beverley,
East Yorkshire HU17 7PN Tel: 01430 810246**

tree some 750 years old. Also overlooking the garden - and thousands of acres of open countryside, are the old stables which have been imaginatively converted to provide 3 charming guest rooms, all of them en suite and with quality furnishings and decorations. This is a delightful hidden place, well worth seeking out whether to enjoy the good fare and hospitality, or to use as a base for exploring the scenic attractions of the Wolds.

BEVERLEY & HOLDERNESS

This southeastern corner of Yorkshire tends to be overlooked by many visitors. If only they knew what they were missing. Beverley is one of the most beguiling of Yorkshire towns and its Minster one of the greatest glories of Gothic architecture. Its parish church, built by a medieval guild, rivals the Minster in its grandeur and in its colourful interior. The whole town has the indefinable dignity you might expect from a community that was a capital of the East Riding in former days when Hull, just six miles to the south, was still a rather scruffy little port.

To the east and south of Beverley lies the old Land of Holderness, its character quite different from anywhere else in Yorkshire. A wide plain, it stretches to the coast where for aeons the land has been fighting an incessant, and losing, battle against the onslaught of North Sea billows. The whole length of the Holderness coast is being eroded at an average rate of three inches a year, but in some locations up to three feet or more gets gnawn away. At its southernmost tip, **Spurn Point** curls around the mouth of the Humber estuary, a cruelly exposed tip of land whose contours get re-arranged after every winter storm. The coastal towns and villages have a bleached and scoured look to them, perhaps a little forbidding at first. It doesn't take long however for visitors to succumb to the appeal of this region of wide vistas, secluded villages and lonely shores.

BEVERLEY   MAP 5 REF L8
8 miles N of Hull on the A1035

"For those who do not know this town, there is a great surprise in store...Beverley is made for walking and living in". Such was the considered opinion of the late Poet Laureate, John Betjeman. In medieval times, Beverley was one of England's most prosperous towns and it remains one of the most gracious. Its greatest glory is the **Minster** whose twin towers, built in glowing magnesian limestone, soar above this, the oldest town in East Yorkshire. More than two centuries in the making, from around 1220 to 1450, the Minster provides a textbook demonstration of the evolving architectural styles of those years. Amongst its many treasures are superb, fine wood carvings from the Ripon school, and a thousand year old *fridstol*, or sanctuary seat. Carved from a single block of stone, the fridstol is a relic from the earlier Saxon church on this site. Under Saxon law, the fridstol provided refuge for any offender who managed to reach it. The canons would then try to resolve the dispute between the fugitive and his pursuer. If after thirty days no solution had been found, the seeker of sanctuary was then given safe escort to the county boundary or the nearest port. The custom survived right up until Henry VIII's closure of the monasteries.

Unlike the plain-cut fridstol, the canopy of the 14th century Percy Shrine is prodigal in its ornamentation - *"the finest piece of work of the finest craftsmen of the finest period in British building"*. The behaviour of some visitors to this glorious Shrine was not, it seems, always as reverent as it might have been. When Celia Fiennes toured the Minster in 1697 she recorded that the tomb of *"Great Percy, Earle of Northumberland was a little fallen in and a hole so bigg as many put their hands in and touch'd the body which was much of it entire"*. Great Percy's remains are now decently concealed once again.

As well as the incomparable stone carvings on the shrine, the Minster also has a wealth of wonderful carvings in wood. Seek out those representing Stomach Ache, Tooth-ache, Sciatica and Lumbago - four afflictions probably almost as fearsome to medieval people as the Four Riders of the Apocalypse.

Close by is the **North Bar**, the only one of the town's five medieval gatehouses to have survived. Unlike many towns in the Middle Ages, Beverley did not have an encir-cling wall. Instead, the town fathers had a deep ditch excavated around it so that all goods had to pass through one of the gates and pay a toll. North Bar was built in 1409 and, with headroom of little more than ten feet, is something of a traffic hazard, albeit a very attractive one. Next door is Bar House, in which Charles I and his sons stayed in the 1630s. Another visitor to the town, famous for very different reasons, was the highwayman Dick Turpin who, in 1739, was brought before a magistrates' hearing conducted at one of the town's inns. That inn has long since gone and its site is now occupied by the Beverley Arms.

St Mary's Church, Beverley

St Mary's Church, just across the road from the Beverley Arms, tends to be over-shadowed by the glories of Beverley Minster. But this is another superb medieval building, richly endowed with fine carvings - many brightly coloured - and striking sculptures. A series of ceiling panels depicts all the Kings of England from Sigebert (623-37) to Henry VI. Originally, four legendary kings were also included, but one of them was re-placed in recent times by a portrait of George VI. Lewis Carroll visited St Mary's when he stayed with friends in the town and was very taken with a stone carving of a rabbit - the inspiration, it is believed, for the March Hare in Alice in Wonderland. Certainly the carving bears an uncanny resemblance to Tenniel's famous drawing of the Mad Hatter.

Tucked away in the historic Wednesday Market area of Beverley, within sight of the famous Minster, **Artlynk Gallery** is a small treasure-house displaying the best of British decorative art, past and present. Housed in an attractive Georgian listed building, the gallery presents an outstanding array of beautiful and exquisite items created by craftsmen and artists from the days of Elizabeth I to Elizabeth II. The founders of Artlynk, which has been established in Beverley for almost 20 years, are Lynde and James Douthwaite. James' speciality is an-

Artlynk Gallery, 14 Wednesday Market, Beverley, East Yorkshire HU17 0DH
Tel: 01482 864902/01964 536941

tique maps; Lynde's expertise is in the field of modern ceramics - "the antiques of tomorrow". But the gallery also displays a wide variety of original paintings and prints, as well as small antiques. Lynde and James make the point that British artists and craftsmen are famed the world over, yet their original works can be collected at less cost than many major manufacturer's limited editions. This is definitely a place for serious browsing - but do note that the gallery is closed on Sundays and Mondays: on other days it's open from 10.30am to 4.00pm.

The wide market square in the heart of the town is graced by an elegant Market Cross, a circular pillared building rather like a small Greek temple. It bears the arms of Queen Anne in whose reign it was built at the expense of the town's two Members of Parliament. At that time of course parliamentary elections were flagrantly corrupt but at Beverley the tradition continued longer than in most places - in 1868 the author Anthony Trollope stood as a candidate here but was defeated in what was acknowledged as a breathtakingly fraudulent election.

The Guildhall nearby was built in 1762, is still used as a courtroom and also houses the town's Tourist Information Centre. The impressive courtroom has an ornate plasterwork ceiling on which there is an imposing Royal Coat of Arms and also the familiar figure of Justice holding a pair of scales. Unusually, she is not wearing a blindfold. When an 18th century town clerk was asked the reason for this departure from tradition, he replied *"In Beverley, Justice is not blind"*.

Housed within a 400 year old listed building, just a few minutes walk from the centre of the town, is the quaint and charming **Highgate Corner Tea Rooms.** Owned and personally run by Margaret Pearce, the tea rooms are laid out on two floors, both beautifully decorated and furnished, giving the establishment a cosy and intimate air. As well as maintaining a very high standard of friendly service, the emphasis at Highgate Corner is on home made and home cooked food of the highest quality. A traditional tea room, which makes this a pleasant change from the bustle of modern snack bars, Highgate Corner's menu offers a wide selection of hot and cold dishes - from tasty sandwiches and salads to filled jacket potatoes, with much more besides. Finally, the mouth-watering selection of cakes and pastries are sure to tempt anyone who sees them and it is well worth making the effort to try some!

Highgate Corner Tea Rooms, 15A Wednesday Market, Beverley, East Yorkshire HU17 0DN Tel: 01482 863131

Beverley can boast three separate museums. The **Beverley Art Gallery and Museum** contains a variety of local antiquities, Victorian bygones and works by the noted local artist, F.W. Elwell RA; the **East Yorkshire Regimental Museum** has six rooms of exhibits chronicling the area's long association with the regiment, and the **Museum of Army Transport** in Flamingate includes an intriguing variety of vehicles. They range from the wagon in which Lord Roberts travelled during the Boer War, to a Beaver military aircraft; from the Rolls Royce used by Field Marshal Montgomery as a staff car in France and Germany, to the only example of a three-wheels-in-a-row motorcycle.

From Beverley, serious walkers might care to follow some or all of the 15 mile **Hudson Way**, a level route that follows the track of the old railway from Beverley to Market Weighton. The Hudson Way wanders through the Wolds, sometimes deep in a cutting, sometimes high on an embankment, past an old windmill near Etton and through eerily abandoned stations.

TICKTON
Map 5 ref L8
2 miles NE of Beverley off the A1035

The magnificent **Crown and Anchor** stands proudly beside the River Hull at Hull Bridge, near Tickton. The appearance both inside and out goes hand in hand with its setting and position which is delightful, particularly in summer months when there is lots of river traffic. Inside the inn are a number of alcoves which make up the main bar area, a lounge and, up a couple of steps, a restaurant which looks out over the river. Alan and Janice Dawson are the landlord and landlady and they are particularly proud of their popular establishment. It is decorated and furnished to a high quality, the atmosphere is friendly and the staff are happy and helpful. The inn is renowned for its food as well as well-kept ales from the Mansfield Brewery Company. In addition to the printed menu, which offers an excellent selection of starters, main courses and desserts, daily spe-

The Crown and Anchor, Hull Bridge, nr Tickton, East Yorkshire HU17 9RY Tel: 01964 542816

cials are written up on the blackboard. The style is that of traditional pub fare with some more exotic dishes as well. The portions are of a good size and the meals are very reasonably priced. The gardens and terraces are by the river bank and are delightful in summer. Bookings for the restaurant are taken for Monday to Thursday, but not for weekends.

To one side of the pub is a small camping and caravan park which can accommodate up to six tourers. Facilities include electric hook-ups, water and a children's play area. The Crown and Anchor can be found by taking the A1035 out of Beverley towards Bridlington. After about two miles, turn right at the Tickton village sign and immediately right again. The pub lies at the end of this road.

HOLDERNESS

"Lordings, there is in Yorkshire, as I guess / A marshy country called Holdernesse". With these words Chaucer begins the Summoner's story in the Canterbury Tales. It's not surprising that this area was then largely marshland since most of the land lies at less than 10m above sea level. The name 'Holderness' comes from Viking times: a 'hold' was a man of high rank in the Danelaw, 'ness' has stayed in the language with its meaning of promontory. The precise boundaries of the Land of Holderness are clear enough to the east where it runs to the coast, and to the south where Holderness ends with Yorkshire itself at Spurn Point. They are less well-defined to the north and west where they run somewhere close to the great crescent of the Wolds. For the purposes of this book, we have taken as the northern limit of Holderness the village of Skipsea, where, as you'll discover in the next entry, some early Norman Lords of Holderness showed a remarkable lack of loyalty to their King.

SKIPSEA
Map 5 ref M7

15 miles NE of Beverley on the B1242

When William the Conqueror granted Drogo de Bevrere the Lordship of Holderness, Drogo decided to raise his castle on an island in the shallow lake known as Skipsea Mere. Built mostly of timber, the castle had not long been completed when Drogo made the foolish mistake of murdering his wife. In the normal course of events, a Norman lord could murder whomever he wished, but Drogo's action was foolish because his wife was a kinswoman of the Conqueror himself. Drogo was banished and his lands granted to a succession of other royal relatives, most of whom also came to a sticky end after becoming involved in rebellions and treasonable acts. The castle was finally abandoned in the mid-13th century and all that remains now is the great motte, or mound, on which it was built and the earth ramparts surrounding it.

ATWICK
Map 5 ref M8

13 miles NE of Beverley on the B1242

Like Hornsea, Atwick once had its own mere. Some years ago, excavations in its dried-up bed revealed fossilised remains of a huge Irish elk and the tusk of an ancient elephant, clear proof of the tropical climate East Yorkshire enjoyed in those far-off days. Atwick is a picturesque village on the coast, just two miles north of Hornsea. It has been a regular winner of local - and, in 1997, county - awards in the Britain in Bloom competition.

HORNSEA
Map 5 ref M8

12 miles NE of Beverley on the B1242/B1244

This small coastal town can boast not only the most popular visitor attraction in Humberside, Hornsea Pottery, but also Yorkshire's largest freshwater lake, Hornsea Mere. **Hornsea Pottery** is an extensive complex which includes the famous pottery where you can watch craftsmen at work and buy their wares, a factory viewing area, a collection of vintage cars, factory shops, a country park, and **Butterfly World** where more than 200 species of colourful butterflies flutter around a tropical greenhouse.

Hornsea Mere, two miles long and one mile wide, provides a refuge for over 170 species of birds and a peaceful setting for many varieties of rare flowers. Human visitors are well provided for, too, with facilities for fishing, boating and sailing. Hornsea is also the home of the **North Holderness Museum of Village Life.** Here, in a converted 18th century farmhouse, period rooms have been recreated, and there are collections of agricultural equipment and the tools of long gone local tradesmen. Excellent sands, a church built with cobbles gathered from the shore, well-tended public gardens and a breezy, mile-long promenade all add to the town's popularity.

The excellent **Hornsea Museum**, established in 1978, has won numerous national awards over the years as well as being featured several times on television. The museum occupies a Grade II listed building, a former farmhouse where successive generations of the Burn family lived for 300 years up until 1952. Their way of life, the personalities and characters who influenced the development of the town or found fame in other ways, are explored in meticulously restored rooms brimming with furniture, decorations, utensils and tools of the Victorian period. The kitchen, parlour, bedroom, have fascinating displays of authentic contemporary artefacts, and the museum complex also includes a laundry, workshop, blacksmith's shop and a barn stocked with vintage agricultural implements. In Swallow Cottage next door, children can undergo the Victorian school experience under the tutelage of "Miss Grim" - writing on

Hornsea Museum, 11 Newbegin, Hornsea,
East Yorkshire HU18 1AB Tel: 01964 533443

slates, having good deportment instilled and, above all, observing the maxim *"Silence is Golden".* The cottage also houses a comprehensive and varied display of early Hornsea pottery, various temporary exhibitions, and, in summer, a refreshment room for visitors. Remarkably, this outstanding museum is staffed entirely by volunteers.

For a satisfying shop-till-you-drop experience, Hornsea Freeport - the 'Independent State of Low Prices - is hard to beat. There are discounts of up to 50% or more on everything from designerwear, childrenswear and sportswear to chinaware, kitchenware and glassware. There are themed leisure attractions and bright, fun-filled play areas to keep the children amused.

Located within the Freeport complex, **The Pavilion Restaurant** is part of the Massarella Catering Group and is a very superior self-service restaurant with seating for 188 inside and a further 150 outside in the attractive tiled courtyard with its Victorian-style covered bandstand. Pleasingly decorated and furnished, the restaurant offers a comprehensive menu with something for everyone. In addition, there are always at least 8 Chef's daily specials. In keeping with the restaurant's name several of the dishes have names with cricketing connotations - the list of starters for instance is headed "The Opener". The food is delicious, the portions generous, the prices extremely reasonable and the service is prompt and courteous. The Pavilion is open all year, except Christmas Day, from 9.30am

The Pavilion, Freeport Hornsea, Hornsea, East Yorkshire HU18 1UT
Tel: 01964 536537

to 6pm. Out of season, you can book a table but during the summer months this is not possible - the restaurant is too busy!

An immense amount of work has gone into making **Orbit** one of East Yorkshire's leading venues for good food, drink and entertainment. The new owner, Richard Hutchins, has made the most of Orbit's favoured position overlooking the sea and added a spacious conservatory with seating for 30 people. The interior has been completely refurbished - both the bar and the separate restaurant where guests can enjoy a candlelit meal. Richard is a chef by profession and offers different menus for the bar and restaurant. A popular innovation has been the Happy Hour between 7 and 8pm when all pump beer, bottles and spirits are served for just £1 a measure. Orbit also provides live entertainment in the

Orbit, Hornsea Burton Road, South Promenade, Hornsea,
East Yorkshire HU18 1TL Tel: 01964 534554

Orbits Club every day, Monday to Saturday, during the season. In addition, the Club has dancing every Friday and Saturday from 10pm until 2am. Since Orbit was built in the 1970s it has had something of a chequered history but is now well on course for establishing itself as the area's premier venue, popular with young and old alike.

SPROATLEY   Map 5 ref M9
7 miles NE of Hull on the B1238

A couple of miles north of Sproatley is **Burton Constable Hall,** named after Sir John Constable who in 1570 built a stately mansion here which incorporated parts of an even older house, dating back to the reign of King Stephen in the 1100s. The Hall was again remodelled, on Jacobean lines, in the 18th century and contains some fine work by Chippendale, Adam and James Wyatt. In the famous Long Gallery with its 15th century Flemish stained glass, hangs a remarkable collection of paintings, amongst them Holbein's portraits of Sir Thomas Cranmer and Sir Thomas More, and Zucchero's Mary, Queen of Scots. Dragons abound in the dazzling Chinese Room, an exercise in oriental exotica that long pre-dates the Prince Regent's similar extravaganza at the Brighton Pavilion. Thomas Chippendale himself designed the fantastical Dragon Chair, fit for a Ming Emperor. Outside, there are extensive parklands designed by - who else could it be? - 'Capability' Brown, and apparently inspired by the gardens at Versailles. Perhaps it was this connection that motivated the Constable family to suggest loaning the Hall to Louis XVIII of France during his years of exile after the Revolution. (Louis politely declined the offer, preferring to settle rather closer to London, at Hartwell in Buckinghamshire). Also in the grounds of the Hall are collections of agricultural machinery, horse-drawn carriages and 18th century scientific apparatus.

The descendants of the Constable family still bear the title 'Lords of Holderness' and along with it the rights to any flotsam and jetsam washed ashore on the Holderness peninsula. Many years ago, when the late Brigadier Chichester Constable was congratulated on enjoying such a privilege, he retorted,

Burton Constable Hall

"I also have to pay for burying, or otherwise disposing of, any whale grounded on the Holderness shore - and it costs me about £20 a time!" The huge bones of one such whale are still on show in the grounds of the Hall.

RYEHILL
9 miles E of Hull off the A1033

Map 5 ref N9

This tiny village is indeed a hidden place, set back from the main Hull to Withernsea road, just east of the much larger village of Thorngumbald. Look out for the sign pointing to the right. The main reason for seeking out Ryehill is to call in at the delightful pub known as **The Crooked Billet**, a traditional country inn where hospitality has been dispensed since the late 1600s. Ancient beams, real fires, lots of local memorabilia and flagstone or quarry-tiled floors all add to the appeal. Originally known as the Royal Oak, the pub's name was changed in 1880 (for reasons unknown) to the Crooked Billet, referring to the

The Crooked Billet, Pit Lane, Ryehill, Thorngumbald,
East Yorkshire HU12 9NN Tel: 01964 622303

kind of rough-hewn staff made from a tree branch and widely used by poorer people as both a walking aid and a defensive weapon. Mine hosts at this charming hostelry with its whitewashed walls and pantiled roof are John and Sylvia Pizer who took over here in 1997 and have made the Crooked Billet such a welcoming and popular place. Sylvia is an accomplished cook and offers an extensive regular menu supplemented by 5 daily specials. Food is available every lunchtime and evening, except on Tuesday evenings, and it's wise to book ahead for Friday and Saturday nights. If you happen to be visiting on a Wednesday evening, feel free to take part in the regular Quiz Night.

HALSHAM

MAP 5 REF N9

14 miles E of Hull off the B1362

Halsham was once the seat of the Constable family, Lords of Holderness, before they moved to their stately new mansion at Burton Constable. On the edge of Halsham village, they left behind their imposing, domed mausoleum built in the late 1700s to house ancestors going back to the 12th century. The mausoleum is not open to the public but is clearly visible from the B1362 Hull to Withernsea road.

WITHERNSEA

MAP 5 REF O9

18 miles E of Hull on the A1033

The next place of interest down the Holderness coast is Withernsea. Long, golden sandy beaches stretch for miles both north and south, albeit a mile further inland than they were in the days of William the Conqueror. The old lighthouse is a striking feature of the town and those energetic enough to climb the 127ft tower are rewarded by some marvellous views from the lamproom. The lighthouse was decommissioned in 1976 and now houses two small museums. One is dedicated to the history of the Royal National Lifeboat Institution; the other to the actress Kay Kendall. Her grandfather helped build the lighthouse in 1892 and was the last coxswain of the deep sea lifeboat. Kay was born in Withernsea and later achieved great success in the London theatre as a sophisticated comedienne but she is probably best remembered for the rousing trumpet solo she delivered in the Ealing Studios hit film *Genevieve*.

South of Withernsea stretches a desolate spit of flat windswept dunes. This is **Spurn Point** which leads to Spurn Head, the narrow hook of ever-shifting sands that curls around the mouth of the Humber estuary. This bleak but curiously invigorating tag end of Yorkshire is nevertheless heavily populated - by hundreds of species of rare and solitary wild fowl, by playful seals, and also by the small contingent of lifeboatmen who operate the only permanently manned lifeboat station in Britain. Please note that a toll is payable beyond the village of Kilnsea, and there is no car park. Access to Spurn Head is only on foot.

PATRINGTON   MAP 5 REF N10

14 miles SE of Hull on the A1033

Shortly after it was built, **St Patrick's Church** at Patrington was dubbed *"Queen of Holderness"*, and Queen it remains. This sublime church took more than a hundred years to build, from around 1310 to 1420, and it is one of the most glorious examples of the eye-pleasing style known as English Decorated. Its spire soars almost 180ft into the sky making it the most distinctive feature in the flat plains of Holderness. St Patrick's has the presence and proportions of a cathedral although only enjoying the status of a parish church; a parish church, nevertheless, which experts consider amongst the finest dozen churches in Britain for architectural beauty. Patrington's parish council go further: a notice displayed inside St Patrick's states unequivocally *"This is England's finest village Church"*. Clustering around it, picturesque Dutch style cottages complete an entrancing picture and just to the east of the village the Dutch theme continues in a fine old windmill.

SELBY & NORTH HUMBERSIDE

Selby is the most southerly of the eight districts that make up the vast, sprawling county of North Yorkshire. Here, the level plains of the Vale of York stretch for miles - rich, agricultural land watered by the four great Yorkshire rivers, Ouse, Wharfe, Derwent and Aire, and by the Selby Canal. It is ideal country for walking and cycling, or for exploring the waterways on which a wide variety of rivercraft is available for hire. Just a few miles away, on the other side of the River Aire, traffic on the M62 hurtles between Leeds and Hull, but here you can still find quiet villages, inviting hostelries, and one of the country's most flamboyant stately homes, Carlton Towers.

SELBY   MAP 4 REF I9

20 miles E of Leeds on the A63

In 1069 a young monk named Benedict, from Auxerre in France, had a vision. It's not known exactly what the vision was but it inspired him to set sail for York. As his ship was sailing up the Ouse near Selby, three swans flew in formation across its bows. (Three swans, incidentally, still form part of the town's coat of arms). Interpreting this as a sign of the Holy Trinity, Benedict promptly went ashore and set up a preaching cross under a great oak called the *Stirhac*. The small religious community he established went from strength to strength, acquiring many grants of land and, in 1100, permission to build a monastery. Over the course of the next 120 years, the great **Selby Abbey** slowly took shape, the massively heavy Norman style of the earlier building gradually modulating into the much more delicate Early English style. All of the Abbey was built using a lovely cream-coloured stone. Over the centuries this sublime church has suffered more than most. During the Civil War it was severely damaged by Cromwell's troops who destroyed many of its statues and smashed much of its stained glass. Then in 1690 the central tower

Selby Abbey

collapsed. For years after that the Abbey was neglected and by the middle of the 18th century a wall had been built across the chancel so that the nave could be used as a warehouse. That wall was removed during a major restoration during the 19th century but in 1906 there was another calamity when a disastrous fire swept through the Abbey. Visiting this serene and peaceful church today it's difficult to believe that it has endured so many misfortunes and yet remains so beautiful. Throughout all the Abbey's misfortunes one particular feature survived intact - the famous Washington Window which depicts the coat of arms of John de Washington, Prior of the Abbey around 1415 and a direct ancestor of George Washington. Prominently displayed in this heraldic device is the stars and stripes motif later adapted for the national flag of the United States.

Devotees of railway history will want to pay their respects to Selby's old railway station. Built at the incredibly early date of 1834 it is the oldest surviving station in Britain.

SOUTH MILFORD   Map 4 ref H9
9 miles W of Selby off the A162

About 9 miles west of Selby, near the village of South Milford, is the imposing 14th century **Steeton Hall Gatehouse**, all that remains of a medieval castle once owned by the Fairfax family. A forebear of the famous Cromwellian general is said to have ridden out from here on his way to carry off one of the nuns at Nun Appleton Priory to make her his bride. He was Sir William Fairfax; she was Isabel Thwaites, a wealthy heiress.

SHERBURN-IN-ELMET   Map 4 ref H9
9 miles W of Selby on the A162

This attractive village was once the capital of the Celtic Kingdom of Elmete. Well worth visiting is All Saints' Church which stands on a hill to the west and dates from about 1120. Its great glory is the nave with its mighty Norman pillars and arcades. A curiosity here is a 15th century Janus cross which was discovered in the churchyard during the 1770s. The vicar and churchwarden of the time both claimed it as their own. Unable to resolve their dispute, they had the cross sawn in half: the two beautifully carved segments are displayed on opposite sides of the south aisle.

RICCALL

MAP 4 REF I8

4 miles N of Selby on the A19

About 3 miles north of Osgodby you come to the ancient village of Riccall, mentioned in the Domesday Book and with a church that was built not long after. The south doorway of the church dates back to about 1160 and its fine details have been well-preserved by a porch added in the 15th century. The village's great moment in history came in 1066 when the gigantic King Harold Hardrada of Norway and Earl Tostig sailed this far up the Ouse with some three hundred ships. They had come to claim Northumbria from Tostig's half-brother King Harold of England but they were comprehensively defeated at the Battle of Stamford Bridge.

Riccall is popular with walkers: from the village you can either go southwards alongside the River Ouse to Selby, or strike northwards towards Bishopthorpe on the outskirts of York following the track of the dismantled York to Selby railway. This latter path is part of the 150 mile long Trans Pennine Trail linking Liverpool and Hull.

Just to the south of Skipwith, the Yorkshire Wildlife Trust maintains the **Skipwith Common Nature Reserve.** This 500 acres of lowland heath is one of the last such areas remaining in the north of England and is regarded as of national importance. The principal interest is the variety of insect and birdlife, but the reserve also contains a number of ancient burial sites.

HEMINGBROUGH

MAP 4 REF J9

5 miles SE of Selby off the A63

Anyone interested in remarkable churches should make the short trip from Selby to **St Mary's Church** at Hemingbrough. Built in a a pale rose-coloured brick, it has an extraordinarily lofty and elegant spire soaring 190ft high and, inside, what is believed to be Britain's oldest misericord. Misericords are hinged wooden seats for the choir which could be folded back when they stood to sing. Medieval woodcarvers delighted in adorning the underside of the seat with intricate carvings. The misericord at Hemingbrough dates back to around 1200AD.

Adjoining this historic church is **The Crown Inn**, a former coaching inn dating back to the early 1800s. It's a lively and popular place and mine hosts Marva and Stan Wilson have made it the hub of village life. The Crown is open all day, every day, except Mondays when it opens at 2pm. There's a wide selection of quality ales on offer, including John Smiths, Tetleys, Caffreys and Boddingtons, and wine

The Crown Inn, Main Street, Hemingbrough,
North Yorkshire YO8 6QE Tel: 01757 638434

is available by the glass or bottle. Marva oversees all the cooking, offering an extensive regular menu along with a choice of five or six daily specials. Food is served every lunchtime and evening, except Mondays of course (unless it's a Bank Holiday), and can be enjoyed either in the bar or in the stylish 40-seater dining room. Those with hearty appetites will really appreciate the "Big Meals" served on a large platter - copious quantities at remarkably reasonable prices. Upstairs, there's a function room with its own bar and seating for 60. This is where the local Folk Club meets on the first Sunday of each month - everyone is welcome!

WHITLEY BRIDGE

Map 4 ref I10

7 miles SW of Selby on the A19

Only minutes from junction 34 of the M62, **The Jolly Miller** provides a very convenient place to break your journey. It's an inviting-looking building with its white-washed walls, hanging baskets and picnic tables set on the side patio. Inside, there are real fires and lots of local memorabilia. Your host, Sandra Nelson, has been in the hospitality business in one capacity or another for some 30 years so she knows how to make her customers feel welcome. Sandra is also an expert cook, offering an extensive menu that ranges from traditional pub favourites such as home-made Steak & Guinness Pie, through fish dishes and cold platters, steaks and omelettes, to vegetarian dishes such as Haddock & Prawn Pasta Mornay. Snacks and toasties are also available and Sandra supplements the menu with daily specials as

The Jolly Miller, Kellington Lane, Whitley Bridge, North Yorkshire DN14 0LB Tel: 01977 661348

well. Food is served all day, 7 days a week, with a special two-course Carvery at Sunday lunchtime. Real Ale fans will find at least two brews available, including John Smiths and Tetleys.

About 4 miles north of Whitley Bridge, near the village of West Haddesley, is **Yorkshire Garden World.** Gardeners will find endless inspiration in these 6 acres of beautiful display and nursery gardens. Organically grown herbs, heathers, ornamental perennials, wild flowers and climbers are all on sale; the gift shop has a huge variety of home made crafts, herbal products, Leeds pottery and garden products; and the many different gardens include a Heather and Conifer Garden, an Aromatherapy Garden, an Open Air Herb Museum, a Lovers' Garden, and the Hall Owl Maze for children.

CAMBLESFORTH
MAP 4 REF 19
4 miles S of Selby on the A1041

A mile or so south of Camblesforth, off the A1041, is **Carlton Towers**, a stately home that should on no account be missed. This extraordinary building, "*something between the Houses of Parliament and St Pancras Station*", was created in the 1870s by two young English eccentrics, Henry, 9th Lord Beaumont, and Edward Welby Pugin, son of the eminent Victorian architect, A.G. Pugin. Together, they transformed a traditional Jacobean house into an exuberant mock medieval fantasy in stone, abounding with turrets, towers, gargoyles and heraldic shields. The richly-decorated High Victorian interior, designed in the manner of medieval banqueting halls, contains a minstrels' gallery and a vast Venetian-style drawing room. Both Beaumont and Pugin died in their forties, both bankrupt. Carlton Towers is now the Yorkshire home of the Duke of Norfolk and is open to the public during the summer months.

The only licensed premises in the country to bear the name, **The Comus Inn** is believed to have been named after the Greek god of hospitality, Comus, the son of Bacchus. The building is around 200 years old and very olde worlde inside, yet at the same time bright and airy - especially in the charming conservatory that overlooks the beer garden and children's play area. Your hosts, Mark Fayers and Sarah Topps, are both qualified chefs and they offer a comprehensive menu along with an ever-changing selection of

The Comus Inn, Selby Road, Camblesforth, nr Selby, North Yorkshire YO8 8HR
Tel: 01757 618234

daily specials. All meals are freshly cooked to order and the majority are home made. Food is available every lunchtime and evening, except for Monday evening, and it's a good idea to book ahead, especially at weekends. On Wednesday lunchtimes there's a Pensioners Special and Thursday evening, between 6pm and 9pm, is "Pie and Pud Night" when special prices apply. This is a lively, welcoming place with live entertainment on Friday evenings and a Quiz Night on Thursday when all are welcome to join in.

A couple of miles east of Camblesforth is the village of Drax which, as well as providing Ian Fleming with a sinister-sounding name for one of the villains in his James Bond thrillers, also provides the National Grid with 10 per cent of all the electricity used in England and Wales. The largest coal-fired power station in Europe, Drax's vast cooling towers dominate the low-lying ground between the rivers Ouse and Aire. Drax power station has found an unusual way of harnessing its waste heat by channelling some of it to a huge complex of glasshouses covering 20 acres; part of the heat goes to specially constructed ponds in which young eels are bred for the export market. Guided tours of the power station are available by prior arrangement.

GOOLE

Map 4 ref J10

12 miles SE of Selby on the A614

Britain's most inland port, some 50 miles from the sea, Goole lies at the hub of a water-ways network that includes the River Ouse, the River Don (known here as the Dutch River), the River Aire and the Aire & Calder Navigation. The **Waterways Museum**, lo-cated on the dockside, tells the story of Goole's development as a canal terminus and also port connecting to the North Sea, displays model ships and many photographs dating from 1905 to the present day, and visitors can explore an original Humber Keel, *Sobriety*, and watch crafts people at work. There are also occasional short boat trips available.

More of the town's history is in evidence at **Goole Museum & Art Gallery** which displays ship models, marine paintings and a changing programme of exhibitions. Other attractions in the town include its refurbished Victorian Market Hall, open all year Wednesday to Saturday, and a well-equipped Leisure Centre which provides a wide range of facilities for all ages.

1999 was a particularly good year for Janet and Peter Haley who run **The Woodlands Hotel** just ten minutes walk from the town centre. Their hostelry was voted "Local Pub of the Year" by the *Goole Courier* and Peter was shortlisted for the award "Most Responsible Licensee of the Year". The Woodlands certainly lives up to the awards, popular with young and old, locals and visitors alike. It's open all day, every day, with excellent food available

The Woodlands Hotel, Rutland Road, Goole DN14 6LX
Tel: 01405 762738

on Thursday, Friday and Saturday evenings, and at Sunday lunchtime when booking is advisable. The Sunday roast lunch offers a choice of either beef, pork, lamb or chicken, served in generous quantities. Children are welcome if eating. John Smiths is the pre-ferred beer here but there's also a good selection of other brews, along with a regularly changing guest ale. The Woodlands is a busy place, full of atmosphere, and if you are visiting on a Sunday evening you can take part in the regular Quiz Night which starts at 9pm. For motorway travellers the hotel is very conveniently located, just minutes from junction 36 of the M62.

HOWDEN

MAP 4 REF J9

11 miles E of Selby on the A63

Despite the fact that its chancel collapsed in 1696 and has not been used for worship ever since, **Howden Minster** is still one of the largest parish churches in East Yorkshire and also one of its most impressive, cathedral-like in size. From the top of its soaring tower, 135ft high, there are wonderful views of the surrounding countryside - but it's not for the faint-hearted! The ruined chapter house, lavishly decorated with a wealth of carved mouldings, has been described as one of the most exquisite small buildings in England.

When the medieval Prince-Bishops of Durham held sway over most of northern England, they built a palace at Howden which they used as a pied-à-terre during their semi-royal progresses and as a summer residence. The Hall of that 14th century palace still stands, although much altered now.

Howden town is a pleasing jumble of narrow, flagged and setted streets with a picturesque stone and brick Market Hall in the market place. The celebrated aircraft designer Barnes Wallis knew Howden well: he lived here while working on the R100 airship which was built at Hedon airfield nearby. It made its maiden flight in 1929 and successfully crossed the Atlantic.

Howden Minster

With its dark beams, low ceilings and olde-worlde atmosphere **Sweet Thoughts** is just the kind of traditional tea room you would hope to find in such an old town. It is tucked away in Vicar Lane, just a few yards off the main road in the centre of Howden. Sweet

Thoughts is owned and run by Cheryl Mell who is noted for her wonderful home made soups, sauces and delicious sweets. Her menu also includes a good choice of snacks, light meals and hearty main courses supplemented by daily specials, and on Wednesdays there's a value for money 1, 2 or 3-course menu for OAPs. The tea room is open Tuesday to Saturday, 9am to 4pm, and Sunday, 10am to 3pm. Sunday lunch, with a choice of four starters and four main courses, is available from 11.30am to 2pm and it's definitely a good idea to book ahead. Children are very welcome and the tea room is non-smoking.

Sweet Thoughts, 5b Vicar Lane, Howden, East Yorkshire DN14 7BP Tel: 01430 431615

Back in November 1992 **Howden Art and Craft Centre** was opened by Margaret Herbert in renovated garages which stood on the site of an old Congregational church. Since then, things have snowballed and the Centre is now one of the leading craft shops in the north of England. Stocking everything that the keen artist and needleworker could possibly need,

Howden Art & Craft Centre, 35-37 Bridgegate, Howden, East Yorkshire DN14 7JG Tel/Fax: 01430 430807

new products arrive at the Centre every day and other crafts now catered for include candle-making, decoupage, quilting, flower arranging and chair seating. Here too is the Pegasus Studio, a meeting place for local societies but also a place where exhibitions are held and, during the winter, a wide variety of workshops and classes are held by visiting tutors. If that were not enough, Margaret has also opened the charming Pastimes Tearoom - she was given a Civic Award for the outstanding renovation of the building in which it is housed. Here visitors can enjoy a cup of tea or coffee whilst tucking into a mouth-watering array of home made scones, cakes and light meals. Yet another attraction is a flower shop, "Dandelion", which sells silk flowers and arrangements, glass paintings and flower-orientated gifts. The facilities at the Centre for disabled visitors are excellent, there's a spacious car park, and coach parties are welcomed.

Built more than a hundred years ago to service travellers on the Selby to Hull railway, **The Station** was for many years owned by the railway company itself. Today it's a welcoming Free House where your hosts Marlene and Ann offer a good range of quality ales, including John Smiths, and bed & breakfast accommodation. At weekends the Station is open all day with light meals, snacks and sandwiches available; during the week the doors open at 5pm. Children are welcome in the lounge, a

The Station, 4 Bridgegate, Howden, East Yorkshire DN14 7AB Tel: 01430 431301 lovely room with panelled walls and decorated with many ornaments and memorabilia. For bed & breakfast guests the Station has two guest rooms, both on the second floor, and both pleasingly decorated and furnished. There's a separate breakfast room for overnight guests.

About 4 miles northwest of Howden are the striking remains of **Wressle Castle**, built in 1380 for Sir Henry Percy and the only surviving example in East Yorkshire of a medieval fortified house. At the end of the Civil War, three of the castle's sides were pulled down and much of the rest was destroyed by fire in 1796. But two massive towers with walls 6ft thick, the hall and kitchens remain. The castle is not open to the public but there are excellent views from the village road and from a footpath that runs alongside the River Derwent. A fine old windmill nearby provides an extra visual bonus.

GILBERDYKE   MAP 4 REF K9
5 miles E of Howden on the B1230

Between Selby and Hull the railway track runs straight as a ruler for 18 miles - the longest such stretch in Britain. Gilberdyke Station stands at almost exactly the halfway point along this line and just across the road from the station is **The Railway Hotel** which has been providing hospitality to travellers since 1869. The hotel is run by Ged and Wendy King, a friendly and welcoming couple who have been in the business for more than 20

The Railway Hotel, Station Road, Staddlethorpe, Gilberdyke, Brough,
East Yorkshire HU15 2ST Tel: 01430 440302

years. The food here is excellent, the menu offering a good range of main meals, (including vegetarian options), pizzas, snacks and sandwiches. Meals can be taken in either the small and cosy restaurant, the carvery, (both non-smoking), in the bar or, in good weather, in the lovely beer garden. The hotel is open all day, every day, except Mondays when it opens at 4pm (unless it's a Bank Holiday). If you're here on a Thursday feel free to take part in the Quiz Night, and on Saturdays you'll find live entertainment from 9pm. Accommodation is also available at the Railway Hotel with 3 guest rooms (1 family, 2 twin) to let and there are special rates for longer stays.

HOLME-ON-SPALDING-MOOR   MAP 4 REF K8
8 miles NE of Howden on the A614/A163

This straggling little town lies at the foot of a hill crowned by a splendid medieval church whose 15th century tower has served as a reliable landmark for centuries of travellers. Its eight pinnacles rise from battlements curiously carved with leafy arches and finials.

The Station Inn was built back in the mid-1800s, first to service the navvies constructing the York to Market Weighton railway line and later to provide refreshment and accommodation for passengers travelling the route. The railway has long since gone but a 9-mile stretch of the track bed between Market Weighton and Bubwith now serves walkers as the 'Bubwith Rail Trail'. Inside the Station Inn there are some interesting memorabilia about the old railway and also the days of World War II when the pub was a popular watering-hole with RAF personnel. Their emblem features on the bar. Today, the inn is owned and run by Graham and Jacqui Hicks who came here in late 1999 after living for many years in Guernsey. Graham is a chef by profession and his quality food is available every lunchtime, (noon until 2.30pm), and evening, (5pm to 7.30pm). Real ales are served, amongst them Tetleys and a changing guest ale.

The Station Inn, Station Lane, Holme-on-Spalding-Moor, York YO43 4AL
Tel: 01430 860335

Situated in the heart of this busy little town **The Hare and Hounds Inn** is a friendly, family run hostelry offering excellent cuisine and comfortable accommodation. A Free House, the inn is owned and run by Norma and John Smith and their daughter Emma who is responsible for the outstanding food. John and Emma were both born at Holme,

Norma has lived here for over 25 years, so between them they have a wealth of local knowledge. The bar has a choice of Real Ales, including John Smiths, Tetleys and a guest ale Emma's comprehensive menu offers a wide choice of

The Hare & Hounds Inn, 57 High Street, Holme on Spalding Moor, York YO43 4EN Tel: 01430 860445

dishes, all freshly cooked to order, and is supplemented by daily specials. Vegetarians can also be catered for. Meals are available every weekday from noon until 2pm, and from 5.30pm until 8pm, while at weekends the kitchen is open continuously from noon until 7pm. Overnight guests stay in 4 chalet-style rooms at the rear of the inn where there's also a children's play area. All the rooms are twin bedded and en suite with breakfast served in the inn itself. Located just a few miles north of the M62, Holme provides a convenient base for exploring the Wolds with the Wolds Way within easy reach.

NORTH NEWBALD

MAP 4 REF K8

8 miles W of Beverley on the A1034

Only a short drive from junction 38 of the M62, **The Gnu Inn** is a delightful find - a traditional country pub with a friendly welcoming atmosphere, offering a whole range of home cooked meals and real ales. Dating back to the early 1800s, the building was originally a farmhouse before becoming a pub in the 1890s. It was known then as the New Inn but during the mid-1900s was bought by a large brewery which named all its pubs after animals. The Gnu Inn, incidentally, is the only pub with this name in the country. Your hosts, Mary and Gordon, have been here since 1996 and have established a solid reputation for quality food and cask ales. Mary is the cook and her regular menu is supplemented each day by at least 12 daily specials.

The Gnu Inn, The Green, North Newbald, York YO43 4SA Tel: 01430 827799

Vegetarian meals are always available. During the season, food is served every lunchtime and evening; out of season, the inn is closed at lunchtime Monday to Thursday. The Gnu Inn also boasts 3 quality letting rooms, available all year round. There's a ground floor family room, a double and a twin, all of them en suite.

SOUTH CAVE

Map 4 ref K9

14 miles W of Hull off the A63

The village of South Cave is, officially, a town with its very own Town Hall in the market place. The name is said to be a corruption of South Cove since the southern part of the parish is set around a backwater of the Humber. The village is separated into two distinct areas by the grounds of the Cave Castle Golf Hotel. This building dates back to Elizabethan times and was once the home of George Washington's great grandfather.

Situated on the outskirts of the village, **Fairways Farm** is a beautiful modern bungalow overlooking the Cave Castle Golf Course and set in 30 acres of grazing parkland for

Fairways Farm, Northfield Close, South Cave, East Yorkshire HU15 2EW Tel: 01430 421285

horses, sheep and cattle. Fairways is the home of Julia and Malcolm Jewitt who offer quality bed and breakfast accommodation in 4 attractively decorated ground floor rooms, (2 family, 2 double), all of them en suite with colour TV and tea/coffee-making facilities. Two of the rooms look out onto the golf course; the other two have peaceful views of pasture land. Children are welcome at Fairways with travel cots and high chairs available if required. An excellent breakfast, served until 9.30am, is included and evening meals can be provided by arrangement. To the front of the house is an inviting patio area where visitors can relax on fairweather days. South Cave itself offers many amenities - there's a sports hall, tennis court, bowling green, play park and the golf course, while the local shops include antiques shop, a tea room, supermarket, bank and hairdressers.

The nearby village of Brantingham, just off the A63, is worth a short diversion to see its remarkable war memorial, once described as *"lovingly awful"*. Conceived on a monumental scale, the memorial was built using masonry recycled from Hull's old Guildhall when that was being reconstructed in 1914. Various stone urns placed around the village came from the same source.

A little further south is the pretty village of **Welton** where a stream flows past the green, under bridges and into a tree-encircled duck pond. It has a church dating from Norman times which boasts a striking 13th century doorway and Pre-Raphaelite windows made by William Morris' company of craftsmen. In the graveyard stands a memorial to Jeremiah Found, a resilient local reputed to have outlived eight wives.

The notorious highwayman Dick Turpin was not a local but his villainous, if romantic, career came to an end at Welton village when he was apprehended inside the Green Dragon inn. Local legend has it that this establishment gave him hospitality before he was taken off to the magistrates at Beverley who committed him to the Assizes at York where he was found guilty and hanged inn 1739.

HULL

During World War II Hull was mercilessly battered by the Luftwaffe: 7,000 of its people were killed and 92% of its houses suffered bomb damage. Hull has risen phoenix-like from those ashes and is today the fastest-growing port in England. The port area extends for 7 miles along the Humber with 10 miles of quays servicing a constant flow of commercial traffic arriving from, or departing for, every quarter of the globe. Every day, a succession of vehicle ferries link the city to the European gateways of Zeebrugge and Rotterdam. Hull is unmistakably part of Yorkshire but it also has the freewheeling, open-minded character of a cosmopolitan port.

Hull's history as an important port goes back to 1293 when Edward I, travelling north on his way to hammer the Scots, stopped off here and immediately recognized the potential of the muddy junction where the River Hull flows into the Humber. The king bought the land from the monks of Meaux Abbey (at the usual royal discount) and the settlement thenceforth was known as "Kinges town upon Hull".

The port grew steadily through the centuries and at one time had the largest fishing fleet of any port in the country with more than 300 trawlers on its register. The port's rather primitive facilities were greatly improved by the construction of a state-of-the-art dock in 1778. Now superseded, that dock has been converted into the handsome Queen's Gardens, one of the many attractive open spaces created by this flower-conscious city which also loves lining its streets with trees, setting up fountains here and there, and planting flower beds in any available space. And waymarked walks such as the Maritime Heritage Trail and the Fish Pavement Trail make the most of the city's dramatic waterfront.

A visit to Hull is an exhilarating experience at any time of the year but especially so in October. Back in the late 1200s the city was granted a charter to hold an autumn fair. This began as a fairly modest cattle and sheep mart but over the centuries it burgeoned into the largest gathering of its kind in Europe. Hull Fair is now a 9-day extravaganza occupying a 14-acre site and offering every imaginable variety of entertainment.

That takes care of October, but Hull also hosts an Easter Festival, an International Festival (some 300 events from mid-June to late July), a Jazz on the Waterfront celebration (August), an International Sea Shanty Festival (September) and a Literature Festival in November.

Throughout the rest of the year, Hull's tourism office modestly suggests you explore its "Magnificent Seven" - a quite remarkable collection of historic houses, art galleries and museums. Perhaps the most evocative is the **Wilberforce House Museum** in the old High Street. William Wilberforce was born here in 1759 and, later, it was from here that he and his father lavished thousands of pounds in bribes to get William elected as Hull's Member of Parliament. Nothing unusual about that kind of corruption at the time, but William then redeemed himself by his resolute opposition to slavery. His campaign took more than 30 years and William was already on his deathbed before a reluctant Parliament finally outlawed the despicable trade. The museum presents a shaming history of the slave trade along with a more uplifting story of Wilberforce's efforts to eliminate it for ever.

Other stars of the "Magnificent Seven" are **The Ferens Art Gallery** which houses a sumptuous collection of paintings and sculpture that ranges from European Old Masters (including some Canalettos and works by Franz Hals) to challenging contemporary art; the **Town Docks Museum** which celebrates seven centuries of Hull's maritime heritage and includes a fine collection of scrimshaw. A more unusual museum is the **Spurn Lightship.** Once stationed on active duty 4.5 miles east of Spurn Point, the 200-ton, 33 metre long craft is now moored in Hull's vibrant Marina. Visitors can explore the 75-year-old vessel with the help of its knowledgeable crew. The city's noisiest museum is the **Streetlife Transport Museum** which traces 200 years of transport history. Visitors are transported back to the days of horse-drawn carriages, steam trains, trams and penny-farthing cycles. There are curiosities such as the "Velocipede", the Automobile à Vapeur (an early steam-driven car), and Lady Chesterfield's ornamental sleigh, caparisoned with a swan, rearing unicorn and a panoply of bells to herald her approach.

You will encounter a marvel of a different kind if you come by road to Hull from the south and drive over one of the most impressive bridges on earth - and also one of the least used. It's been described as the least likely place in Britain to find a traffic jam. Opened in 1981, the **Humber Bridge** is one of the world's longest single-span bridges with an overall length of 2,428 yds (2,220m). That means that for more than a third of a mile only four concrete pillars, two at each end, are saving you from a watery death. From these huge pylons, 510ft (155m) high, gossamer cables of thin-wired steel support a gently curving roadway. Both sets of pylons rise vertically, but because of the curvature of the earth they actually lean away from each other by several inches. The bridge is particularly striking at night when the vast structure is floodlit.

Before leaving the city, one should mention two of its more unusual features. Firstly, visitors to Hull soon become aware of its unique public telephones. They are still the

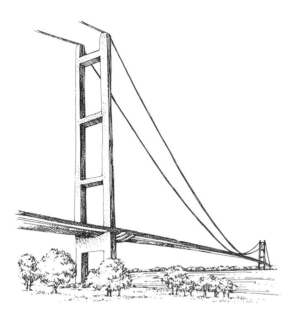

Humber Bridge

traditional, curvy-topped, heavily-barred boxes but with the distinctive difference that Hull's are all painted a gleaming white. What isn't apparent is that by some bureaucratic quirk, Hull remained the only municipally owned telephone company in Britain until it was floated on the Stock Exchange early in 2000. The sale brought the City Council a huge windfall. The second unusual feature of Hull: in Nelson Street you can avail yourself of award-winning loos. These spotless conveniences, complete with hanging baskets of flowers, have become a tourist attraction in their own right.

HESSLE   Map 5 ref L9
5 miles W of Hull off the A63

At Hessle the River Humber narrows and it was here that the Romans maintained a ferry, the *Transitus Maximus*, a vital link in the route between Lincoln and York. The ferry remained in operation for almost 2000 years until it was replaced in 1981 by the Humber Bridge whose mighty pylons soar more than 800ft above the village. The great bridge dwarfs Cliff Mill, built in 1810 to mill the local chalk. It remained wind-driven until 1925 when a gas engine was installed. Although it is no longer working the mill provides a scenic feature within the **Humber Bridge Country Park**. This well laid out park gives visitors a true back-to-nature tour a short distance from one of modern man's greatest feats of engineering. The former chalk quarry has been attractively landscaped, providing a nature trail, extensive walks through woodlands and meadows, picnic and play areas, and picturesque water features.

4 The Northern Dales

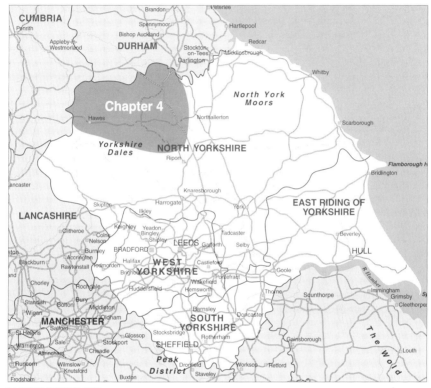

SWALEDALE

For many, Swaledale is the loveliest of the Yorkshire Dales. From historic Richmond town it runs westwards through countryside that ranges from the dramatic lower dale with its steep-sided wooded hills to austere upper reaches, - a terrain where your nearest neighbour could be several miles away. Its rugged beauty makes quite a contrast to the pretty and busier Wensleydale just to the south. There are several other noticeable differences: the villages in Swaledale all have harsher, Nordic sounding names, the dale is much less populated, and the rivers and becks are more fast flowing mountain streams.

At one time Swaledale was a hive of activity and enjoyed a prosperous century and more when the lead mining industry flourished here. The valley of the River Swale still bears many of the scars left behind since the mining declined and the dale once again became a remote and underpopulated place. The attractive market town of Richmond, first settled by the Romans, has for many years been the major focal point of this northerly region of Yorkshire. With several interesting museums, a fine Norman castle, and excellent shopping facilities, Richmond is still the key town in the northern dales.

Swaledale sheep will be a familiar sight to anyone who spends more than a few minutes in the Dales. Recognised by their black faces, white muzzle, and grey speckled legs, the Swaledale sheep were introduced to the area in the 1920s. Each flock knows its own territory - they are said to be *'heafed'* to the moor. The sheep have to cope with extremely wild weather and their hardiness is typified by the warmth and durability of their wool. No surprise to find that the ram has been adopted as the emblem of the Yorkshire Dales National Park.

There are several side dales to Swaledale: the small, thriving market town of Reeth lies at the junction of Arkengarthdale and the valley of the River Swale. First settled by Norsemen who preferred wild and remote countryside, the valley of Arkle Beck was not considered important enough to gain an entry in the Domesday Book. There is much evidence of the old lead-mining days and the dale is now chiefly populated by hardy Swaledale sheep. At the head of this rather bleak and barren dale lies England's highest inn, Tan Hill. Finally, though only a short section of the River Tees flows through Yorkshire, the section of Teesdale around Piercebridge is particularly charming and well worth a visit.

REETH   Map 1 ref E4
11 miles W of Richmond on the B6270

Considered the capital of Upper Swaledale, this small town is poised at the junction of the River Swale and its main tributary, Arkle Beck. The local lead mining industry, which was begun by the Romans, served the town well for many years, until competition from abroad gradually caused its decline and Reeth became chiefly an agricultural centre. Noted in the Domesday Book, whilst everything else in the area was written off as untaxable wasteland, Reeth prospered and it is still today a much visited place.

Until the end of the 19th century a total of four fairs were held here annually, as well as a weekly market. Today, the annual agricultural show in September, held on the sprawling village green, is still a magnet for farmers from the entire length of the dale and beyond. Along the top of the green is **High Row**, with its inns and shops and outstanding Georgian architecture, reflecting the affluence of the town in the 17th century when the trade in wool and lead was booming.

The **Swaledale Folk Museum**, housed in what was once the old Methodist Sunday School, is the home for exhibits of local farming methods, crafts, and mining skills, as well as displays on local pastimes, the impact of Wesleyan Methodism, and the exodus of the population to the industrial areas of the south Pennines when the lead mines closed.

This little town is noted for its variety of craft shops. There's a cluster of them at the **Reeth Craft Workshops** near the green. Here you'll find a cabinet maker, a guitar maker, a pottery shop, a clock maker and restorer, 'Shades of Heather' which has everything for rag rug making and 'Stefs Models' where visitors can see the production of beautifully crafted animal models.

Just to the south of Reeth lies the quiet village of **Grinton** whose parish **Church of St Andrew** served the whole of the dale for centuries. The building dates back to the 13th and 15th centuries, though there are still some Norman remains as well as a Leper's Squint (a small hole through which those afflicted by the disease could follow the service within).

For those people living in the upper reaches of Swaledale who died, there was a long journey down the track to Grinton which became known as the **Corpse Way**.

Running northwestwards from Reeth, **Arkengarthdale** is a small and remote valley. It was first settled by Norsemen and their presence is still reflected in the dale's place names - Booze, Eskeleth, and Wham. Overlooked completely during the Domesday survey, when it was considered of no value, lead mining brought about a period of prosperity in the 18th and 19th centuries.

LANGTHWAITE MAP 1 REF E4
3 miles NW of Reeth off the B6270

Langthwaite, the main village of Arkengarthdale, will seem familiar to many who have

Langthwaite Village

never been here before as its bridge featured in the title sequence of the popular television series *All Creatures Great and Small*. Just outside this beautiful place lies the cryptically named CB Hotel - named after Charles Bathurst, an 18th century lord of the manor who was responsible for the development of the lead mining industry in the dale. His grandfather, Dr John Bathurst, physician to Oliver Cromwell, had purchased the land here in 1659 with the exploitation of its mineral wealth in mind.

TAN HILL MAP 1 REF D3
10 miles NW of Reeth off the B6270

Standing at the head of Arkengarthdale on the border with County Durham, 1732 feet above sea level, is England's highest pub, the **Tan Hill Inn**. Why on earth should there be a pub here, in one of the most remote and barren stretches of the north Pennines, frequently cut off and in total isolation during the winter? A century ago, the inn's patrons didn't need to ask. Most of them were workers from the Tan Hill coal mines; others were drivers waiting for their horse-drawn carts to be filled with coal. The coal mines have long since closed but an open coal fire still burns in the inn 365 days a year and some 50,000 visitors a year still find their way to Tan Hill. Many of them are walkers who stagger in from one of the most gruelling stretches of the Pennine Way Walk and, clutching a pint of Theakston's *'Old Peculier'*, collapse on the nearest settle.

During the long winters when at times the moorland roads have disappeared under 12ft deep snowdrifts and, despite cellar walls 3ft thick, the pub's beer-pumps have frozen, trade tends to fall off a bit. It revives spectacularly on the last Thursday in May. This is when the **Tan Hill Sheep Fair** takes place and, if only for a day, Tan Hill Inn becomes the centre of agricultural Yorkshire. "It's the Royal Show for Swaledale Sheep is Tan Hill" said one proud farmer scrutinizing his flock, "and I've got some princes and princesses here". In cash terms the value of the prizes awarded at the Fair is negligible - just a few pounds for even a first class rosette. But at the auction that follows it's a different story. In 1990 one particularly prized Tupp Hogg (a young ram) was sold for £30,000.

HEALAUGH
MAP 1 REF E4

2 miles W of Reeth on the B6270

In the 12th century an Augustinian Priory was founded here but none of the remaining fragments date from earlier than the 15th century. However, the village **Church of St Helen and St John**, which dates from around 1150, not only has outstanding views over the dale to the Pennines but also has a bullet hole which, it is alleged, was made by a Cromwellian trooper on his way to Marsden Moor.

LOW ROW
MAP 1 REF D4

4 miles W of Reeth on the B6270

In medieval times the track along the hillside above Low Row formed part of the **Corpse Way** along which relays of bearers would carry the deceased in a large wicker basket on journeys that could take two days to complete. Along their route, you can still see the large stone slabs where they rested their burden. Even more convenient was the 'Dead Barn' above Low Row where the carriers could deposit the body and scramble downhill for a convivial evening at the **Punch Bowl Inn.** This ancient inn is still one of the dale's most popular hostelries. A superb location, quality food and drink, and a welcoming atmosphere all contribute to the appeal and mine hosts, Sheila and Doug, make sure their customers are well looked after. Food is available from noon until 2pm and again from 6.30pm until 9pm and meals can be taken in any one of the three dining areas which in total can seat 80 people comfortably.

Punch Bowl Inn, Low Row, Richmond,
North Yorkshire DL11 6PF Tel: 01748 886233

Children are welcome and there are non-smoking areas. If you are planning to stay in this lovely dale, the Punch Bowl has 16 guest rooms, five of them en suite. And if you are travelling on a budget, there's also a comfortable Bunkhouse which can accommodate up to 12 people.

Located on the edge of the village, **Hazel Brow Farm** provides a popular family day out. Set in glorious Swaledale scenery the 200-acre traditional family run farm offers children the opportunity of bottle feeding lambs, riding a pony or helping to feed the calves, sheep and pigs. The farm also has a tea room, children's play area and gift shop.

Just west of Low Row, a road to the left attracts many visitors with its signpost pointing to 'Crackpot'. Don't bother: all you will find is a perfectly sensible-looking cluster of working farmhouses. Crackpot simply means a place where crows (*crack*) congregate around a deep hole in the hills (a *pot*).

GUNNERSIDE   MAP 1 REF D4

5 miles W of Reeth on the B6270

This charming Dales village in the heart of Swaledale was, until the late 19th century, a thriving lead mining village. Gunnerside became known as the Klondyke of Swaledale and, although the boom centred around lead rather than gold, the Old Gang Mines are the most famous in Yorkshire. The paths and trackways here are mainly those trodden by the many successions of miners travelling to their work and the valley's sides still show the signs of the mine workings. In the village, one can visit tearooms that offer such delights as *'Lead Miners' Bait'* and the delicious *'Gunnerside cheese cake'* made from a recipe handed down from mining days.

After the closure of the mines, many families left the village to find work elsewhere in northern England whilst others emigrated to America and even as far afield as Australia. For many years afterwards one of the village's most important days was Midsummer Sunday when those who had left would, if able, return and catch up with their families and friends.

MUKER   MAP 1 REF D4

8 miles W of Reeth on the B6270

An old stone bridge leads into this engaging village which consists of a collection of beige-coloured stone cottages overlooked by the **Church of St Mary** which dates back to the time of Elizabeth I - one of the very few to be built in England during her reign. Most church builders until that time had spared no expense in glorifying the house of God. At Muker they were more economical: the church roof was covered in thatch, its floor in rushes. No seating was provided. Despite such penny-pinching measures, the new church of 1580 was warmly welcomed since it brought to an end the tedious journey for bereaved relatives along the Corpse Way to the dale's mother church at Grinton, some 8 miles further to the east.

The good people of Muker devised means of making further savings. For many years, the thrifty mourners of the parish shared a communal coffin. Year after year the same coffin would bear the departed to the churchyard where the shrouded body was removed, placed in the grave and the coffin retrieved for use at the next funeral. It wasn't until 1735 that the vicar decreed that everyone buried in his parish deserved the dignity of a personal coffin.

On the gravestones in the churchyard local family names, such as Harker, Alderson, and Fawcett feature prominently as they do among the villagers still living here. Swaledale cuisine is equally durable: specialities on offer in the local tearooms include Swaledale Curd Tart, Yorkshire Rarebit, and Deep Apple Pie with Wensleydale cheese. And the main crafts still revolve around the wool provided by the hardy Swaledale sheep, in great demand by carpet manufacturers and for those impermeable jumpers worn by fell walkers, climbers, and anyone else trying to defeat the British weather.

Housed in one of Muker's many picturesque stone cottages, **Swaledale Woollens** has revitalised the local cottage industry of hand-knitting woollen items using wool from the famous Swaledale sheep. With their black faces, grey noses and curled horns, Swaledale sheep look remarkably intelligent and they were certainly sensible enough to grow separate coats of wool dense enough to cope with the dale's sometimes savage winters. An outer covering of rugged wool shrugs off rain and snow, beneath that an even tougher coat preserves the sheep's body heat. For generations, the lead miners of Swaledale and their families supplemented their meagre incomes by producing knitted and

Swaledale Woollens, Muker, Richmond,
North Yorkshire D11 6QG Tel/Fax: 01748 886251
website: www.yorkshirenet.co.uk/swaledalewoollens

crocheted items such as sweaters, cardigans and socks from this hardy wool but this practice was steadily dying out until Swaledale Woollens was established in 1974.

Today, Swaledale Woollens' cottage shop provides a thriving centre for the collection, display and sale of hand and machine-knitted woollen garments, with many of the items carrying a label bearing the name of its creator. The shop also stocks a range of various natural yarns on cone or in packs for those who do their own hand or machine knitting, and there's an interesting exhibition on the history of Swaledale sheep. A mail order catalogue is available on request.

THWAITE
MAP 1 REF D4
9 miles W of Reeth on the B6270

Surrounded by dramatic countryside which includes Kisdon Hill, Great Shunnor, High Seat, and Lovely Seat, this is a tiny village of ancient origins. Like so many places in the area the name comes from the Nordic language, in this case *thveit*, meaning a clearing in the wood. The woodlands which once provided shelter and fuel for the Viking settlers have long since gone.

To the southwest of the village lies **Buttertubs Pass**, one of the highest and most forbidding mountain passes in the country. The Buttertubs themselves are a curious natural feature of closely packed vertical stone stacks rising from some unseen, underground base to the level of the road. A local Victorian guide to the Buttertubs, perhaps aware that the view from above was not all that impressive, solemnly assured his client that "some of the Buttertubs had no bottom, and some were deeper than that". No one is quite sure where the Buttertubs name comes from. The most plausible explanation is that farmers used its deep-chilled shelves as a convenient refrigerator for the butter they couldn't sell immediately.

Unusually, these potholes are not linked by a series of passages as most are, but they are free-standing and bear only a slight resemblance to the objects after which they are named - a place where farmers placed their butter to keep it cool. The narrow road from Thwaite across the Buttertubs Pass is not for the faint-hearted driver. Only a flimsy post and wire fence separates the road from a sheer drop of Alpine proportions. In any case, it's much more satisfying to cross the pass from the other direction, from Hawes: from the south, as you crest the summit you will be rewarded with a stupendous view of Swaledale that stretches for miles.

KELD
Map 1 ref D4

9 miles W of Reeth on the B6270

The little cluster of stone buildings that make up the village stand beside the early stages of the River Swale. The place is alive with the sound of rushing water and it comes as no surprise that the word *keld* is Nordic for spring. For lovers of green woodlands and breath-taking waterfalls, this village is definitely well worth a visit and it has also managed to retain an impression of being untouched by modern life.

Wain Wath Force, with rugged Cotterby Scar providing a fine backdrop, can be found alongside the Birkdale road. **Catrake Force**, with its stepped formation, can be reached from the cottages on the left at the bottom of the street in the village. Though on private land the falls and, beside them, the entrance to an old lead mine can still be seen. For less adventurous pedestrians **Kisdon Force**, the most impressive waterfall in Swaledale, can be reached by a gentle stroll of less than a mile from the village along a well-trodden path. For really serious walkers, Keld is the most important crossroads in northern England. Here the south-to-north **Pennine Way** and the east-to-west **Coast to Coast** long distance walks intersect.

RICHMOND
Map 2 ref F4

4 miles SW of Scotch Corner on the A6108

The former county of Richmondshire (which still survives as a parliamentary constituency), once occupied a third of the North Riding of Yorkshire. Alan Rufus, the 1st Earl of Richmond, built the original **Richmond Castle** in 1071 and the site, 100ft up on a rocky promontory with the River Swale passing below, is imposing and well chosen. The keep rises to 109ft with walls 11ft thick, while the other side is afforded an impregnable defence by means of the cliff and the river. Richmond Castle was the first Norman castle in the country to be built, right from the foundations, in stone. Additions were made over subsequent years but it reached its final form in the 14th century. Since then it has fallen into ruin though a considerable amount of the original Norman stonework remains intact. With such an inspiring setting, it is hardly surprising that there is a legend suggesting that King Arthur himself is buried here, reputedly in a cave beneath the castle. The story goes that a simple potter called Thompson stumbled across an underground passage which led to a chamber where he discovered the king and his knights lying in an enchanted sleep, surrounded by priceless treasures. A voice warned him not to disturb the sleepers and he fled, predictably, unable to locate the passage again. Another legend associated with the castle tells how a drummer boy was sent down the passageway. Beating his drum as he walked, the boy's progress was followed by the soldiers on the surface until, suddenly, the drumming stopped. Though the passageway was searched the boy was never seen again but, it is said, his drumming can still be heard.

In 1315, Edward II granted Richmond the right to protect the town by a stone wall after Scottish raiders had caused considerable damage in the surrounding area. By the 16th century, the walls were in a state of disrepair and little survives today. Two road bridges cross the River Swale in the town. The elder of the two, Green Bridge, was erected in 1789 to the designs of John Carr after the existing bridge had been swept away by flood water. Its picturesque setting is enhanced by the massive cliff crowned by Richmond Castle that towers above it.

During the Middle Ages, the markets of Richmond gave the town much of its prosperity and

Richmond Castle

its influence spread across Yorkshire to Lancashire. Also, like many North Yorkshire towns and villages, the textile industry played an important role in the continuation of the town's wealth and, for some time, Richmond became famous for its knitted stockings.

The **Green Howards Museum**, the regimental museum of the North Riding's infantry, is based in the old Trinity Church in the centre of the cobbled market square. The regiment dates back to 1688, when it was founded, and the displays and collections illustrate its history with war relics, weapons, uniforms, medals, and regimental silver. Also housed in the museum is the town's silver. The church itself was founded in 1135 and, though it has been altered and rebuilt on more than one occasion, the original Norman tower and some other masonry has survived.

One of the grandest buildings in the town is the **Culloden Tower**, just off the town green. It was erected in 1747 by the Yorke family, one of whose members had fought at the Battle of Culloden the previous year. Unlike most follies, the interior of the 3-storey tower is elaborately decorated in the rococo style and since it is now in the care of the Landmark Trust it is possible to stay there. It is not surprising that a town steeped in history should have several museums and the **Richmondshire Museum** traces the history of this old place and its county. There is also a reconstruction of James Herriot's veterinary surgery taken from the popular television series as well as other period costumes and displays.

Richmond is also home to England's oldest theatre, the **Georgian Theatre Royal**, which originally formed part of a circuit that included Northallerton, Ripon, and Harrogate. Built in 1788 by the actor and manager Samuel Butler, it had at that time an audience capacity of 400. The connection with the theatrical Butler family ended in 1830 and from then until 1848 it was used, infrequently, by travelling companies. After the mid 19th century right up until the 1960s, the theatre saw a variety of uses, as a wine cellar and a corn chandler's amongst others, and it did not re-open as a theatre until 1963 and only then after much restoration work had been carried out. The **Georgian Theatre Royal Museum** was also opened and it contains a unique collection of original playbills as well as the oldest and largest complete set of painted scenery in Britain.

Top of the range in every respect, **West End** is a wonderful stonebuilt guest house offering bed and breakfast accommodation, with adjacent garden cottages providing self-catering accommodation. Set in three-quarters of an acre of lovely gardens, this peaceful retreat serves as a marvellous base from which to explore the delights of this part of the county. There are five guest bedrooms: three doubles, one twin - all en suite - and one single with private facilities. The home-cooked breakfast uses fresh local produce whenever possible. A friendly, homely atmosphere pervades this comfortable and beautifully appointed home. There are four self-catering

**West End, 45 Reeth Road, Richmond,
North Yorkshire DL10 4EX Tel: 01748 824783**

units in all, available for weekly lets or shorter breaks. All are furnished and decorated to a high standard of comfort and quality, and all offer every modern amenity. Each has two bedrooms, an attractive lounge/dining area with fully fitted kitchen and its own paved patio area with garden furniture. There's also a handy on-site laundrette, and off-street parking.

Just outside the town lies **Easby Abbey**, a delightful monastic ruin which looks down to the River Swale. Founded in 1155 by Roald, Constable of Richmond Castle, its order of monks were of more modest leanings than the Cistercians, and the building certainly possesses none of the

Easby Abbey, nr Richmond

grandiose lines of Rievaulx and Fountains, although the riverside setting is a common feature. The abbey's most notable feature is its replica of the Easby Cross, an Anglo-Saxon cross dating from the 9th century and the extensive ruins can be reached by a pleasant riverside walk that is well sign-posted.

HUDSWELL
MAP 2 REF F4
2 miles SW of Richmond off the A6108

This ancient village, which was well established by the time it was recorded in the Domesday Book, stands high above the River Swale and over the years the village has gravitated to a more sheltered spot. The present St Michael's Church was built in the late 19th century on the site of an older building and the view from the churchyard is considered to be one of the finest in Richmondshire.

The walk from the village down to the river leads through pleasant woodland and also takes in some 365 steps. About half way down, below a path leading off to an old lime kiln, can be found **King Arthur's Oven**, a horizontal crack in the limestone which, it is claimed, has connections with Richmond Castle and the legend of King Arthur.

Character and atmosphere comes in abundance at the **George and Dragon Inn**, a sturdy stone building dating back some 300 years. Lots of gleaming copper, wood panelling and a cosy snug all contribute to the charm. Your hosts at this popular Free House are Jackie and Clive Town who took over here in early 1999 and quickly established a reputation for hospitality, fine ale and good food. All the food is home cooked and the menu offers a varied choice ranging from a freshly-prepared sandwich to Whitby scampi, from hearty steaks to a vegetable Tikka Masala. Food is available every lunchtime and evening except Monday lunchtime, (unless it's a Bank Holiday), and Monday evenings

George & Dragon Inn, Hudswell, Richmond, North Yorkshire DL11 6BL Tel: 01748 823082

during the winter. Enjoy your meal anywhere throughout the pub or, in good weather, on the rear patio overlooking Swaledale and National Trust woodland where there are some delightful woodland trails. Every third Sunday, the George & Dragon hosts a fun quiz and about once a month there's live entertainment, usually on a Friday evening.

CATTERICK VILLAGE
MAP 2 REF F4
5 miles SE of Richmond off the A1

Ever since the time of the Romans, when the settlement was known as Cataractonium, Catterick has been associated with the armed forces. Located on the Roman highway between London and Hadrian's Wall, the garrison was also close to the place where Paulinus, Bishop of York baptised 10,000 Christians in the River Swale. Today, the large army camp is some way from the village but there are many reminders of its military connections. The connections with Nelson are not immediately obvious but it was Alexander Scott, vicar of Catterick in 1816, who was at Nelson's side when he died at Trafalgar. Also, the Admiral's sister-in-law, Lady Tyrconnel, lived at nearby **Kiplin Hall**, a beautiful Jacobean country home famed for its wonderful interior plasterwork and medieval fishponds. The hall also contains many mementoes of Nelson and Lady Hamilton and, on display in the Blue Room, is a folding library chair from the Admiral's cabin on *HMS Victory*.

MOULTON   MAP 2 REF F4
5 miles NE of Richmond off the A1

This small village is home to two fine 17th century manor houses that were built by members of the Smithson family. The Manor House, in the village centre, was originally built in the late 16th century and was improved greatly in the mid 17th century. Just to the south lies **Moulton Hall**, built by George Smithson following his marriage to Eleanor Fairfax in 1654. Similar in size to the original Smithson family home and somewhat resembling it, Moulton Hall is now in the hands of the National Trust.

MIDDLETON TYAS   MAP 2 REF F3
5 miles NE of Richmond off the A1

Situated in a sheltered position yet close to the Great North Road, the position of the village church, away from the village centre and at the end of a long avenue of trees seems strange. However, when the Church of St Michael was built it served not only Middleton Tyas but also Moulton and Kneeton, (the latter no longer in existence), between which Middleton lay. During the 18th century, the village saw a period of prosperity when copper was found and mined from the fields near the church. Several grand houses were built including **East Hall**, which belonged to Leonard Hartley, who founded the industry, though his son, George, had a grander house on the outskirts of Middleton that was designed by John Carr of York.

RAVENSWORTH   MAP 2 REF F3
6 miles NW of Richmond on minor road off the A66

Lying in the small and forgotten dale of Holmedale, the Methodist chapel here, built in 1822, is the oldest chapel on the Richmond circuit. To the south-east of the village are the remains of the Fitzhughs' Norman castle which is believed to have been in existence in 1180. However, the present ruins suggest that the demolished building was of a 14th century construction. The castle is privately owned with no public access

The Bay Horse Inn makes a very pretty picture with its mellow stone walls, cobbled front patio, colourful hanging baskets and tubs of flowers, and backed by a cluster of mature trees. The interior is just as inviting. A stone door case, 17th century or older, was almost certainly salvaged from Ravensworth Castle, the rest of the building dates back to 1725. Your hosts, Sue and Charlie, bought the inn a few years ago when it had fallen on hard times but have transformed the Bay Horse into a popular hostelry with a reputation for good ale and excellent food. Charlie's *very* extensive menu caters for every palate, including vegetarians and children. There are Cheese Soufflés amongst the starters, a home made Beef Crumble as a main course, delicious fish dishes such as Salmon in watercress sauce, and an irresistible choice of desserts. An interesting feature of the restaurant decor is its collection of memorabilia associated with the Grand National near-winner "Crisp" whom Sue used to look after. On the first Sunday of each month, the Bay Horse hosts a quiz, (eve-

Bay Horse Inn, Ravensworth, Richmond, North Yorkshire, DL11 7ET Tel: 01325 718328

ryone welcome), and the inn also has an en suite twin guest room available all year round.

EAST LAYTON

MAP 2 REF F3

8 miles N of Richmond off the B6274

The summer of 1999 saw the opening of a major new visitor attraction in North Yorkshire. **Miniature World** offers families and school groups a wonderful day out, giving

them the opportunity of meeting a wide range of small animals, (including rare breeds), enjoying pony rides, honing their orienteering skills and much more. Do note that Miniature World is open by appointment only: Gill and Stephen Sims, who created this unique project, like to make sure that each visit is individually tailored to suit the visiting party. This is a magical place for children. They can touch and hold the smaller animals, feed the ducks; there's a Barn Owl which will sit on your shoulder, a very tame Red Deer to nuzzle up to, and rare breeds of hens, geese, pheasants and peacocks to wonder at. Perhaps the most popular animals are the miniature breeds: Buddy - a miniature horse 30 inches high; George, Mildred and family - small Vietnamese pot-bellied pigs; Wally - a tiny wallaby; and a family of pygmy goats. Miniature World is an ideal place for

Miniature World, West Grange, East Layton, Richmond, North Yorkshire DL11 7PB Tel: 01325 718038

birthday parties, when you will have the 26 acre site all to yourself, and if you live locally, you can take advantage of "Holiday Hutch", the only holiday home in the area for your rabbits, guinea pigs and other small animals.

ALDBROUGH
MAP 2 REF F3
7 miles N of Richmond off the B6275

To the west of the village lies the enormous complex of earthworks known as **Stanwick Camp.** The series of banks and ditches were excavated in the 1950s and their discovery also revealed that the constructions had been carried out in the 1st century. The site, open to the public, is now owned by English Heritage.

FORCETT
MAP 2 REF F3
8 miles N of Richmond on the B6274

The mainly Norman village Church of St Cuthbert underwent a drastic restoration programme in 1859 and the interior is now chiefly Victorian. Nearby Forcett Park, which is privately owned, is a particularly outstanding example of an early Georgian house, complete with stables, lodges, and a fine dovecote. The dovecote and the splendid east gate can be seen from the road leading to the park from the village.

CALDWELL
MAP 2 REF F3
9 miles N of Richmond on the B6274

Tucked away in the countryside but only a couple of miles or so from the A1 and A66, the **Brownlow Arms** is a charming building of local stone dating back to the 1700s. Your hosts, Tim and Carole, are both Yorkshire folk - Tim in fact was born and bred in the neighbouring village. Since they took over here in 1990 they have established the inn's reputation for good food and well-kept ales. Carole is an inspired chef and her ever-changing restaurant menu offers an extensive choice ranging from home made soup of the day and starters such as Cold Poached Salmon with Tzatziki, to a Steak Menu, fish and poultry dishes, along with vegetarian and pasta choices. Bar meals, sandwiches, and lunchtime snacks such as filled jacket potatoes or a Ploughman's Platter, are also available. Booking is recommended if you want to eat in the separate restaurant on Friday or

The Brownlow Arms, Caldwell, Richmond, North Yorkshire DL11 7QH
Tel: 01325 718471/718971

Saturday evening, or at Sunday lunchtime. The olde-worlde bar at the Brownlow is well-stocked with quality real ales, including Theakstons Best and Beamish Black, as well as 2 draught lagers and "Scrumpy Jack". Tim and Carole also arrange occasional live entertainment and, by the time you read this, they hope to also offer quality accommodation.

PIERCEBRIDGE   MAP 2 REF F3
9 miles NE of Richmond on the A67

This picturesque village, in upper Teesdale, was once an important Roman fort, one of a chain of forts linking the northern headquarters at York with Hadrian's Wall: another fort in the chain can be found to the south at Catterick. The Romans are thought to have originally chosen Piercebridge as a suitable river crossing back in AD 70, when Cerialis attacked a British camp at Stanwick. The remains of the fort, which are visible today, can be dated from coin evidence to around AD 270. The site is always open though the finds from the excavations are housed in the Bowes Museum at Barnard Castle.

The attractive River Tees forms part of the northern boundary of North Yorkshire and though Teesdale is not, strictly, a Yorkshire Dale it is well worth visiting. In its upper reaches, the river is noted for its waterfalls though the narrow valley soon widens to give attractive meadow land.

WENSLEYDALE

Wensleydale perhaps above all the others is the one most people associate with the Yorkshire Dales. At some 40 miles long it is certainly the longest dale and it is also softer and greener than many of its neighbours. The pasture land, grazed by flocks of Wensleydale sheep, is only broken by the long lines of dry stone walls and the dale is, of course, famous for its cheese whose fortunes have recently been given an additional boost by Wallace and Gromit who have declared it to be their favourite!

Wensleydale is the only major dale not to be named after its river, the Ure, although until fairly recent years most locals still referred to the area as Yoredale, or Uredale. The dale's name comes from the once important town of Wensley where the lucrative trade in cheese began in the 13th century. Wensley prospered for many years until 1563 when the Black Death annihilated most of its people and Leyburn became the trading centre of the lower dale. Wensleydale is also recorded in the 12th century as Wandelesleydale - *Waendel's woodland clearing in the valley.* Waendel has disappeared into the mists of time but undoubtedly his clearing was somewhere near this attractive little village.At the western end of the dale is Hawes, derived from the Norse word *hals* meaning neck and, indeed, the town does lies on a neck of land between two hills. Home of the **Dales Countryside Museum** and the **Wensleydale Creamery**, Hawes is an ideal starting point for exploring the dale. It is widely believed that the medieval monks of Jervaulx Abbey were responsible for introducing the manufacture of cheese to the dale some 700 years ago (they were of French origin after all). It was first made from ewe's milk but by the 1600s the milk of shorthorn cows was used instead since the sheep were becoming increasingly important for their wool and mutton. Originally just a summer occupation and mainly the task of the farmer's wife, the production of Wensleydale cheese was put on a commercial footing when the first cheese factory was established at Gayle Beck, near Hawes, in 1897.

Using Hawes as a base, visitors can also follow the **Turner Trail** which takes in the scenic sights that so impressed JMW Turner when he visited Wensleydale and neighbouring Swaledale in 1816. As it flows down the dale, the Ure is fed by a series of smaller rivers and becks, many of which have their own charming dale. Among the better-known are Coverdale, the home of some of England's finest racehorse stables, and peaceful Bishopdale with its ancient farmhouses. Remote Cotterdale, with its striking waterfall, and the narrow valley of the River Waldern are also well worth exploring.

Wensleydale, along with Swaledale and area around Thirsk, are commonly referred to as **Herriot Country** since it was this region of fells and friendly villages that provided many locations for the BBC series *All Creatures Great and Small*. Based on the working life of the real life vet, Alf Wight (1916-95), the stories recount the working life of Dalespeople between the 1930s and 1960s with humour and affection.

HAWES
Map 1 ref D5

17 miles W of Leyburn on the A684

The present town expanded greatly in the 1870s after the arrival of the railways but there's still plenty of evidence of the earlier settlement in street names relating to ancient trades: Dyer's Garth, Hatter's Yard and Printer's Square. Now the commercial and market centre of the upper dale, Hawes offers a good range of shopping, accommodation and visitor attractions.

Built in the late 17th century and ideally located in the centre of this lively market town, **The Fountain Hotel** was originally a coaching inn. Its main purpose then was to accommodate and feed the many travellers passing through. Today, the theme remains exactly the same except that the horses and carriages have gone and the old stables now provide an extra dining area and conference room. The Fountain's owners, Angus and Mandy McCarthy, have been here since 1988 and they have constantly upgraded the 12 en suite bedrooms, all of which have colour TV, tea/coffee facilities and BT direct dial telephone. There is a mixture of double, twin, family and single rooms. The Fountain's bar menu, available both at lunchtime and in the evening, seven days a week, offers a wide selection of good home cooking and fine cuisine, with a traditional roast every Sunday. The Public Bar stocks a wide selection

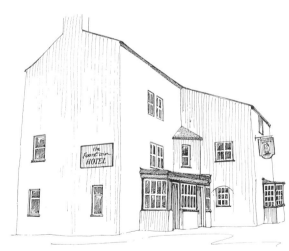

**The Fountain Hotel, Market Place, Hawes,
North Yorkshire DL8 3RD
Tel: 01969 667206 Fax: 01969 667085**

of traditional local ales, lagers and fine wines and convincingly claims to serve "the best beer in town!". From November to Easter, Friday nights at The Fountain are disco nights, with youngsters welcome from 7.30pm and adults from 10.30pm.

Housed in the former railway station, the **Dales Countryside Museum** tells the story of how man's activities have helped to shape the Dales' landscape. Providing fascinating historical details on domestic life, the lead mining industry, hand-knitting and other trades as well as archaeological material the museum covers many aspects of Dales' life from as far back as 10,000BC.

One of those local industries was rope-making and at **The Hawes Ropeworkers**, adjacent to the museum, visitors can still see it in operation, with experienced ropers twisting cotton and man-made fibres to make halters, hawsers, picture cords, dog leads, clothes lines and other 'ropy' items. The gift shop here stocks a comprehensive range of rope-related items along with an extensive choice of other souvenirs of the dale.

Wensleydale's most famous product, (after its sheep), is its soft, mild cheese, and at the **Wensleydale Cheese Experience** not only can you sample this delicacy but also learn about its history through a series of interesting displays. With a museum, viewing gallery of the production area, cheese shop, gift shop and licensed restaurant, there's plenty here for the cheese lover to enjoy.

One of the most popular eating places in this busy little town is the **Wensleydale Pantry** in Main Street. This spacious, first floor café/restaurant is owned and run by three brothers, David, Alan and Robert Blades, and run by Robert's daughter, Jackie. Her menus, chalked up on blackboards, offer a comprehensive choice of tasty, wholesome dishes, all carefully cooked to order. In the evening, from 6.30pm, even more options are added to the wide range already on offer. Crisp, creamy-white tablecloths and flowers on each table add to the pleasure of eating here, and the bar is well-stocked with beverages to accompany your meal. The waitress/counter service at the Wensleydale Pantry is prompt and friendly, and non-smokers have their own separate area. Such is the popularity of this welcoming restaurant, that it's advisable to book well ahead for Sunday lunch. The Pantry is open

Wensleydale Pantry, Main Street, Hawes, North Yorkshire DL8 3QW Tel: 01969 667202

daily all year except Christmas Day, Boxing Day and New Year's Day, from 8am until 9pm in the summer. During the winter, hours may vary - it's advisable to phone ahead.

Situated at the peaceful end of this picturesque market town, **Steppe Haugh Guest House** is a lovely 17th century stone building offering a wealth of character and atmosphere while at the same time providing all the modern facilities required by today's tourist. Dating back to 1643, this former farmhouse is covered with climbing plants and, during the summer months, together with the tubs of flowering plants, make the outside a riot of colour. Steppe Haugh offers its guests comfortably furnished double, twin and single rooms, all with central heating, tea/coffee making facilities, and all with pleasant views over the dale. Steppe Haugh is owned and run by Margaret and Edward Grattan

who bought the property some 5 years ago and wanted to make their guest house the kind of place in which they themselves would be happy to stay. So you'll find traditional Yorkshire hospitality, a breakfast spread sufficient to appease the heartiest appetite, a wonderfully relaxing residents' lounge with a glowing fire in the grate, and friendly hosts who are dedicated to making your stay as pleasant and enjoyable as possible.

Steppe Haugh Guest House, Town Head, Hawes, North Yorkshire DL8 3RH Tel: 01969 667645

For a really satisfying Cream Tea with home made scones, or a light meal, the place to seek out in Hawes is **Beckindales**, a stylish tea room just across from the Dales Museum and next door to the famous Hawes Ropemakers. To accompany your tea or snack, there's a choice of some 18 different kinds of tea, including decaffeinated. Beckindales owners, Paul Carpenter and Brenda McDermid also offer a good selection of cafetière coffees which range from a mild American Roast to a full

Beckindales, Burtersett Road, Hawes, North Yorkshire DL8 3NP Tel: 01969 667784

strength High Mountain Roast. Beckindales also serves a beverage not often seen on tea room menus - a hot Oxo drink, served with bread. The light meals available include jacket potatoes, (one of the fillings, naturally, is Wensleydale cheese), salads, sandwiches and filled baguettes. Not to be missed is the Yorkshire delicacy of Liz's home-made fruit cake accompanied by a slice of Wensleydale cheese. Outside tables provide an airy alternative to the non-smoking interior, and Beckindales also stocks an interesting range of crafts and gifts, most of them from the dales, some of them from Hawes itself.

HARDRAW

Map 1 ref D5

1 mile N of Hawes off the A684

Located in a natural amphitheatre of limestone crags, **Hardraw Force** is the highest, unbroken waterfall in England above ground, a breathtaking cascade 98ft high. Due to an undercut in the cliff, walkers can view the water from behind as both Turner and Wordsworth famously did. It shows at its best after heavy rain as, generally, the quantity of water tumbling over the rocks is not great. On two separate occasions, in 1739 and 1881, the falls froze solid into a 100ft icicle.

The amphitheatre here provides superb acoustics, a feature which has been put to great effect in the annual brass band competitions which began here in 1885 and have recently been resumed. Access to Hardraw Force is through the Green Dragon pub where a small fee is payable. The inn itself is pretty venerable with records of a hostelry on this site since at least the mid-13th century. At that time the land here was a grange belonging to the monks of Fountains Abbey who grazed their sheep nearby.

COTTERDALE

Map 1 ref C4

3 miles N of Hawes off the A684

The small valley of Cotter Beck lies below the vast bulk of Great Shunner Fell which separates the head of Wensleydale from Swaledale. **Cotter Force**, although smaller than Hardraw, is extremely attractive though often neglected in favour of its more famous neighbour.

BAINBRIDGE

Map 1 ref D5

5 miles E of Hawes on the A684

Back in the Middle Ages this area of Upper Wensleydale was a hunting forest, known as the Forest and Manor of Bainbridge and the village itself was established around the 12th century as a home for the foresters. One of their duties was to show travellers the way through the forest. Should anyone still be out by nightfall a horn was blown to guide them home. The custom is still continued between the Feast of Holy Rood (September 27th) and Shrove Tuesday when the present horn is blown at 9pm.

Just to the east of Bainbridge is **Brough Hill** (private) where the Romans built a succession of forts known collectively as *Virosidum*. First excavated in the late 1920s, they now appear as overgrown grassy hummocks. Much easier to see is the Roman road that strikes south-westwards from Bainbridge, part of their trans-Pennine route to Lancaster. It passes close to the isolated lake of **Semer Water**, one of Yorkshire's only two natural lakes. (The other is Lake Gormire, near Thirsk). Semer Water stretches for half a mile in length and teems with wild fowl. To the north the lake is drained by the River Bain which, at little more than 2 miles long, is the shortest named river in England.

An enduring legend claims that a town lies beneath the depths of Semer Water, cast under water by a curse. A poor traveller once sought shelter but was turned away by the affluent inhabitants. The next day he stood on the hill above the town, pronounced a curse, and a great flood engulfed the town immediately. There's an intriguing postscript to this tale. During a severe drought the level of the lake dropped to reveal the remains of a Bronze Age town, clear proof that the story was true.

STALLING BUSK
6 miles SE of Hawes off the A684

MAP 1 REF D5

Home Farm is a wonderfully picturesque building, its ancient stone walls almost smothered in creeper. This outstanding guest house enjoys a lovely position in this small hamlet overlooking Semer Water, North Yorkshire's largest lake. The farmhouse is a gracious 17th century building, replete with beamed ceilings and log fires. Maureen and Bill Orme have refurbished it in traditional style with lots of antique furniture: downstairs in English oak

Home Farm, Stalling Busk, nr Bainbridge, Wensleydale, North Yorkshire
Tel: 01969 650360

and upstairs with antique pine, Victorian brass beds and patchwork quilts. The food at Home Farm is definitely something to look forward to, with home made bread, home produced eggs and traditional cooking being the order of the day. The optional evening meal is strongly recommended since the Ormes maintain a small suckler herd of 25 cows and a Limousin bull, so the home produced, naturally fed beef is a Home Farm speciality, together with locally reared lamb, pork and game in season. The farmhouse has a licence so you can also enjoy a drink with your meal. For dessert, there's Treacle Pudding, Spotted Dick, Ginger Pear Pudding, Plum Lattice Tart, Bakewell Tart with custard, and many more, all of them home made. (Please note that Home Farm is only suitable for children over the age of eight).

ASKRIGG
5 miles E of Hawes off the A684

MAP 1 REF D5

Once an important market town, Askrigg became better known to television viewers as Darrowby, a major location for the long-running series *All Creatures Great and Small*. The 18th century Kings Arms Hotel often featured as "The Drovers Arms" and Cringley House doubled as "Skeldale House", the fictional home of the TV vets. The village has been popular with tourists since the days of Turner and Wordsworth when the chief attractions here were the two waterfalls at Whitfield and Mill Gill. Despite its olde worlde atmosphere Askrigg was one of the first places in the dales to be supplied with electricity.

That was in 1908 when the local miller harnessed the power of Mill Gill Beck.

Askrigg is bountifully supplied with footpaths radiating out to other villages, river crossings and farmsteads. One of the most scenic takes little more than an hour and takes in two impressive waterfalls, **Whitfield Gill Force** and **Mill Gill Force**. The route is waymarked from Mill Lane alongside the church.

AYSGARTH   MAP 1 REF E5
7 miles W of Leyburn on the A684

The village is famous for the spectacular **Aysgarth Falls** where the River Ure thunders through a rocky gorge and drops some 200ft over three huge slabs of limestone which

divide this wonderful natural feature into the Upper, Middle and Lower Falls. They provided a perfect location for the battle between Robin Hood and Little John in Mel Gibson's film *Robin Hood, Prince of Thieves*.

Close to the falls stands the **Church of St Andrew**, home of the Jervaulx Treasures - a vicar's stall that is made from the beautifully carved bench ends salvaged from Jervaulx Abbey. During the Middle Ages, Aysgarth enjoyed the distinction of being the largest parish in England though the parish has long been subdivided into more manageable areas.

The Dales National Park has a Visitor Information Centre here, with a spacious car park located close to the Church and Falls and also just a short walk from the **Yorkshire Carriage Museum** where a collection

Aysgarth Falls

of nearly 60 Victorian coaches are housed in the 200-year-old mill which overlooks the Falls.

Offering quality bed and breakfast just a short walk along a bridle way from Aysgarth Falls, **Field House** is a charming detached house looking out over superb Wensleydale countryside. Built in 1876, Field House was bought in 1997 by Ros and Bob who carried out a comprehensive refurbishment of the house and also completely overhauled the garden. The results are splendid. The

**Field House, East End, Aysgarth,
North Yorkshire DL8 3AB Tel: 01969 663556**

house has two guest rooms, one of which is en suite, the other has use of a lavishly appointed and sumptuous bathroom. The bedrooms are decorated and furnished to the highest standard, with lots of little extras, and both enjoy splendid views. An excellent breakfast is provided and Ros and Bob are happy to serve an evening meal, with vegetarian options available if required. Open from March to November, Field House is non-smoking and not suitable for children. The idyllic setting, close to one of Wensleydale's top scenic attractions, makes this an ideal place to relax and unwind.

THORALBY
Map 1 ref E5

8 miles W of Leyburn off the A684

Situated on the north slope of Bishopdale, opposite its sister village Newbiggin, Thoralby was once a centre for lead mining and although lead is no longer extracted here the mine can still be found on maps of the area. A side dale of Wensleydale, Bishopdale was once covered by a glacial lake that has given rise to its distinctive wide valley base. Here can be found many of Wensleydale's oldest houses.

NEWBIGGIN-IN-BISHOPDALE
Map 1 ref E5

9 miles SW of Leyburn on the B6160

As might be supposed, the name of this Bishopdale village means 'new buildings' and it is indeed a relatively new settlement having been first mentioned in 1230! There is only one road along Bishopdale, a beautiful unspoilt valley with hay meadows, stone barns and traditional Dales long houses. Look out for the **Street Head Inn** which makes a pretty picture indeed with its whitewashed walls draped with Virginia creeper. An old

Street Head Inn, Newbiggin-in-Bishopdale, Leyburn, North Yorkshire DL8 3TE Tel/Fax: 01969 663282 e-mail: streetheadinn@daelnet.co.uk

coaching inn established around 1730, the Street Head Inn has original oak and elm beams, open fires and a feature window created from the original coach entrance. You'll find a good selection of Yorkshire-brewed ales along with a range of malt whiskies, wines, spirits and soft drinks. Delicious espresso and cappuccino coffee is available in the bar, and there's a pleasant beer garden which enjoys superb views of the surrounding fells. A varied menu includes traditional, continental and oriental options as well as a children's menu, all cooked freshly on the premises and also available to take away. Vegetarian meals are usually on the menu or will be made to order. Jane and Mike who own and run the Inn, base their hospitality on down to earth principles - don't expect "nouveau cuisine" here! The guest bedrooms at Street Head Inn are all centrally heated and provided with colour TV and tea/coffee making facilities; 2 of them are en suite, the third has its own private shower and toilet.

REDMIRE   MAP 1 REF E5
4 miles W of Leyburn off the A684

Throughout its long history this village is thought to have occupied several sites in the vicinity. However, Redmire has been at its present location for many years and on the village green stands an old oak tree, supported by props, which is estimated to be at least 300 years old. When John Wesley preached in the village during his two visits in 1744 and 1774 it is believed that he stood in the shade of this very tree.

A sturdy building of local stone, located in the heart of this pretty village, **The Bolton Arms** has a history stretching back some 250 years. Since the spring of 1999 the inn has been owned and run by Beryl and Geoff Stoker who have revived the place, given it style and atmosphere, and above all established a reputation for creating a warm and friendly inn with all the characteristics one expects of a Dales' pub - traditional furnishing and decorations, fine ales - and good food which is available daily except Mondays (unless it's a Bank Holiday). Beryl is in charge of the cooking and if you plan to eat here at weekends it's definitely a good idea to book ahead. The former stable block at The Bolton Arms has been imaginatively converted into 3 quality letting rooms, all of them en suite, spotlessly clean

The Bolton Arms, Redmire, Leyburn, North Yorkshire DL8 4EA Tel: 01969 624336 website: www.boltonredmire.freeserve.co.uk

and attractively furnished. The rooms are available from February to December and provide an excellent base from which to explore this lovely part of Yorkshire.

WEST BURTON   MAP 1 REF E5
7 miles SW of Leyburn off the B6160

One of the most picturesque villages in Wensleydale, West Burton developed around its large central green where a busy weekly market used to take place. A distinctive feature of the green is the market 'cross' - actually a pyramid erected here in 1820. Just to the east of the village a path leads across a small packhorse bridge to **Mill Force**, perhaps the most photogenic of the Wensleydale waterfalls.

West Burton lies at the bottom of Walden, a narrow, steep-sided valley that provides a complete contrast to neighbouring Bishopdale. Secluded and with just a scattering of houses and farms, Walden was one of the last places in Yorkshire where wild red deer were seen.

CASTLE BOLTON   Map 1 ref E4
5 miles W of Leyburn off the A684

Bolton Castle has dominated mid-Wensleydale for more than six centuries and is one of the major tourist attractions of the area. In 1379 the lord of the manor, Richard le Scrope, Lord Chancellor of England to Richard II, was granted permission to fortify his manor house and, using stone from a nearby quarry and oak beams from the Lake District, the

Bolton Castle

building was completed some 18 years later. To-day, this luxurious fortified manor house is still occupied by a direct descendant of the 1st Lord Scrope and it remains an impressive sight with its four-square towers acting as a local landmark. The halls and galleries are remarkably well-preserved as are some of the private apartments used by Mary, Queen of Scots when she was a reluctant visitor here between 1568-69. Indeed, modern day visitors can take tea in the grand room where she spent many melancholy days. If you climb to the battlements you will be rewarded with some breathtaking views along the dale.

WEST WITTON   Map 1 ref E5
4 miles W of Leyburn on the A684

Recorded in the Domesday Book as Witun this village was then the largest in Wensleydale and exceptional in having stone rather than wooden houses. West Witton is well known for its annual feast of St Bartholomew, patron saint of the parish church. It takes place on August 24th when an effigy of a man, known as the Bartle, is carried through the village. According to legend, Bartle was an 18th century swine that was hunted over the surrounding fells before being captured and killed. The culmination of the three days of celebration is the burning of the effigy at Grassgill End.

The oldest inhabited site in the village is believed to be where the **Fox & Hounds Inn** now stands. The houses here were linked to the famous Jervaulx Abbey, a few miles further down the dale, and beneath the Inn are cellars which were hewn out of the solid rock some time in the 1400s. When the Inn was recently refurbished a small chamber was found here, just big enough for one person. Historians believe that it was probably a place of penance for sinners. This historic hostelry is owned and run by Andrew and Nola Blackburn, both of them born and bred in West Witton and both of them possessing a wealth of local knowledge! The Fox & Hounds enjoys a good reputation for the food on offer which is available daily at both lunchtime and in the evening. You can enjoy your meal either in the bar, in the non-smoking restaurant with its inglenook fireplace and rare "beehive" oven, or in the lovely beer garden overlooking the dale. And if you are tempted to linger in

Fox & Hounds Inn, Main Street, West Witton, Leyburn, North Yorkshire DL8 4LP   Tel: 01969 623650

this enchanting corner of the Dales, the inn has 1 family, en suite room which enjoys a superb view of Pen Hill.

CARLTON-IN-COVERDALE   MAP 1 REF E5

4 miles SW of Leyburn on minor road off the A684

Carlton is Coverdale's principal village - with a population of less than a hundred. Nevertheless it has its own pub and is a wonderfully peaceful base for walking, hiking, fishing or touring the Dales National Park.

A delightful place to stay for bed & breakfast in this charming little village is **Abbots Thorn**, a 200-year-old traditional stone-built Dales farmhouse but one of the few distinguished by round chimney stacks. The stones for these are believed to have been cannibalised from Middleham Castle. Abbots Thorn has been lovingly converted into a warm and comfortable place to spend your holiday.

Abbots Thorn, Carlton-in-Coverdale, Leyburn, North Yorkshire DL8 4AY   Tel: 01969 640620 e-mail: abbots.thorn@virgin.net website: http://business.virgin.net/patricia.lashmar

Pat and John have 3 guest rooms available, two of them en suite, and all the rooms feature country pine furniture and doors, along with colour TV, thermostat-controlled central heating and tea/coffee making facilities complete with fresh milk and biscuits. Window seats provide a vantage point from which to enjoy the stunning views of Coverdale that unfold from the sunny south-facing location. After a good night's sleep, a full Yorkshire breakfast awaits and dinner is available each evening if you wish, offering you good, home cooked food based on fresh, local produce wherever possible. Abbots Thorn doesn't have a drinks licence, but feel free to bring your own and Pat and John will do the rest.

WENSLEY

MAP 1 REF E5

1 mile W of Leyburn on the A684

This peaceful little village beside the River Ure was once the main settlement in mid-Wensleydale and such was its importance it gave its name to the dale. However, in 1563, the town was struck by plague and those who could fled up the hill to Leyburn which was thought to be a healthier place.

The stately **Church of the Holy Trinity** is one of only two surviving medieval structures in Wensley (the other is the graceful bridge nearby) and it is thought to have been built on the site of an earlier Saxon church. Inside can be seen the unusual Bolton family pews which are actually a pair of opera boxes that were brought here from London during the 1700s when a theatre was being refurbished.

The Bolton family still live at nearby Bolton Hall, a massive 18th century pile which is closed to the public although its splendid gardens are occasionally open during the summer months.

"*Purveyors to the Military, Colonies, Overseas Missions, Churches and the Cinematograph Industries*" runs the proud claim in the brochure for **White Rose Candles Workshop**. "*Patronised by the Nobility and Gentry*" it continues; "*Cathedrals supplied include Ripon and Norwich*". One of Wensleydale's most popular attractions, the workshop is housed in a 19th century water mill - the water wheel still exists and mills have been recorded on this site since 1203. The workshop is very much a family business with Jennie and Mick White, along with their daughter Rachel, each pursuing their own area of expertise. Visitors may observe the various processes involved in the manufacture of candles, including traditional dipping techniques and casting methods. Naturally, there's a huge choice of candles on sale in a wide variety of colours, sizes and shapes: - eggs, snowballs and even a bomb are among the more unusual. To quote the brochure once again, "*Once you have tried a White Rose Candle you are bound to Return for More!*"

White Rose Candles, Wensley Mill, Wensley, Leyburn, North Yorkshire DL8 4HR Tel/Fax: 01969 623544

About a mile to the west of Wensley, on the Tupgill Park Estate, **The Forbidden Corner** is an unusual attraction. Strange and exotic buildings are scattered around the park, some of them underground, and visitors are given a list but must discover these fantastic constructions by themselves. *"In parts you might find your heart's delight"* says the brochure *"In others you'll tremble with fear"*. There's also a shop, refreshment room, and toilets which are all accessible to the disabled but some parts of the garden are only reached by way of steps. Admission is by pre-booked tickets only and they can be obtained at Leyburn Tourist Information Office.

LEYBURN

Map 2 ref E5

17 miles E of Hawes on the A684

The main market town and trading centre of mid-Wensleydale, Leyburn is an attractive town with a broad market place lined by handsome late-Georgian and Victorian stone buildings. Friday is market day and the little town is even busier than usual. There's an interesting mix of traditional family-run shops and surprisingly large supermarkets behind deceptively small frontages.

The town has several interesting connections with famous people. Lord Nelson's surgeon, Peter Goldsmith, once lived in the Secret Garden House on Grove Square (and is buried in Wensley church, just a mile up the road). Flight Lieutenant Alan Broadley DSO, DFC, DFM, the 'F for Freddie' of Dam Busters fame, is named on the War Memorial in the main square, and just a few yards away is the birthplace of the *Sweet Lass of Richmond Hill*. Many believe that the popular song refers to Richmond Hill in Surrey rather than Richmond, North Yorkshire. Not so. Frances I'Anson was born in her grandfather's house on Leyburn High Street and his initials, WIA, can still be seen above the door of what is now an interior decorator's shop. It was her husband-to-be, Leonard McNally, who composed the immortal song.

The Shawl, to the west of the town, is a mile-long limestone scarp along which runs a footpath offering lovely panoramic views of the dale. A popular legend suggests that it gained its unusual name when Mary, Queen of Scots dropped her shawl here during her unsuccessful attempt to escape from Bolton Castle. However, a more likely explanation is that Shawl is a corruption of the name given to the ancient settlement here.

Spring is a good time to visit since that is when both the Swaledale and Wensleydale festivals take place, as well as the prestigious Dales Music Festival.

Continuing the musical theme, Leyburn is also home to **The Violin Making Workshop** where visitors have the rare opportunity of watching this ancient and fascinating craft. Little has changed in the art of violin making over the centuries and the traditional tools and methods used by such master craftsmen as Stradivari are still employed today. The workshop is open every day during the high season, and every day except Saturday between Easter and the end of September.

Close by, at **The Teapottery**, you can see other craftspeople at work - in this case creating a whole range of witty and unusual teapots - anything from a grand piano to a bathtub complete with yellow duck. The finished pots can be purchased in the showroom where there's also a tea room with your tea served, naturally, in one of the astonishing teapots produced here.

About 2 miles west of Leyburn, off the A684, the **Sheepshop** at Cross Lanes Farm in Garriston is a treat for anyone who appreciates good knitwear which can be specially knitted to the customer's requirements. You can see the raw material grazing in the surrounding fields - rare Wensleydale longwool sheep. The Sheepshop also stocks an extensive range of hand knitting yarns and patterns for the enthusiast.

SPENNITHORNE
MAP 2 REF F5
2 miles SE of Leyburn off the A684

This pleasant little village dates back many years. The present Church of St Michael and All Angels stands on the site of a Saxon church although the only remains of the ancient building to be seen are two ornamental stones set into the walls of the chancels and a Saxon monument in the vestry.

Two of Spennithorne's earlier residents are worth mentioning. John Hutchinson was born here in 1675 and went on to become steward to the 6th Duke of Somerset - and a rather controversial philosopher. He vehemently disagreed with Sir Isaac Newton's Theory of Gravity and was equally ardent in asserting that the earth was neither flat, nor a sphere, but a cube. Though there are no records mentioning that Hutchinson was ever considered as of unsound mind, another resident of Spennithorne, Richard Hatfield, was officially declared insane after he fired a gun at George III.

MIDDLEHAM
MAP 2 REF E5
2 miles S of Leyburn on the A6108

Middleham is an enchanting little town which, despite having a population of fewer than 800, boasts its own Mayor, Corporation and quaint Town Hall. It also is the site of one of Yorkshire's most historic castles; 12 of England's most successful racing stables and not just one, but two, Market Places. It is almost totally unspoilt, with a wealth of handsome Georgian houses and hostelries huddled together in perfect architectural harmony.

Rising high above the town are the magnificent ruins of **Middleham Castle** (English Heritage), a once-mighty fortress whose most glorious days came in the 15th century when most of northern England was ruled from here by the Neville family. The castle's most famous resident was the 'evil' Richard III who was sent here as a lad of 13 to be trained in the *"arts of nobilitie"*. Whatever crimes he committed later down in London, Richard was popular locally, ensuring the town's prosperity by granting it a fair and a twice-yearly market. The people of Middleham had good reason to mourn his death at the Battle of Bosworth in 1485.

Middleham is often referred to as the 'Newmarket of the North', a term you'll understand when you see the strings of thoroughbred racehorses clip-clopping through the town on their way to training runs on Low Moor. It was the monks of Jervaulx Abbey who founded this key industry. By the late 18th century races were being run across the moorland and the first stables established. Since then, they have produced a succession of classic race winners with one local trainer, Neville Crump, having three Grand National winners to his credit within the space of twelve years.

Just a few steps from the Castle, the **Millers House Hotel & Restaurant** offers top quality cuisine, friendly service and excellent accommodation in a superb Georgian house set back from one of Middleham's two squares. The interior has been meticulously furnished to the standards of a modern first class hotel and the quality of the cuisine on offer is indicated by the fact that the restaurant has won several awards, amongst them the AA's Red Rosette. At your candlelit dinner you'll find an imaginative menu based on a variety of the very best local produce, along with herbs and vegetables from the hotel's own garden. The wine list (also an award winner) is well balanced and very sensibly priced. The hotel has 7 entirely individual bedrooms, six of them with en suite facilities. One of them boasts a splendid 4-poster bed and a free-standing Victorian roll top bath. The owners of Millers House Hotel, Ann and James Lundie, go out of their way to ensure that your stay is a pleasant one, adding many thought-

**Millers House Hotel & Restaurant, Middleham, Wensleydale, North Yorkshire DL8 4NR
Tel: 01969 622630   Fax: 01969 623570
e-mail: hotel@millershouse.demon.co.uk**

ful touches such as a comprehensive information pack in each bedroom and welcoming home-made biscuits.

COVERHAM
Map 2 ref E5

3 miles S of Leyburn off the A6108

Lying beside the River Cover in little-visited Coverdale, this village is perhaps best known for the remains of **Coverham Abbey** (private). Built in the late 1200s, only some decorated arches remain, along with a Norman gateway. The nearby 17th century manor house, as well as other surrounding buildings, have clearly used the Abbey's stones in their construction - in some of the walls effigies from the old building can clearly be seen.

EAST WITTON
Map 2 ref F5

3 miles SE of Leyburn on the A6108

An attractive village set beside the confluence of the rivers Cover and Ure, East Witton was almost entirely rebuilt after a great fire in 1796. The new buildings included the well-proportioned Church of St John although the old churchyard with its many interesting gravestones remains. Some two decades after that conflagration the village was struck by another calamity. In 1820, twenty miners perished in a coal mine accident at Witton Fell. They were all buried together in one grave in the new churchyard.

Just to the west of the village is **Jervaulx Abbey**, one of the great Cistercian sister houses to Fountains Abbey. The name Jervaulx is a French derivation of Yore, (or Ure), and Vale, just as Rievaulx is of Rye Vale. Before the Dissolution, the monks of Jervaulx Abbey owned huge tracts of Wensleydale and this now-solitary spot was once a busy trading and administrative centre. Despite its ruination, Jervaulx is amongst the most evocative of Yorkshire's many fine abbeys. The grounds have been transformed into beautiful gardens with the crumbling walls providing interesting backdrops for the sculptured trees and colourful plants and shrubs.

Jervaulx Abbey, nr East Witton

CONSTABLE BURTON
MAP 2 REF F5
4 miles E of Leyburn on the A684

Surrounded by walled and wooded parkland **Constable Burton Hall** is famous for its gardens (open March to October) and in particular its spacious, romantic terraces. The house itself is not open to the public but its stately Georgian architecture provides a magnificent backdrop to the fine gardens, noble trees and colourful borders.

HUNTON
MAP 2 REF F4
5 miles NE of Leyburn off the A684

Located at the heart of this peaceful little village, **The New Inn** has been dispensing hospitality for a hundred years or more. A few years ago it was forced to close down, a sad blow to village life. Fortunately, it was bought by Ian and Helen Vipond who undertook a thorough refurbishment of the building, being careful to retain the inn's appealing traditional features. The New Inn now enjoys an excellent reputation for its welcoming atmosphere, quality ales and first class

The New Inn, Leyburn Road, Hunton, Bedale, North Yorkshire DL8 1QL Tel: 01677 450009

food. Ian's menu, chalked up on the blackboard, changes daily but it always offers a choice of at least 16 appetising dishes, with fish and game a speciality. If you plan to eat in the restaurant over a weekend, you are strongly advised to make a booking. Ian also holds occasional themed food nights, with a carefully thought-out menu exploring one particular cuisine. In addition to the restaurant fare, The New Inn also offers a range of wholesome bar meals and snacks. Food is available every evening except Tuesday; and at lunchtimes Thursday to Sunday, and on Bank Holiday Mondays.

CRAKEHALL   MAP 2 REF F5
2 miles NW of Bedale on the A684

Sometime around 1090AD the Domesday Book commissioners arrived in Crakehall and noted details of a mill on the beck that runs through this picturesque village. More than 900 years later there's still a mill on the very same spot. The present **Crakehall Water Mill** building dates from the 1600s; its mighty machinery from the 18th and 19th centuries. It's still a working mill - visitors can watch the whole process in operation and then, if they wish, purchase a bag or two of the top quality flour it produces.

Housed in a former Methodist chapel dating back to 1840, the **Museum of Badges and Battledress** is a private collection displaying uniforms, equipment, cap badges, formation signs, trade badges and photographs of all branches of the Armed Forces. The exhibits include more than 60 mannequins dressed in various uniforms along with military equipment and ephemera dating from 1900 to the present day. The museum is open from Easter to September inclusive but parties and guided tours are available at any time by prior arrangement.

Overlooking the village green and cricket pitch, **The Bay Horse Inn** is a natural home for the Crakehall cricket team, especially since the inn's landlord, John Shephard, is also the chairman of the cricket club. John and his wife Dianne have been here since 1993 and by virtue of their warm and friendly hospitality have made the Bay Horse something of a social centre for the village. The attractive old building with its red pantiled roof dates back to the late 17th century when it began life as a blacksmith's smithy which also sold ale. By the beginning of the 18th century, the inn side of the business took over from the smithying and it

The Bay Horse Inn, The Green, Crakehall, Bedale, North Yorkshire DL8 1HP Tel: 01677 422548

has remained a licensed premises ever since. Dianne offers a choice of up to a dozen different main courses, all detailed on the blackboard along with a separate menu for desserts. Meals are available Tuesday to Sunday, and also on Bank Holiday Mondays. The beer at the Bay Horse is of equally high quality and, as well as the popular Theakstons and John Smiths, there is always a selection of guest ales from which to choose. Cosy, and comfortably decorated and furnished, the inn hosts a quiz night once a month to which all are welcome, and there are occasional barbecues on summer weekends.

BEDALE   Map 2 ref F5
12 miles E of Leyburn on the A684

This pleasant little market town developed around the point where the Saxon track from Ripon joined the route from Northallerton to Wensleydale. Traders met here and in 1251 Henry III granted a charter for a weekly market which still flourishes today. The market cross stands at the top of Elmgate, a narrow street leading from the river to the market place. As commercial activity increased, water power was harnessed from the **Bedale Beck** for the processing of wool. Skinners and tanners worked down by the ford and the town was a lively hub of cottage industry.

The curving main street leads to the beautiful parish **Church of St Gregory** at the northern end. Recorded in the Domesday Book and incorporating architectural styles from the 11th to the 16th centuries, the building has a fine fortified tower. Just inside the churchyard is an old building dating from the mid-1200s which served as a school in the 18th century.

Across the road from the church is **Bedale Hall** which houses the library and local museum. The north front of the building is a particularly fine example of the Georgian architecture which gives Bedale its special character. Another building of interest is the 18th century **Leech House**, so called because it was once used by the local chemist to store his leeches.

Overlooking the broad Market Place, **The Kings Head** is one of the many attractive Georgian buildings in this unspoilt little town. The broad alley to one side reveals the Kings Head's origins as a coaching inn and the interior evokes the old world atmosphere of those days, a tradition reflected in the outstanding hospitality on offer here. Your hosts, Steve Reed and Adam Lawrence, though, are very much up-to-date and have made the inn popular with young

**The Kings Head, 40 Market Place, Bedale,
North Yorkshire DL8 1GQ Tel: 01677 422763**

as well as older patrons. Adam is the chef, offering quality meals at lunchtime all year round, and evening meals from 5.30 to 7.30 during the spring and summer months. The Kings Head is also highly regarded for its fine ales, with a choice that includes John Smiths, Tetley, Guinness, four draught lagers and Scrumpy Cider. Entertainment here includes karaoke on Thursday and Sunday evenings, and a disco on Friday and Saturday evenings from 8pm until 11.15pm. Bedale is just a mile or so from the A1 so it's a very convenient place to stay while exploring Wensleydale and the Kings Head has two out-standing double guest rooms, both en suite with excellent bathrooms with showers. By the time you read this, additional en suite rooms should be available.

A popular family attraction located just west of the town is **The Big Sheep and Little Cow Farm.** There are guided tours which include bottle feeding the lambs, bathing George (the pig), holding poultry and going into the fields to meet a menagerie of other animals. You don't have to take the tour - you can relax next to the old mill race and sample the delicious Oakwoods Speciality Ice Cream which is produced on the farm from the milk of ewes grazed on the old water meadows next to the Watermill. Pony rides are available, there's an all weather children's play area and a picnic area.

SNAPE
MAP 2 REF F5
2 miles S of Bedale off the B6268

This quiet and unspoilt village, where the original timber-framed cottages stand side by side with their more modern neighbours, is still dominated by its castle as it has been for centuries. Reached via an avenue of lime trees, **Snape Castle** has a famous, if somewhat complicated, royal connection as it was the home of Lord Latimer of Snape (a member of the Neville family), the first husband of Catherine Parr, Henry VIII's last wife. The Nevilles owned the castle for over 700 years and its beautiful chapel, still used by the villagers, saw the marriages of many Latimers and Nevilles.

Set in over 1000 acres of parkland, **Thorp Perrow Arboretum** is unique to Britain, if not Europe, in that it was the creation of one man, Col. Sir Leonard Ropner (1895-1977). Sir Leonard travelled all over the world col-lecting rare and unusual species for Thorp Perrow and today the hundreds of trees he enthusias-tically collected are in their prime. The arbo-retum was initially Sir Leonard's private hobby but after his death his son, Sir John Ropner, decided to open the 85-acre garden to the public and the arboretum is now one of the area's prime attractions. A

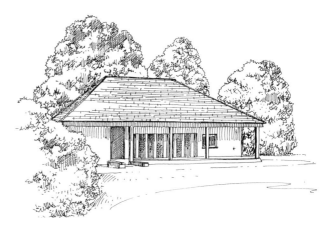

Thorp Perrow Arboretum, Snape, Bedale, North Yorkshire DL8 2PR   Tel/Fax: 01677 425323

treasure trove of specimen trees, woodland walks, nature trail, tree trails, a large lake, picnic area and children's play area, the Arboretum also embraces the **Milbank Pinetum**, planted by Lady Augusta Milbank in the mid-19th century, and the medieval Spring Wood dating back to the 16th century. Thorp Perrow provides interest all year round but perhaps the most popular time is the spring when you can witness one of the finest and most extensive plantings of daffodils in the north of England, amongst them some old and unusual varieties. In addition to the fascinating collection of trees, visitors will also find an information centre, a tea room and a plant sales area. An additional attraction at Thorp Perrow opens in the spring of 2000. **The Falcons of Thorp Perrow** is a brand new bird of prey, captive breeding and conservation centre which has been created within a large, formerly derelict walled garden.

WELL

MAP 2 REF F5

3 miles S of Bedale off the B6268 or B6267

This pretty village takes its name from **St Michael's Well** which was already being vener-ated long before the Romans came here and one of them built a spacious villa near the well. Part of the tessellated pavement of that villa is now on display in the parish church, which is itself a venerable building with foundations that date back to Norman times. The church's greatest treasure is a font cover dating from 1325, one of the oldest in the country. It was a gift to the church from Ralph Neville, Lord of Middleham, who also founded the line of almshouses near the church which were rebuilt by his descendants in 1758.

This historic little village also boasts a traditional Yorkshire inn, **The Milbank Arms**, which dates back to the 17th century. It was then an alehouse serving the workers on Lord Milbank's extensive estate, hence the name. The range of fine ales and good food on offer

has expanded con-siderably since those days. Mark and Samantha Wilson now provide their patrons with a range of constantly chang-ing real ales, with at least 5 available at any one time. Mark is the chef and he commands a com-prehensive and varied repertoire of tasty, wholesome dishes. Once a month, the Milbank

The Milbank Arms, Church Street, Well, nr Bedale, North Yorkshire DL8 2PX   Tel: 01677 470411/470200

hosts a themed food night and Mark is also much in demand for outside catering. If you're visiting the inn on a Friday evening, you'll be entertained with live music from 9pm and on Sunday evening there's a popular quiz. The engaging old world atmosphere of the Milbank makes it the kind of place where you'll feel inclined to linger. Fortunately, Mark and Samantha can provide you with a choice of lovely, ground floor, guest rooms. All of them are en suite, and attractively decorated and furnished.

MASHAM
MAP 2 REF F5
5 miles SW of Bedale on the A6108

Set beside the River Ure, Masham (pronounced *Massam*) is a very picturesque place with a huge market place at its heart. The ancient **Church of St Mary** stands in one corner, a school founded in 1760 in another, while at the centre is the market cross surrounded by trees and flowers. The size of the market place reflects Masham's historical importance as a market town and its position, between the sheep-covered hills and the corn growing lowlands, certainly helped to support its flourishing trade. The sheep fairs held in the town in the 18th and 19th century were among the largest in the country and in September the Masham Sheep Fair revives those heady days, giving visitors the chance of seeing many rare breeds of sheep and goats as well as witnessing events such as dog agility and sheep racing!

The town is famed for its beer, boasting two celebrated breweries - Theakston's and Black Sheep. **Theakston's Brewery**, noted for its Old Peculier brew, was founded in 1827 by two brothers, Thomas and Robert. Adjoining the brewery today is a modern visitor centre which illustrates the process of brewing and the art of cooperage. Those taking the tour (which must be pre-booked) should be aware that there are two flights of steep steps along the route and the tour is not suitable for children under 10. Interestingly, the name of the famous brew derives from the fact that Masham in medieval times had its own Peculier Court (meaning special rather than odd) - an ecclesiastical body with wide-ranging powers.

The **Black Sheep Brewery** is also well worth a visit. It too offers a guided tour and visitors get the chance to sample the traditionally made ale. In addition to the working brewery, the old Maltings building is home to a "sheepy" shop and a popular bistro.

Just a 2-minute walk from Masham's delightful Market Place, **Bank Villa** is a friendly, welcoming home offering quality bed and breakfast accommodation. The substantial old house, some 200 years old, was once a doctor's home and surgery, and was built on a grand scale. The former surgery is now an impressive, high-ceilinged dining-room; the doctor's parlour a peaceful room where you can settle down with a good book. There's also a comfortable residents' lounge, complete with colour TV. The 6 beautifully furnished and decorated guest bedrooms are all different in character and size. Three of them are en suite and one has its own bathroom which is a real eye-opener, especially if you like frogs - look out for Ferdinand! Bank Villa

Bank Villa, Masham, nr Ripon, North Yorkshire HG4 4DB
Tel/Fax: 01765 689605

is the home of Lucy and Bobby Thomson, a welcoming couple who provide their guests with a generous breakfast and will also serve you a tasty evening meal if you wish. Since the house is licensed, you can enjoy the beverage of your choice with your dinner. To the rear of the house, there's a lovely terraced garden which is ideal for relaxing on fair-weather days.

Silverdale, Silver Street, Masham, North Yorkshire HG4 4DX
Tel: 01765 688180 Fax: 01765 635224

If you love browsing around antique shops, there's a treat in store for you at **Silverdale** where you'll find a tempting blend of fine pieces from both the past and the present. Located in the heart of the town and housed in a handsome late-18th century house, Silverdale is owned and run Angela and John Shevels who have stocked their elegant showroom with a huge range of artefacts. They specialize in 19th and 20th century china but you'll also find a wealth of quality prints and water-colours, glass items of every kind and much, much more. Once inside the shop, it's unlikely you will leave without buying something since there are items to suit just about every budget. John is an experienced craftsman who restores antique furniture and also creates attractive Country Oak Furniture to commission. Silverdale is open on Wednesday, Friday and Saturday, 10am to 5pm, and on Sunday from noon until 5pm.

WEST TANFIELD
MAP 2 REF F5
3 miles SE of Masham on the A6108

This attractive village on the banks of the River Ure is home to a remarkable Tudor gatehouse known as the **Marmion Tower**. Overlooking the river and with a beautiful oriel window, the tower is open to the public.

For many years, West Tanfield was associated with the powerful Marmion family and the 14th century Church of St Nicholas contains many effigies belonging to the family. Though the purpose of the **Thornborough Circles**, which lie just outside the village, remains a mystery, these late Neolithic or early Bronze Age oval earthworks are well worth finding.

GREWELTHORPE
MAP 2 REF F6
3 miles S of Masham off the A6108

It was long thought that the Romans had a camp to the north of this leafy village and the discovery early this century of the complete skeleton of a Roman soldier confirmed the story. The remains were reburied in the churchyard at Kirkby Malzeard but the soldier's sandals are on view in the York Museum. Just north of the village are the beautiful **Hackfall Woods** through which the River Ure flows.

During the 19th century the Victorians developed the woodland, creating waterfalls and transforming the 18th century follies that had been built here into splendid vantage points. Following a period of neglect which began with the sale of the woodland in the 1930s, the Hackfall Woods are now in the care of the Woodland Trust and the area is being gradually restored to its 19th century condition.

KIRKBY MALZEARD   MAP 2 REF F6
4 miles S of Masham off the A6108

Dating back to the 11th century, the **Church of St Andrew** is noted for its associations with witchcraft. Apparently, the north-eastern corner of the churchyard was favoured by practitioners of the black arts for conducting their strange rituals and charms. Black magic aside, the church has been pealing its bells for over 400 years and records show that in 1591 one of the bells was recast - the process taking place inside the church building.

This traditional Yorkshire village is also one of the few places in the country that can boast its own Sword Dance. Certainly a pagan ritual, thought to date back to prehistoric times, the performance of the dance is supposed to make the grass grow tall and to wake the earth from her winter's sleep.

Many of the farms around the village are dairy farms and at **Kirby Malzeard Dairy** they still produce the traditionally made Coverdale cheese. Very much a local speciality, it is one of the few remaining Dales' cheeses still made though, at one time, each dale had its own particular variety.

ILTON   MAP 2 REF F5
3 miles SW of Masham off the A6108

This village is close to one of the area's most interesting and unusual features - the **Druid's Temple**. Though the name suggests that this was an ancient meeting place for pagan worshippers, the charming folly was built in the 1820s by William Danby of the nearby Swinton Estate. Resembling a miniature Stonehenge, the folly was inspired by a similar temple Danby saw on his travels in Europe and his building project was intended to provide work for local unemployed people. It is considered one of the best Druidic follies in the country. From Ilton village it can be reached by following part of the long distance footpath known as the **Ripon Rowel Walk**.

5 The Southern Dales

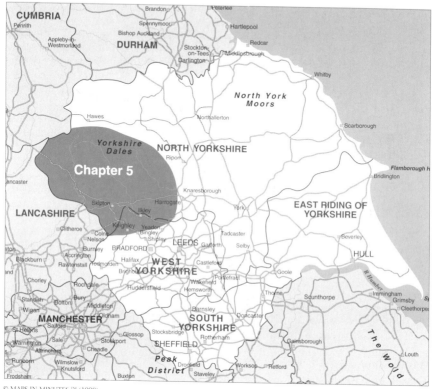

© MAPS IN MINUTES ™ (1998)

NIDDERDALE

This typical Yorkshire dale with its dry stone walls, green fields, and pretty stone villages was christened Little Switzerland by the Victorians. Indeed, the upper reaches of the valley of the River Nidd are steep and wooded, with the river running through gorges, and with a covering of snow in winter it is easy to see the resemblance. It is this natural beauty that draws many people to the dale and there are also several remarkable features that are well worth exploring.

The history of the dale is similar to that of its neighbours. The Romans and Norsemen both settled here and there are also reminders that the Dale was populated in prehistoric times. It was the all powerful Cistercian monks of Fountains and Byland Abbeys who began the business-like cultivation of the countryside to provide grazing for cattle and sheep and the space to grow food. This great farming tradition has survived and, though prosperity came and went with the lead mining, a few of the textile mills established in the golden age of the Industrial Revolution can still be found.

Best explored from Pateley Bridge, keen walkers will delight in the wide variety of landscape that can be covered within a reasonable amount of time. High up on the moorland, famed for its brilliant colour in late summer, there are several reservoirs, built to provide water for the growing population and industry in Bradford. This area is a must for bird watchers as there are excellent opportunities for spotting a number of species of duck as well as brent geese and whooper swans. Further down the valley, in the rich woodland, wildlife again abounds and the well-signposted footpaths help visitors reach the most spectacular sights.

The dry stone walls that are such a feature of the countryside in the Yorkshire Dales originated from the new demand for the scientific management of the land by enclosure following the Agricultural Revolution in the 18th century. The arrow-straight dividing walls sprang up high on the hillsides and the enclosures are still easily recognised by their geometric shapes. The walls are constructed by packing small stones on top of a firm foundation and tying these together with 'troughs' - stones spanning the width of the wall. Their mortarless construction remains a fascinating feature and the clumsy, irregular shaped stones require extremely skilful selection and placement.

PATELEY BRIDGE

MAP 2 REF F6

12 miles SW of Ripon on the B6265

Considered one of the prettiest towns in the Dales, Pateley Bridge is perfectly situated as a base from which to explore Upper Nidderdale. Considering its compact size, the town is remarkably well connected by roads which have been here since the monastic orders established trade routes through the town for transporting their goods. A street market, whose charter was granted in the 14th century, has however, been abandoned for some time although sheep fairs and agricultural shows still take place here.

Pateley Bridge is more than just a market centre - the nearby lead mines and spinning and hand-loom weaving also provided employment for the local community. The construction of the turnpike road to Ripon in 1751, followed by the opening of a road to Knaresborough in 1756, gave the town a further economic boost. In the early 19th century, the brothers George and John Metcalfe moved their flax spinning business to nearby Glasshouses and they expanded rapidly. The lead mines too were expanding, due to the introduction of new machinery, and the town saw a

Pateley Bridge

real boom. The arrival of the railway in 1862 maintained this flourishing economy, making the transportation of heavy goods cheaper and the carriage of perishable foods quicker.

Much of the Pateley Bridge seen today was built in those prosperous years. A town of quaint and pretty buildings, the oldest is **St Mary's Church**, a lovely ruin dating from 1320 from which there are some fine panoramic views. Another excellent vista can be viewed from the aptly named **Panorama Walk**, part of the main medieval route from Ripon to Skipton.

The **Nidderdale Museum**, a winner of the National Heritage Museum of the Year, is housed in one of the town's original Victorian workhouses and presents a fascinating record of local folk history. The exhibits include a complete cobbler's shop, general store, Victorian parlour, kitchen and schoolroom, chemist's, haberdasher's, joiner's shop, solicitor's office as well as an agricultural, transport and industrial display.

The bridge at Pateley is a long established crossing which was used by the monks of Fountains Abbey. The original ford was replaced by a wooden bridge in the 16th century and the present stone structure dates from the 18th century.

The Willow Restaurant is a cosy country restaurant offering traditional English fare in a quiet and intimate atmosphere. Up to 30 guests can be accommodated in the restaurant at one time and there is a separate bar and coffee lounge where guests may relax

before or after dining. The attractive Georgian cottage premises offer diners a warm welcome in the form of the varying lunchtime menu, with a more extensive à la carte dinner menu for evenings - or table d'hôte alternatives for either. Rack of Nidderdale Lamb is a local favourite but there is a constantly changing variety of meat and fish courses, as well as vegetarian. All dishes are freshly prepared on the premises by chef/proprietress Margaret Ninness using local produce wherever possible. A considerable selection of wines is available, from a very acceptable house wine to something for the more discerning. The Willow is also open for morning coffee and afternoon teas - tea with hot home-made scones and

The Willow Restaurant, Park Road, Pateley Bridge, Harrogate, North Yorkshire HG3 5JS
Tel: 01423 711689

cream is a favourite! The Willow is open every day from spring to autumn inclusive but closes on Mondays during the winter. If you plan to stay a night or two in still unspoilt Nidderdale, Margaret can offer bed and breakfast with an en suite double room and attached sitting-room above the restaurant.

A few minutes walk from the town centre, **Greengarth** is a large detached bungalow standing in its own grounds, the home of Joan Ravilious who has been welcoming bed and breakfast guests here since 1994. Joan assures her visitors a warm welcome, excellent food and a pleasant, comfortable stay. All the bedrooms in this no-smoking house are on the ground floor, with easy access for wheelchairs. Two of them are en suite and all bedrooms have central heating, washbasins, shaver points, radio/alarm clocks and tea/coffee making facilities. Children over 3 years old are welcome. Joan provides her guests with a good choice at breakfast time, with

Greengarth, Greenwood Road, Pateley Bridge,
North Yorkshire HG3 5LR Tel: 01423 711688

vegetarian options also available. Located in the heart of this Area of Outstanding Natural Beauty, Greengarth is an ideal centre for walking, touring the Yorkshire Dales, or just for enjoying a relaxing break in lovely surroundings. The spectacular North Yorkshire scenery stretches for miles to the north and west, and when you're ready for some urban amusements, Harrogate lies just 14 miles to the east.

RAMSGILL

MAP 2 REF E6

5 miles NW of Pateley Bridge off the B6265

This pleasant village, clustered around its well kept green, was the birthplace of Eugene Aram in 1704. The son of a gardener at Newby Hall, Aram was arrested in 1758 in Kings Lynn for the murder of Daniel Clark in Knaresborough 13 years before. The trial took place in York and Aram caused a stir by conducting his own defence. However, he was convicted and later executed before his body was taken to Knaresborough where it was hung from a gibbet. The gruesome story has been the centre of many tales and songs including a very romantic version by Sir Bulwer Lytton.

Ramsgill is situated at the head of **Gouthwaite Reservoir**, built in the early 20th century by Bradford Corporation to satisfy the demand from the rapidly expanding town. Gouthwaite, along with the other two reservoirs in the Dale (Scar House and Angram), is now a popular and important site for wildfowl.

LOFTHOUSE

MAP 2 REF E6

7 miles NW of Pateley Bridge off the B6265

This is a small dales' village lying in the upper valley of the River Nidd and, unlike neighbouring Wharfedale, the stone walls and rocky outcrops are of millstone grit though the valley bottom consists of limestone. As a result, only in excessive weather is there water under the bridge here as, in normal conditions, the river drops down two sumps:

Manchester Hole and Goydon Pot. The monks of Fountains Abbey certainly had a grange here but it is also probable that the village was first settled by Norsemen.

Nearby **How Stean Gorge**, in the heart of Nidderdale, is often called Yorkshire's Little Switzerland and for good reason. This spectacular limestone gorge, which is up to 80 feet deep in places, through which the Stean Beck flows is a popular tourist attraction though little known outside the area. A narrow path with footbridges guide the visitor along the gorge where the waters rush over the large boulders below. However, there are also many sheltered areas of calm water where fish hide under the rocks. As well as taking a stroll up this fascinating path, visitors can also step inside Tom Taylor's Cave and, along the walk, marvel at the wide variety of plant life that grows in this steep ravine.

MIDDLESMOOR
Map 2 ref E6

8 miles NW of Pateley Bridge off the B6265

This tucked away village of stone built cottages and houses lies at the head of Upper Nidderdale and is reached by a single, winding road. The existence of ancient settlers can be seen in the present 19th century Church of St Chad where an early 10th or 11th century preaching cross, bearing the inscription *"Cross of St Ceadda"* can be seen.

BEWERLEY
Map 2 ref F6

1 mile SW of Pateley Bridge on the B6265

Recorded as *Bevrelie* (a clearing inhabited by badgers) in the Domesday Book, this is Nidderdale's oldest settlement. It was also the site of the earliest and most important of

Fountains Abbey's many granges and not only were they farming here but lead was being extracted from the nearby moor. The recently restored Chapel, built here by one of the last abbots, Marmaduke Huby, acted for many years as the village school.

In the 17th century the Yorke family moved to the embellished hall at Bewerley following their purchase of the former lands of Byland Abbey in Nidderdale. During the subsequent years, the family laid out the parkland as well as rebuilding some of the village and, though the estate was sold in the 1920s and the hall demolished, the park remains and plays host to the annual Nidderdale Show. The name of the village's most influential family, however, is not lost to the village as Yorke's Folly, two

Bewerley Chapel

stone stoops, still stand on the hillside overlooking Bewerley.

WILSILL   MAP 2 REF F7
1 mile E of Pateley Bridge on the B6165

A traditional Dales building of local honey-coloured stone, **The Birch Tree Inn** enjoys
outstanding panoramic views over Nidderdale. Dating back to the late 1700s, when it
began life as a sim-
ple alehouse, this
friendly country inn
with its real fires and
exposed stone walls
is well known lo-
cally for its quality
home made food
and well kept ales
which include real
ales such as Black
Sheep   and
Theakstons Best.
The inn used to be
Dennis   and
Christine Bell's local
until they bought it
in 1998 and quickly

**The Birch Tree Inn, Wilsill, Pateley Bridge, Harrogate,
North Yorkshire HG3 5EA Tel: 01423 711131**

established an excellent reputation. The inn's head cook, Anne Carrington, is renowned
for her old fashioned, traditional British recipes, regularly featuring dishes such as
Huntingdon Fidget Pie, Dorset Jugged Steak, Cumberland Tatie Pot, Glamorgan Sausages
and, naturally, Yorkshire Fishcakes. For
lighter appetites, snacks and hot or cold
sandwiches are also available. Food is
served daily from noon until 2pm, and
from 6.30pm until 9pm, (7pm to 9pm on
Sunday).

About 2 miles east of Wilsill are
Brimham Rocks (National Trust), an extraordinary natural sculpture park.
Formed into fantastic shapes by years of
erosion, these great millstone grit boulders lie atop a steep hill amidst some 400
acres of heathland. Some of the shapes
really do resemble their names - the 'Dancing Bear' in particular, but perhaps the
most awe-inspiring is 'Idol Rock', a huge
boulder weighing several tons which rests
on a base just a foot in diameter. The
National Trust has provided large scale
maps showing suggested itineraries and
the positions and names of the major formations.

Brimham Rocks

FELLBECK

Map 2 ref F6

2 miles NE of Pateley Bridge on the B6265

This tiny hamlet a mile or so to the north of Brimham Rocks rarely appears on maps but it's well worth seeking out for **The Half Moon Inn** which has been a fully licensed hostelry since the late 1700s. The interior is everything you would expect of a traditional inn in the Dales, with features such as a wood-burning stove, old beams and low ceilings. The

Half Moon is very much a family business. The owners, Colin and Tracey Sidley, along with Tracey's Mum and Dad, David and Sheila Crosby, and barmaid Joan Bagshaw who has been serving here for more than 30 years, create a wonderfully welcoming atmosphere. The inn's quality real ales and good pub food (available every lunchtime and evening) have earned it an entry in the *Good Pub & Beer*

The Half Moon Inn, Fellbeck, Pateley Bridge, Harrogate, North Yorkshire HG3 5ET
Tel: 01423 711560 Fax: 01423 712548

Guide and The Half Moon's rural location, standing in open countryside with lovely panoramic views, have made it a popular base for holiday-makers. Accommodation is provided in a separate stone building next door to the inn and by the time you read this the Sidleys should also be offering 2 self-catering properties. If you enjoy an active holiday, Colin can arrange facilities for horse riding, shooting, clay pigeon shooting, fishing and even paragliding.

SUMMERBRIDGE

Map 2 ref F7

3 miles SE of Pateley Bridge on the B6165

In 1825 Summerbridge was just a small settlement with a bridge and a corn mill, but in that year New York Mill, a large flax mill, was built here and by the mid-19th century Summerbridge was flourishing with five mills in operation, a rope works, and a foundry.

It's now a peaceful this riverside village with a welcoming old inn at its heart. **Ye Olde Oak Inn** is a sturdy building of local stone, originally a group of cottages but converted into an inn back in the early 1800s. The interior is warm and inviting, decorated with lots of paintings and an interesting collection of wall plates. Mine hosts, Vicki and Bill Barker, have many years experience in the licensed trade and although they only took over here in mid-1999 they have already established the inn's reputation for good food, excellent ales and a lively atmosphere. There always seems to be something going on at Ye Olde Oak

- dominoes on Mondays and Thursdays, darts on Tuesdays, a fun quiz on Wednesdays, and live entertainment every other Friday. Vicki is an accomplished cook and her menu offers a good choice of traditional dishes along with a selection of sandwiches, snacks, a children's menu and vegetarian options. Her traditional Sunday lunch is very popular so do book ahead if you want to eat in the restaurant. Inci-

Ye Olde Oak Inn, Low Laithe, Summerbridge, Harrogate,
North Yorkshire HG3 4BD Tel: 01423 780247

dentally, Vicki makes a point of ensuring that none of the food she serves contains genetically modified ingredients.

BURNT YATES

MAP 2 REF F7

6 miles SE of Pateley Bridge on the B6165

Located at one of the highest points in the dale, Burnt Yates enjoys some fine views of the surrounding hills and moors. Its tiny village school of 1750 still stands. Its original endowment provided for 30 poor boys to be taught the three Rs and for an equivalent number of poor girls to learns the skills of needlework and spinning.

Set within a 350-acre working farm, historic **Brimham Lodge** offers a choice of either bed & breakfast or self-catering accommodation. This imposing 3-storey building dates back to 1661 and stands on land that once belonged to Fountains Abbey. Close by is the boundary of the royal hunting grounds of the Forest of Knaresborough and the village's curious name, Burnt Yates, is believed to be a contraction of "Boundary Gates". Brimham Lodge is the home of Neil and Sue Clarke - Neil's family has lived here for more than half a century. Old oak beams, mullioned windows and open fires testify to the antiquity of the house and help create a wonderful olde worlde atmosphere. There are 2

Brimham Lodge, Burnt Yates, Ripley, Harrogate,
North Yorkshire HG3 3HE Tel: 01423 771770

bedrooms for bed & breakfast guests while the self-catering apartment can accommodate up to 6 people plus babies. B&B guests will find a hearty farmhouse breakfast and although evening meals are not available, Sue can advise you on good eating places in the neighbourhood and will even make the booking for you. Brimham Lodge is open all year except over the Christmas and New Year period.

Set next to the delightful Church of St Andrew is **The Bay Horse Inn** where excellent cuisine and first class accommodation are just part of the hostelry's appeal. You'll also

find a warm family atmosphere since the owners, Tony and Linda Robinson, are ably assisted by daughter Heather and son Richard. The restaurant here serves a mixture of traditional British and French cuisine with a 4-course table d'hôte menu and an extensive à la carte menu, including vegetarian dishes, served

The Bay Horse Inn, Burnt Yates, Harrogate,
North Yorkshire HG3 3EJ Tel: 01423 770230
Fax: 01423 771894 e-mail: enquiries@bayhorseinn.co.uk

every evening from 7pm to 9.30pm. In the cosy bar with its open fire, hand-pulled traditional ales are served by friendly staff and tasty bar meals are available every lunchtime and evening. The Bay Horse has 16 guest bedrooms, all en suite, some of which are in the main building, the remainder in an attractive stone annex that overlooks the inn's peaceful beer garden. The Robinsons will be happy to arrange fishing, golf breaks, pony trekking or clay pigeon shooting for you, and if you want to bring your pet with you, accommodation for other than guide dogs can be arranged at nearby kennels.

The distinctive and gracious stonebuilt self-catering cottages offered by **Dinmore Cottages** date back to the late 17th century. Surrounded by what was a working farm up

Dinmore Cottages, Dinmore House, Burnt Yates, nr Harrogate, North Yorkshire
HG3 3ET Tel/Fax: 01423 770860 email: aib@dinmore-cottages.freeserve.co.uk

until 1972, these former farm buildings were converted to use as accommodation in 1984, and have won awards for their outstanding conversion. Set in seven acres of beautiful grounds that offer wonderful walks and opportunities for bird-watching, there is an abundance of natural wildlife in the area. The three top of the range cottages feature exposed beams, open stone fireplace or log-burning stove, and a wealth of original features. Sleeping between two and five people, they are both cosy and spacious, offering a truly peaceful and relaxing retreat. Each cottage has been individually designed and comfortably furnished, with fitted carpets and well-equipped kitchens. Each also boasts its own private grassed area or terrace. Children welcome. No pets. ETB 4 Keys Highly Commended.

HAMPSTHWAITE   MAP 2 REF F7
7 miles SE of Pateley Bridge off the A59

This picturesque Nidderdale village lies on an ancient Roman way between Ilkley and Aldborough and traces of Roman tin mining have been found in the area. The village Church of St Thomas has remnants of a Saxon building in the tower and, in the churchyard, is buried Peter Barker. Known as *"Blind Peter"*, Barker was a local character very much in the tradition of Jack Metcalfe and he did not let his disability hinder him: he was a skilled cabinet maker, glazier, and musician. The mysterious portrait of the bearded man hanging in the church, painted by the local vicar's daughter, may well be of Blind Peter.

RIPLEY   MAP 2 REF G7
8 miles SE of Pateley Bridge off the A61

In the outer walls of the parish church, built around 1400, are holes said to have been caused by musket balls from Cromwell's firing squad, who executed Royalist prisoners here after the battle of Marston Moor. Inside, there is a fine Rood Screen dating from the reign of King Stephen, a mid-14th century tomb chest, and the stone base of an old weeping cross (where one was expected to kneel in the stone grooves and weep for penance) survives in the churchyard.

Ripley, still very much an estate village, is a quiet and pretty place, with cobbled streets, a castle, a wonderful hotel, and an interesting history. The title was granted to Thomas Ingilby in the 1300s for killing a wild boar in Knaresborough Forest that was charging at King Edward III. Visitors strolling around Ripley cannot fail to notice the Hotel de Ville - the Town Hall. Sir William Amcotts Ingilby was responsible for this when, in 1827, he began to remodel the entire village on one which he had seen in Alsace Lorraine. The original thatched cottages were replaced with those seen today and now Ripley is a conservation area with every pre-1980 dwelling being a Grade II listed building.

Magnificent **Ripley Castle** has been home to the Ingilby family for over 600 years. The castle is open to the public and is set in an outstanding 'Capability' Brown landscape, with lakes, a deer park, and an avenue of tall beeches over which the attractive towers only just seem to peek. Its tranquillity belies the events that took place here after the battle at Marston Moor, when Cromwell, exhausted after his day's slaughter, camped his Roundheads here and chose to rest in the castle.

The Ingilbys, however, were Royalist and his intrusion was met with as much ill-will as possible; they offered neither food nor a bed. Jane Ingilby, aptly named *"Trooper Jane"* due to her fighting skills, was the house's occupant and, having forced the self-styled Lord Protector of England to sleep on a sofa with two pistols pointing at his head, declared the next morning, *"It was well that he behaved in so peaceable a manner; had it been otherwise, he would not have left the house alive."* Cromwell, his pride severely damaged by a woman ordered the immediate execution of his Royalist prisoners and left Trooper Jane regretting staying her hand during the previous night.

WHARFEDALE

The valley of the River Wharfe, **Wharfedale**, is the longest of the Yorkshire Dales following the river from its origins on **Cam Fell** for over 70 miles to Cawood, where it joins the River Ouse. At its source, almost 2,000 feet above sea level, the river is nothing more than a moorland stream and, even in mid-Wharfedale, it is little more than a mountain river, broad, shallow, and peat brown in colour. The Romans named a local Goddess, Verbeia, after the river and those who visit will understand why as the goddess was known for her treachery as well as her beauty. Wharfedale is one of the most spectacular and most varied of the Yorkshire dales, and no one who sees the river charging through the narrow gorge at The Strid, near Bolton Abbey, will deny that the power of the river is to be respected.

For many years, Wharfedale has been the place to which those working in the grim industrial towns of Yorkshire came to for clean air and solitude. Today, it is probably the most popular of all Yorkshire's dales and there is certainly a lot on offer to those who visit here. The chief towns of the dale are little more than villages and they have retained much of their charm despite the various invasions of industry and tourism. Perhaps, this is because they were first invaded some 10,000 years ago by the hunter-gatherers of the mesolithic age.

There is much to see in Wharfedale and, in keeping with much of the Yorkshire Dales National Park, there is a variety of landscape to discover. From the high moorland and fell to the deep, eroded limestone gorges the landscape varies almost, it seems, with every turn of the River Wharfe. This section of Wharfedale has, over the years, inspired many of Britain's poets, writers, and painters. Both Coleridge and Wordsworth were taken with its beauty and, in the case of Wordsworth, with the local stories and legends. Ruskin enthused about its contrasts and Turner painted several scenes that also capture something of the dale's history and mystery.

KETTLEWELL

Map 1 ref D6

13 miles N of Skipton on the B6160

Surrounded by the beautiful countryside of Upper Wharfedale, Kettlewell is a popular centre for tourists and walkers. At the meeting point of several old packhorse routes, which now serve as footpaths and bridleways, the village was a busy market centre and, at one time, the home of 13 public houses which catered to the needs of the crowds. The market charter, granted in the 13th century, is evidence that Kettlewell was once a more important place than it is today and the various local religious houses of Bolton Priory, Coverham Abbey, and Fountains Abbey all owned land in the area.

Today, however, Kettlewell is a conservation area, a charming place of chiefly 17th and 18th century houses and cottages. Its original 13th century waterfall, later converted into a textile mill, has gone though evidence of a local lead mining industry remains. The late 19th century **Church of St Mary** attracts many visitors to its attractive churchyard and lychgate built on the site of a 12th century building.

Just a few steps across the road from St Mary's Church, **The Kings Head Inn** offers top class food, drink and accommodation. The building dates back some 300 years and at one time served as the area's workhouse. There's no sign of those grim days now in the warm and welcoming bar with its open fire, stone walls and flag-stone floors. Paul and Sheila Revel are the owners of this popular Free House where the quality ales include Tetley's and Black Sheep, supplemented by a guest ale. Paul is the chef, offering qual-ity meals at lunchtime and in the evening, daily throughout the season. (The kitchen is closed on Tuesday and Wednesday lunchtime during November, January and February).

The Kings Head Inn, The Green, Kettlewell,
North Yorkshire BD23 5RD Tel: 01756 760242

If you are planning to stay in the area, The Kings Head has 5 guest rooms, (2 doubles, 2 twins and 1 family), all of them offering value for money accommodation. Located in the heart of Wharfedale, The Kings Head provides an excellent base for exploring this spectacularly scenic region of Yorkshire, and is also close to Coverall and Wensleydale.

STARBOTTON
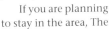
MAP 1 REF D6

2 miles N of Kettlewell on the B6160

This quiet little Wharfedale village was the scene in 1686 of a disastrous flood when a huge head of water descended from the surrounding fells and swept away many of the houses and cottages. The damage was such that a national appeal was started and aid, in the form of money, was sent from as far afield as Cambridgeshire.

BUCKDEN
MAP 1 REF D6

4 miles N of Kettlewell on the B6160

Marking the beginning of Wharfedale proper, Buckden is the first full sized village of the dale and proudly boasts that it is also home to Wharfedale's first shop. Unusually for this area, the village was not settled by the Anglo-Saxons but, later, by the Normans and it was the headquarters of the officers hunting in the forest of Langstrothdale. As the forest was cleared to make way for agriculture, Buckden became an important market town serving a large part of the surrounding area. Wool was one of the important sources of income for the dalesfolk and the local inn here still has some of the old weighing equipment from the days when the trade was conducted on the premises.

Designated in Norman times as one of the feudal hunting forests, **Langstrothdale Chase** was governed by the strict forest laws. Just to the south of the village, which lies on the edge of the Chase, can be seen an old stone cross which was used to mark the forest boundary. Buckden's name means the "valley of the bucks" but its last deer was hunted and killed here in the 17ᵗʰ century.

HUBBERHOLME
MAP 1 REF D6
5 miles N of Kettlewell off the B6160

This small village was originally two places: Hubberholme proper and Kirkgill, which takes its name from the nearby Church of St Michael and All Angels that was, at one time, a forest chapel. Each year, on New Year's Day, the villagers gather at the local pub for the **Hubberholme Parliament**. For that night, the public bar becomes the House of Commons, where the farmers congregate, whilst the room where the vicar and churchwardens meet is the House of Lords. Bidding then takes place between the farmers for the rent of a field behind the church and, encouraged by the vicar, the highest bidder gains the lease for the coming year.

YOCKENTHWAITE
MAP 1 REF D5
6 miles NW of Kettlewell off the B6160

The unusual name of this small village is Viking in origin and, though once a prosperous place, Yockenthwaite is now a collection of old stone farms. On the surrounding fells lies a well-preserved Bronze Age stone circle and **Giant's Grave**, the remains of an Iron Age settlement.

LITTON
MAP 1 REF D6
5 miles NW of Kettlewell off the B6160

This pretty village lends it name to the dale, **Littondale**, which is actually the valley of the River Skirfare. Once part of a Norman hunting forest, the dale was originally called

Litton Village

Amerdale (meaning deep fork) and this ancient name is preserved in Amerdale Dub, where the River Skirfare joins the River Wharfe near Kilnsey.

Outstanding self-catering cottages can be found at **Stonelands Farmyard**. Found amidst panoramic and scenic countryside in Littondale on the outskirts of Litton, the properties and location are certainly a cut above the rest. Converted from old farm buildings and opened back in 1993, some of the buildings date back to the 18th century, and feature comfortable furnishings and decor. There are 10 cottages in all, ranging from the luxurious one-bedroom units to the three cottages eminently suitable for families

Stonelands Farmyard Cottages, Litton, Skipton, North Yorkshire BD23 5QH Tel: 01756 770293 Fax: 01756 770321 website: www.stonelands.co.uk

and the three "suites" in the main farmhouse. Each facility is spacious and welcoming, sleeping from two people up to six. Most boast four-poster beds and all have spa baths. Other superb amenities include the indoor heated swimming pool, sauna, video library and laundry room. A home-cooked "welcome meal" greets new guests on their arrival. This family-run business is owned by the Cowan family: Tom and Brenda, together with their sons Mark and Roger, Mark's wife Ruth and Roger's wife Mandy. Mark is a qualified chef who prepares the mouth-watering "welcome meal" as well as offering an extensive a la carte menu on subsequent evenings, all delivered to guests' cottages. Weekly, weekend and mid-week breaks available.

ARNCLIFFE
MAP 1 REF D6

3 miles W of Kettlewell off the B6160

Situated in Littondale, the village name dates back to Saxon times when the valley was referred to as Amerdale. This is a quiet, tranquil dale and life has remained the same here for many years in this small village. Many of the buildings around the central village green are listed and, in its early years, the long running television series *Emmerdale* was filmed here.

Near the village bridge, over the River Skirfare, stands a house, **Bridge End**, that was once the home of the Hammond family. Whilst staying with the Hammonds, author Charles Kingsley was so taken with the village and Littondale that he incorporated the house and his hostess in his famous work *The Water Babies*.

KILNSEY
MAP 1 REF D6

3 miles S of Kettlewell on the B6160

This small hamlet, on the opposite bank of the River Wharfe from Conistone, is a great place from which many anglers fly fish and the Kilnsey Angling Club has its home in the village pub. This quiet and peaceful place has been overlooked by the now uninhabited Old Hall which was originally built as a grange for the monks of Fountains Abbey.

Set in six acres of beautiful Yorkshire countryside, overlooked by the renowned Kilnsey Crag, **Kilnsey Park and Trout Farm** offers a variety of leisure activities and facilities for all the family.

The restaurant/coffee shop overlooks the two trout lakes and Kilnsey Crag, and is recommended far and wide for the quality of its food. Open every day from 9-5.30 (later in summer), it is very cosy and

**Kilnsey Park and Trout Farm, Kilnsey, North Yorkshire
BD23 5PS Tel: 01756 752150 Fax: 01756 752224**

the hospitality offered warm and genuine. The menu features a fine range of hearty and delicious meals and snacks; there are also tempting daily specials. Many naturally feature trout, and visitors can partake in some fly fishing on one of the two wonderful trout

Kilnsey Crag

lakes. While the grown-ups enjoy their meal the children can either go for some supervised "fun fishing", have a go with a radio-controlled boat, play in the adventure playground or see how the trout are reared. Then the whole family can enjoy the aquarium or see the endangered Red Squirrels being bred here. Next to the restaurant is the marvellous deli - with lots of fresh trout, cheeses, preserves and more locally produce are for sale. This superb centre, designated a Site of Scientific Interest, also offers visitors a glimpse of rare orchids and features a specialist herb and alpine centre, a conservation centre and a fascinating nature trail.

The striking outline of **Kilnsey Crag** is unmistakable as one side of this limestone hill was gouged out by a passing glacier during the Ice Age. One of the most spectacular natural features in the dales, the crag has a huge 'lip' or overhang which presents an irresistible challenge to adventurous climbers.

CONISTONE
MAP 1 REF D6
4 miles S of Kettlewell off the B6160

This ancient settlement, whose name suggests that it once belonged to a king, is clustered around its maypole and village green. The village Church of St Mary is thought to have been founded in Saxon times and there are certainly two well-preserved Norman arches to be seen. The land surrounding Conistone is unusually flat and it was once the bottom of a lake formed by the melt water from the glacier that carved out Kilnsey Crag.

GRASSINGTON
MAP 1 REF E7
8 miles N of Skipton on the B6265

One of the best loved villages within the Yorkshire Dales National Park, Grassington in many ways typifies the Dales' settlement with its characteristic market square. Known as the capital of Upper Wharfedale, the historically important valley roads meet here and the ancient monastic route from Malham to Fountains Abbey passes through the village.

Dating back to the 1600s, **The Foresters Arms** was formerly a coaching inn and that long tradition of hospitality, spanning more than 3 centuries, is maintained today by mine hosts Rita and Phil. The Foresters offers a warm and friendly atmosphere where you'll find traditional ales and home cooked food available at both lunchtime and in the evening. The lunchtime menu ranges from home made sandwiches to a hearty 16oz grilled ham, while the extensive evening menu offers a good choice of steak, fish and poultry dishes along with a vegetarian dish of the day. Meals are served in the attractive dining room with its open fire and olde-worlde appearance where, next morning, overnight guests are served a full English breakfast. The Foresters Arms has 7 guest bed-rooms, all of them en

**The Foresters Arms, 20 Main Street, Grassington,
nr Skipton, North Yorkshire BD23 5AA
Tel: 01756 752349 Fax: 01756 753633**

suite and equipped with colour TV and tea/coffee-making facilities. Children and pets are both welcome. If you happen to be staying at The Foresters on a Monday night, do take part in the fun quiz which has some worthwhile prizes for the winners!

Occupying a lovely position overlooking the River Wharfe and ancient woodland protected by the Woodland Trust, **Greenways House** is the home of Stephen and Julia Oxby who have been welcoming bed & breakfast guests here since 1995. Their magnificent Edwardian house was originally Grassington Girls School, which explains its grand scale and spacious rooms. The charming guest sitting room has panoramic views along

Greenways House, Wharfeside Avenue, Grassington, North Yorkshire BD23 5BS Tel: 01756 752598

the Wharfe valley, vistas which can also be enjoyed from the extensive grounds where, in summer, guests can enjoy a quietly lethal game of croquet. Greenways House has 3 quality guest rooms, (2 doubles, 1 twin), all of them attractively decorated and en suite, with one of them, the Garden Room, furnished with a 4-poster bed. Breakfast here is definitely something to look forward to, with an extensive choice and provision for special diets if required. Evening meals are not available but there are many excellent eating places in this area of outstanding natural beauty.

Grassington's origins are rooted in ancient history; there was certainly a Bronze Age settlement here, the remains of an Iron Age village have been found, a Celtic field system lies on nearby **Lea Green**, and the village was mentioned in the Domesday Book. However, the settlement seen today is Anglian and, having passed through various families, is now part of the estate of the Dukes of Devonshire. With its narrow streets lined with attractive Georgian buildings, Grassington is a delightful place to wander around.

Housed in two 18th century lead miners' cottages, in Grassington Square, is the **Upper Wharfedale Folk Museum**. Containing many exhibits and displays relating to the lives of those who have lived in the dale, the museum is open (afternoons only) at the weekend during the winter and daily throughout the summer. Throughout the year, there were many festivals and holidays observed by the dales people and one, the **Feast Sports**, still takes place here on a Saturday in October. Among the many traditional events which are carried out there is the tea cake eating race, where children have to eat a tea cake, and race to the other end of the field. The winner is the first child to whistle a tune.

THRESHFIELD

MAP 1 REF D7

1 mile W of Grassington on the B6160

Across the river from Grassington, Threshfield has at its heart a small village green called the Park, complete with the original village stocks and surrounded by charming 17th century houses. Perhaps the most striking building is the Free Grammar School built in 1674. According to local people its porch is haunted by a fairy known as Old Pam the Fiddler. Threshfield was once famed for the production of besoms, (birch brooms) but the last family to make them, the Ibbotsons, died out in the 1920s.

Originally a farmhouse and built in the traditional style using local limestone, **Long Ashes Inn** is full of charm and character. The emphasis here is on wholesome traditional food, home made by the Inn's chef using the best of local produce. There's a wide choice and the menus are changed daily for both lunch and evening meals. The extensive wine list is modestly priced and the bar features a selection of hand-pulled ales including Theakston's and Black Sheep, all kept in the time-honoured way.

Long Ashes Inn, Long Ashes Park, Threshfield, Skipton, North Yorkshire BD23 5PN Tel: 01756 752434 Fax: 01756 752937 e-mail: info@longashesinn.co.uk website: www.longashesinn.co.uk

The inn also serves morning coffee and, in the summer, afternoon tea. There are 5 attractive and comfortable en suite bedrooms, elegantly furnished in pine, one of them boasting a 4-poster bed. Each room has colour television, direct dial telephone, hairdryer, trouser press, tea/coffee-making facilities - and fresh flowers. Children are most welcome, with a cot available if required, and well-behaved dogs are also accepted by arrangement but guests are asked to bring food and bedding for their pets. Overnight guests have free use of the adjacent leisure centre with its heated indoor pool, squash court, jacuzzi, steam room and sauna, and for over-16s the fitness room.

LINTON

MAP 1 REF D7

1 mile SW of Grassington off the B6160

This delightful and unspoilt village, that is more correctly called Linton-in-Craven, has grown up around its village green through which runs a small beck. This flat area of land was once a lake and around its edge was grown flax which the villagers spun into linen. The village is also the home of the **Church of St Michael and All Angels**, a wonderful building that is a fine example of rural medieval architecture. Probably built on the site of a pagan shrine the church lies some way from the village centre though its handsome bell-cote is a suitable landmark. Among the 14th century roof bosses can be seen the Green Man, an ancient fertility symbol of a man's head protruding through foliage, which was adopted by the Christian church. Spanning Linton beck is a graceful 14th century packhorse bridge that was repaired by Dame Elizabeth Redmayne in the late 17th century. During the repair work, Dame Elizabeth had a narrow parapet added to the bridge to prevent carts from crossing because, so it is said, the local farmers refused to contribute to the cost of the repairs.

CRACOE

MAP 1 REF D7

3 miles SW of Grassington on the B6265

The village contains several 17th century houses that are typical examples of the building style of the day. Constructed from stone quarried on nearby Cracoe and Rylstone Fell, the cavity between the 3 foot thick walls was filled with rubble. Above the village, on top of the fell, is a cairn built in memory of local men who died in World War I. Construction of the cairn began in the early 1920s but the professional masons experienced great difficulty as high winds tore down their work over night. Eventually, a local man was hired for the task and, instead of coming down from the fell each night, he pitched his tent close to the cairn and remained on-site until it was completed.

THORPE
MAP 1 REF E7
2 miles SE of Grassington off the B6160

This small hamlet, the full name of which is Thorpe-sub-Montem (meaning 'below the hill'), lies in a secluded hollow between drumlins - long low alluvial mounds. As well as taking advantage of its hidden position, ideal for secreting valuables and family members here during Scots raids, the village was also known for its cobblers. Their fame was such that the monks of Fountains Abbey were among their regular customers. However, the influence of the monks did not prevent the high spirited cobblers from stealing nearby Burnsall's maypole and planting it on their own village green. The maypole did, eventually, return to its home village but not until the villagers of Burnsall had organised a rescue party.

HEBDEN
MAP 1 REF E7
3 miles E of Grassington on the B6265

From this quiet hamlet it is only a short distance to the wonderful 500,000 year old cave at **Stump Cross Caverns**. The large show cave holds a fantastic collection of stalactites and stalagmites which make it one of the most visited underground attractions in the area. During excavations, the remains of animals were found here and they can be seen on display at the visitor centre where there is also a gift shop and a tea room.

BURNSALL
MAP 1 REF E7
2 miles S of Grassington on the B6160

The village is very dramatically situated on a bend in the River Wharfe with the slopes of Burnsall Fell as a backdrop. Of ancient origins it is thought that, prior to the 8th century, Wilfrid Bishop of York, founded a wooden church, on the site of which now stands the village's 12th-century church. The only remains of Wilfrid's building is the font which can still be seen at the back of **St Wilfrid's Church**. The churchyard is entered via a unique lychgate and here can be seen two hogback tombstones and various other fragments which date back to the times of the Anglo-Saxons and the Danes.

However, it is not this sturdy Dales' church which draws visitors to Burnsall but its bridge. Today, this typical Dales' bridge of 5 stone arches is the start of the annual **Classic Fell Race** which takes place on a Saturday towards the end of August. Over the years, the flood waters of the River Wharfe have washed away the arches on several occasions but the villagers have always replaced them as this is the only crossing point for 3 miles in each direction.

For a good idea of what to expect from a stay at **The Devonshire Fell** in Burnsall just send for their brochure which contains photographs of every one of the 12 en suite guest rooms, each one with its own distinctive decor and comprehensively equipped. This outstanding hotel was purchased early in 1999 by the Duke and Duchess of Devonshire's estate and six months were spent refurbishing and modernising the impressive 19th century building to the standards of a modern London hotel. As you might expect, the cuisine at The Devonshire Fell is definitely something special. Created by Head Chef Michael Ward, the menu offers a versatile selection of dishes prepared from the

The Devonshire Fell, Burnsall, Skipton, North Yorkshire BD23 6BT Tel: 01756 729000 Fax: 01756 729009

finest ingredients along with a daily selection of market fresh fish, crustacea and game listed on the blackboard. For simplicity, all courses are one set price and whatever your choice you'll find a good selection of reasonably priced wines, available by the bottle, small glass or large glass, to accompany it. Overnight guests also receive complimentary membership of the Devonshire Health, Beauty and Fitness Club at nearby Bolton Abbey.

APPLETREEWICK
MAP 1 REF E7

4 miles SE of Grassington off the B6160

This peaceful village, which is known locally as Aptrick, lies between the banks of the River Wharfe and the bleak moorland and is overlooked by the craggy expanse of **Simon's Seat**, one of Wharfedale's best loved hilltops. Dating back to monastic times, lead has been mined on the surrounding moorland for many centuries and the northern slopes were the property of the monks of nearby Bolton Priory. The village was also the home of William Craven, a Lord Mayor of London, who returned to spend much of his amassed wealth on improvements and additions to Appletreewick's fine old buildings. The cottage where he was born was largely furnished by the similarly legendary Robert Thompson of Kilburn. Known as the Dick Whittington of the Dale, William Craven was born in 1548 and he moved to London when he became apprenticed to a mercer (a dealer in textiles and fine fabrics).

Just to the north of Appletreewick lie **Parcevall Hall Gardens**, a wonderful woodland garden which includes many varieties of unusual plants and shrubs. Though the 16 acre gardens are high above sea level, (which provides the visitor with splendid views), many of the plants still flourish in these beautiful surroundings. The gardens, which are open between Easter and October, have a special quality of peace and tranquillity - appropriately enough since the lovely old Hall is now a Bradford Diocesan Retreat and Conference Centre. The nearby gorge of **Trollers Gill** is said to be haunted by a fearsome ghost dog, with huge eyes and a shaggy coat, that drags a clanking chain. A local story, recorded in 1881, tells how a man, somewhat foolishly, went to the gorge in the middle of the night. He failed to return and his body, on which there were marks not made by human hand, was later found by shepherds. A little further down river is the stately ruin of **Barden Tower**, a former residence of Lord Henry Clifford, owner of Skipton Castle. It was built in the 15th century but allowed to fall into decay and, despite repair in 1657, it is once more a ruin. Nearby is the attractive **Barden Bridg**e, a 17th century arch now designated as an ancient monument.

STORITHS
MAP 1 REF E7
8 miles SE of Grassington off the A59 or B6160

Just across the river from Bolton Abbey, but tucked away as the address suggests "at back o' th'hill", **Buffers Coffee Shop** is a hidden gem that really must be tracked down. There are at least two very good reasons for seeking it out. The first is the tea room itself, housed in an early 17th century byre converted by Keith and Pamela Blackburn and their son

Howard, who also farm the surrounding land. The menu offers a good choice of snacks, sandwiches, salads and light meals, all freshly prepared to order by Pamela who also bakes the home made cakes and biscuits. The coffee shop's name provides a clue to the other major attraction here: - an extraordinary working model railway and what must be one of the most comprehensive collections of model locomotives, rolling stock

Buffers Coffee Shop, Back o' th'Hill Farm, Storiths, Bolton Abbey, North Yorkshire BD23 6HU Tel: 01756 710253

and railway paraphernalia in the country. What began as a childhood hobby for Keith has grown into this fascinating display. Keith is also a stockist of all Hornby and Bachmann model railway equipment: - if he doesn't have what you want in stock, then neither has Hornby! Also on display is another huge collection of Britain's agricultural toys and models. Not to be missed.

BOLTON ABBEY
MAP 1 REF E7
8 miles SE of Grassington on the B6160

The village is actually a collection of small hamlets which have all been part of the estate of the Dukes of Devonshire since 1748. Bolton Abbey itself lies on the banks of the River Wharfe whilst the hamlets of Storiths, Hazelwood, Deerstones, and Halton East lie higher up.

The main attraction in the village is the substantial ruin of **Bolton Priory**, an Augustinian house that was founded in 1155 by monks from Embsay. In an idyllic situation on the banks of the River Wharfe, the ruins are well preserved whilst the nave of the priory church, first built in 1220, is now incorporated into the parish church.

After the Dissolution of the Monasteries the priory was sold to the 2nd Earl of Cumberland, Henry Clifford and it has since passed into the hands of the Dukes of Dev-

Bolton Abbey

onshire, the Cavendish family. The 14th century priory gatehouse, Bolton Hall, is the present duke's shooting lodge. Visitors walking to the priory ruins from the village pass through a hole in the wall which frames one of the most splendid views of the romantic ruins.

Whether you're "hiking, biking, working, shirking, fancy a quick brunch, long business lunch, office meeting or need a hundred seating", **The Cavendish Pavilion** caters for all tastes and occasions. The Cavendish began as a small tea room in the days when charabancs would bring customers down from the old station. Since then, it has been greatly extended over the years. Totally refurbished in 1993, this striking building has been owned by the Rogers family for more than half a century and is now run by Barbara Rogers and her two sons, David and Gary. There's extensive seating outside where you can enjoy a lovely view of the River Wharfe, while inside the elegantly decorated Pavilion is divided into two parts: a restaurant with waitress service, and a self service tea room. The Rogers family pride themselves on the

The Cavendish Pavilion, Bolton Abbey, Skipton, North Yorkshire, BD23 6AN Tel: 01756 710245 Fax: 01756 710684

quality of the food they serve and the standard of service they provide. Not surprisingly, The Cavendish enjoys an excellent reputation for its fine food and warm hospitality. The Pavilion is located about a mile north of Bolton Priory, on a minor road off the B6160, and is open daily throughout the season: the café from 10am until 6pm; the restaurant from 12 noon until 5pm. From November to February, the café and restaurant are only open at weekends, Christmas and during school holidays.

The Strid

In and around this beautiful village there are some 75 miles of footpaths and nature trails, skirting the riverbanks and climbing up onto the high moorland. Upstream from the Priory however lies one of the most visited natural features in Wharfedale, a point where the wide river suddenly narrows into a confined channel of black rock through which the water thunders. This spectacular gorge is known as **The Strid** because, over the centuries, many heroic (or foolhardy) types have attempted to leap across it as a test of bravery.

ADDINGHAM

5 miles E of Skipton off the A65

MAP 6 REF E8

Although Addingham dates back to Saxon times, (it was named after a Saxon chieftain, Adda), the village enjoyed its greatest prosperity in the 18th century when no fewer than 5 water mills lined the banks of the Wharfe. Four of them were textile mills and no longer operate, but the fifth, a timber mill, is still working.

Housed in a later, splendidly-proportioned Victorian mill **Manor Barn Fine Furniture** offers a magnificent range of meticulously crafted oak and pine furniture, pieces which would add style and distinction to any home. The 'Jacobus' collection of solid oak furniture is based on beautiful, classic 17th century styles which combine good looks with comfort and practicability. Constructed and finished by hand, using selected and well-seasoned timber,

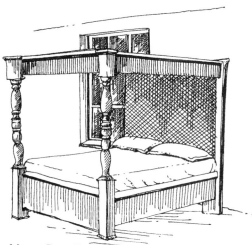

Manor Barn Fine Furniture, Burnside Mill,
Main Street, Addingham, nr Ilkley LS29 0PJ
Tel: 01943 830176 Fax: 01943 830991
e-mail: manorbarn@addingham40.freeserve.co.uk
web site: www.manorbarn.com

each individual piece is hand made and therefore unique. Equally attractive is the 'Country Pine' range of carefully co-ordinated reproductions reflecting many of the best features of country craftsmen over the past 150 years. In addition to these collections, Manor Barn also stocks a very large range of antique and original furniture, including an interesting selection of Georgian, Victorian and Edwardian furniture constructed in oak, mahogany, walnut, satin and other hardwoods. Shoppers at Manor Barn have the additional benefit of being able to talk to the people who actually make these fine pieces and who genuinely care about them.

Built of mellow local stone, **The Swan** inn is some 200 years old and boasts many attractive features - a lovely, old-fashioned snug, flagstone and wooden floors, and a real fire housed in a traditional Yorkshire range. Mine hosts at The Swan are Dick and Julia Barrow who have lived in the village since 1985. For many years The Swan was their local but in 1997 they were able to take it over and have made it well-known for its quality ales and delicious home made food. The menu might include a pheasant casserole or a hearty wholesome stew but there are plenty of other choices too. Food is available every lunchtime and evening, except Sundays, noon until 2pm, and 5pm until

The Swan, 106 Main Street, Addingham LS29 0NS
Tel: 01943 830375

8pm (6pm to 9pm Friday and Saturday). Ales on offer include Tetley's, Abbots and Ruddles plus a guest ale. Children are welcome if eating. Devotees of pub quizzes should make a date at The Swan for Wednesday evening and the pub also hosts occasional fund raising events for charity.

ILKLEY
8 miles SE of Skipton on the A65

MAP 6 REF E8

Originally an Iron Age settlement, Ilkley was eventually occupied by the Romans who built a camp here to protect their crossing of the River Wharfe. They named their town *Olicana*, so giving rise to the present name with the addition of the familiar *ley* (Anglo-Saxon for pasture). Behind the medieval church is a grassy mound where a little fort was built and in the town's Museum are altars carved in gritstone, dedicated to the Roman gods. The spring at **White Wells** brought more visitors to the town in the 18th century. A small bath house was built where genteel and elderly patients were encouraged to take a dip in the healing waters of the heather spa. Early Victorian times saw the development of the Hydros - hydropathic treatment hotels - providing hot and cold treatments based on the idea of Dr Preissnitz of Austria who, in 1843, became the director of Britain's first Hydro at nearby Ben Rhydding. The coming of the railways from Leeds and Bradford in the 1860s and 70s, during a period of growth in the Yorkshire woollen industry, saw the town take on a new rôle as a fashionable commuter town. Wool manufacturers and their better-paid employees came, not only to enjoy the superb amenities, but to build handsome villas. If Bradford and Leeds were where people made their brass, so it was said at the time, then it was usually at Ilkley that it was spent. Even today, Ilkley sports some remarkable and opulent Victorian architecture as proof of this. Ilkley's patrons and well-to-do citizens gave the town a splendid Town Hall, Library, Winter Gardens and King's Hall and a sense of elegance is still present along The Grove. It is still a delight to have morning coffee in the famous Betty's coffee house and discerning shoppers will find a wealth of choice, some in a perfectly preserved Victorian arcade complete with beautiful potted palms and balconies.

Anyone over 50 will find childhood memories of their local sweet shop come flooding back when they visit **The Candy Box** in The Grove Promenade. Whatever age you are, you'll find your mouth watering when you see the incredible array of sweet things on

display here. There are more than 50 different kinds of loose chocolates, most of them made in Belgium or at Whittakers in Skipton; boxes of Belgian chocolates, fudge and liqueur chocolates; and a marvellous selection of old-fashioned sweets such as dolly mixture, bulls' eyes, fruit drops and liquorice strings, all stored in the traditional screw-top jars. If you have a wedding in the offing, you should know that the shop will make up almond Bridal Favours and wedding keepsakes to order. The Candy Box is open 9.30am to 5.30pm, Monday to Saturday, and 1pm to 5pm on Sunday. Bob Alcantarilla, who owns this sweet-lover's paradise, also runs an old-fashioned tobacconist's

The Candy Box, 15 The Grove Promenade, Ilkley, West Yorkshire LS29 8AF
Tel: 01943 608705 Fax: 01943 690705

shop in Bow Street, Keighley, where loose tobacco is still sold and the persecuted fraternity of smokers will find all their favourite brands, however obscure, and receive knowledgeable advice - and moral support!

Also in The Grove Promenade and one of the gems of the town is **Browns Wine Bar & Restaurant** which is housed in a rather imposing Victorian house with an elegant conservatory and white-painted frontage. It takes its name from Chris and Pam Brown who bought the restaurant in 1995 and have made it a popular venue, well-known for its quality food and wines and the relaxed atmosphere. One of the specialities of the house is its tapas menu which offers a wide choice of generous snacks such as Assorted Seafood Dim Sum with Plum Sauce and Chorizo Sausage cooked with onions and red wine, all at remarkably modest prices. There's also a good selection of lunchtime 'bites' and an extensive evening menu with a Mediterranean flavour which changes every 6 weeks or so. Both menus include fish fresh from the market. Early diners benefit from a substantial discount, children are welcome and non-smokers have their own designated areas. Except for Sunday and Monday lunchtime, Browns is open every lunchtime from noon until

Browns Wine Bar & Restaurant, 60 The Grove, Ilkley, West Yorkshire LS29 9PA Tel: 01943 816477 Fax: 01943 817853

2pm; evenings 6pm to 10pm, and booking is strongly recommended for Friday and Saturday evenings.

Another fascinating establishment in The Grove, housed in a splendid late-Victorian building, is **Sweet Indulgence** which offers both a top-quality tea room and a wonderfully old-fashioned sweet shop. The ground floor is a chocaholic's dream of heaven where Michael Beck offers confectionery from Belgium and Whittakers of Skipton, a comprehensive range of fudges, and serried ranks of bottles containing traditional toothsome favourites such as Tom Thumb Drops, Cinnamon Rock and Barley Sugar. Upstairs, Maggie Turner's charming little tea room presents customers with a wide choice of teatime treats as well as wholesome, home made dishes such as Stilton Vegetable Casserole, Cod and Parsley or Chicken and Broccoli Bake, and Courgette and Aubergine Crumble. Round off your meal with a delicious home made pudding or one of the many ice cream varieties on offer. The tea room is open 7 days a week, 10am to 4pm (Monday to Saturday); 12.30pm to 4pm (Sunday). Either the tea room or the sweet shop would be worth a special visit in themselves; together, they should certainly not be missed.

Sweet Indulgence, 8 The Grove, Ilkley LS29 9EG Tel: 01943 816927

Muffins of Ilkley, 14a Brook Street, Ilkley,
West Yorkshire LS29 6DE Tel: 01943 817505

For home cooking at its very best, visitors to Ilkley need go no further than **Muffins of Ilkley**. It is owned and personally run by Heather and David Phillips, ably assisted by their daughter, Lucinda, and since they arrived here in 1996 the family have turned Muffins into an excellent establishment with an enviable reputation. In pleasant, airy surroundings visitors can sit in comfort in either the upper or lower area and be waited on by smiling, cheerful staff. The appetising menu is complemented by a list of daily specials - a home made country vegetable quiche, perhaps, or tasty Ciabatta filled with cream cheese, smoked bacon and herbs. Famous for its scones, Muffins also has a wide range of delicious cakes from which to choose and, as it has a licence, visitors can enjoy a glass of wine with their meal. Open all day, seven days a week, this is a popular place so bookings are taken so that no one will be disappointed. A recipient of the Roy Castle Clean Air Award, Muffins is a no smoking establishment and also has good access for disabled people to its lower level.

The Midland Hotel, Station Road
Ilkley LS29 8HA Tel: 01943 607433

Standing across the road from Ilkley railway station, **The Midland Hotel** was built in the mid-1800s to service travellers on the London, Midland & Scottish Railway during the great days of steam. The building has retained many of its Victorian features - twin bay windows, stained glass panels, antique fireplaces and prints of the period. The Midland is a popular resort for lovers of real ale: John Smiths and Marston Pedigree are always available, along with regularly changing guest ales. Andrea and Christopher Hems are 'mine hosts' at the Midland, which has been run by the

Hems family since 1989, and as part of the hospitality on offer provide a good choice of wholesome, reasonably-priced food - home made Steak Pie, giant Yorkshire puddings with a variety of fillings, jacket potatoes likewise, sandwiches and additional daily specials which are chalked up on the board. Food is available every lunchtime between noon and 2pm and the bar itself is open all day, every day.

Work starts early at **Michael's of Ilkley** - around 2.30am, in fact, when the first master baker arrives to begin preparing the day's supply of bread, rolls and home made cakes for the shop's many customers and for its very own tea room. The lucky people of Ilkley have been enjoying Michael's wholesome products for many years and since Kathryn Firth took over in 1995 the bakery's reputation has if anything become even more stellar. The display area presents an appetising array of bakery products, all of which can also be enjoyed in the attractively decorated tea room. The menu here offers a good choice of light meals and snacks with something to suit everyone's taste. There's ramp access for the disabled and

Michael's of Ilkley, 45/47 Brook Street, Ilkley LS29 8AG Tel: 01943 600105

a special area for non-smokers. Michael's should definitely not to be missed by anyone who appreciates good, wholesome food. The shop, (which also sells sandwiches to take away), and the tea room are open Monday to Saturday, 8am to 4.30pm (5-ish on Saturday).

One of the most famous West Yorkshire attractions has to be **Ilkley Moor**, immortalised in the well-known song and a visit is a must. Like any of the Yorkshire moors, Ilkley Moor can look inviting and attractive on a sunny day but ominous and forbidding when the weather takes a turn for the worse. The River Wharfe runs along the edge of the moor and through the town of Ilkley which is clustered within a narrow section of the valley in the midst of heather moorland, craggy gritstone and

Ilkley Moor

wooded hillside. Few places in the north can equal Ilkley Moor or, more correctly, Rombalds Moor. The moorland, much of it still covered in heather, is also an area of national importance for its archaeology. There is a series of mysteriously marked cup and ring stones dating from the Bronze Age. Almost in the centre of the moor is an ancient stone circle, no doubt a site of some religious importance. Only the keen walker is likely to find these, located high up on the moor, but there is a fine example of a cup and ring stone in the lower part of St Margaret's churchyard in Queen's Road.

Looking at a map of the area, many people's attention is drawn to the curiously named **Cow and Calf Rocks** which form a striking moor-edge landmark above Ben Rhydding. The Cow is a great gritstone outcrop concealing an old quarry, popular with climbers, while the free-standing Calf is a giant boulder.

Standing on top of Ilkley Moor and enjoying spectacular views overlooking Wharfedale, the **Cow and Calf** takes its name from the famous rock formation nearby. The inn stands on the site of the Ben Rhydding Hydropathic Hotel, built in 1844 and the first of its kind in England. It was replaced in 1877 by Highfield House, a private residence until the late 1800s when it became a boarding house. It finally became the Cow and Calf in 1949 and is now part of Vintage Inns who completely renovated it in 1999 with fixtures, fittings and an ambience unmistakably Yorkshire crafted. The inn is run by

**Cow & Calf, Hangingstone Road, Ilkley, West Yorkshire LS29 8BT
Tel: 01943 607335 Fax: 01943 604712**

Sue and Paul Spedding who take particular pride in the quality of the food and drink, offering a superb selection of excellent food all day, every day - and in generous portions too! Patrons can also enjoy cask-conditioned ales and a wide selection of fine wines from around the world. The Cow and Calf has 16 en suite guest bedrooms, all comfortable, traditionally decorated and individual in character. The inn is also very well-equipped for business people who like to do business in informal surroundings but with all the necessary facilities they need on hand.

BEN RHYDDING
MAP 6 REF F8

1 mile E of Ilkley off the A65

"A few weeks spent at Ben Rhydding seem to effect a complete change in the system" wrote one Victorian visitor to the spa. *"I have seen delicate women, scarcely able to walk feebly round the garden on their first arrival, become strong enough to walk to the Hunting-tower, a lovely point in the heart of the moor at some distance from the house".*

The original Ben Rhydding Hydropathic Hotel, opened in 1844 by a consortium of Leeds businessmen, was built in the Scottish baronial style so popular at the time. By 1908, interest in hydropathy had declined and the exuberant building became the Ben

Rhydding Golf Hotel. Later it was turned into flats but finally demolished in 1955.

Athough the name suggests some Scottish connection - and the surrounding scenery certainly has a Caledonian grandeur - 'Ben Rhydding' is actually derived from nearby Bean Rhydding, or bean clearing.

The centre of Ben Rhydding retains much of its spa town charm and one of its gems is **The Wheatley Hotel**. Family-run hostelries always seem to be that little more welcoming and The Wheatley Hotel is no exception. In this case it's the Haw family: Chris and Irene, who have been run-
ning the hotel for more than 20 years and their daughter Vicky and son-in-law Paul. They all take pride in offer-ing comfortable surroundings, a friendly atmosphere and first class customer service. The Wheatley is well-known locally for its excellent food which, thanks to Chris and Paul, has won nu-merous catering awards. The extensive choice of around 130 dishes includes Chi-nese, Indian, pasta and

The Wheatley Hotel, 101 Wheatley Lane,
Ben Rhydding, West Yorkshire LS29 8PP
Tel/Fax: 01943 607266

vegetarian options. Please note, though, that no food is available on Sunday and Monday evenings and at other times it's always a good idea to book ahead. If you are planning to stay in this popular town, The Wheatley has 4 en suite rooms (2 doubles, 2 twins), all comfortably furnished and well-equipped. Incidentally, the imposing Victorian building which the hotel occupies was once, it is believed, known as the Cow and Calf - a belief supported by an attractive stained glass window depicting the famous rocks.

BURLEY IN WHARFEDALE
MAP 6 REF F8
12 miles SE of Skipton on the A65

Mentioned in the Anglo-Saxon Chronicle in 972AD as *Burhleg* and in the Domesday Book as *Burghelai* remained a small riverside settlement until the 1790s when the Indus-trial Revolution reached the village. Many of the terraces of stone-built cottages, designed for the mill workers, have survived and are now highly desirable residences. Burley's population has doubled since the 1920s but the Main Street is still lined with Yorkshire stone cottages and houses, and the surrounding hills frame every view.

Patrons of Rick's Just for Starters restaurant in Harrogate will be delighted to know that its owner, Rick Hodgson, has recently opened **Cutlers Bar and Brasserie** in a splen-did old Victorian mansion in the village of Burley in Wharfedale. Cutlers is based on the same principle - customers choose from a range of starters which can also be ordered as a main course. Have two starter courses if you wish - gravadlax of salmon perhaps with a beetroot and raspberry relish, followed by a Cutlers Pastry Box of sauté chicken livers in a

Cutlers Bar and Brasserie, Main Street, Burley in Wharfedale
LS29 7DN Tel: 01943 852207 Fax: 01943 865748
website: www.cutlers-brasserie.com

piquant sherry sauce. In this way you can create a meal to suit your appetite and food preferences, your pocket and perhaps your diet. However, if you prefer a traditional main course meal, then check the blackboard menu for dishes such as Baked Halibut, Lamb Cutlets or Fillet Steak. Cutlers also offers a children's menu and if you order your meal before 7pm there's a 20% discount (except on Saturdays). This outstanding restaurant is open every day from noon until 2pm, and 6pm to 10pm (Monday to Saturday); noon until 2.30pm and 6pm to 9pm (Sunday).

OTLEY

MAP 6 REF F8

14 miles SE of Skipton on the A660

Although it now forms part of the Leeds Metropolitan District, Otley has retained its distinctive character, still boasting a busy cobbled market place with a maypole standing on the site of the old market cross, many little alleyways and courtyards. Each May the Wharfedale Agricultural Show, founded in 1799 and the oldest show of its kind in England, is held in a nearby field. Even older is Prince Henry's Grammar School, founded in 1602 by James I and named after his eldest son. On the front of the building in Manor Square is a statue of Thomas Chippendale, the great furniture maker who was born in Otley in 1718. In 1754 Chippendale published *The Gentleman and Cabinet-Maker's Director*, which was immensely influential in both Britain and the USA. His own workshop produced a comparatively small number of pieces but he gave his name to a style that dominated a generation and is still highly prized. Otley's parish church dates from Saxon times although the main body was constructed in the 11th century. An unusual memorial, close by, is a stone model of **Bramhope Railway Tunnel** with its impressive crenellated entrance portals. It was built in the 1830s on the Leeds-Thirsk railway line and more than 30 labourers died during its construction - a tragic loss of life which the model commemorates. An attractive feature of the town is The **Chevin Forest Park**, a forested ridge above the town which can be reached by a delightful walk that starts alongside the River Wharfe.

Back in the town centre, there's been a fish restaurant on Cross Green since the 1920s and since 1998 **Maypole Fisheries** has been owned and run by Heather and Neal Hodnett who provide their customers with excellent food and a friendly service. The front part of the premises is devoted to the takeaway counter with the restaurant hidden away at the back. It takes its name incidentally from the Otley Maypole, approximately 50 yards away. There's an interesting mirrored painting dating back to the 1950s, which shows children dancing around a maypole. Another feature of the restaurant is a very varied collection of teapots. The menu offers plenty of choice, servings are generous and all at very reasonable prices. Children's and pensioners' specials are also available. The quality of the food on offer here is reflected in the Friers Quality Award presented by the Seafish Industry Authority in recognition of Maypole Fisheries' high standard of product, premises and handling practices. The restaurant is open for lunch from 11.30am to 1.15pm (Tuesday to Saturday), and for tea/supper from 4.45pm to 9pm (Tues to Fri).

Maypole Fisheries, 28 Cross Green, Otley LS21 1HD Tel: 01943 462625

Lovers of real ale and connoisseurs of pubs with lots of character should immediately make their way to **The Bowling Green** in Bondgate. The building itself has had a varied history - built in 1757 as a chapel it has served as a school, a courthouse and assembly rooms before opening as an inn in 1865. Step inside and you'll find an astonishing collection of memorabilia crowding every available surface. Stuffed animal heads, vintage signs and advertising plaques -in fact anything that caught the eye of mine hosts Judith Walker and Trevor Wallis who have owned and run this unique inn since 1982. They serve only real ales here with pride of place given to Briscoe's fine ales which are actually produced in premises at the rear of the pub. Master brewer Paul Briscoe is an enthusiastic fell runner so he names his beers after major fell races such as 'Burnsall Classic' and 'Chevin Chaser'. So far he has produced more than a dozen of these outstanding brews. If you enjoy good beer full of character and flavour then you should definitely visit The Bowling Green and if you'd like to see how these fine beers are created, tours of the brewery are available by arrangement. Another attraction here is the

The Bowling Green, 18 Bondgate, Otley LS21 3AB
Tel: 01943 461494

Thursday evening entertainment, "Hippie Chick Night", when a popular DJ presents a variety of music that "ranges from Lithuanian to Bedouin"!

In addition to the statue on the front of the Grammar School, Otley's most famous son is commemorated by a plaque on the wall of **Browns Gallery** which records that

Thomas Chippendale was born in 1718 in a cottage that stood on this spot. The present building used to be a building society office, (its vault is still there), but now houses Peter Brown's gallery of original paintings and prints, many by famous artists such as David Shepherd, Russell Flint and Stephen Townsend. Local artists are also featured in the constantly changing displays and in special exhibitions. Peter also owns and runs **The Picture Shop**, across on the other side of the Market Place, where you'll find a further choice of collectable works of art. If you are

Browns Gallery, Wesley Street Chambers, Wesley Street, Otley, West Yorkshire LS21 1AZ
Tel: 01943 464656 Fax: 01943 464328

looking for a specific topic, or even an individual painting, Peter will be happy to search for it and if you have a picture to sell he'll do his best to find a buyer. Both Browns Gallery and the Picture Shop are open 9.30am until 5pm (Monday to Thursday); 9am to 5pm (Friday and Saturday); and on Sunday afternoons.

Occupying a prime corner site in the centre of the town, **The Black Horse Hotel** is a stately late-Victorian building erected in 1901 in the ornate architectural style that was all the fashion at the time. The interior also has lots of character with wooden floors, comfortable easy chairs dotted around and some interesting bygones on display. The hotel bar is open all day, every day, offering a good choice of ales, (with Tetley's as the main handpull beer), and food served either in the sepa-

The Black Horse Hotel, Westgate, Otley LS21 3AS
Tel: 01943 461047

rate restaurant or in the bar. In addition to the regular menu there's always a choice of daily specials. On most Friday and Saturday evenings The Black Horse's landlords, Alex and Maria McHarrie, lay on live entertainment - varying between folk, rock and jazz. The hotel also has 7 guest rooms, 5 of them en suite, all of them spacious and well-equipped with some having good views over the town centre. And if you are looking for a venue for some special event, the Black Horse has an upstairs function room which can cater for up to 100 people.

Tucked away in the corner of Bay Horse Court, (behind the Bay Horse public house) in the centre of the town, only a short walk from Courthouse car park, **The Bells of Otley** is well worth seeking out by anyone with a taste for top quality cuisine. Attractively and stylishly decorated with honey-coloured pine tables and chairs, mirrored windows and lots of interesting bygones

The Bells of Otley, 3 Bay Horse Court, Otley LS21 1SB Tel: 01943 468888

and memorabilia around the walls, this popular restaurant offers outstanding menus supplemented by daily specials. These might include oysters or smoked salmon and prawn croquettes amongst the starters and Scampi Thermidor or slowly roasted Lamb Shank in a rich jus as main courses. Martin is the chef who produces these appetising dishes and, together with his business partner Karin, opened the Bells of Otley in 1997. Such has been their success that anyone wishing to eat here would be well-advised to make a booking. The restaurant is open from noon until 2pm (Tuesday to Sunday), and from 7pm onwards, Wednesday to Saturday.

A former farmhouse and now a listed building, the **Three Horseshoes** is a charming traditional pub where Joe and Winnie Toole offer visitors excellent food, ales and accommodation. There's always a good choice of real ales with Tetley's Bitter and Tetley's Mild permanently on tap and another four guest ales which change regularly. Food is served Friday, Saturday and Sunday lunchtimes from noon until 2pm (2.30pm on Sundays) and in addition

Three Horseshoes, Bridge Street, Otley LS21 1BQ Tel: 01943 461222

to the printed menu, daily specials are also available. Joe and Winnie also lay on a good range of entertainment. On Wednesday evening there's a folk group; Thursday is Quiz Night; and on Friday and Saturday evenings live bands entertain - all begin at 9pm. If you are planning to stay in this pleasant old town, the Three Horseshoes has 6 comfortable and attractively furnished guest rooms, (5 twins and 1 single). Joe and Winnie also have a 6-berth caravan, sited at Skirlington near Hornsea in East Yorkshire and available to rent between Easter and October.

Gloucesters Tea Rooms, 22 Newmarket, Otley LS21 3AE Tel: 01943 850730
e-mail:neilmcgowan@gloucesters.fsnet.co.uk

Tucked away in the quiet area of Newmarket, **Gloucesters Tea Rooms** with seating on two floors is *the* place to seek out for good, wholesome food freshly prepared to order and served with a smile. Diane and Neil McGowan bought the business in 1997 and have since extensively refurbished it. The Tea Rooms is a very inviting place with brightly-coloured chequered tablecloths, potted plants and fresh flowers all adding to the relaxing ambience and appeal. The appetising menu includes a good choice of light meals and snacks with hot and cold sandwiches, "Gloucester specialities" and delicious home made soups. Gloucesters are renowned locally for their quality coffee in filter, espresso, cappuccino and latte styles plus cafetieres of various types along with flavoured varieties such as Cinnamon and Hazelnut, Tiramisu and Irish Cream. There is also a wide range of teas available to suit every taste along with cold drinks and milk shakes. Children are very welcome, with toys, books and high chairs available. Smoking is permitted in the upstairs room. Gloucesters is open Monday to Saturday from 9am until 4.30pm and should not be missed!

Although only 2 miles from Leeds/Bradford airport, **Chevin Lodge Country Park Hotel** provides "The Complete Retreat". Set amid 50 acres of woodland and lakes, this privately owned independent hotel offers a perfect, peaceful environment for both business and leisure. It would be easy to think you were in Scandinavia or Canada since the main building here is the largest log building in Britain and all of the 50 guest rooms are constructed of prime timber from Finland. All rooms are en suite, fitted to the highest standards and all enjoy views of the grounds. An elegant lakeside restaurant forms the centrepiece of this unique hotel, serving a cuisine commended by all the major guides. All dishes are freshly prepared on the premises by a team of talented chefs - with not a frozen vegetable in sight! There's also a lakeside patio where, on fine days, refreshments can be ordered. Guests at the Chevin Lodge have free membership of the Lodgix Leisure Club where the facilities include an 11m x 7m pool, jacuzzi, sun bed room (for which a

Chevin Lodge Country Park Hotel, Yorkgate, Otley, West Yorkshire LS21 3NU
Tel: 01943 467818 Fax: 01943 850335

small charge is made), and sauna. Or you could enjoy a game of tennis on the all-weather court, fish for roach and carp in the hotel's main lake or go for a ride on a mountain bike.

AIREDALE

The *"Gateway to the Dales"*, Skipton, has long been a starting point for any tour of the Yorkshire Dales and, though still a bustling centre for Airedale and its neighbour Malhamdale, the town's old industries have given way, to a large degree, to tourism. The source of the River Aire lies in Malhamdale, just to the north of Malham, and it flows through both dales before finally joining the River Ouse. For some of its length, in Airedale, the river lies side-by-side with the Leeds and Liverpool Canal. The construction of a navigable waterway, linking the two great industrial areas of Lancashire and Yorkshire, changed the lives of many living in the Dales and certainly played a major part in establishing the textile mills in the area. However, the importance of farming has never been lost and market day is a key event in the daily lives of the dalesfolk. As well as the sheep, other constant features of the countryside are the dry stone walls; a familiar sight to all those visiting the Yorkshire Dales.

Of the many and varied attractions in Airedale and the area surrounding Skipton, the most impressive feature is the beautiful limestone formations found to the north of Malham. The spectacular and enormous curved cliff of Malham Cove, created by glacial action during the last Ice Age, the limestone pavements above the cove, the deep gorge of **Gordale Scar**, and the remote natural lake, Malham Tarn, are all well worth a visit.

This dramatic scenic area has been designated a Site of Special Scientific Interest and, as well as the wonderful formations themselves, the area supports a wide range of animals, birds, and plant life. As there is a variety of terrain, from bleak, bracken strewn moorland to coniferous plantations, there too is a wide variety of flora and fauna. Birdwatchers, particularly, will delight in the opportunity to catch sight of red grouse and short-eared owls on the moors whilst also having the chance to view the many wading birds which populate the lakes and reservoirs of the area.

SKIPTON
Map 6 ref D7

22 miles W of Harrogate

Often called the "Gateway to the Dales", Skipton's origins can be traced to the 7th century when Anglian farmers christened it Sheeptown. Featuring in the Domesday Book, the Normans decided to build a castle here to guard the entrance to Airedale and Skipton became a garrison town. **Skipton Castle**, home of the Cliffords, was begun in 1090 and the powerful stone structure seen today was devised in 1310 by Robert de Clifford, the 1st Earl of Skipton. The Cliffords were a fighting breed and, throughout the Middle Ages, wherever there was trouble a member of the family was sure to be found. The 8th Lord Clifford, Thomas, and his son John were both killed whilst fighting for the House of Lancaster during the War of the Roses. Later, George Clifford, Champion to Queen Elizabeth I and a renowned sailor, fought against the Spanish Armada and, as well as participating in many voyages of his own, he also lent a ship to Sir Walter Raleigh.

Skipton Castle

One of the most complete and well preserved medieval castles in England, it is thanks to Lady Anne Clifford that visitors to Skipton can marvel at its buildings. Following the ravages of the Civil War, from which the castle did not escape, Lady Anne undertook a comprehensive restoration programme and, though little of the original Norman stonework remains, much of the work of the 1st Lord Clifford still stands.

As well as an enormous banqueting hall, a series of kitchens still remain with some of their original fittings, and a beautiful Tudor courtyard. There is also a rather unusually decorated room whose walls are lined with shells that were collected by George Clifford in the 19th century whilst he was travelling in the South Seas. However, the most striking feature of the castle is the impressive 14th century gateway, which is visible from the High Street, and carries the Clifford family motto *Desormais* meaning Henceforth.

Adjacent to the castle, at the top of the High Street, lies the parish **Church of the Holy Trinity** which was originally built in the 12th century and replaced in the 1300s. There is a wealth of interest inside the building which has been topped by a beautiful oak roof since the 15th century. It is possible to spend much time discovering the centuries of artefacts in the church and the various tombs and memorials are just as interesting and include the many tombs of the Clifford family. The church too suffered damage during the Civil War and, again, Lady Anne Clifford came to the rescue, restoring the interior and rebuilding the steeple in 1655. Inside the church, among the many tombstones, is that of the Longfellow family, which included the uncle of the American poet, Henry Wadsworth Longfellow. As well as the fine castle and church, the Normans also established Skipton as a market town and it received its first charter in 1204. The market today is still thriving and is very much an important part of daily life in the area.

For many years Skipton remained a market town, then, with the development of the factory system in the 19th century, the nature of the town began to change. Textile mills were built and cottages and terraced houses were constructed for the influx of mill workers. However, not all were happy with the changes that the Industrial Revolution brought about and, in 1842, a group of men, women, and children set out from the Pennine cotton towns and villages to protest at the mechanisation taking place. By the time the group had reached nearby Broughton, their number had grown to 3,000 and the Skipton magistrates urged them to turn back and return home. But the protesters continued, surging on Skipton, and the worried magistrates sent for military help. Moving from mill to mill, the mob stopped the looms and created panic amongst the townspeople. Special constables were quickly sworn in to help contain the situation and the Riot Act was read from the town hall steps. Though the mob retreated to nearby Anne Hill, they refused to disperse and the soldiers were ordered to charge. During the ensuing violence, one soldier was killed and a magistrate blinded but the mob, bar six of the leaders who were arrested, fled as the first shots were fired.

The **Leeds and Liverpool Canal**, which flows through the town, provided a cheap form of transport as well as linking Skipton with the major industrial centres of Yorkshire and Lancashire. The first of three trans-Pennine routes, the 127 mile canal has 91 locks along the full length as well as two tunnels, one of which is over a mile long. Today, the canal basin, behind the town centre, is busy with pleasure craft and boat journeys can be taken along a section in the direction of Gargrave. The towpath was also restored at the same time as the canal and there are a number of pleasant walks which includes a stretch along the cul-de-sac Spring Branch beside the castle walls. Before the days of the canal, travelling by road, particularly in winter, was often a hazardous business. One local tale tells how, on Christmas Eve, during a bad snow storm, a young waggoner set out from the town for Blubberhouses. Though an inn keeper tried to dissuade him, the young man carried on into the night - thinking only of his betrothed, Ruth. He soon lost his way in a snow drift and chilled by the fierce northerly winds, he fell to the ground in a comatosed sleep. Safe in her cottage, Ruth suddenly awoke and ran out of the house crying that her John was lost. Two men hurried after her and by the time they had caught up with Ruth she was digging out John with her bare hands. He was none the worse for his misadventure and the couple married on New Year's Day.

A walk around the town is also worth while and there are many interesting buildings to be found here. One, in particular, is the Town Hall which is now also the home of the **Craven Museum** (free). Dedicated to the surrounding area, there are many interesting displays relating to the geological and archaeological treasures that have been found locally, including a piece of Bronze Age cloth which is considered the oldest textile fragment in the country. Closer to the present day, there are displays of furniture illustrating the fine craftsmanship that went into even the most mundane household item and also farming exhibits which reflect the changing lives of many of the people who lived off the surrounding countryside.

Almost opposite the Town Hall, on the High Street, are the premises of the **Craven**

Herald, a newspaper that was established in 1874 although the publication was produced for a short time in the 1850s. The building is fortunate in having retained its late Victorian shop front, as well as the passageway to one side, and it was first occupied by William Chippendale in the late 18th century. A trader in textiles, Chippendale made his money by buying then selling on the cloth woven by the farmers in their own homes. Close to the newspaper's offices is the **Public Library** which opened in 1910 and was funded by Andrew Carnegie. A large, ornate building, it is in contrast to the town's older buildings and stands as a reminder to the change in character which Skipton underwent in the late 19th century. It seems fitting that, in a town which over many years has been dedicated to trade and commerce, Thomas Spencer, co-founder of Marks and Spencer, should be born here in 1851. Skipton, too, was the home of Sir Winston Churchill's physician, Lord Moran, who grew up here as the son of the local doctor.

As with many historic market towns, Skipton has its fair share of inns and public houses which provided farmers with refreshment during the busy markets. The **Black Horse Inn** is one such pub and its date stone of 1676 is well worth a second look as it is carved with symbols of the butcher's trade: axes, animal heads, and twisted fleeces. Originally called The King's Head, the inn was built by, not surprisingly, a butcher, Robert Goodgion. In the 19th century it served as a headquarters to Lord Ribblesdale's cavalry when they held their annual training in the town.

Another hostelry of interest and where you can be assured of a warm welcome is **The Unicorn Hotel**, located in the centre of the town close to the High Street. The hotel's history goes back many years to the days when it was known as the Bentley Yorkshire Brewery Building and was then welcoming guests attending Skipton's famous Cattle Market. Over the years many changes have taken place and whilst the Cattle Market is still

one of the largest in the county, Skipton itself is very much a tourist town attracting many other kinds of visitors wanting to spend a few days touring the peaceful surrounding countryside. The Unicorn Hotel is well designed to meet the needs of both overnight visitors as well as those staying longer. Its facilities include a comfortable lounge to relax in. A choice of evening meals is served in the dining room from 7pm to 9pm, and there are many varied restaurants within walking distance. A traditional Yorkshire breakfast is served in the dining room. The guest bedrooms

The Unicorn Hotel, Devonshire Place, Keighley Road, Skipton, North Yorkshire BD23 2LP
Tel: 01756 794146 Fax: 01756 793376

at The Unicorn are on the first and second floors, and each has its own individual character. All of them are very tastefully furnished, en suite, and comprehensively equipped with features such as colour TV and direct dial telephones.

EMBSAY
MAP 6 REF D7

1 mile N of Skipton off the A59

The village is home to the **Embsay Steam Railway** which is based at the small country station. As well as taking a scenic steam train journey to the end of the line, a couple of miles away, there are over 20 locomotives, both steam and diesel, on display together with railway carriages. Special events are arranged throughout the year and opening times vary though the trains run every Sunday.

Well before the days of railways, Embsay was home to an Augustinian priory, founded in 1130. However, for some reason the monks found life difficult here and, in 1145, they crossed Embsay Moor and moved to what is now Bolton Abbey. Those choosing to walk over the moor to the north of the village should take care as the area is peppered with old coal pits and disused shafts. However, the view from **Embsay Crag** (1,217 feet high) is well worth the effort of climbing.

RYLSTONE
MAP 6 REF D7

5 miles N of Skipton on the B6265

On Rylstone Fell, above this Pennine village, stands **Rylstone Cross** which was, originally, a large stone that looked rather like a man. In 1885, a wooden cross was erected on top of the stone to commemorate peace with France and the initials DD and TB, carved on the back of the cross, refer to the Duke of Devonshire and his land agent, Mr T Broughton.

At the beginning of the 19th century, when Wordsworth was touring the area, he heard a local legend which became the basis for his poem *The White Doe of Rylstone*, published in 1815. The story, set in the 16th century, concerns the local Norton family and, in particular, Francis who gave his sister Emily a white doe before he went off to battle. Francis survived the conflict but he was murdered in Norton Tower on his return. Emily was struck down with grief and she was comforted by the same white doe, returned from the wild, and it also accompanied her on her visits to her brother's grave. Long after Emily's death, a white doe can still be seen lying on Francis's grave.

BROUGHTON
MAP 6 REF D8

4 miles W of Skipton on the A59

The Tempest family has been associated with this farming community for the past 800 years and their family home, **Broughton Hall** dates back to 1597. Enlarged in the 18th and 19th centuries, the hall is open to the public on Bank Holidays when guided tours are conducted around this interesting building. Those lucky enough to visit on the last Sunday in June will also be witness to the Broughton Hall Game Fair, a well-attended event which covers all manner of country sports and pursuits. The building itself may seem familiar since it, as well as the grounds, have been used frequently by film crews as a historic location.

EAST MARTON
MAP 6 REF D8

6 miles W of Skipton on the A59

This pleasant little village sits beside the Leeds and Liverpool Canal and is well known to walkers along the Pennine Way for its outstanding hostelry. Set endways on to the road,

ELSLACK
MAP 6 REF D8

4 miles SW of Skipton off the A56

Overlooking the village is the 1,274 ft high Pinhaw Beacon from which there are some fine panoramic views over the heather covered moorland. During the Napoleonic Wars in the early 19th century, when there was great fear of an invasion from France, the beacon, one in a countrywide chain of communication beacons, was manned 24 hours a day. Unfortunately, during a raging blizzard on a January night in 1805, the lookout, Robert Wilkinson, died and was buried on the moor. His body was later exhumed and his grave can be seen in the parish churchyard to the northeast of the village.

THORNTON-IN-CRAVEN
MAP 6 REF D8

5 miles SW of Skipton on the A56

This attractive village stands on the Pennine Way and from here there are magnificent views of Airedale and, towards, the west, Pendle Forest in Lancashire. Now a quiet place, during the Civil War the manor house was ruined by Royalist soldiers shortly after Cromwell had stayed here to attend a local wedding. The present house is situated opposite the original site. Past parish records associated with the 12th century Church of St Mary too are lost as, unfortunately, they were accidentally burnt by the local rector.

EARBY
MAP 6 REF D8

6 miles SW of Skipton on the A56

Though the Yorkshire Dales are thought of as a once thriving textile producer, lead mining, for many centuries, was also a key industry. Housed in an old grammar school, that was founded in 1591 by Robert Windle, is the **Museum of Yorkshire Dales Lead Mining** which was opened in 1971. The large collection, as well as the substantial documentation and indexing, has been put together by several local interest groups who began their work in 1945 when the Earby Mines Research Group was formed within the Earby Pothole Club. The museum, which has limited opening, has many excellent displays including mine tubs, photographs, mine plans, small implements, mining machinery, and miners' personal belongings.

GARGRAVE
MAP 6 REF D7

5 miles NW of Skipton on the A65

This picturesque small village in Upper Airedale was once a thriving market town and it also became a busy transport centre after the Leeds and Liverpool Canal was built. Lead from the nearby mines was loaded on to the barges at the five wharves here, whilst other goods were unloaded ready for distribution to the surrounding area. The village too played a part in the textile boom and there were two cotton mills in the village. Now no longer in commercial use, like the canal, some of the mills have been turned into residential accommodation whilst the canal is very much alive with pleasure boats.

The remains of Celtic crosses found within the village Church of St Andrew indicate that, although the present building is chiefly Victorian, there has been a church here for centuries. The original church was destroyed by the Scots during a raid in 1318. To the south of the village, at **Kirk Sink**, is the site of a Roman villa that was excavated in the 1970s. Relics recovered from the building can be seen in Skipton and Cliffe Castle Museums and the site has since been recovered. An ideal location for family or walking holidays, **Eshton Road Caravan Site** is a small friendly family-run camp site with the Leeds/Liverpool canal running through it. This well-established site is set in 1½ acres and can accommodate up to 20 caravans and 10 tents. There's plenty to keep visitors occupied - fishing in the canal, walks (the Pennine Way passes right through the site), horse riding, swimming baths (3 miles), pitch & putt and golf are all available within easy reach. There

**Eshton Road Caravan Site, Eshton Road, Gargrave, Skipton,
North Yorkshire BD23 3PN Tel: 01756 749229**

are good shopping facilities in Gargrave, (a 5-minute walk away), as well as in the market towns of Skipton (4 miles), Settle (10 miles), Grassington (8 miles) and the popular village of Malham is also just 8 miles distant. The site is open all year round and the facilities have been recently modernised, now providing hot and cold showers, shaving points, mains water points, electricity hook-ups and flush sanitation. Dogs are welcome if exercised on leads off the site.

CONISTON COLD   MAP 6 REF D7
7 miles NW of Skipton on the A65

Lying midway between Skipton and Settle, this small village lies on the old route to the Lake District. Like most places situated on once busy routes, the village had its share of coaching inns and one in particular was the Punch Bowl Inn (until recently it acted as the post office) which has an unusual circular indentation on the front outside wall. In days gone by the inn's patrons would stand a few yards from the wall and try to kick a ball to this mark.

AIRTON   MAP 6 REF D7
8 miles NW of Skipton off the A65

This charming Airedale village is well known to long distance walkers as it lies on the Pennine Way. Though small there are a couple of buildings of interest including a corn mill (now converted into flats) that was first recorded in 1198. As sheep farming took over from corn, the mill, like so many in the southern dales, turned to cotton spinning though, with the advent of steam powered machinery, the industry moved to nearby Skipton. At the beginning of the 18th century, Airton became a Quaker community and the **Meeting House**, which was built on land donated by the well-known Quaker weavers William and Alice Ellis, can still be seen by the village green. Another legacy of the village's Quaker community is the absence of a public house as the drinking of alcohol was strictly forbidden by the Friends. Also found on the village green is a 17th century squatter's cottage so called because, according to the law, any person building a house and having smoke rising from the chimney within 24 hours was granted the freehold of the property including the land within a stone's throw of the front door.

MALHAM

Map 6 ref D7

11 miles NW of Skipton off the A65

Malham village was originally two settlements, Malham East and Malham West, which were separated by the beck. Each came under the influence of a different religious house: Bolton Priory and Fountains Abbey respectively. United after the Dissolution of the Monasteries, the focal point of Malham became the village green where the annual sheep fairs were held. This pretty village of farms and cottages is one of the most visited places in the Yorkshire Dales though it is not the charming stone built dwellings which visitors come to admire but the spectacular limestone scenery which lies just to the north. However, the two ancient stone bridges in the village centre are also worth a second glance. The New Bridge, which is also known as the Monks' Bridge, was built in the 17th century whilst the Wash-Dub Bridge dates from the 16th century and is of a clapper design (limestone slabs placed on stone supports).

The way to the ancient glacial grandeur of **Malham Cove** is from the Langcliffe road beyond the last buildings of the village, down a path alongside the beck that leads

Malham Cove

through a scattering of trees. The 300ft limestone amphitheatre is the most spectacular section of the mid-Craven fault and, as recently as the 1700s, a massive waterfall that was higher than Niagara Falls cascaded over its edge! These days the water disappears through potholes at the top, called water-sinks, and reappears through the cavern mouth at Aire Head near the village. A steep path leads to the limestone pavement at the top, with its characteristic clints and grykes, where water has carved a distinctive natural sculpture through the weaknesses in the limestone.

From here it is not too far to reach the equally inspiring **Gordale Scar**, a huge gorge carved by glacial melt water with an impressive waterfall leaping, in two stages, from a fissure in its face. Further on still is another waterfall known as Janet's Foss. Beside the waterfall is a cave which Janet, a friendly fairy, is reputed to inhabit. Three miles north of the scar is **Malham Tarn**, a glacial lake which by way of an underground stream is the source of the River Aire, and Malham Tarn House, where such famous names as Ruskin, Darwin, and Charles Kingsley (author of *The Water Babies*) received inspiration.

**Hill Top Farm, Malham, nr Skipton, North Yorkshire BD23 4DJ
Tel: 01729 830320**

Located on the outskirts of this popular village, surrounded by perfect walking country and within easy reach of all the local amenities, **Hill Top Farm** offers the choice of a self-catering cottage or a self-catering bunk barn. Annie and John Heseltine have lived on this 320-acre working farm since 1951 and in 1989 they converted an early 17th century barn into quality accommodation suitable for family or school parties, youth groups and Pennine Way walkers. Sleeping accommodation for up to 32 people is provided in 6 separate bedrooms, of varying sizes, on the ground floor where there's also a large drying room and separate toilet and shower for people with disabilities. On the first floor are toilets, washbasins and showers, and a well equipped kitchen with electric cooking, fridge and other facilities. The large dining and recreation room enjoys magnificent views of Malhamdale. The self-catering accommodation at Hill Top Farm is provided in a charming, self-contained cottage adjoining the main house. There are 3 bedrooms in all - a double bedroom, a bunk room and a single room, which together can accommodate up to 5 people.

SILSDEN   MAP 6 REF E8
4 miles SE of Skipton on the A6034

This well-contained stone built industrial town, which spreads uphill from the Leeds and Liverpool Canal, owes its development to the textile industry. Rows of terraced cottages and houses lie on the steep hillsides and there is newer housing on the outskirts of the town. It was the birthplace of Augustus Spencer, Principal of the Royal College of Art (1900-20), whose memorial can be seen in the 18th century parish church.

Outside **The Kings Arms**, in the centre of the village, stands an old mounting block, a survival from the days when

**The Kings Arms, 9 Bolton Road, Silsden,
Keighley BD20 0JY Tel: 01535 653216**

this was a coaching and post house inn. The resident ghost probably dates back to that era as well! Don't worry, he won't spoil your enjoyment of the quality food and ales on offer here. Eileen and Ken North have been running this atmospheric old pub since 1997 and it's Eileen who can take the credit for the excellent food which is available all day, every day (except Sunday when the pub closes between 3pm and 7pm). A particularly customer-friendly feature is the fact that the kitchen stays open until 10.45pm. For special occasions, The Kings Arms has an attractive function room which can accommodate up to 100 guests. Eileen and Ken make sure that their customers don't get bored - there's a Quiz Night on Sunday evening from 9pm, and frequent karaoke, disco and theme nights.

EASTBURN
MAP 6 REF E8

4 miles NW of Keighley off the A629

When the Keighley to Kendal turnpike was built in 1789, an enterprising farmer decided to convert his farmhouse into an inn and named it The Red Lion. For many years it provided accommodation and refreshment for both travellers and horses, and westward-bound coaches would double up on their horses here for the strenuous climb into Lancashire. The inn was later rechristened **The White Bear**, the name by which this

friendly and welcoming inn is still known. Alan Slack and Marina Reynolds took over here in 1998 when the pub had fallen on hard times and by dint of much expense and effort have given the White Bear a new lease of life. They have retained its traditional character - the old beams are still in place, for example, and vintage prints of bygone days enhance the olde-worlde atmosphere. The food

The White Bear, Main Road, Eastburn, Keighley BD20 7SN
Tel: 01535 653000

here is especially recommended. Marina commands the kitchen and her regular menu is supplemented by at least 12 mouth-watering daily specials. Complement your food with one of the two real ales on offer. Meals are available every lunchtime and evening except Sunday evenings and, during the winter months, Monday lunchtimes.

LOTHERSDALE
MAP 6 REF D8

7 miles NW of Keighley off the A629

A dramatic stretch of the Pennine Way passes through this village set in a deep valley in the heart of the moors. Charlotte Brontë knew the village well and in *Jane Eyre* the house she calls Gateshead is modelled on Lothersdale's Stonegappe, up on the hillside near the church. Standing in open farmland and enjoying spectacular views along the Aire valley, **Street Head Farm** is a traditional 18th century Dales farmhouse which has been recently renovated and now provides a superb location for self-catering holidays. Great care was taken to retain a wealth of old oak beams, open stone fireplaces, stone flagged floors and mullioned windows with window seats. Modern comforts

Street Head Farm, Lothersdale, Skipton BD20 8HY
Tel/Fax: 01535 632535 E-mail: streethead@towtop.co.uk

include central heating, double glazing throughout, a log burner in the large sitting room, colour TV and video in a second sitting room, and well-equipped kitchen and utility rooms. No wonder the Street Head Farm has been awarded a 5 Keys Highly Commended rating by the English Tourist Board. The house comfortably sleeps ten in five bedrooms, one of which is on the ground floor. Children are welcome, with a cot and high chair available on request, and so are smokers and well-behaved pets. The area is a walker's paradise with the Pennine Way just a mile or so away and the scenic attractions of Dales National Park extend for miles to the north.

With its striking black and white frontage **The Hare & Hounds** looks an inviting sort of hostelry, an impression fully confirmed when you step inside the bar with its old beamed ceiling, stone fire surrounds and lots of bygone memorabilia. This is a family run inn with Joseph and Tracey Currie in partnership with Tracey's mum, Janet. Tracey and Janet are responsible for the excellent food on offer and their regular menu is always supplemented by a good selection of daily specials. A sample choice might include a 'War of the Roses', (Lancashire Hot Pot in a Yorkshire Pudding), Wild Boar Sausages, Roast Thai Chicken or Pink Scottish Trout. Real Ale lovers have a choice of two regular brews and a third

The Hare & Hounds, Dale End, Lothersdale,
nr Keighley BD20 8EL Tel: 01535 630977

which changes every two weeks. As we go to press a new, non-smoking dining room is nearing completion and should be functioning fully by the time you read this. Children are welcome at the Hare & Hounds and there's a delightful beer garden and aviary to the rear of the inn where they can play in safety.

KILDWICK

MAP 6 REF E8

6 miles NW of Keighley off the A629

This picturesque little village, on the north bank of the River Aire, is approached over a bridge that was built in the early 14th century by the canons of Bolton Priory. The village **Church of St Andrew** was also rebuilt around the 14th and 15th centuries, though the choir was extended to its unusually long length sometime later which gives the church is local name Lang Kirk o'Craven.

The River Aire is not the only waterway which passes through the village as it also lies on the banks of the Leeds and Liverpool Canal. Once a hive of industry with many spinning and weaving mills in the village and the surrounding area producing wool and silk yarn and cloth, the decline of the textile industry has caused many of the mills to close though some have now been converted to provide interesting accommodation or as offices for small business units. The canal, which until the 1930s was still in commercial use, is now the preserve of pleasure craft and Kildwick is a popular overnight mooring.

KEIGHLEY

MAP 6 REF E8

10 miles NW of Bradford on the A650

Lying at the junction of the Rivers Worth and Aire, this bustling textile and engineering town, despite its modern redevelopment, still retains a strangely nostalgic air of the Victorian Industrial Revolution. It was that era of rapid growth that created the town seen today, beginning at Low Mill in 1780, when cotton spinning on a factory scale was first introduced. Reminders of hardship endured by the many factory workers of that time can be seen in the labyrinth of ginnels and terraces which lie amid the many elaborately decorated mills. There are delightful carvings and on one early mill chimney are three heads, one wearing a top hat; in contrast is the classical French-styled **Dalton Mill** in Dalton Lane with its ornate viewing gallery.

Just a short walk from the town centre, **Victoria Fine Art** stocks a vast range of original paintings, prints and engravings by artists from every period and from all over the country. Whatever your preference - landscapes or seascapes, villages or animal pictures, you'll find a huge choice within each genre, all of them attractively displayed and offered at very reasonable prices. Victoria Fine Art was established in 1990 by Jean and Keith Blackburn, a helpful and knowledgeable couple who started the business when Keith retired. He had been a master butcher in this very building which

Victoria Fine Art, 230 Oakworth Road, Keighley, West Yorkshire BD21 1QX Tel/Fax: 01535 602002

at that time was a butcher's shop. Jean, a former hairdresser, had always been keenly interested in art and her expertise is evident in the quality of the work on sale here. Victoria Fine Art also provides an excellent bespoke framing service, offering a wide choice of styles and colours and specialising in the framing of tapestries and embroidery. The shop is open from 9am to 5.30pm, Tuesday to Saturday, and telephone enquiries are welcome.

The centre of Keighley is dominated by impressive Victorian civic buildings and a beautifully set out covered shopping precinct, where the statue of legendary local giant, Rombald, stands. The parish church, also in the centre, is famous as the site where Patrick Brontë often officiated at marriages. The graveyard contains 15th century headstones, as well as a crude cross made from four carved heads which is believed to be Saxon in origin. Above the town, by way of escaping the industrial past, one might enjoy a walk in Park Woods, taking the cobbled path to Thwaites Brow, which affords magnificent views of the town below.

Outside the town centre is **Cliffe Castle** which, despite its deceptive name, is in fact a grand late-19th century mansion complete with a tower, battlements, and parkland, which once belonged to local mill owners, the Butterfields. It now houses **Keighley Museum**, which concentrates on the fascinating local topography and geology of Airedale as well as the history of the town. Also housed in the museum is the hand loom, complete with unfinished cloth, that was used by Timmy Feather, the last hand loom weaver in England. Part of the building is still furnished and decorated in the lavish style of the 1880s.

Another attraction within the castle grounds is **Café Cliffe Castle**. Here you'll find a wide selection of snacks, main courses, sweets and cakes as well as vegetarian dishes and a children's menu. In addition to the printed menu, there are also daily specials. The café has seating for 56 people inside and a further 20 on the verandah outside if you are lucky with the weather. There's good access for the disabled and a secure play area for children. Café Cliffe Castle is open all year round, (10am to 5pm in summer; 11am to 3pm in winter) but is closed on Mondays except during school holidays. The café is owned and

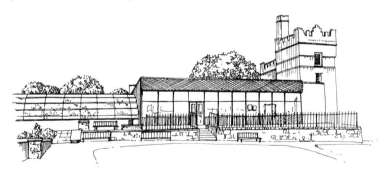

Café Cliffe Castle, Spring Gardens Lane, Keighley BD21 6LH
Tel: 01535 606593

run by Barry and Margaret Doveston who also run an outside catering business. They can cater for anything from 25 to 150 people and provide either cold foods or hot meals cooked at your venue. Select one of their sample menus, choose from their "Create your own Buffet" leaflet, or make a selection from their à la carte menu.

To the south of Keighley runs the line of the **Keighley and Worth Valley Railway** to Haworth. This restored steam railway line passes through some attractive small villages and some notable stations. Keighley Station itself is Victorian and the 5 miles of railway that runs to Oxenhope is run by volunteers.

HAINWORTH
MAP 6 REF E8
1 miles SE of Keighley off the A650

The **Worth Way** is an interesting 5 mile walk from the heart of industrial Keighley to the eastern edge of the Worth Valley at Oxenhope. This landscape has changed little since the time when Mrs Gaskell wrote about the area whilst visiting Charlotte Brontë in 1856. En route, the Worth Way passes close to the village of Hainworth. Here, standing high on the hillside and commanding some grand views of Harden Moor, **The Guide Inn** is a popular watering-hole for walkers and is well worth seeking out by anyone who appreciates good food and ale in an unspoilt country setting. An interesting feature of the inn is the series of murals painted on both the exterior and interior walls. Jim and Linda Rosie

took over here in the summer of 1999 and they keep the inn open all day, every day, with food available from noon until 7pm, Monday to Saturday, and noon until 5pm on Sunday. Linda's home made Steak & Mushroom Pie has already acquired a formidable reputation but you'll also find a wide choice of other dishes, either from the regular menu or from the

The Guide Inn, Keighley Road, Hainworth, Keighley BD21 5QP Tel: 01535 272138

daily specials on the board. Sunday lunch is particularly good value with a choice of 2 starters, 3 main courses and 4 sweets. Other attractions at the inn include live entertainment on Sunday evenings from 8.30pm and a children's disco once a fortnight from 6pm to 9.30pm. Also, there's a field adjacent to the inn where campers and touring vans are welcome to set up and which is provided with hot and cold water facilities.

UTLEY
MAP 6 REF E8
1 mile N of Keighley off the A629

Lovers of good food who live in this part of Yorkshire will already know about the outstanding cuisine on offer at **Headley's Restaurant**; visitors to the area have a treat awaiting them. The restaurant occupies a rather striking building which dates from the early 1900s and was originally the Co-operative Bakery. The owners, Phillip Binns and Robert Storton, are both accomplished chefs and their frequently changing menus display a versatile repertoire of dishes to suit every palate. Wild Mushroom Tagliarini as a starter, for example, Seared Medallions of Salmon or Roasted Stuffed Pepper amongst the main courses, and a mouth-watering choice of desserts that includes a wonderful Egg Nog Crème Brulée and a Timbale of Fresh Fruits. There's an excellent wine list and the restaurant hosts regular "Call My Bluff" wine tasting sessions. Open every evening, except Sunday and Monday, and also Thursday and Friday lunchtime, Headley's is a place to savour in every sense. Many patrons join the restaurant's Q-Card

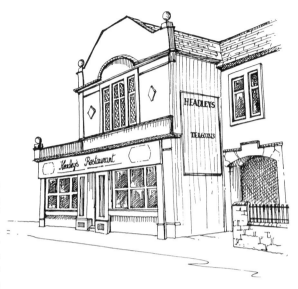

Headley's Restaurant, 398 Skipton Road, Utley, Keighley BD20 6HP Tel: 01535 607375 Fax: 01535 210489

programme which entitles them to substantial discounts from local shops, theatre and concert performances, excursions and holidays.

RIDDLESDEN

Map 6 ref E8

1 mile NE of Keighley off the A629

Parts of **East Riddlesden Hall**, now a National Trust property, date back to Saxon times. The main building, however, was constructed in the 1630s by James Murgatroyd, a wealthy Halifax clothier and merchant. A fine example of a 17th century manor house, the gabled hall is built of dark stone with mullioned windows, and it retains its original centre hall, superb period fireplaces, oak panelling, and plaster ceilings. The house is furnished in Jacobean style, which is complemented by carved likenesses of Charles Stuart and Henrietta Maria. East Riddlesden Hall also has one of the largest and most impressive timber framed barns in the North of England which now houses a collection of farm waggons and agricultural equipment. The hall is said to be haunted by the ghost of a lady dressed in blue who wanders along the building's passageways and it is probably this ghost which sets rocking the child's cradle.

RIBBLESDALE AND THE THREE PEAKS

The River Ribble, the source of which lies high up on bleak moorland to the northeast of Ingleton, flows through several ancient settlements before leaving the county of Yorkshire and flowing on into the mill town country of Lancashire. At the Aire Gap, and on opposite banks of the river, lie Settle and Giggleswick, which are overlooked by the towering white limestone cliffs of Castleberg Crag and Langcliffe Scar, parts of the mid-Craven fault. Further north from these two market towns lies one of the most popular tourist centres in the Dales, Ingleton, and high above the village are the famous **Three Peaks** of Ingleborough, Pen-y-ghent, and Whernside. The surrounding countryside is dominated by caves, potholes, and waterfalls and it is ideal country for all those who enjoy the outdoors.

The layer of limestone which lies across this whole area was laid down around 400 million years ago, when the shells of dead sea creatures along with mud accumulated at the bottom of the warm sea that covered a huge area of northern England. Much later, the layer of sandstone, known as millstone grit, was formed over the top. Much is talked about the **Craven Fault** and, though it was formed by a series of mighty earthquakes, this all happened well over 30 million years ago so visitors need not worry about visiting the area. However, the line of the fault, where the land to the northwest was lifted up and the land to the southeast slipped down, is all too evident today. It was the action of water, seeping into the limestone, which froze during the Ice Age that has created the many caves and potholes of the area. Erosion, though this time on the surface, near Malham and elsewhere, formed the magnificent limestone pavements whilst the Three Peaks, as they are capped by millstone grit, have stood the test of time and still stand proud. This is very much farming country and the traditional agricultural methods, along with the abundance of limestone, have given this region its own distinctive appeal. The high fells, composed of grits and sandstone, support heather moorlands and here can be found the only bird unique to Britain, the red grouse, and several birds of prey. Meanwhile, the limestone areas support a much more varied plant life, though the woodlands are chiefly of ash. In these shaded places, amongst the wild garlic and lily of the valley, visitors might be lucky enough to come across roe deer, badgers, and foxes.

SETTLE

This small market town, which received its charter in 1249, still retains its thriving weekly market on Tuesdays. A busy stopping place in the days of the stagecoach, when travellers journeying between York and Lancaster and Kendal called here, Settle is now a popular place for visitors, walkers, and cyclists who stop in the town to take full advantage of the wide range of inns and hotels.

However, for most, Settle is the home of the famous **Settle-Carlisle Railway**, a proudly preserved memento of the glorious age of steam and the line is still flanked by charming little signal boxes and stations that are a real tourist magnet. This attractive railway was built in the midst of great controversy and even greater cost, in both money and lives, earning it the dubious title of *"the line that should never have been built."* There is a churchyard at St Leonard's in Chapel-le-Dale where over 100 of the workers and miners, who laboured under the most adverse conditions, lie buried. Today, the trains still thunder over the 21 viaducts, through the 14 tunnels, and over the numerous bridges for which they gave their lives.

Settle town itself is dominated by one of these huge viaducts as well as the towering limestone cliffs of **Castleberg Crag** and it is worth spending some time here. Settle's architecture is very distinctive, in the main being Victorian sandstone buildings that all look as if they are born of the railway culture. Buildings of note include the arcaded Shambles, originally butcher's slaughter houses, the French-style Town Hall, the Victorian Music Hall, and the oldest building, Preston's Folly, described as an extravaganza of mullioned windows and Tudor masonry, and so called because the man who created this anomalous fancy impoverished himself in the process! The composer, Edward Elgar, was a frequent visitor to the town and whilst here he stayed at the house of his friend, Dr Buck.

Apart from the grander structures on the main streets, there are charming little side streets, lined with Georgian and Jacobean cottages, and criss-crossed with quirky little alleyways and ginnels with hidden courtyards and workshops of a time gone by. In Chapel Street is the **Museum of North Craven Life**, which gives a historical, topographical, and geological background to the area. The imaginative displays tell the story of the local farming traditions and also the history of the building of the Settle-Carlisle Railway.

Just outside the town, housed in a refurbished 19th century cotton mill, is the **Watershead Mill Visitor Centre**. This charming place, on the banks of the River Ribble, offers a unique shopping experience with the Dalesmade Centre offering a collection of 35 crafts all made in the region and much more besides.

The features of the surrounding countryside are equally interesting and, in particular, there is the fascinating Victorian Cave. Discovered in 1838 by Michael Horner, the cave has yielded finds of Roman relics, Stone Age artefacts, and even 120,000 year old mammoth bones. Unfortunately, the instability of the rock in the area has caused the cave and the surrounding land to be closed to the public.

GIGGLESWICK   MAP 1 REF C7
1 mile W of Settle off the A65

This ancient village, which lies below the limestone scar that is part of the Craven fault, is home to several interesting places including the 15th century **Church of St Alkelda** and the well-known **Giggleswick School**. Alkelda is thought to have been a Saxon saint who was strangled for her faith whilst the school, founded by James Carr, was granted a Royal Charter in 1553 by Edward VI. The school's fame stems from its observatory which was used by the Astronomer Royal in 1927 to observe an eclipse of the sun. The school's chapel, the copper dome of which is a well-known local landmark, was built to commemorate the Diamond Jubilee of Queen Victoria by Walter Morrison, a school governor who lived at Malham Tarn House. Just to the north of Giggleswick can be found the famous **Ebbing and Flowing Well**, one of many in the area which owe their unusual name to the porous nature of the limestone of the area which causes there sometimes to be water here and sometimes not.

RATHMELL   MAP 1 REF C7
2 miles S of Settle off the A65

From this small village, set beside the River Ribble, there are many footpaths along the riverbanks, through the nearby woods, and up to Whelpstone Crag. An old farming community, the oldest farm here is dated 1689 and a little row of farm cottages called Cottage Fold are from around the same period. The unusual name stems from the 17th century when Richard Frankland founded a nonconformist college in the village.

Located on the edge of this peaceful village **Layhead Farm Cottages** offer exceptionally attractive self-catering accommodation in 3 ingeniously converted old farm buildings. Set within a 200-acre sheep farm, they provide a haven of peace and quiet although only 4 miles from the busy little market town of Settle. Two of the properties, "Cobblestones"

**Layhead Farm Cottages, Field House, Rathmell, Settle,
North Yorkshire BD24 0LD
Tel: 01729 840234 Fax: 01729 840775**

and "Craggs Barn", have been created by the conversion of an old stone barn. Every modern comfort has been provided in this careful transformation whilst retaining many of the original features, including oak beams and exposed stonework. Both cottages can sleep 5 people in 2 bedrooms and an additional 2 people can be accommodated on a bed settee in the lounge. The third property, "The Stables", has 2 light and airy beamed bedrooms with imaginative furnishings and en suite bathrooms. With an additional chair bed in each bedroom, up to 6 people can be accommodated. If you wish, you can have a hearty Dales breakfast, made with local organic produce where possible, cooked for you in "The Stables" own kitchen.

LONG PRESTON
MAP 1 REF C7

3 miles S of Settle on the A65

Though it may be hard to imagine today, this pleasant village which straddles the main road was once larger than Leeds. Close to the pretty Church of St Mary's, which dates back in part to the 12th century, the remains of a Roman encampment have been discovered. The other interesting building in Long Preston is Cromwell House which, so the legend goes, once gave refuge to the Puritan leader.

FEIZOR
MAP 1 REF C6

3 miles NW of Settle off the A65

The village dates back to monastic times when it lay on the route from Kilnsey to the Lake District which was much used by the monks of Fountains Abbey. Although both Fountains Abbey and Sawley Abbey had possessions in the area, there are few reminders of those times today. However, the **Yorkshire Dales Falconry and Conservation Centre** does bring visitors to this village. With demonstration flights held throughout the day when the centre's wide range of birds of prey are seen flying free and much else on offer it does make an interesting and unusual day out.

AUSTWICK
MAP 1 REF C6

4 miles NW of Settle off the A65

This ancient village of stone cottages and crofts, dry stone walls, abandoned quarries, and patchwork hills was originally a Norse settlement: the name is Nordic for Eastern

Settlement. The largely 17ᵗʰ century buildings, with their elaborately decorated stone lintels, flank what remains of the village green where the ancient cross stands as a reminder of when this was the head of a dozen neighbouring manors and the home of an annual cattle fair.

The most peculiar feature of the surrounding area has to be the **Norber Boulders**: a series of black boulders which stand on limestone pedestals which, despite their contrived appearance, are a completely natural feature. They are also known locally as the Norber Erratics because they are anomalous - the grey silurian slate they are composed of usually occurs beneath limestone rather than on top. The mystery of their existence is explained

Norber Boulders

by the fact that these huge rocks were originally deposited by glacial action at the end of the last Ice Age. Another distinctive local feature is the clapper bridge, a medieval structure made from large slabs of rock that span the local becks.

CLAPHAM   MAP 1 REF C6
6 miles NW of Settle off the A65

By far the largest building in the village is **Ingleborough Hall**, once the home of the Farrer family and now a centre for outdoor education. One member of the family, Reginald Farrer, was an internationally renowned botanist and he was responsible for introducing many new plant species into the country. Many examples of his finds still exist in the older gardens of the village and in the hall's grounds and there is a particularly pleasant walk, the **Reginald Farrer Nature Trail**, which leads from Clapham to nearby Ingleborough Cave.

Though the whereabouts of **Ingleborough Cave** was known for centuries, it was not until the 19ᵗʰ century that its exploration was begun. One of the explorers, geologist Adam Sedgwick, is quoted as saying *"we were forced to use our abdominal muscles as sledges and our mouths as candlesticks"* which gives an excellent indication of the conditions the early pot-holers had to endure. However, their work proved very much worth while and the system is extremely extensive. Those visiting the caves today see only a small part of the 5 miles of caverns and tunnels though, fortunately, this easily accessible portion is spectacular. As well as exotic cave formations and illuminated pools there is **Eldon Hall Cavern**, home to a vast mushroom bed!

This is an area that has a great abundance of natural waterfalls but the waterfall seen near the village church is one of the very few which owes its existence to man. In the 1830s the Farrer family created a large lake, covering some 7 acres of land, and the waterfall is the lake's overflow. As well as providing water for the village, a turbine was placed at the bottom of the waterfall and, with the help of the electrical power, Clapham was one of the first villages in the country to have street lighting. This is perhaps not as surprising as it might seem as Michael Faraday, the distinguished 19th century scientist, was the son of the village blacksmith.

Overlooked by Ingleborough, close to the village is the giant pothole known as **Gaping Gill**. Some 340 feet deep, the hole is part of the same underground limestone cave system as Ingleborough Cave and the main chamber is similar in size to York Minster. Twice a year, the public can gain access via a bosun's chair on a winch that is operated by local caving clubs.

NEWBY
7 miles NW of Settle off the A65

MAP 1 REF B6

This tiny hamlet was originally found about a mile south of its present position because, in the 17th century, the Great Plague decimated the village's population. The survivors moved away and rebuilt Newby and many of the buildings date from this time.

The village came under the direction of the monks of Furness Abbey and the remains of their walled garden can still be seen. By the Victorian era, Newby had become a thriving weaving community. However, the cottage industry was soon overtaken by the new factory systems and, by 1871, the village had once again returned to peace and quiet.

INGLETON
10 miles NW of Settle off the A65

MAP 1 REF B6

Mentioned in the Domesday Book, the name means Beacon Town and Ingleton is certainly one of the most visited villages in the Dales. As a gateway to the Three Peaks, it is also popular with walkers. From as long ago as the late 18th century, Ingleton has been famous for the numerous caves and other splendid scenery that lie within a short distance though some are harder to find and even harder to reach. The coming of the railway, which gave those working in the towns easy and cheap access to the countryside, greatly increased the numbers of visitors looking for clean, country air. Though Ingleton is no longer served by trains, the village is still dominated by the railway viaduct that spans the River Greta. The river, which is formed here by the meeting of the Rivers Twiss and Doe, is famous for its salmon leaps.

Discovered in 1865 by Joseph Carr, the **Ingleton Waterfalls**, which were not immediately made accessible to the public, have been delighting visitors since 1885. Along the 4 miles

Ingleton

of scenic walks, the stretch of waterfalls includes those with such interesting names as Pecca Twin Falls, Holly Bush Spout, Thornton Force, and Baxengill Gorge.

The second principal network of caves in the area which are open to the public are **White Scar Caves**. Discovered in 1923, this cave network has been under exploration ever since and today the main features include two waterfalls, beautiful stalactites, and the longest show cave in Britain.

Finally, there is **Ingleborough** which, at 2375ft, is the middle summit of the **Three Peaks**. For over 2000 years, the peak has been used as a beacon and a fortress and, as a result, it is perhaps the most interesting. A distinctive feature of the horizon for miles around as it is made of several layers of rock of differing hardnesses, there are several paths to the summit most of which begin their journey in Ingleton. As well as the fine views, on a clear day, there are also several interesting features on top of the peak. The most recent of these are the remains of a tower that was built by a local mill owner, Mr Hornby Roughsedge. Though the intended use of the building is not known, its short history is well documented. A grand opening was arranged on the summit and the celebrations, probably helped by a supply of ale, got a little out of hand when a group of men began tearing down the structure! At the highest point is a triangulation point whilst, close by, a cross-shaped shelter has been built which offers protection from the elements whatever their direction. The shelter acts as a reminder that the weather can change quickly in this area and a walk to the summit, however nice the day is at lower levels, should not be undertaken without careful thought as to suitable clothing. To the east, on the edge of the summit plateau, are the remains of several ancient hut circles and, beyond, the remains of a wall. The Romans are known to have used Ingleborough as a signal station but the wall may have been built by the Brigantes whose settlement on the mountain was called Rigodunum.

Enjoying a grand view of famous Ingleborough Hill, **Ferncliffe Country Guest House** is a charming, creeper-covered stone house just a short walk from the centre of the village. Built in 1897, Ferncliffe is the home of Peter and Susan Ring who offer quality bed and breakfast accommodation boasting a 4-diamond rating from the Tourist Board.

Susan's hobby is patchwork and some fine examples of her work are scattered around the various rooms, including the comfortable residents' lounge. Ferncliffe has 5 guest bedrooms, (4 twins and 1 double), all of which are en suite and attractively furnished and decorated. A substantial breakfast awaits you each morning, served in the pleasant dining room with its Welsh dresser and fresh flowers on the tables. Evening meals are also available by arrangement and Susan will

Ferncliffe Country Guest House, Main Street, Ingleton, North Yorkshire LA6 3HJ Tel: 015242 42405

happily supply you with a packed lunch if required. Open from Valentine's Day weekend to the end of October, Ferncliffe provides a perfect base for exploring the Dales, the Forest of Bowland and the Southern Lakes area.

THORNTON IN LONSDALE   MAP 1 REF B6
1 mile NW of Ingleton off the A65

This small village of a few houses, an inn, and an interesting church dates back to at least the 12th century though it is probably much older. The 13th century **Church of St Oswald** was unfortunately burnt almost to the ground in 1933 and only the tower remains of the original building. The rest of the church was rebuilt to resemble the extensive restoration work that was undertaken here in 1870. On an outside wall of the tower is an unusual carving, of a rose, a thistle, and a shamrock, which is believed to commemorate the union of England and Wales with Scotland and Ireland in 1801.

FAR WESTHOUSE   MAP 1 REF B6
2 miles NW of Ingleton off the A65

Gatehouse Farm, just off the A65, offers excellent bed and breakfast accommodation in a sturdy old farmhouse built in 1740 which commands panoramic views over open countryside. This is great walking country where you will hear the call of the curlew, see lapwings circling over the limestone crags and enjoy the wild flowers as you wander round the country lanes. Gatehouse Farm is the home of Bryan and Nancy Lund who together with their son farm the surrounding 250-acre sheep and dairy farm. Guests are welcome on either a B&B, or dinner, B&B basis. Nancy is an excellent cook, offering hearty breakfasts and tasty, beautifully prepared dinners. All the rooms here feature original beams and there's a comfortable guest lounge with colour TV and open fires on chilly evenings. If you are travelling with

Gatehouse Farm, Far Westhouse, Ingleton,
North Yorkshire LA6 3NR Tel: 015242 41458 / 41307

a caravan, the farm has a caravan site about ¾ mile away with electric hook-ups and running water, and there's also a self-catering caravan available from March to October.

CHAPEL-LE-DALE   MAP 1 REF C6
5 miles NE of Ingleton on the B6255

Whernside, to the north of the village, is the highest of the **Three Peaks**, at 2418ft, and also the least popular of the mountains - consequently there are few paths to the summit.

Just below the top are a number of tarns. Here, in 1917, it was noticed that they were frequented by black-headed gulls. Those walking to the top of the peak today will also see the birds, a reminder that the northwest coast is not so far away.

KEASDEN
Map 1 ref B6

4 miles S of Ingleton off the A65

Today, Keasden is a scattered farming community that is easily missed but evidence from the 17th century church records tell a different story. At that time there were some 40 farms here (now there are around 15) as well as many associated trades and craftsmen. The name Keasden comes from the Old English for 'cheese valley' and some of the farms still retain the vast stone weights of the cheese presses though, unfortunately, the recipe for the local cheese has been lost.

LOW BENTHAM
Map 1 ref B6

3 miles S of Ingleton on the B6480

Lying close to the county border with Lancashire and on the slopes of the Pennines, this village is pleasantly situated in the valley of the River Wenning, a tributary of the River Lune. Like many Pennine villages in the late 17th and early 18th centuries, Low Bentham was taken over by the textile industry and there was a linen mill here. After a time, the mill changed hands, and also direction, taking on the specialised task of spinning silk before that too ceased in the 1960s as a result of the increasing use of man-made fibres.

The growth in textiles in the area coincided with an increase in Quakerism within the parish and, in 1680, a meeting house was set up in the village. Established as a place of nonconformist worship, the village was also well known as a place of Weslyan Methodism by 1800.

LANGCLIFFE
Map 1 ref C6

1 mile N of Settle on the B6479

As its name suggests, Langcliffe lies in the shelter of the long cliff of the Craven fault where the millstone grit sandstone meets the silver grey of the limestone. Although the majority of the houses and cottages surrounding the central village green are built from the limestone, some sandstone has also been used which gives this pretty village an added charm. The Victorian urn on the top of the **Langcliffe Fountain** was replaced by a stone cross, after World War I, in memory of those villagers who died in the conflict.

STAINFORTH
Map 1 ref C6

1 mile N of Settle on the B6479

This sheltered sheep farming village owes its existence to the Cistercian monks who brought those animals to this area. The monks were also responsible for building the 14th century stone packhorse bridge which carries the road over the local beck, a tributary of the River Ribble. Although the village is certainly old, there are few buildings which date beyond the days of the Civil War: during those turbulent times, much of Stainforth was destroyed. **Catrigg Force**, found along a track known as Goat Scar Lane, is a fine waterfall which drops some 60 feet into a wooded pool, whilst to the west is **Stainforth Force** flowing over a series of rock shelves.

Many of the earliest customers of the famous **Craven Heifer Hotel** would have passed over the old packhorse bridge which still spans Stainforth Beck at this picturesque spot. Your hosts at this small friendly pub are Barbara and Robert. Barbara is in charge of the kitchen, offering traditional home-cooked pub food as well as an extensive restaurant menu which can be enjoyed in the intimate dining room. Robert looks after the well-

tended ales in the cosy bar with its open fire, wood panelling and stained glass windows. There's a separate bar specially for the muddy boots brigade, walkers enjoying this glorious corner of the Dales, and outside a delightful beer garden overlooking the beck. The hotel is residential, with 5 letting bedrooms, all with

**Craven Heifer Hotel, Stainforth, Settle,
North Yorkshire BD24 9PB Tel: 01729 822599**

hot & cold water, and tea/coffee-making facilities. Colour televisions are available on request. Guests are served a generous breakfast, with vegetarian and special diets catered for by arrangement, and packed lunches are also available if required.

HELWITH BRIDGE   Map 1 ref C6
5 miles N of Settle on the B6479

Railway enthusiasts will be delighted with the location of **The Helwith Bridge** since the steam trains of the famous Settle to Carlisle railway run past the hotel on the other bank of the River Ribble. During the construction of the railway, the pub was a popular

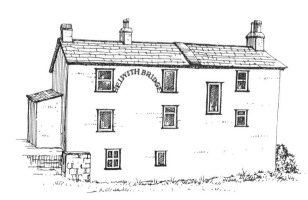

watering hole for the navvies although at that time it was little more than a rough and ready alehouse. Even earlier, the premises were used as a canteen for workers in the slate quarry and saw mills in the village. In the autumn of 1999 however, the pub was purchased by railway enthusiast Colin Hall and has had some refurbishment while retaining such features as the open fire. Good ale is available with at least 4 real ales on of-

**The Helwith Bridge, Helwith Bridge, Horton in
Ribblesdale, nr Settle, North Yorkshire BD24 0EH
Tel: 01729 860220**

fer including Theakstons and Marstons Pedigree, and bar snacks are served throughout the day. The pub enjoys a lovely position beside the River Ribble, famous for its quality salmon and sea trout, and there are some impressive rapids nearby.

HORTON IN RIBBLESDALE
6 miles N of Settle on the B6479

Map 1 ref C6

First mentioned in the Domesday Book, the village, whose name means literally the settlement on the muddy land or marsh, was probably in existence long before the 11th century. The oldest building here is the 12th century **St Oswald's Church** which still shows signs of its Norman origins in the chevron designs over the south door. Inside, peculiarly, all the pillars lean to the south and, in the west window, there is an ancient piece of stained glass show-

ing Thomas à Becket wearing his bishop's mitre.

This village is the ideal place from which to explore the limestone landscapes and green hills of Upper Ribblesdale. To the east lies **Pen-y-ghent** (2273ft high), one of the famous **Three Peaks**. For particularly ener-getic visitors to Horton, there is the demanding Three Peaks Challenge which is organised by the Pen-y-ghent Café. The

St Oswald's Church

24 mile hike takes in not only Pen-y-ghent but the other two peaks, Ingleborough and Whernside, and those completing the trek within 12 hours qualify for membership of the Three Peaks of Yorkshire Club. Less energetic walkers will be glad to hear that the café not only supplies well earned refreshments but also has a whole host of local information and runs a highly efficient safety service.

The whole of this area has been designated as being of Special Scientific Interest, mainly due to the need to conserve the swiftly eroding hillsides and paths. This is an ancient landscape, well worth the efforts to preserve its relic ash woodlands, primitive earthworks, and rare birdlife such as peregrine falcon, ring ouzel, and golden plover. There are also a great many caves in the area, which add to the sense of romance and adventure one feels in this place. There are several listed buildings in the area including Lodge Hall, which was formerly known as Ingman Lodge. Before the 20th century, a judge would travel around the countryside on horseback stopping to try cases rather than villagers commuting to major towns for their trials. Here, if anyone was found guilty, they were brought to Ingman Lodge to be hanged.

RIBBLEHEAD
10 miles N of Settle on the B6479

Map 1 ref C5

Lying close to the source of the River Ribble is the impressive structure, the **Ribblehead Viaduct**, which was built to carry the **Settle-Carlisle Railway**. Opened in 1876, after taking 5 years to construct, its 24 arches span the dark moorland and it is overlooked by

Ribblehead Viaduct

Whernside. A bleak and exposed site, the viaduct is often battered by strong winds which on occasion can literally stop a train in its tracks.

6 West Yorkshire

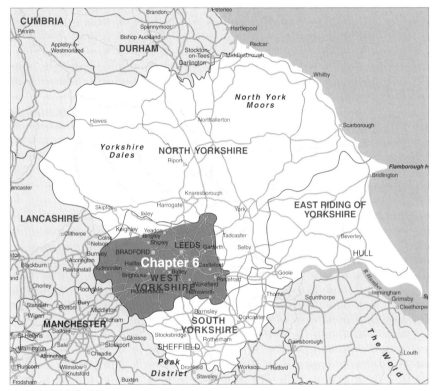

© MAPS IN MINUTES ™ (1998)

BRONTË COUNTRY

This area of West Yorkshire, surrounding the Brontë family home at Haworth, is dominated by the textile towns and villages along the valley bottom and the wild and bleak moorland above. The land has been farmed, mainly with sheep, since the Middle Ages and, in order to supplement their wages, the cottagers took to hand loom weaving in a room of their home. The advances in technology, beginning in the 18th century, replaced the single man powered looms with water powered machinery that were housed in the large mill buildings in the valley bottom and close to the source of power.

During the 19th century there was an explosion of building and the quiet riverside villages grew into towns and the South Pennine textile boom was in full flow. At first the conditions in the mills were grim as, indeed, were the living conditions for the mill workers but, with the reduction in the hours of the working day, people were able to take the opportunity to discover, and in some cases rediscover, the beauty of the surrounding moorland.

Not all the villages were completely taken over by the mills and, in many, the old stone built weavers cottages, with their deep windows to let in light for the worker within, survive. This, then, was the landscape of the area to which the Brontë family moved in 1820 when their father, Patrick, took up the position of rector. In the first five years of the family living in Haworth, both Maria Brontë (the mother) and two of the five girls died; the harsh climate having begun to take its toll. Though all the remaining children did receive an education it was in a somewhat haphazard way and they spent much of their time with each other isolated at the parsonage. After various attempts at working, generally as teachers, the girls, and their brother Branwell, all returned to the parsonage in the mid-1840s and this is when their writing began in earnest.

HAWORTH   MAP 6 REF E9
12 miles N of Halifax off the A6033

Once a bleak, moorland town in a dramatic setting that fired the romantic imaginations of the Brontë sisters, Haworth has been transformed into a lively, attractive place, with wonderful tea houses, street theatre, and antique and craft shops, very different to how it must have been in the Brontë's days. It was then a thriving industrial town, squalid amidst the smoke from its chimneys, filled with the noise of the clattering looms, which were rarely still. It is, however, worth exploring the ginnels and back roads off the steeply rising high street, to get a feeling of what the place was like in the days of the Brontës.

The Parsonage, built in 1777, is the focus of most Brontë pilgrimages and is now given over to the **Brontë Parsonage Museum**. The Brontë Society have restored the interior to be as close as possible to the house in which the sisters lived with their father and brother. There are exhibitions and displays of contemporary material, personal belongings, letters, and portraits, as well as a priceless collection of manuscripts, first editions, and memorabilia in the newer extension. The Brontë family moved to the fine Georgian house in 1820 when Patrick Brontë, the sisters' father, became the local parson.

Brontë Parsonage Museum

Taking their inspiration from the surrounding bleak and lonely Haworth Moor and from the stories they made up as children the three sisters, Anne, Charlotte, and Emily, under their male pen names, all became published authors whilst Branwell, though by all accounts a scholar, sought refuge in the beer at the local inn. Then the tuberculosis that had attacked the family earlier returned and, one by one,

Patrick Brontë's children succumbed to the terrible disease. The story of the Brontë family is one of tragedy but the circumstances of their deaths were all too common in the 19th century and graphically illustrates the harshness of life just 150 years ago.

Many visitors are drawn to the area by the story of the family and the **Brontë Way**, a 40 mile linear footpath with a series of four guided walks, links the places which provided inspiration to the sisters. The most exhilarating and popular excursion is that to **Top Withins**, a favourite place of Emily's and the inspiration for the 'Wuthering Heights' of the novel. The route also takes into account a great variety of scenery, from the wild moorlands to pastoral countryside.

Brontë enthusiasts can also sit in the Black Bull, where Branwell sent himself to an early grave on a mixture of strong Yorkshire ale, opium, and despair (although the last two are not available here these days). The Post Office, from where the sisters sent their manuscripts to London publishers, is still as it was, as is the Sunday School at which they all taught. Sadly the church which they all attended no longer exists, although Charlotte, Emily, and Branwell (Anne is buried in Scarborough) all lie in a vault in the new church which dates from 1879.

In such an historic little town one expects to find a traditional tea room and that expectation is amply fulfilled at **Heather Cottage Tea Rooms** which enjoy a 3-Diamond tourist board rating. The old stone building, located in the centre of Haworth, was formerly two weavers cottages and dates back some 260 years. It has a wonderfully olde-worlde atmosphere with many original features such as the flag-stoned floors and beamed ceilings still in place. The tea rooms are owned and run by Trevor Craven who offers his customers a wide selection of home cooked meals, snacks and a variety of home made cakes and pastries, all freshly baked on the premises. Trevor is the cook and in addition to the outstanding fare featured in his regular menu he also cooks for special Theme Nights about once a month. (In April, it's Mexican Night; in June, a Murder Nite). And if you are planning to stay in the Haworth area, Heather Cottage has 3 quality guest rooms to let, all of them with en suite facilities, central heating, colour television, hair dryers and tea/coffee-making facilities. A Visitors' Lounge and Garden Patio are both available to guests.

Heather Cottage Tea Rooms, 25-27 Main Street, Haworth, West Yorkshire BD22 8DA
Tel: 01535 644511
e-mail: heathercott@haworthmsfreeserve.co.uk

Awarded a 3-Diamond rating by the tourist board, **The Old Registry** is a striking building more than a hundred years old which once housed the office of the Registrar of

Births, Marriages and Deaths. Standing on the old cobbled main street, this characterful house is now the home of Marilyn and Michael Herdman, a welcoming couple who do everything they can to make their guests' stay here very special. The beautifully decorated en suite rooms with their co-ordinated soft furnishings are all well-equipped with colour television, hair dryer, toiletries, welcoming tray (with biscuits) and much more. For that extra special treat, why not book the elegant Four Poster Room? Guests can stay at The Old Registry on either a B&B, or Dinner, Bed & Breakfast arrangement. The house is non-smoking and ideally located for exploring this historic little town. It over-looks the park and across to the

The Old Registry, 2-4 Main Street, Haworth, West Yorkshire BD22 8DA Tel/Fax: 01535 646503 e-mail: oldregistry.haworth@virgin.net

steam railway with the famous Haworth Parsonage just a short stroll from the house.

The Flappit is the only pub in the country with this unusual name, a name which goes back to the days when there was a flay pit here where the hides of animals, particu-larly cattle, were flayed (stripped and cleaned) before being sent to the local tannery. So although the pub's original name was the Stone House Inn, the locals' name for it is the one that has survived. The Flappit is run by Simone and Wayne Lerigo who arrived here in 1999 and have stamped their personalities on the place. Well-decorated and furnished inside, there's also a charming beer garden to the rear of the pub which is understandably very popular in good weather. When it's cold out-side though, the roaring fires inside certainly add to the warm and friendly atmosphere. The food here is quite outstanding, with a menu that offers no fewer than 83 differ-ent main courses. Everything is freshly cooked to order, with the menu high-lighting Sizzler

The Flappit, Flappit Springs, Haworth, West Yorkshire BD21 5PU Tel: 01535 643117

Steaks on Tuesdays and Wednesdays, seafood on Thursday, and a carvery with a choice of three roasts on Sunday. For lovers of good food The Flappit is a place not to be missed.

As well as devotees of the Brontë legend, Haworth is popular with devotees of steam railways. The town is the headquarters of the **Keighley & Worth Valley Railway,** a thriving volunteer-run railway which serves 6 stations (most of them gas-lit) in the course of its 4¾ mile length. The railway owns an extensive and varied collection of locomotives and everything combines to re-create the atmosphere of the days of steam. There are daily services during July and August and intermittent services throughout the rest of the year. To listen to the talking timetable, telephone 01535 643629.

Just across the street from the Haworth station is the **Royal Oak Inn**, built in the mid-1800s at the same time as the railway came to Haworth. Used by rail passengers since then, the inn is still a popular place with visitors to the village. As might be imagined, there is a railway theme inside the pub, especially in the Railway Room where old pictures, photographs and all kinds of railway memorabilia adorn the walls. Those not so interested in the vintage railway artefacts may enjoy looking at the fine collection of old brass keys displayed above the bar area. Mine hosts, Alan and Ann, gained wide experience of the hospitality business all around the UK before taking over here in late 1999. Their menu offers a good choice of tasty dishes, supplemented by daily specials. (Reduced prices for OAPs). On Wednesday evenings there's live entertainment from 9pm and Monday evening is Folk Night when customers are encouraged to bring their own instruments and play, or simply join in the singing.

**Royal Oak Inn, 2 Mill Hey, Haworth,
West Yorkshire BD22 8NQ Tel: 01535 643257**

The countryside around Haworth inspires the modern visitor as much as it did the Brontës. This is excellent walking country and it is worth taking a trip via the Penistone Hill Country Park, following the rough track by old moorland farms to the Brontë Falls and stone footbridge. For the energetic the path eventually leads to the deserted ruins of Top Withins Farm, said to have been the inspiration for the setting of *Wuthering Heights*. It is said that the ghost of Emily Brontë has been seen walking, with her head bowed, between the Parsonage and Top Withins Farm.

OAKWORTH

MAP 6 REF E8

1 mile N of Haworth on the B6143

Those visiting Oakworth may find its Edwardian station, on the Keighley and Worth Valley Railway line somewhat familiar. In fact, not only did it feature in the classic children's film, *The Railway Children*, but also in episodes of the television series *Sherlock Holmes*.

STANBURY

MAP 6 REF E9

2 miles W of Haworth off the B6143

Close to the village lies **Ponden Mill** which was, in the heyday of Yorkshire's textile industry, one of the largest working mills in the country. At the height of production, cloth from Ponden Mill was exported around the world. Though the vast majority of the mills have now closed and the Yorkshire textile industry is almost a thing of the past, Ponden Mill is still open, this time as a retail centre selling all manner of textiles from home furnishings and linens to country clothing. To round off your visit, have a look in the clog shop where traditional methods of manufacture are still on show.

If you take the country lane that leads from Haworth alongside Ponden reservoir towards the moors, you leave behind the stress of 21st century life. Here you will find the peace of another era, especially if you are staying at **Ponden Guest House** where Brenda Taylor, her family and friends, offer hospitality to guests from far and near with not a TV, video, newspaper or computer to be seen. "We can even hide the clock!" says Brenda. After 22 years at Ponden Hall, Brenda continues to offer a warm and relaxing Yorkshire welcome. Her ample breakfasts include fruit juices, fresh and stewed fruits, yoghurt, cooked dishes, toast and home made jams and marmalades. Home cooked evening meals are also available by arrangement. The fresh, flavoursome and innovative dishes are served by

**Ponden Guest House, Stanbury, nr Haworth,
West Yorkshire BD22 0HR Tel: 01535 644154**

candlelight at the large dining room table. After the meal guests can relax around a log fire with a glass or two of wine and with no worries about driving home. Ponden House enjoys an outstanding position, set in 7 acres of its own grounds and with glorious views down to the reservoir and across to the moors. Three miles away are the Brontë Parsonage, Haworth and the Worth Valley Steam Railway, while Top Withers, the original of Wuthering Heights, is a walk away. Long distance walkers will also find that the Pennine Way actually passes the front door!

OXENHOPE
MAP 6 REF E9

1 miles S of Haworth on the A6033

This village contains over 70 listed buildings, including a **Donkey Bridge**, two mile-stones, a mounting block, a cowshed, and pigsty. The early farmhouses had narrow mullioned windows which gave the maximum light for weaving and some had a door at first-story level so that the pieces could be taken out. The first mill here was built in 1792 and, during the 19th century, there were up to 20 mills producing worsted.

Many scenes for *The Railway Children* were set here in 1970 using local views and local people and a station on the Keighley and Worth Valley Railway also serves the village.

The Dog & Gun lies just outside the centre of this attractive village, on the main road to Denholme. When it was built in the 16th century, a team of horses was kept here for the

passing stage coaches. Today there are no horses but the Dog & Gun still offers excellent refreshments to travellers and wayfarers. Well known for the delicious meals served here at both lunchtimes and evenings (except Sunday evenings and all

The Dog & Gun, Denholme Road, Oxenhope, Keighley BD22 9SE Tel: 01535 643159

day on Mondays), the hosts Kathryn and Michael Roper also provide a range of well-kept ales, amongst them Timothy Taylor's 'Landlord' which was voted Supreme Champion Beer of Britain in 1999. The Dog & Gun's intimate dining room and the cosy bar area both have the added warmth of roaring log fires in the winter months and the walls are adorned with all manner of old and interesting items. Popular with locals and visitors alike, this is a lively pub with plenty of character and those who enjoy pub quizzes should make sure to call in on Monday evening.

HEBDEN BRIDGE
MAP 6 REF E9

5 miles NW of Halifax on the A646

This mill town is characterised by the stepped formation of its houses which were stacked one on top of the other up the steep sides of the Calder valley. There has been a village here for many years centred around the crossing point of the River Calder. When the first bridge was built is not known but as early as the beginning of the 16th century its state of repair was causing concern and, in a style typical of this area of Yorkshire, a stone bridge was erected close by.

The **Rochdale Canal**, which flows through the town, was completed in 1798. It was constructed to link the Calder and Hebble Navigation with the Bridgwater and Ashton canals from Lancashire. Used by commercial traffic since 1939, the canal has been re-

Hebden Bridge

paired and sections of it, including that between Hebden Bridge and Todmorden, are now open to traffic though, now, it consists mainly of pleasure craft. Horse drawn or motor boat cruises are available from the marina.

One of the first purpose built industrial towns in the world, Hebden Bridge grew rapidly as the demand for textiles boomed. Over the years, the town has seen many changes of fortune and, today, though textiles have now gone, it is a place of bookshops, antique shops, restaurants, and a market.

Located in the heart of this picturesque little town, **The Shoulder of Mutton** is a popular traditional pub offering first class ales and food. The old stone buildings date back to the 17th century and were originally cottages and a workshop. The interior still has a welcoming olde-worlde atmosphere, a relaxing ambience where locals and visitors mix freely. Mine hosts here are the brothers Bob and John Taylor, and since their arrival in 1997 they have made the Shoulder of Mutton a lively

The Shoulder of Mutton, Bridge Gate, Hebden Bridge, West Yorkshire HX7 8EX Tel: 01422 842585

social centre. They organise many events to raise funds for charity, - just call them for details. The pub is open all day, every day, and there's a good range of ales, amongst them

The Swiss Connection, 17 Market Street, Hebden Bridge HX7 6EU Tel: 01422 845524

Flowers IPA, Oak Best and Speckled Hen. Food is available every lunch time until 4pm with a menu that offers all the traditional favourites, - Pie & Peas, Liver & Onions, Shepherd's Pie, and much more.

A rather surprising sight in the town's Market Street is a flag displaying a bold white cross on a red background, - the Swiss national flag. It hangs above **The Swiss Connection**, an inviting tea room and café which takes it name from the Swiss background of the owner, Monika Clay, and Hebden Bridge's strong links with Switzerland. For many years the Swiss communities in Great Britain have celebrated their National Day, August 1st, at Hardcastle Crags a couple of miles outside the town, an area reminiscent of the Rütli meadows where to this day the Swiss commemorate their folk hero William Tell. Monika's menu offers a wide range of appetising savouries, (including of course a choice of Röstis), breakfasts, salads, grills, and afternoon teas. A speciality of the house is its wonderful selection of Swiss ice creams. There are always at least 17 delicious varieties to choose from and in summer as many as 25. Definitely not to be missed, The Swiss Connection is open every day from 11am until 5pm; children are welcome, baby-changing facilities are available and there is good access for wheelchairs.

The Nutclough House Hotel, Keighley Road, Hebden Bridge, West Yorkshire HX7 8EZ Tel: 01422 844361

An excellent place to stay in Hebden Bridge is **The Nutclough House Hotel**, conveniently located on the edge of the town centre. The sturdy stone house dates back to 1725 when it was built as a Mill Manager's town residence. Before that the site was occupied by a Toll House and the ground floor of that building is now the hotel's cellar. The Nutclough is owned and run by Andy and Pat Brown and they have preserved many of the original features of the

18th century building, - stone-flagged floors and exposed brick walls, for example, attractively set off by comfy sofas and stylish decoration. The hotel, a free house, is renowned for its quality real ales, at least 5 of them available at any one time. Timothy Taylor's 'Landlord' and Theakston's Best are permanent features with an ever-changing choice of guest ales. Pat is an accomplished cook, offering a menu which is notable for its vegetarian dishes along with a good choice of home made dishes and daily specials. The Nutclough also has 5 superior en suite guest bedrooms, one of them a family room with its own toilet and shower.

HEPTONSTALL

MAP 6 REF D9

7 miles NW of Halifax off the A646

The village, one of the main tourist centres in Calderdale, overlooks Hebden Bridge and **Hardcastle Crags**. This beautiful wooded valley is protected and cared for by the National Trust and, from the crags there are several interesting walks along the purpose built footpaths. It is also one of only three places in Britain where two churches occupy the same churchyard. In this case, the original church, which dates from 1256, was struck by lightning in the 1830s and a new church was built next to the ruin. Every year, on Good Friday, the **Paceggers Play** takes place in Weavers Square. An ancient method of story-telling, the actors, dressed in elaborate costumes, tell the legend of St George.

Set in the heart of this picturesque conservation village, **The Cross Inn** is a very friendly village pub serving well-kept beer and good food. It's one of the family of 'Timothy Taylor Pubs', some 20 hostelries located in and around the brewery's home town of Keighley. All of them serve fine cask ales, a wide choice of other drinks and in most you'll find good home-cooked pub food. You certainly will at The Cross Inn, - Jane is a qualified chef and offers a good selection of home made dishes every lunchtime from noon onwards. By the time you read this, The Cross will also be offering evening meals from 6.30pm. Together with her partners

The Cross Inn, 46 Towngate, Heptonstall,
Hebden Bridge HX7 7NB Tel: 01422 843833

Anthony and Alvin, Jane took over here in November 1999 and quickly established a fine reputation. Built in the mid-1700s, the inn is full of character and dog lovers will be pleased to know that their pets are also welcome and even receive a complimentary dog chew on arrival!

BLACKSHAW HEAD
MAP 6 REF D9

8 miles NW of Halifax off the A646

Set high on the hillside overlooking Colden Water and Hebden Bridge, **The New Delight Inn** really lives up to its name. It stands beside an old Drovers road and dates back to the

The New Delight Inn, Jackbridge, Blackshaw Head, nr Hebden Bridge HX7 7HT Tel: 01422 846178

early 1700s. The sturdy old building began life as a farmhouse, later became an alehouse and then an inn. Inside, the flagstone floors, real fires and stone exposed walls create a setting full of character. Your hosts are Julie and Steve Hunter who moved to the village a few years ago, fell in love with the pub and when it became available, bought it.

Julie is a gifted cook, renowned for her delicious home made pies, - melt in the mouth Steak & Ale or Steak & Kidney for example. The New Delight is a lively place with quiz nights on Tuesday evenings during the season and occasional themed nights. During the summer, customers can enjoy their refreshments in the attractive beer garden with its soothing views of unspoilt countryside. You may well want to linger a while here: if so, the inn has a charming double room available all year round which can be rented for either B&B or self-catering accommodation.

TODMORDEN
MAP 6 REF D9

8 miles W of Halifax Bridge on the A646

This is another, typical mill town that grew with the expansion of the textile industry.

Todmorden Town Hall

Before the 19th century, Todmorden had been a spartan place with many of the villagers eking out frugal lives by hand loom weaving. Following the building of the first mill here Todmorden began to grow and the highly ornate and flamboyant public buildings were, in the main, built by the mill owners. Though many towns which owe their existence to industry also bear the scars, Todmorden has retained all its charm and character and is an excellent place to visit for those interested in architecture. It boasts a magnificent **Town Hall** designed by John Gibson and opened in 1875. One of the finest municipal buildings of its size in the country, the grand old building stands half in Yorkshire and half in Lancashire. So the ornate carving in the pediment represents the farming and iron trades of Yorkshire in the right panel; the cotton trade of Lancashire in the left.

MYTHOLMROYD   Map 6 ref E9
5 miles W of Halifax on the A646

Prior to the 1600s, the valley bottom in what is now Mytholmroyd, was marshy and of little use as foundations for a village, though some of the outlying farms in the area date from the late 14th century. However, with the need to build more mills, close to a supply of water, the land was improved and Mytholmroyd joined the age of the Industrial Revolution.

Each spring the town is host to the **World Dock Pudding Championships**. Dock Pudding is unique to this corner of the county and is made from the weed *Polygonum Bistorta* or sweet dock (which should never be confused with the larger docks that are commonly used for easing nettle stings. In spring the plant grows profusely and local people pick it by the bagful. The docks are then mixed with young nettles and other essential ingredients and cooked to produce a green and slimy delicacy the appearance of which is found by many to be rather off-putting. It is usually served with bacon after having been fried in bacon fat and is believed to cure acne and cleanse the blood.

Set beside the River Elphin on the back road to Littleborough, **The Shoulder of Mutton** has been showered with awards for its outstanding food and well-kept ales. It has featured in the *Camra Good Food Guide* every year for 10 years, is recommended by the *Camra Good Beer Guide 1999*, received Whitbread's 'Gold Award' 1996-97, has been nominated by the *Halifax Evening Courier* as 'Pub of the Year' and was a runner-up in the Guinness Scotland, Wales and North Pub Food Competition. The credit for this impressive record goes to John and Lyn Hartley, who have been running the pub since 1976, and their 'right hand lady', Lisa. Their value-for-money menu offers a good choice of main meals, (including 4 different roasts), snacks and desserts, with smaller meals available for

The Shoulder of Mutton, New Road, Mytholmroyd,
nr Halifax HX7 5DZ Tel: 01422 883165

children and OAPs. Everything served here has been home cooked using fresh local produce. Food is available every lunchtime (11.30am to 2pm) and evening (7pm to 8.30pm) except Tuesday evenings. At least six hand pulled real ales are always available to complement your meal and Pub Quiz fans should make a note to be at the Shoulder of Mutton on Monday evening for 9pm!

LUDDENDEN FOOT
MAP 6 REF E9
3 miles W of Halifax off the A646

Located about halfway between Hebden Bridge and Halifax, **Rockcliffe West** is reached by way of a long wooded drive. It's an imposing and spacious house built for a Halifax mill owner in 1872. The builders used a honey-coloured local sandstone which is very easy on the eye and, together with the mature trees and attractive gardens, make this a very pleasant and soothing setting. Rockliffe West has been the home of Ginny Hodgson for more than 30 years and for the last seven or so of those years she has been welcoming guests for bed & breakfast. There are two guest rooms with lovely views over the garden and surrounding hillside, - 1 double which is en suite, and a twin with its own

Rockcliffe West, Luddendenfoot, Halifax, West Yorkshire HX2 6HL Tel: 01422 882151 Fax: 01422 881421

private bathroom. The rooms are spacious and the attractive decorations include watercolours painted by Ginny, along with owls, owls and more owls. Ginny is fascinated by these wide-eyed creatures and collects owl ornaments of every kind. This is a charming place to stay, (ETB-inspected and awarded a 4-Diamond rating), and in addition to the breakfast included in the tariff, evening meals are also available by arrangement.

HALIFAX
MAP 6 REF E9
6 miles SW of Bradford on the A629

Halifax boasts one of Yorkshire's most impressive examples of municipal architecture, the glorious 18th century **Piece Hall**. It possesses a large quadrangle where regular markets are held on Fridays and Saturdays, surrounded by colonnades and balconies behind which are some forty specialist shops. On Thursdays a flea market is held here and there's a lively and varied programme of events for all the family throughout the season. There's also an art gallery with a varied programme of contemporary exhibitions and workshops, a museum and tea room.

The **Town Hall** is another notable building, designed by Sir Charles Barry, architect of the Houses of Parliament, and there's an attractive Borough Market, constructed in cast iron and glass with an ornate central clock. In Gibbet Street stands a grisly reminder of the past, - a replica of guillotine, the original blade being kept in the Piece Hall Museum. There are many hidden places in old Halifax to explore: from Shear's Inn, an old weavers' inn near the town centre, one can walk up the cobbled **Boy's Lane**, very little changed from Victorian times, or trace out the ancient *Magna Via*, a medieval path to the summit of Breacon Hill.

Halifax also boasts the largest parish church in England. Of almost cathedral sized proportions, it dates from the 12th and 13th centuries although most of the present building is from the 1400s. It has a lovely wooden ceiling, constructed in 1635, and visitors should look out for '*Old Tristram*', a life-sized wooden effigy of a beggar, reputedly based on a local character, which served as the church poor box - and still does.

Piece Hall, Halifax

Right next door to Piece Hall, the **Calderdale Industrial Museum** houses still-working looms and mill machinery, hand textile demonstrations and amongst the many displays one celebrating the town's greatest contribution to modern travel, the cats-eye! From the Great Wheel to the Spinning Jenny, from mining to moquette, from steam engines (in live steam) to toffee, the museum provides a riveting insight into Halifax's industrial heritage. Situated next to Halifax railway station, **Eureka!** is Britain's first and only interactive museum designed especially for children between 3 and 12 years old. With more than 400 larger than life exhibits and exciting activities available, Eureka! opens up a fascinating world of hands-on exploration. A team of 'Enablers' help children make the most of their visit, there are regular temporary exhibitions, and the complex includes a café and gift shop.

Shibden Hall and Park, about a mile out of town, is somewhere very special that should not be missed. The Old Hall itself lies in a valley on the outskirts of the town and is situated in 90 acres of parkland. The distinctive timber framed house dates from 1420 and has been carefully furnished to reflect the various periods of its history. The 17th century barn behind the Hall houses a fine collection of horse drawn vehicles and the original buildings have been transformed into a 19th century village centre with a pub, estate worker's cottage, saddler's, blacksmith's, wheelwright's and potter's workshop.

Also on the outskirts of the town is the **Bankfield Museum**, the home between 1837 and 1886 of Edward Akroyd, the largest wool manufacturer in Britain. He lavished money and attention on the building, transforming it from a modest town house into a magnificent Italianate mansion with elaborate ceilings, staircases and plasterwork. After his death, his sumptuous home became a museum and now houses an internationally important collection of textiles and costumes from around the world. Contemporary crafts are also featured and the museum hosts an interesting programme of temporary exhibitions, workshops, seminars, master classes and gallery demonstrations.

AMBLER THORN
MAP 6 REF E9

3 miles N of Halifax on the A647

Located on the A647 Queensbury to Halifax road, **The Royal Oak Inn** is a handsome Victorian building, the home of the Harney family who offer their customers a warm welcome, good ale and fine food. There are five members of the family: Brian, Susan, (who is in charge of the kitchen), their son John and daughters Michelle and Christine.

The pub is open all day, every day with food available every lunchtime (noon until 2pm) and evening (5.30pm to 8.30pm) except Sunday and Monday evenings. Susan's menu offers plenty of choice, - from shoulder of lamb to scampi, from rump steak to omelettes, and the vast majority of the dishes are home made. To comple-

The Royal Oak Inn, Ambler Thorn, Queensbury,
Bradford BD13 2DJ Tel: 01274 880531

ment your meal there's a good selection of ales, including Tetleys and Black Sheep, along with draught lagers, ciders and Guinness. There's a separate, non-smoking dining room, for which bookings are advisable, or you can enjoy your meal in the lounge bar.

QUEENSBURY
MAP 6 REF E9

4 miles NE of Halifax on the A647

The hamlet of West Scholes lies on the old Thornton Road between Queensbury and Thornton. This hidden place is well worth seeking out in order to visit **The Junction Inn** where you'll find an outstanding combination of good food, good beer and a warm

Yorkshire welcome. The inn was refurbished towards the end of 1997 and the addition of a large conservatory provides an excellent dining area, - ideal for business lunches, informal dinners, or party bookings in a lovely setting overlooking well-kept gardens. Your hosts, Irene and Paul Grayson, concentrate on quality food - served as bar snacks in the warm friendly pub or as main meals in the stylish conservatory restaurant. Their menu includes a fine

The Junction Inn, West Scholes, Queensbury, Bradford BD13 1NQ Tel: 01274 880278

selection of starters, steaks, grills, chicken and seafood, roasts, home made pies, pasta, vegetarian options and home made sweets. In addition, there's a choice of blackboard specials, - constantly changing, adventurous and different. Food is available every lunchtime and evening, (except Monday lunchtime, unless it's a Bank Holiday), and is complemented by at least three hand-pulled ales and a fine choice of wines.

CLAYTON HEIGHTS

Map 6 ref E9

4 miles W of Bradford on the A647

History, hospitality and 'mine hosts' with a great sense of humour all combine to make **The Old Dolphin Inn**, which was voted Bradford Pub of the Year 1999, a place you really should seek out. History first. The oldest parts of the Old Dolphin have been in place for some 800 years, pre-dating King John's signing of Magna Carta in 1215 by a decade or more. Oliver Cromwell and his men were billeted here in 1647 and in more recent times, the inn was regularly frequented by Percy Shaw, the inventor of 'Cats' Eyes', and by John Foster who used to play music here before going on to create the world-famous Black Dyke Mills Brass Band. Your hosts at the Old Dolphin are Colin ("Fat Boy") and Angie ("Little Mama")

The Old Dolphin Inn, 192 Highgate, Clayton Heights, Bradford BD13 1DR Tel: 01274 882202

Clarke. Angie is a superb cook, serving up delicious food lovingly prepared in Little Mama's Kitchen, - big steaks, big grills and big meals including vegetarian, diabetic, pensioners and children's menus. If you have a hearty appetite, why not try the 80oz steak? If you finish it, you get 5 free pints and a free pudding. No one has yet managed to claim their free pints! Meals are served every lunchtime and evening with an 'Early Bird' discount on food between 5.30pm and 7pm Tuesday to Friday. The fame of Angie's cooking is such that you'd be wise to book ahead at weekends. Real Ales and a good range of traditional keg beers and lagers add to the dining pleasure here and on Friday and Saturday evenings there's entertainment on the piano and Thursday evening is Quiz Night. Incidentally, you won't find any 'bandits' here, or a juke box - only pleasant background music. Other attractions at the Old Dolphin include real log fires and a large beer garden with a children's play area.

The owner of **The Nags Diner** in Clayton Heights knows this welcoming establishment very well, - June Calvert worked here for a couple of years before buying the café in the summer of 1999. It's a popular place, well-known locally for its friendly atmosphere and value-for-money food. June opens up at 7.30am every day, offering a choice of a hearty breakfast or a 'Mega' breakfast and from then on until 1pm she serves a wide range of wholesome food. The menu includes home made pies, scampi, chicken dishes, lasagne, and of course roast beef and Yorkshire pudding. In

The Nags Diner, 78 Highgate, Clayton Heights, Bradford BD13 1ES Tel: 01274 818366

addition, there's always a daily special. If there's something you particularly fancy and it doesn't feature on the menu, just ask. If June has the ingredients to hand she will happily cook it for you. All the food at the Nags Diner is also available to take away.

MOUNTAIN
MAP 6 REF E9

4 miles W of Bradford on the A644

When you come across a pub called **Mad Ma Jones** you may wonder what you are going to find inside. In fact, you'll find a warm and welcoming hostelry, run by Linda Walker and offering quality ales and food. Strangely, no-one seems to know who Mad Ma Jones was, but one would like to think that she was a wonderfully eccentric landlady. Today, the inn serves excellent food every evening until 8.45pm (except on Monday evenings) and a range of fine ales that includes Tetleys and a regularly changing guest ale. Such is the pub's reputation for good food, it's definitely a good idea to book ahead. If you fancy your skills in pub quizzes, then make sure you call in on Mad Ma Jones on a Wednesday when the Quiz begins at 9.30pm.

Mad Ma Jones, Brighouse and Denholm Road, Mountain, Bradford BD13 1LN   Tel: 01274 882605

THORNTON

MAP 6 REF E9

4 miles W of Bradford on the B6145

Thornton is an essential stopping place on the Brontë trail for it was here that the three sisters were born, at No. 74 Market Street, now open to the public as the **Brontë Birthplace**. Their father was the vicar of Thornton and one of the treasures of his parish church is a font, inscribed with the date 1687, in which Charlotte, Emily and Anne were all baptised. Charlotte was only 4 years old, her two sisters still toddlers, when the family moved a few miles northwest to Haworth where their father had been appointed Rector.

Today, Thornton has an additional claim to fame. Since it opened in 1982 the **Villa Roma Pizzeria-Ristorante** has established a reputation as probably one of the finest Italian eating-places in the country. The Villa Roma was created by Franco Arcuri whose son Richard is now the Head Chef here. Richard's 10-page menu offers a mind-boggling range of Italian treats. There are half a dozen soups, a dozen hot starters, 17 cold starters, and about the same number each of pasta dishes and varieties of pizza. Chicken, scampi, trout, veal, fillet and sirloin also are all available in a

Villa Roma Pizzeria-Ristorante, 1519 Thornton Road, School Green, Thornton, Bradford BD13 3DB Tel: 01274 882480

diverse range of presentations, along with a wide choice of vegetarian dishes. And then there are the house specials: Capriolo alle Pesche, for example, (venison sautéed in butter, topped with peaches & served in a madeira sauce), or Anatra Tropicale, (a half duckling served in a sauce of tropical fruits and liqueur). To complement the outstanding cuisine, the Villa Roma wine list offers a choice selection of Italian wines, available by the glass, ½ carafe or ½ bottle, carafe or bottle. This outstanding restaurant is open every evening, except Monday, from 6pm until 11pm (11.30pm on Friday and Saturday).

DENHOLME
MAP 6 REF E9

6 miles W of Bradford on the A629

Set high on the hillside, this little town enjoys magnificent views across the moors and also boasts an outstanding inn. A Grade II Listed Building with a history that goes back some 200 years, **The Brown Cow** is a smartly refurbished hostelry offering top quality food and drink. In August 1999, landlord Ben Loftus and his father took over the lease of this ancient inn, completely renovated the premises and introduced an excellent, varied

and constantly changing menu which includes dishes based on rabbit and ostrich along with 16oz T-bone steaks, Baked Halibut, and Lobster Thermidor. The menu is supplemented by daily specials and customers will find an impressive wine list that includes Chateauneuf du

The Brown Cow, 1370 Thornton Road, Denholme, Bradford BD13 4HQ Tel: 01274 833077

Pape and Barolo. À la carte meals are served in the restaurant every day, all day from noon on Saturday and Sunday, and Monday to Friday from noon until 2pm, and from 5pm to 9pm. There's a special lunchtime (noon until 2pm) and early evening (between 5pm and 7pm) set menu. The waiter/waitress service is prompt and courteous; children are welcome and there are separate smoking and non-smoking areas.

BRADFORD
MAP 6 REF F9

8 miles W of Leeds on the A647

Bradford is a city with much to offer the visitor. In terms of numbers, the most popular attraction is undoubtedly the **National Museum of Photography, Film and Television** which houses IMAX, one of the largest cinema screens in the world. If you suffer from vertigo you'll need to close your eyes as the huge, wrap-around screen shows such heart-stopping scenes as roller-coaster rides and Alpine mountaineering. There's plenty to keep you occupied here for hours, - virtual reality exhibits, the Kodak Gallery which leads you on a journey through the history of popular photography, an extensive television display which ranges from the world's first TV pictures to the very latest, and much, much more.

A recent addition is a vast new space presenting world-class exhibitions on photography, film, television and new media. Of related interest is Britain's only **Museum of Colour**. 'The World of Colour' gallery looks at the concept of colour, how it is perceived and its importance. Visitors can see how the world looks to other animals, mix coloured lights and experience strange colour illusions. In the 'Colour and Textiles' gallery you can discover the fascinating story of dyeing and textile printing from Ancient Egypt to the present day. Computerised technology allows you to take charge of a dye making factory and decorate a room. While both these museums look to the future, the **Bradford Industrial Museum and Horses at Work** celebrates the city's industrial heritage. It is housed in an original worsted spinning mill complex built in 1875 and recreates life in Bradford in late Victorian times. Open all year, the museum offers horse-bus and tram rides, a Shire Horse centre, a reconstructed mill owner's house and the workingmen's back to back cottages. The complex also includes a café, shop and picnic area.

Architecturally, the most striking building in Bradford must be **Lister's Mill**. Its huge ornate chimney dominates the city skyline and its claimed that it is wide enough at the top to drive a horse and cart around. The mill fell silent some years ago though its exterior has been cleared up and there are plans to use to house a museum to the industry that brought the city its wealth - wool. A rather quirkier sign of the city's former riches is **Undercliffe Cemetery**. Here the wool barons were buried, each in a more opulent Gothic mausoleum than the last. It is easy to spend an hour here admiring the Victorian funereal art on show with the cityscape laid out before you. The fact that the city has a **Cathedral** is an indication of its importance. The first evidence of worship on the site is provided by the remains of a Saxon preaching cross. Today the Cathedral contains many items of interest, including beautiful stained glass windows, some of which were designed by William Morris, carvings and statuary.

SHIPLEY

MAP 6 REF F9

4 miles N of Bradford on the A6037

Although Shipley is mainly industrial, **Shipley Glen** is a very popular area for tourists. Within the grounds is a narrow gauge, cable hauled tramway, built in 1895, that carries passengers a quarter of a mile up the side of a steep hill, passing en route through Walker Wood, famous for its bluebells.

SALTAIRE

MAP 6 REF F8

4 miles NW of Bradford off the A657

Saltaire is the model village created by Titus Salt for the workers at his mill. Salt was a very benevolent employer and determined to provide his workers with everything essential for a decent standard of living. Built between 1851 and 1876, the facilities in the village were designed to cater for all their needs, - health, leisure and education, but there were no public houses. The spiritual needs of the work force were attended to by the elegant Congregational church which has been described as the most beautiful Free Church in the north of England. A statue of Titus Salt stands in nearby Robert's Park (where swearing and gambling were banned) above the figures of a llama and an alpaca whose wool he imported for spinning in his mills.

The **Victoria Boat House** was built in 1871 and has been beautifully restored, with an open fire, pianola and wind-up gramophone, all recreating a traditional parlour atmosphere where you can enjoy cream teas and attend special Victorian Evenings in the dress of that time. Also in Saltaire is the **Museum of Victorian Reed Organs** which has a collection of more than 45 instruments, including harmonicas and an American organ, which are demonstrated from time to time, and some of which are available for visitors to try. Saltaire isn't completely locked in the past. The former Salt's Mill has been converted into the **1853 David Hockney Gallery** which displays the world's largest collection of paintings by the internationally acclaimed artist who was born in Bradford in 1937.

GUISELEY
MAP 6 REF F8

5 miles N of Bradford on the B6151

At the village of Guiseley lies the most famous fish and chip shop in the world, **Harry Ramsden's**. Harry's career as the world's most successful fish frier began in Bradford where he was the first to offer a sit-down fish and chip meal. He moved to Guiseley in 1928 and the original white-painted wooden hut, 10ft by 6ft, in which he started business is still on the site today. The present building holds its place in the *Guinness Book of Records* as the world's busiest fish and chip restaurant, serving nearly 1 million customers each year.

HAREWOOD
MAP 7 REF G8

8 miles N of Leeds on the A61

One of the grandest stately homes in the country, **Harewood House** was built at a time when many of the most illustrious names in the history of English architecture, interior decoration, furniture making and landscape gardening were all at the peak of their powers. For the creation of Harewood in the mid-1700s, Edwin Lascelles was able to employ the dazzling talents of Robert Adam, John Carr, Thomas Chippendale and 'Capability Brown'.

Harewood House

Edwin's son, Edward, was one of the first to patronise a young artist named JMW Turner and many of Turner's paintings are still here along with hundreds by other distinguished painters collected by later generations of the family. Many of the finest of them are displayed in a superb Gallery that extends along the whole west end of the house, 76ft long, 24ft wide, 21ft high. Amongst the masterpieces on show are works by Bellini, Titian, Veronese, El Greco and Tintoretto, while family portraits by Reynolds, Hoppner and Gainsborough look down from the silk-covered walls of the opulent drawing rooms.

Along with superb gardens, charming walks, a Bird Garden which is home to some 120 exotic species, an Adventure Playground, boat trips on the lake, and an extensive events and exhibitions programme, Harewood House is indisputably one of Yorkshire's 'must-see' visitor attractions.

LEEDS

In recent years, the city of Leeds has seen something of a renaissance. Its waterfront, neglected and derelict for so long, is now buzzing with new developments. Abandoned warehouses have been imaginatively transformed into fashionable bars, restaurants and tourist attractions, all less than 15 minutes walk from the shopping centre. Debenhams has recently opened a new flagship store in the heart of the city and other high profile stores are also flocking to the city. Perhaps the most talked about store is Harvey Nichols whose Knightsbridge emporium enjoyed a heightened reputation in the 1990s thanks to the BBC series *Absolutely Fabulous*. In parallel with these developments the Aire and Calder Navigation, which is set to celebrate its 300th birthday, is being transformed to enable leisure traffic to use the waterway as well as freight.

The city is also a major European cultural centre with its own opera and ballet companies, Northern Ballet Theatre and Opera North, while the West Yorkshire Play-house, regarded as the 'National Theatre of the North', is a showcase for classic British and European drama as well as work by new Yorkshire writers. The Leeds International Film Festival, held every October since 1986, has provided major world premieres for films such as *Brassed Off*. The city also boasts some outstanding galleries and museums. Located right next to the monumental City Hall, the **Leeds City Art Gallery** boasts an exceptional collection of Victorian and French Post-Impressionist paintings along with major works by Courbet, Lowry, Sickert, Stanley Spencer and Bridget Riley. Linked to the gallery is the Henry Moore Institute, the first centre in Europe devoted to the display and study of sculpture of all periods. There's also a Craft & Design shop selling cards, jewellery and pottery, and an art library.

The **Thackray Medical Museum**, one of the largest museums of its kind in Europe, possesses more than 25,000 extraordinary objects in its collection. They range from a surgical chain saw and Prince Albert's Medical Chest through to a 17th century Correction Frame. Visitors can listen in to the thoughts and feelings of a surgeon, his assistants and Hannah Dyson, an 11 year old girl whose leg has been crushed in a factory accident, as they prepare for the amputation of Hannah's leg. Or you might prefer to walk through a giant gut in Bodyworks and find out exactly why your tummy rumbles.

Opened by the Queen in 1998, the **Royal Armouries** traces the development of arms and armour from the 5th century BC to modern times. The museum utilises interactive computer displays, videos, films, music and poetry to tell the story of arms and armour in battle, self-defence, sport and fashion. Outside, the Tiltyard features jousting and hunting tournaments daily from April to September, while a bustling Menagerie Court includes displays of falcons, hunting dogs and horses.

Lovers of real ale may well want to take advantage of a joint ticket which gives admission to both the Royal Armouries and **Tetley's Brewery Wharf**. Here you can learn how Joshua Tetley founded his great empire and learn the secret of his famous brew. Costumed actors depict how the English pub has played an important part in British life throughout the centuries and the centre also includes traditional pub games, working Shire horses, a shop and café.

AROUND LEEDS

To the northwest of the city, **Kirkstall Abbey** is one of the most complete ruins in this part of Yorkshire. Building started in 1152 by the Cistercians and was completed within a generation, so Kirkstall is regarded by many as representing Cistercian architecture at its most monumental. It was executed with the typical early Cistercian austerity as can be seen in the simplicity of the outer domestic buildings. The bell tower, a 16th century addition, was in contravention of the rule of the Order that there were to be no stone bell towers as they were considered an unnecessary vanity.

A few miles north of Leeds city centre is one of the UK's most popular garden tourist attractions and home to the largest collection of tropical plants outside Kew Gardens, - **Tropical World**. Visitors can follow the 'Tropical Trail' into the Amazon rain forest, for example, where waterfalls tumble into jungle pools and birds of every hue fly through the trees. There's also a 'Desert World' and a Nocturnal House where fruit bats, monkeys, bush babies and rock cavies reside, - animals that can normally only be seen during twilight hours.

About 8 miles to the northeast, **Bramham Park** is one of Yorkshire's most exquisite country houses and is special for a number of reasons. The house itself dates from the Queen Anne era, built by Robert Benson, Lord Bingley, between 1698 and 1710, and superbly proportioned in an elegant and restrained classical style. The final effect is more French than English and indeed the gardens were modelled on Louis XIV's Versailles, with ornamental canals and ponds, beech groves, statues, long avenues and a superb arboretum with a collection of rare and unusual trees. The interior contains elegant furniture and paintings by artists such as Kneller and Sir Joshua Reynolds.

A couple of miles southwest of the city is **Temple Newsam House**, known as the Hampton Court of the North. Set in 1200 acres of parkland (entry to which is free), this Tudor-Jacobean gem boasts extensive collections of decorative arts displayed in their original room settings. Amongst them is one of the largest collections of Chippendale furniture in the country. Adjacent to Temple Newsam House is the country's largest approved Rare Breeds Centre - **Home Farm**. Visitors to this working farm will see pigs, goats, horses and poultry alongside interesting displays of vintage farm machinery and past farming methods.

PONTEFRACT
MAP 7 REF H10
9 miles SE of Leeds off the M62/A1

Shakespeare alluded to the town in his plays as 'Pomfret', - a place of influence and power, often visited by kings and their retinues. The great shattered towers of **Pontefract Castle** stand on a crag to the east of the town. Built by Ilbert de Lacy in the 11th century it was one of the most formidable fortresses in Norman England. In medieval times it passed to the House of Lancaster and became a Royal Castle. Richard II was imprisoned here and tragically murdered in its dungeons on the orders of Henry Bolingbroke who then assumed the crown as Henry IV.

The castle was a major Royalist stronghold during the Civil War, after which it was destroyed by Cromwell's troops. Today it remains as a gaunt ruin with only sections of the inner bailey and the lower part of the keep surviving intact. There is an underground chamber, part of the dungeons where prisoners carved their names so that they might not be utterly forgotten. Perhaps the unfortunate Richard II may have been incarcerated in this very chamber.

Only a short walk from the famous castle, the **Hope & Anchor Inn** has had almost as long a history. It was recorded as a drinking establishment as long ago as the 15th century and is mentioned in accounts of the first and second sieges of Pontefract Castle. Representatives of the warring sides met at the inn to try to settle their differences. In later times, the Hope & Anchor was a coaching inn but the present building is an imposing Victorian structure erected in 1892. The inn is a 'wet house' only and landlords Colin and Linda Byford are well known for the quality of the ales they offer, - John Smith's is the main bitter with Whitbread Trophy, two lagers and cider all on draught. As befits

The Hope & Anchor Inn, North Bailgate/Mill Dam Lane, Pontefract, West Yorkshire WF8 1ES Tel: 01977 702292

a traditional hostelry, plenty of time honoured pub activities take place here. There are darts and domino matches on Monday and Wednesday; domino handicap games on Tuesday and Sunday, and a Quiz and Bingo on Thursday.

Many of the streets of Pontefract evoke memories of its medieval past with names such as Micklegate, Beast Fair, Shoe Market, Salter Row and Ropergate. Modern development has masked much of old Pontefract but there are still many old Georgian buildings and winding streets.

The town's most famous products, of course, are Pontefract Cakes. Liquorice root has been grown here since monastic times and there's even a small planting of liquorice in the local park. The town celebrates this unique heritage with the 5-day **Pontefract Liquorice Fayre** in mid-August which includes two days of jousting, archery and battle re-enactments at Pontefract Castle.

Just a short walk from the centre of the town is **The Yorkshire Penny**, a smart modern pub with a traditional olde-worlde atmosphere. It's run by Danny and Paula Chambers, a friendly and welcoming couple who took over here in 1998. A particularly attractive feature of the inn is the elegant conservatory which overlooks the children's play area and serves as a quality restaurant at weekends. At present, food is available every lunchtime Tuesday to Sunday from noon until 2pm (Tuesday to Thursday); 4pm (Friday and Saturday), and 3pm (Sunday). You should definitely book ahead for the popular Sunday lunch. By the time you read this, meals should also be available in the evenings.

**The Yorkshire Penny, Cobblers Lane, Bondgate, Pontefract,
West Yorkshire WF8 2HN Tel: 01977 602894**

The Yorkshire Penny is a lively place with quiz nights on Wednesday and Sunday from 9pm and occasional live bands on either Friday or Saturday. During the summer, Danny and Paula also host Fun Days. (Please note that the pub is only open from 7pm on Monday evenings).

Enjoying a central location with the M1, M62 and A1 all within easy reach, **The Queens Hotel** is a magnificent Grade II listed Victorian building offering the very best in food, drink and accommodation. The 23 guest rooms are all en suite and provide outstanding levels of guest comfort at highly competitive rates. Nine of the rooms are on the ground floor and for that special occasion there's a bridal suite with a four-poster bed and en suite sunken jacuzzi. Non-residents are welcome in both the lounge bar or the 50-seater restaurant, the Brasserie Victoria. Food is available every day from noon until 2pm and again from 5pm to 9pm and guests can complement their meals with either traditional hand-pulled ales or a selection from the excellent wine list. For weddings, the entire first floor is made

**The Queens Hotel, Front Street, Pontefract, West Yorkshire
WF8 4DH Tel: 01977 702228 Fax: 01977 798305**

available for the exclusive use of the wedding party and The Queens is also ideal for business meetings since it can accommodate from 2 to 120 people in Theatre, Banquet or Boardroom styles.

WAKEFIELD

MAP 7 REF G10

8 miles S of Leeds on the A642

One of the oldest towns in Yorkshire, Wakefield stands on a hill guarding an important crossing of the River Calder. Its defensive position has always been important and it was the Battle of Wakefield in 1460, when the Duke of York was defeated, that gave rise to the mocking song *The Grand Old Duke of York*.

Many students of the Robin Hood legends claim that the famous outlaw had his origins in Wakefield. As evidence they cite the Court Rolls in which one 'Robin Hode' is noted as living here in the 14th century with his wife Matilda before fleeing to the woods of Sherwood Forest. Also medieval in origin are the Wakefield Miracle Plays which explore Old and New Testament stories in vivid language. The 600 year old cycle is performed in the Cathedral precincts as part of the city's annual Festival.

There are four main streets in the city, Westgate, Northgate, Warrengate and Kirkgate, which still preserve the medieval city plan. One of the most striking surviving buildings of that time is the tiny Chantry Chapel on Chantry Bridge which dates from the mid-1300s and is the best of only 4 such examples of bridge chapels in England. It is believed to have been built by Edward IV to commemorate the brutal murder of his brother Edmund. Grandest of all though is **Wakefield Cathedral** which was begun in Norman times, rebuilt in 1329 and refashioned in 1470 when its magnificent 247ft high spire, - the highest in Yorkshire - was added. The eastern extension is a 20th century addition, considered necessary after the church became a Cathedral in 1888. Other interesting buildings in the town include the stately Town Hall, the huge County Hall, the recently restored Edwardian Theatre Royal and many fine Georgian and Regency terraces and squares.

Wakefield's cultural attractions include **Wakefield Art Gallery**, housed in an attractive former Victorian vicarage just a short stroll from the town centre. Collections include many early works by locally born sculptors Henry Moore and Barbara Hepworth along with important work by many other major British modern artists. **Wakefield Museum**, located in an 1820s building next to the Town Hall, was originally a music saloon and then a Mechanics' Institute. It now houses collections illustrating the history and archaeology of Wakefield and its people from prehistoric times to the present day. There is also a permanent display of exotic birds and animals garnered by the noted 19th century traveller, naturalist and eccentric Charles Waterton who lived at nearby Walton Hall where he created the world's first nature reserve. Also of interest are the **Stephen G Beaumont Museum** which houses an unusual exhibition of medical memorabilia and the **National Coal Mining Museum** at Caphouse Colliery in Overton, a few miles southwest of Wakefield. A visit here includes a guided tour 450ft underground, indoor exhibitions and videos, outdoor machine displays and some friendly pit ponies.

Over to the southeast from Wakefield, **Nostell Priory** is one of the most popular tourist venues in this area. The word 'priory' is misleading since it evokes the picture of an ecclesiastical structure. But Nostell is in fact a large Palladian building erected on the site of an old Augustinian priory. It was in 1733 that the owner, Sir Rowland Winn, commissioned James Paine to build a grand mansion here. Paine was only 19 at the time and this was his first major project. Thirty years later, only half the state rooms were constructed and Sir Rowland's son, also named Rowland, engaged an up and coming young designer to complete the decoration. The young man's name was Robert Adam and between 1766 and 1776 his dazzling designs produced an incomparable sequence of interiors.

There was a third man of genius involved in the story of Nostell Priory, - the cabinet

Nostell Priory, nr Wakefield

maker Thomas Chippendale. What is believed to be his 'apprentice piece', made around 1735, is on display here, - an extraordinary Doll's House 6ft high and replete with the most elaborate detail, every minuscule door, window or desk drawer functioning perfectly. Today, Nostell Priory can boast the most comprehensive collection in the world of Chippendale's work.

DEWSBURY
MAP 7 REF F10

8 miles SW of Leeds on the A653

Dewsbury is an extremely old town which once had considerable influence. It has one of the region's oldest town centres with an imposing Town Hall designed by Henry Ashton and George Fox. It also has a number of other notable public and commercial buildings, a substantial shopping area (with some 443,500 sq. ft of retail floorspace) and a famous open market.

According to legend, **Dewsbury Minster** is situated at the very spot where, in 627AD, St Paulinus baptised converts to Christianity in the River Calder. The church dates from the 12th century although the tower was erected in 1767 to a design by the eminent York architect, John Carr. The interior has some interesting features, amongst them fragments of an Anglo-Saxon cross and coffin lids. The Minster is perhaps best known for its custom of tolling the 'Devil's Knell' on Christmas Eve to ward off evil spirits with a bell known as Black Tom. There are Brontë connections here. Patrick Brontë was curate of Dewsbury between 1809-11, and Charlotte taught at Wealds House School nearby. The school was run by a Miss Wooler who later gave her away when she was married.

HUDDERSFIELD
MAP 6 REF F10

14 miles SW of Leeds off the M62

With its steep, often cobbled streets, millstone grit cottages and larger Victorian dwellings, Huddersfield has a very distinctive character all its own. The town flourished in Victorian times and its most impressive buildings date from that era. The stately railway station was designed by James Pigott of York and built between 1846-50. It was followed by the Italianate Town Hall and culminated in the lofty **Jubilee Tower**, built in 1897 to celebrate Queen Victoria's Diamond Jubilee, which crowns the summit of **Castle Hill** on the outskirts of the town. Inside the tower there's a museum which traces the hill's 4000 years of history. One thousand feet high, **Castle Hill** has been occupied as a place of defence since Stone Age times. Simple tools, flints, bone needles, combs and pottery dating back to 2000BC have been unearthed here. The much later ramparts of an Iron Age fort, built here around 600BC can still be seen. In 1147 the Normans repaired the earthworks and built a motte and bailey castle which was apparently used as a base for hunting. The hill was also used as a beacon when England was threatened by the Spanish Armada, and again during the Napoleonic wars.

Back in the town, the **Tolson Memorial Museum** has displays that range from the tools of the earliest settlers in the area to modern day collections contributed by local people. One of the most

Castle Hill and Jubilee Tower

popular exhibits is the collection of vintage vehicles and motoring memorabilia in the 'Going Places' collection. Other displays trace the story of the Industrial Revolution, so important to the growth of the town, and the political protests it engendered.

Just a five minute drive from the M62 **The Lodge Hotel & Restaurant** occupies a splendid mid-Victorian mansion designed by Edgar Wood, a much sought after architect of that time. Garry and Kevin Birley bought the house in 1989 and have restored the hotel to its former state of grace, complete with walnut panelled private dining and conference rooms and elegant reception rooms. Quality period furnishings and decorations are in evidence throughout the Lodge and an exquisite glass door is inscribed with the hotel's encouraging motto: *Welcome ever Smiles*. There are eleven magnificent en suite rooms and a beautiful 50-cover restaurant which is well-known for its excellent innovative cuisine which makes

The Lodge Hotel & Restaurant, 48 Birkby Lodge Road, Birkby, Huddersfield HD2 2BG Tel: 01484 431001 Fax: 01484 421590

use of the freshest foods in season. To complement your meal there's an extensive wine list featuring not only classic European but also popular New World wines. Set in attractive grounds and with its own private car park, The Lodge is ideal for small conferences, weddings and private dinner parties and in summer, guests can enjoy traditional cream teas on the lawn.

SCAPEGOAT HILL
Map 6 ref E10

3 miles W of Huddersfield off the A62 or A640

About a mile south of the oddly-named Scapegoat Hill the **Colne Valley Museum** is housed in three 19th century weavers' cottages near the parish church. Visitors can see a loom chamber with working hand looms and a Spinning Jenny; a weavers' living room of 1850 and a gas-lit clogger's shop of 1910. On two weekends a year, a craft weekend is held when many different skills are demonstrated. Light refreshments are available and there's also a museum shop. Run entirely by its members, the museum has featured many times on television and is open at weekends and Bank Holidays throughout the year but party visits can be arranged at other times.

Standing high on the hillside **The Scapehouse Inn** enjoys some breathtaking views across the Pennine Hills. The building dates back to the mid-1800s and in those days it was known as the New Inn. It became The Scapehouse Inn back in the 1960s but its regulars always refer to it as "The Scape". Frank and Janet Crampton took over here in the

summer of 1999 but know the pub well since they used to work here before taking on the tenancy. The inn has kept much of its Victorian charm with real fires and lots of by-gones all adding to its character. (See how long it takes you to spot the old farm cart which provides an unusual feature of the decor!) At least 4 different Jennings brews are on offer here, along with a changing guest ale.

The Scapehouse Inn, 74 High Street, Scapegoat Hill, Golcar, Huddersfield HD7 4NJ Tel: 01484 654144

Excellent food is available every lunchtime and evening with the Wednesday evening menu specialising in steaks and salmon. And if you are visiting The Scapehouse on Thursday evening, feel free to take part in the regular Pub Quiz.

MELTHAM
Map 6 ref E11

5 miles SW of Huddersfield on the B6107/B6108

A typical Pennine mill town, Meltham is mostly Victorian but with a handsome Georgian parish church dating from 1786 which is challenged in size by the spacious Baptist Chapel, rebuilt in 1864. Only two mills have survived but the Meltham Mills Band, founded in

1845, is still thriving and has won many competitions throughout the country, including the British Championship. Some customs of the past have also managed to survive. On Collap Monday, (the day before Shrove Tuesday) the town's shopkeepers distribute free sweets to children; there is carol singing on Christmas Eve in the centre of the village; and on Whit Monday the different congregations of churches and chapels join in the Whitsuntide Walk around the town accompanied by the brass band.

Right in the centre of Meltham, where the B6107 meets the B6108, two pubs stand side by side. Unusually, both the **Waggon & Horses** and the **Rose & Crown** are run by the same two partners, Jonny and Tricia. Both pubs are sturdy, stone built Victorian properties and both have a welcoming, hospitable atmosphere. Both serve a good selection of quality beers with more than

The Waggon & Horses, 16 Huddersfield Road, Meltham, Huddersfield HD7 3AE Tel: 01484 850269

20 different draught ales available between them. So which hostelry do you choose? If you are looking for food then it has to be the Waggon & Horses which offers a really extensive choice of bar snacks. There's a Giant Yorkshire Pudding Menu, with a choice of 10 different fillings, an appetising range of vegetarian meals, lots of tasty main meals, light bites and jacket potatoes, along with a special menu for kids. Food is available from 11am to 2pm every day except Monday. On Thursday evenings the Waggon & Horses hosts live entertainment or a disco, from 9pm, but the Rose & Crown is the place to be if you enjoy jazz (Wednesday evening); live bands (Friday) or a 60s and 70s disco (Saturday). By the time you read this, the Rose & Crown will also be offering comfortable B&B accommodation.

"West Yorkshire's Warmest Welcome" is the promise made by the King family who own and run the **Durker Roods Hotel**, an impressive Victorian mansion built in 1870 by a local businessman as his pri-

Durker Roods Hotel, Bishopsway, Meltham, Huddersfield HD7 3AG Tel: 01484 851413 Fax: 01484 851843

vate residence. It was converted into a hotel in 1975 and has been an integral part of local life ever since. More recently it was taken over by Maria and Spencer King and her brother Matthew, all of them dedicated to ensuring the future success of this historic hotel. A great deal of thought has gone into providing their guests with a wide selection of traditional British food. An extensive table d'hôte menu is supplemented by daily specials whilst theme evenings and dinner dances offer the opportunity of sampling more exotic dishes. There's also a wide range of dishes on the hotel's popular bar menu which can be enjoyed in the relaxed and informal atmosphere of the main hotel bar. The Durker Roods has 30 guest bedrooms, - doubles, twins and spacious family rooms, all equipped with en suite bath or shower, colour TV, direct dial telephone and tea/coffee-making facilities. Guest with disabilities are more than welcome, - ground floor rooms and disabled toilets are both available.

HONLEY

Map 6 ref F10

3 miles S of Huddersfield off the A616

The centre of this delightful little Pennine village has been designated as a site of historic interest. There are charming terraces of weavers' cottages and lots of interesting alleyways, and the old village stocks still stand in the churchyard of St Mary's. The Coach and Horses Inn has strong connections with the Luddite movement of the early 1800s. It was here, in 1812, that two Luddites, Benjamin Walker and Thomas Smith, spent the night drinking after murdering a mill owner at nearby Marsden. They were later arrested, convicted and executed at York. Not far from the inn is another interesting feature, - an old well dated 1796 whose date stone warns passers-by they will be fined 10 shillings (50p) for 'defouling' the water.

Lupton Square Gallery, 1-2 Lupton Square, Honley,
Huddersfield HD7 2AD Tel: 01484 666144
Fax: 01484 661221 e-mail: geoff@luptonsquaregallery.co.uk
website: www.luptonsquaregallery.co.uk

Located in a beautifully renovated 18th century house in the centre of the village, the **Lupton Square Gallery** offers the opportunity to view a wide range of original quality works of art in a friendly and informal setting. The opening of the Gallery in 1996 represented the fulfilment of an ambition for its owner, Geoff Harrop, who has had a lifelong interest in art. Now he presides over a constantly changing array of paintings, ceramics, sculpture and original prints displayed on three floors, including a bright vaulted cellar at the foot of a lovely spiral staircase. If you don't see precisely what you are looking for, Geoff will be pleased to discuss any requests you might have: with his extensive network he will take pleasure in finding your exact requirements. The Gallery has pieces to suit every pocket and also participates in Art£oan, the interest-free easy payment purchase scheme operated by Yorkshire Board. The Gallery hosts around six exhibitions each year, - if you'd like an invitation to the previews, just give the gallery a call. Lupton Square Gallery is open Friday, Saturday, Sunday and Bank Holidays from 10am to 5pm; at other times by appointment.

FARNLEY TYAS
MAP 6 REF F10
3 miles SE of Huddersfield off the A626 or A629

Farnley Tyas is another attractive Pennine village with scattered stone farmhouses and barns, and 18th and 19th century workers' cottages grouped around the crossroads. It is mentioned in the Domesday book as *'Fereleia'*: the Tyas part of its name comes from the Le Teyeis family which owned much of the land hereabouts from the 13th century.

Although the centre of Huddersfield is just three miles away as the crow flies, **The Golden Cock Inn** is surrounded by hundreds of acres of open Pennine countryside. This handsome old stone-built hostelry is particularly recommended for the quality of the

The Golden Cock Inn, 2 The Village, Farnley Tyas, Huddersfield HD4 6UD
Tel/Fax: 01484 666644

cuisine on offer. A quick glance at the menu confirms that food is taken seriously here. Amongst the starters for example there's a Sauté of Foie Gras set upon toasted Ciabatta finished with red onion marmalade and shallot jus, and the main courses include Mexican style 'Sizzling Plates', steaks, and dishes such as Braised Oxtails on a bed of horseradish mash with a rich red wine jus. The regular menu is supplemented by equally appetising daily specials. Ken Pratt owns and runs this outstanding inn, a free house where you'll find Black Sheep real ale along with another guest ale. As we go to press, plans are under way for the addition of 6 en suite guest bedrooms and these should be available by the time you read this.

THONGSBRIDGE
MAP 6 REF F11

5 miles S of Huddersfield on the A616

Upperthong, Netherthong and Thongsbridge derive the common element of their names from the Danish word *'thing'* meaning an assembly or council. Thongsbridge is set beside a tributary of the River Holme and is very much a part of the *Last of the Summer Wine* country.

There's been a hostelry on the site where **The Sycamore Inn** now stands since at least 1689, - a map dated that year clearly shows an inn on this spot. In those days it was a posting inn where teams of horses were changed and The Sycamore still retains much of the atmosphere of those days with its flagstone floors, ancient beams and fascinating bygones displayed around the rooms. Today the inn is well-known locally for its well-maintained real ales, including Tetleys and Timothy Taylors, and its outstanding food. Your hosts, Phil and Sue Craner, both contribute to the cooking, offering a wide range of wholesome home made dishes at remarkable value-for-money prices. Along with tradi-

The Sycamore Inn, 15 New Mill Road, Thongsbridge, Huddersfield HD7 2SH
Tel: 01484 683458

tional favourites such as steaks, Bangers & Mash and Giant Yorkshire Puddings, the house specialities include Paella, Lasagne, Chicken Tikka Masala and Vegetable Stir Fry. Meals are available every lunchtime and evening except for Mondays (unless it's a Bank Holiday) and it's advisable to book ahead at weekends. The Sycamore hosts a Quiz Night on Mondays, a Disco on Thursdays, the last Saturday of each month is Golden Oldies Disco night, and there are regular Irish nights, - just phone for details.

SHEPLEY
MAP 6 REF F11

8 miles SE of Huddersfield on the A629

Hidden away in its own spacious grounds, **Spring Head House** is an imposing mid-19th century building which was originally the home of a brewer named Seth Senior. His brewery was actually located at the rear of the house with the maltings and bottling plants just down the road. For the last 20-odd years Spring Head has been the home of Tim and Trauti Hard who have been providing quality bed and breakfast accommodation here since 1990. There are just 2 guest bedrooms, a twin en suite and a single, both of

them cosy and attractively decorated. Both rooms are well-equipped with colour TV and tea/coffee-making facilities and they enjoy lovely views over the garden towards Emley Moor and its famous mast. Spring Head House truly is a Hidden Place but to find it all you have to do is get to the crossroads of the A635 and A629 in Shepley, take the

Spring Head House, 15 Holmfirth Road, Shepley, Huddersfield, West Yorkshire HD8 8BB
Tel: 01484 606300 Fax: 01484 608030

road signposted to Holmfirth and the house is about half a mile along the road, on the left.

HOLMFIRTH
MAP 6 REF F11

6 miles S of Huddersfield on the A6024/A635

BBC-TV's longest running situation comedy, *Last of the Summer Wine*, has made the little Pennine town of Holmfirth familiar to viewers around the world. Visitors can enjoy an authentic bacon buttie in the real 'Sid's Café', gaze at Nora Batty's cottage and sit in the famous pub. The rest of the town offers a network of side lanes, courts and alleyways while the terraces of weavers' cottages are typical of a town famous for its production of wool textiles.

As with so many of these moorland villages, there is a lot of surrounding water and in its time Holmfirth has suffered three major floods. The worse occurred in 1852 when the nearby Bilbury Reservoir burst its banks, destroying mills, cottages and farms, and killing 81 people. A pillar near the church records the height the waters reached. Holmfirth has a lovely Georgian church, built in 1777-8 in neo-classical style to the designs of Joseph Jagger. The gable faces the street and the tower is constructed at the eastern end against a steep hillside.

A popular attraction in the town is the **Holmfirth Postcard Museum** which has a comprehensive collection of the traditional saucy seaside postcard produced by Bamfords of Holmfirth in the first half of the 20th century. The company also produced hymn sheets and, rather surprisingly, many early silent movies. The museum displays also include other vintage postcards, including patriotic cards from World War I, less sentimental ones from World War II, and a moving audio-visual documentary presentation of the 1852 flood.

A short walk from many of the locations immortalised in *Last of the Summer Wine*, **Prickleden House** is a charming stone building some two hundred years old, its walls covered with luxuriant creeper. Prickleden House is the home of Joan and Wilf Beck who have lived here for almost 30 years and for the last 12 years or so have been offering rather special bed and breakfast accommodation. There's just the one guest bedroom, a twin

Prickleden House, 29 Woodhead Road, Holmfirth,
Huddersfield HD7 1JU Tel: 01484 683962

with its own bathroom, so visitors are very well looked after indeed. There's a wonderfully relaxed atmosphere and the Becks are proud of the fact that many of their guests are repeat visitors. The interior of the house is a picture, - flagstone floors in the wood-panelled hallway that leads to the original Georgian staircase, and some lovely stained glass in the leaded window on the landing. The guest room enjoys splendid views over Holme Moss and is provided with lots of thoughtful little extras. In the morning, you'll find that breakfast at Prickleden House observes the best traditions of Yorkshire hospitality!

Set right in the heart of this popular little town, **The Shoulder of Mutton** is a sturdy early 19th century house built in local creamy-grey stone. Sue Hobson took over this

The Shoulder of Mutton, 2 Dunford Road,
Holmfirth HD7 1DP Tel: 01484 684414

traditional Yorkshire hostelry in January 2000 and has swiftly established the pub's reputation for good food, drink and accommodation. It's open all day, every day, and quality food is served every lunchtime (noon until 3pm) except on Mondays. The resident chef offers a extensive choice with something to suit every palate, including a hugely generous Mixed Grill for those with really hearty appetites. The ales on offer include Tetley's, Boddington's and Worthington Creamflow, along with a wide range of other beverages. This is a lively pub, hosting a disco on Friday evening, live music on Saturday evening, and a karaoke session on Sunday evening. You may well want to stay longer. If so, the Shoulder of Mutton has 4 guest bedrooms, 1 of them en suite, and visitors can stay on either a B&B, or dinner, B&B basis.

HOLMBRIDGE
7 miles SW of Huddersfield on the A6024

MAP 6 REF E11

This charming village stands at the head of a steep-sided valley and enjoys picture post-card views of the Pennines and the Holme valley. There are cottages here dating from the 1700s and the area is known for its unusual style of architecture, 4-decker cottages dug into the hillside. The lower cottage is approached from the front, the upper cottage is reached by a steep flight of stone steps leading round the back.

One of the highlights of the village year is the **Sunday School Feast**. With the Hinchcliffe Mill Brass Band leading the way, Sunday school children, teachers, relatives, friends and members of the congregation proceed around the village, stopping at certain places to sing a few verses of the chosen feast hymns on their way to Dam Head. Here they hold a United Sing and a short open air service. Everyone then repairs to the parish hall for tea, a feature of which is the 'School Cake', a fruity and spicy bread cake.

"Accommodation at its Best" is the promise made by Kathleen and Trevor Bellamy of **Corn Loft House** in the heart of Holmbridge. The premises were built in 1853 for a corn merchant and the arched gateway where the horse-drawn carts were loaded still stands. The house later became a shop, then an off licence but is now a welcoming guest house, full of character. There are 5 guest rooms, two of which have 4-poster beds. The ground floor room has its own entrance while the Corn Loft Suite is particularly attractive with its beamed ceiling, wooden floors and balcony sleeping area. All the rooms are attrac-

tively decorated and furnished, and very spacious. A hearty breakfast is included in the tariff and if you wish you can have it served in your room. Packed lunches are available on request and guests are wel-come to bring a takeaway to their room in the evening, - Trevor runs the lo-cal fish & chip shop so what more could a visitor ask? The Bellamys will also happily loan bicycles

Corn Loft House, 146 Woodhead Road, Holmbridge, Holmfirth, West Yorkshire HD7 1NL Tel: 01484 683147

and even, when the weather is appropriate, sledges and skis!

HEPWORTH
2 miles SE of Holmfirth on the A616

MAP 6 REF F11

What does one make of a village that lies on the River Jordan, has a house which has always been known as 'Solomon's Temple' (although no-one knows why), and a parcel of land called 'Paradise', the only place, it is said, where fruit trees will grow. There are some other curious names. **Meal Hill** is where the Romans brought their hand-mill stones to grind corn, and **Barracks Fold** was the area where, during the plague, the healthy barricaded themselves against the infected. There are still some triangular patches of land in the village which are believed to contain the common graves of the plague victims.

Located in the centre of this village in the heart of *Summer Wine* country, **The Butchers Arms** is a truly traditional Yorkshire inn with old beams, flagstone and wood floors, and welcoming real fires. Proprietor Dominic Kirkup has been in the hospitality business for more than 14 years and certainly runs an excellent house - the ales available in this free house include Marstons Pedigree and Mansfield Ale along with rotating guest ales. There is also a very popular restaurant offering constantly changing menus of creative fresh foods. The blackboard menu changes about three times a week and a typical bill of fare might include Blue Marlin, Guinea Fowl Supreme, Inshore Baby Dover Sole, or Chicken Breast filled with Brie and spinach. The starters are just as appetising, - headless King Prawns, for example, Greenlip Mussels or Asparagus spears. Food is available Tuesday to Saturday evenings, from 7pm until 9.30pm, and on Saturday and Sunday lunchtimes from noon until 2.30pm. The

The Butchers Arms, 38 Towngate, Hepworth, Huddersfield HD7 1TE Tel/Fax: 01484 682857

pub itself is open from 5.30pm, weekday evenings, and all day on Saturday and Sunday. Definitely well worth seeking out!

Renowned for its outstanding food, **The Chase Inn & Restaurant** stands high on a hillside looking out across the splendid scenery of the West Yorkshire moors. When Brian and Pauline Walker arrived here in the early 1980s they took

The Chase Inn & Restaurant, Sheffield Road, Hepworth, Huddersfield HD7 1TN Tel: 01484 683775

possession of three cottages and a barn, parts of which dated back to 1800. They have tastefully renovated the old property and created a welcoming and hospitable hostelry that attracts lovers of good food from miles around. Brian is the chef and his extensive menu offers a huge choice of superbly prepared and presented dishes, - the à la carte menu for example offers no fewer than 16 main courses ranging from steaks to Duckling à l'orange, from Rack of Lamb to Grilled Salmon. Meals are served in the restaurant with its attractive countryside views. There's also a bar menu which has almost as many dishes to choose from. Food is available every evening (except Monday), and also at Sunday lunchtime, and since The Chase Inn is a free house there's a wide selection of fine ales and wines available to complement the excellent food.

DENBY DALE   MAP 6 REF F11
8 miles SE of Huddersfield on the A635/A636

Denby Dale is, of course, famous for its production of gigantic meat pies. The first of these Desperate Dan-sized dishes was baked in 1788 to celebrate George III's return to sanity; later ones marked the victory of Waterloo and Queen Victoria's Jubilee. The 1928 monster meal was organised to raise funds for the Huddersfield Royal Infirmary but the festivities were almost cancelled when the organisers discovered that a large part of the pie had gone bad. Four barrowloads of stinking meat were secretly spirited away. Perhaps because of that mishap, no more great pies were attempted until 1964 when it was decided to commemorate the four royal births of that year. On this occasion two walls of Mr Hector Buckley's barn, in which the pie had been baked, had to be demolished to get it out. The most recent pie was made in 1987 and the dish used is now on display just outside the village.

Signposted from the centre of Denby Dale, Springfield Mill is a former weaving mill which closed in 1970 and now houses the **Worlds Apart Crafts & Antique Centre**. The Centre opened in 1995 but the owners, Sharon and Chris Dawson, have been in antiques for many years. Sharon had always wanted to open an antique shop so when they found the right location the business was established. The front half of the Centre houses a wondrous array of collectables, anything from Toby jugs to coal mining memorabilia with just about everything else in between. There's something here for every taste

**Worlds Apart Crafts & Antique Centre, Unit 6a Springfield Mill,
Norman Road, Denby Dale, Huddersfield HD8 8TH
Tel: 01484 866713 Fax: 01484 865169**

and every pocket. The rear half of the Centre is stocked with an equally varied range of antiques of all periods and styles, - furniture, pottery, glassware, to mention just a few of the items for sale. Worlds Apart is open Tuesday to Saturday, 10am to 5pm, Sunday from noon until 5pm, but is closed on Mondays unless it's a Bank Holiday.

CLAYTON WEST
MAP 6 REF F10

8 miles SE of Huddersfield on the A636

A popular attraction at Clayton West is the **Kirklees Light Railway**, a 15″ gauge steam railway which runs along the old Lancashire & Yorkshire Clayton West branch line. The track runs through gently rolling farmland for about 4 miles with a quarter-mile long tunnel adding to the thrill. The large station/visitor centre at Clayton West provides

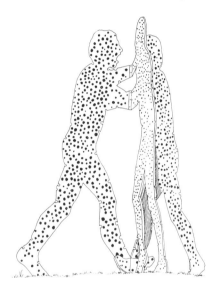

Yorkshire Sculpture Park

passengers with comfortable, spacious surroundings to await their train or take advantage of the light refreshment café and the souvenir shop. The railway operates daily during the season and every weekend throughout the year. For train times and other information, telephone 01484 865727.

One of the leading attractions of the area is found about 3 miles northeast of Clayton West, conveniently close to Junction 38 of the M1. The **Yorkshire Sculpture Park** draws in some 200,000 visitors a year and since you only pay a small charge for parking it represents amazing value for money. Changing exhibitions of sculpture are set in the beautiful 18th century parkland of Bretton Hall, 200 acres of historic landscape providing a wonderful setting for some of the best sculpture to be seen in Britain today by artists from around the world. Alongside the programme of indoor and outdoor exhibitions, more permanent features include the YSP collection of works in many different styles, (from 19th century bronzes by Rodin to contemporary sculptures), and a display of monumental bronzes by Henry Moore sited within the adjacent 100 acre Bretton Country Park.

7 South Yorkshire

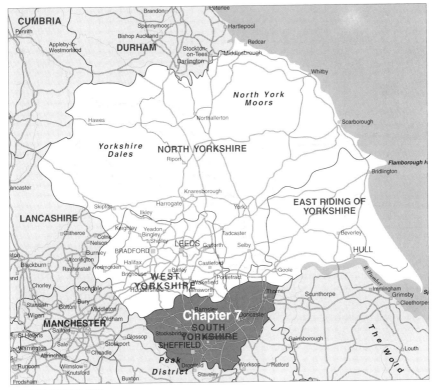

© MAPS IN MINUTES ™ (1998)

INTRODUCTION

Lacking the spectacular scenery of the Yorkshire dales, moors and coastline, South York-shire tends to be overlooked as a tourist venue. But there's a great deal here to occupy and entertain the visitor. Its main centre, Sheffield, quite rightly claims to be England's green-est city and the wild open spaces of the Pennine moors roll right up to its western boundaries. The city boasts many open spaces and gardens, some excellent museums and galleries and for shoppers a choice that ranges from the small independent shops in Orchard Square to the shopaholic's paradise of Meadowhall, one of the largest shopping malls in the UK. Heritage sites in South Yorkshire include Roche Abbey, Conisbrough Castle and the appealingly faded Victorian grandeur of Brodsworth Hall.

SHEFFIELD

In recent years Sheffield has re-invented itself. England's fourth largest city, it is still busy with its steel, cutlery, engineering and toolmaking industries but is also a vibrant, international, multi-cultural city whose image was given a fillip by the worldwide success of *The Full Monty* which was filmed in and around Sheffield. The city is also a world class centre for sport, a base for the Government backed UK Sports Institute and with an impressive array of international venues. There are excellent facilities for swimming, athletics, ice skating, dry skiing as well as two indoor climbing centres.

The city is also home to the unique **National Centre for Popular Music**. The story of music through the ages and from many cultures is told using live performances, interactive exhibits, real and virtual instruments, audio-visual simulations and items of rare memorabilia. Visitors can try their hand at playing an instrument, mixing a hit record, being a DJ or experience an unforgettable journey through the world of music in 'Soundscapes' - the Centre's unique 3-dimensional surround-sound auditorium. The city's premier museum is the **Kelham Island Museum** which tells the story of Sheffield in a living museum. Visitors can see the mighty River Don Engine in steam - the most powerful working steam engine in Europe; reconstructed workshops; the 'Little Mesters' working cutler; and craftspeople demonstrating traditional 'Made in Sheffield' skills. For children up to 9 years old, 'The Melting Shop' provides an interactive experience

Sheffield Town Hall

where they can "clock on" to become a piece of steel - including being rolled and hammered! Sheffield's industrial heritage is also celebrated at the **City Museum and Mappin Art Gallery** (free) in Weston Park. The museum houses the city's collection of cutlery, metalwork, ceramics, coins, archaeology and natural history. The Mappin Art Gallery has a permanent display of Victorian paintings and organises an imaginative programme of temporary exhibitions.

Sheffield's most picturesque museum is undoubtedly the **Bishop's House Museum** which dates from around 1500 and is the earliest timber-framed house still standing in the city. Many original features survive and the Bedchamber and Great Parlour are furnished

Bishop's House Museum

in the style of the home of a prosperous 17th century yeoman. There are also displays on Sheffield in Tudor and Stuart times, and changing exhibitions on local history themes. A museum of a very different nature is the **Sheffield Bus Museum**, housed in the Tinsley Tram sheds on Sheffield Road. The collection includes many types of bus and other transport-related exhibits such as destination blinds, old timetables and models. The museum also houses the Tinsley Model Railway layout.

Of related interest is the **South Yorkshire Railway** in Meadowbank. As well as displaying more than 60 locomotives, there are vintage carriages and wagons, and a signal box. Plans are under way to run a steam-hauled passenger service on the 3½ miles line from Meadowhall to Chapeltown.

The city offers a wide range of restaurants and cafés but for top class continental-style cuisine in Sheffield the place to seek out is **Maria's**. The chef here is Stephen Attwell who named the restaurant after his lovely wife when they bought the business in September 1998. Stephen has been a chef for more than 30 years, working in top hotels and restaurants in England, Italy and France. He offers an extensive menu with a wide range of dishes from all around the world - Californian sirloin steaks, for example, or Thai prawns,

Maria's, 216a Crookes, Sheffield S10 1TH
Tel: 0114 268 5555

along with pizzas and pasta dishes. In addition to the main menu, there are always at least 6 extra starters and 6 main courses listed on the specials board. Discreet background music adds to the relaxed atmosphere and service is prompt and courteous. Maria's is not licensed but guests are welcome to bring their own beverage of choice. This outstanding restaurant is open only in the evening, from 5.30pm until late, and if you plan to eat here at weekends you would be wise to book ahead.

Sheffield has three outstanding galleries devoted to the visual arts. **The Ruskin Gallery** (free) houses the fascinating collection formed for the people of Sheffield in 1875 by the Victorian artist, critic and sage John Ruskin. It includes paintings, water-colours and drawings, minerals, plaster casts and architectural details, illuminated manuscripts and books. Adjoining the gallery is the Ruskin Craft Gallery which has displays of contemporary craft products, some of which are for sale. Nearby, the **Graves Art Gallery** (free) displays a wide-ranging collection of British art from the 16th century to the present along with European paintings and a fine collection of water-colours, drawings and prints. One of its major treasures is the Grice Collection of Chinese ivories which forms the centrepiece of a display of non-European artefacts. Another gallery of interest, the **Site Gallery** (free), is devoted to photographic and new media exhibitions and events. One of the largest contemporary visual art and media centres in the country, the gallery also offers darkroom and digital imaging facilities, as well as photographic and digital courses in the recently created education suite.

Winner of the RAC "Little Gem Best Small Hotel in Eastern England, 1999", **The Cooke House** is a quite exceptional hotel/restaurant, tucked away in the leafy suburb of Fulwood. It's the family home of Maureen and Peter Cooke who in 1997, with retirement approaching and their two children having flown the nest, decided to convert their imposing detached house into a mini-hotel and restaurant. There are just 3 guest bedrooms, all en suite, beautifully furnished and decorated, and well-equipped with extras such as Sky TV and video channels. The sitting and dining rooms have open fires that bestow a warm and pleasurable atmosphere. As the many accolades testify, the cuisine at The Cooke House is outstanding. Maureen is queen of the kitchen and all the ingredients she uses are carefully sourced - beef from a Scottish supplier, free range poultry and

The Cooke House, 78 Brookhouse Hill, Fulwood,
Sheffield S10 3TB Tel: 0114 230 8186 Fax: 0114 263 0241
e-mail: enquiries@cookehouse.co.uk
website: www.cookehouse.co.uk

eggs, and the freshest of fish from local suppliers. The restaurant is open most evenings for residents but since everything is freshly cooked, residents should book in advance. Prebooked groups of non-residents can also be accommodated and in this circumstance the Cookes provide "purpose-built" menus agreed beforehand between themselves and their guests. The Cooke House is licensed and Peter will be happy to discuss the comprehensive range of wines stored in his well-stocked cellar.

Standing in its own grounds, **The Martins Guest House** is a commodious Victorian house dating back to the 1860s. It was built for a wealthy steel magnate and much of the original decor, like the original plasterwork on the ceilings, is still in place and the whole

The Martins Guest House, 397 Fulwood Road, Ranmoor, Sheffield S10 3GE Tel: 01142308588

house has a relaxed, comfortable atmosphere. The Martins is the home of Balthazar and Odette Martins who have been welcoming bed & breakfast guests here for some years. They have 4/5 rooms available to let, most of them with their own facilities. All of the rooms are spacious, well-furnished and decorated and one of them is on the ground floor. A hearty breakfast awaits guests each morning, taken in the delightful breakfast room overlooking the garden. The Martins do not provide evening meals but there are numerous eating places within walking distance. Open all year round, The Martins Guest House is conveniently located for Sheffield's manifold attractions and as a base for exploring the scenic splendours of the Peak National Park.

OWLER BAR
7 miles SW of Sheffield on the A621

MAP 7 REF G13

Located on the edge of the Peak District, **The Peacock Hotel** is a family run 16th century coaching inn offering panoramic views and ideally situated within 10 minutes drive of both Sheffield and Chesterfield. Parts of the handsome stone building date back some 400 years and it takes its name from the coat of arms of the Dukes of Rutland who at that time owned the land here. Their delightful Tudor home, Haddon Hall, is just a few miles away. The Peacock is noted for its restaurant which offers an intimate candle-lit setting

The Peacock Hotel, Baslow Road, Owler Bar, Sheffield S17 3BQ
Tel: 0114 236 1789

for evening diners and is also available for private functions and wedding receptions. Bar meals are available at lunchtime and non-residents are welcome. The hotel also boasts 11 en suite rooms, 4 of them on the ground floor, and all well appointed with TV and tea/coffee-making facilities. As well as being conveniently located for Sheffield and Chesterfield, The Peacock is also an ideal base for walking in the Peak District, visiting the historic market town of Bakewell, Castleton with its Blue John Caverns, Peveril Castle and the palatial Chatsworth House.

LODGE MOOR
Map 7 ref G12

5 miles W of Sheffield off the A57

"*.....an old world inn, it boasts no modern fads / A real old country calling-place, it's called* **Three Merry Lads**". Those lines come from a poem printed on the menu at this delightful pub on the outskirts of Sheffield, close to the Redmires Reservoir. It was originally a farmhouse but when the reservoirs were being constructed in the 1870s it became an alehouse for the navvies. According to an old story, the pub was given its name when the owner looked out one day and saw his sons playing happily in the fields. Today, Anne and John Savage are your hosts at the Three Merry Lads. Anne is in charge of the food which is truly outstanding and with something to pamper every palate - Thai Fish Cakes or local Black Pudding amongst the starters, Beef & Mushroom Stroganoff or Vegetable Lasagne as main courses; filled baguettes or jacket potatoes; and a special separate menu for Young

The Three Merry Lads, 610 Redmires Road, Lodge Moor, Sheffield S10 4LJ Tel: 0114 230 2824

Adults. In addition to good food, cask ales and enchanting views across to the Peak District, the Three Merry Lads also provides live entertainment on Thursdays (often with John on the guitar) and occasional themed nights - just call for details.

CROSSPOOL
Map 7 ref G12

4 miles W of Sheffield on the A57

Intriguingly, it was a fit of pique that led to the building of **The Bell Hagg Inn**. Back in the 1830s a certain Dr Hodgson offered the vicar of Stannington (a village across the River Rivel from Crosspool) a large donation for the church funds. But Hodgson was well known as a gambler and frequenter of pubs so the vicar declined the generous offer. Incensed by this rebuff, Hodgson bought the land directly opposite the church and built the pub there, a monument to drinking that no-one attending Divine Service at Stannington church could possibly overlook. It clings to the cliff side, a defiant piece of architecture

The Bell Hagg Inn, Manchester Road, Crosspool, Sheffield S10 5PX Tel: 0114 230 2082

obviously intended to make a statement. Amazingly, the pub survived Dr Hodgson and today it's owned and run by John and Genine Chidlaw who offer their customers excellent food, well-maintained ales, varied entertainment and comfortable accommodation. The restaurant is open all day for breakfast and bar meals, and there's also an appetising à la carte menu available between noon and 2.30pm, and again from 5pm until 8pm (except on Sunday evenings). The Bell Hagg hosts a Folk Night on Tuesday, a music night on Thursday, and there's a Singalong each Friday, Saturday and Sunday evening. This is the kind of inn where one wants to linger - fortunately, the Bell Hagg has 9 guest rooms, (a mixture of single, double and family), all of which are en suite.

OUGHTIBRIDGE
Map 7 ref G12

5 miles NW of Sheffield on the A6102

This pleasing village is set on the west bank of the River Don looking across to the tree-covered slopes of **Wharncliffe Wood**. The settlement dates back to Saxon times at least but surprisingly there is no church and no evidence of there ever having been one. But the village does offer visitors two good eating places.

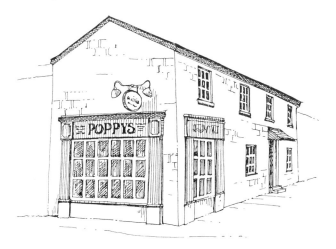

Leading back from the main road in Oughtibridge, a row of stone-built Victorian cottages have been stylishly converted into two outstanding, and complementary, eating places - **Brearley's Restaurant** and **Poppy's Café**. This is a well-run family business with Stephen and Jean Brearley mainly concerned with the restaurant while their daughter Wendy looks

Brearley's Restaurant & Poppy's Coffee Shop, 7-9 Langsett Road South, Oughtibridge, Sheffield S35 0GY Tel: 0114 286 2261

after the coffee shop with its accompanying craft shop. Everything served in the coffee shop is fresh and home made - pies, quiches, sausage rolls, and the menu also includes soup, light meals, sandwiches and cakes. The upstairs restaurant, open every lunchtime and evening except on Mondays, offers both table d'hôte and à la carte menus. Chef Jonathan Elliott specialises in English and French cuisine and his inventive menus, which change every couple of months, include dishes such as Kangaroo Medallions with Port Sauce along with more traditional offerings like steaks, chicken and lamb. Jonathan is particularly renowned for his "Crustacean Creations" - oysters, moules, prawns or scallops, each prepared in its own distinctive style.

WHARNCLIFFE SIDE   MAP 7 REF G12
5 miles NW of Sheffield on the A6102

Nestling in the valley below **Wharncliffe Crags**, Wharncliffe Side is a community of some 2000 souls and a popular location for commuters to Sheffield and Stocksbridge. An old tradition in the village tells of the 'Dragon of Wantly' which lurked in the recesses of the crags and terrorized the local people until a knight by the name of More did battle with the monster and killed it. A cave up on the crags is still called the 'Dragon's Den' and local children experience an enjoyable frisson of terror by shouting into its depths. Another ancient tradition in the village is the Whitsuntide walk when Sunday school children process around Wharncliffe Side stopping at various points to sing hymns.

STOCKSBRIDGE   MAP 7 REF G11
11 miles NW of Sheffield on the A616

This large town extends across the hillside with Underbank Reservoir to the west and the glorious scenery of the Peak National Park stretching for miles to the south and west. This is grand walking country and a favourite watering-hole for walkers is **The Silver Fox**, a spacious modern pub with a lively and welcoming atmosphere - "a place for all to meet, of all ages and from all walks of life". Your hosts, Rita and Trev Goldsworthy, are local people and they seem to have arranged for something to be happening almost every night. There's a Family Night when, between 5 and 8pm, children accompanied by an adult can tuck in to beefburgers or sandwiches and strut their stuff in a disco. Tuesday is Quiz Night when you can test your general knowledge, and on Friday and Saturday

The Silver Fox, 839 Manchester Road, Stocksbridge, Sheffield S36 1DR Tel: 0114 288 5655

evenings there's a disco for grown-ups starting at 8pm. Food is available every evening and at lunchtimes on Saturday and Sunday. The Carvery - on Sunday lunchtimes from noon till 2.30pm, offers a choice of two roasts and is very popular so booking is definitely recommended. The Silver Fox also offers a good selection of ales, with John Smith's Smooth the favoured brew. The pub is pleasantly furnished and decorated with Rita's collection of teapots of every size and shape providing an interesting talking point.

BRADWAY   MAP 7 REF G13
5 miles S of Sheffield off the A61

The Castle Inn has stood in Bradway village for well over a hundred years. It's believed it began as an alehouse for the navvies working on the Bradway-Dronfield railway tunnel which runs nearby or possibly for workers in the brick field which once operated here. The inn has gone up in the world since those days and it now offers quality food and ales in comfortable, attractive surroundings. June and Ken Cottrell took over here in the summer

of 1999 and their experience in the hospitality business has quickly brought The Castle an excellent reputation. The inn offers anything up to 7 different ales and a first class regular menu which is supplemented by at least half a dozen daily specials. Look out for the dishes listed under "Big Platters for the Really Hungry" - each one a feast in itself and outstanding value for money. Other specialities of the house are the fish dishes, prepared daily from freshly delivered fish. Booking is recommended for the (non-smoking) restaurant at weekends.

The Castle Inn, Twentywell Road, Bradway,
Sheffield S17 4PT Tel: 0114 236 2955

MOSBOROUGH   MAP 7 REF G13
5 miles SE of Sheffield off the A616

It's difficult to believe nowadays that the quiet little lane known as South Street was once the main Sheffield to London road. From the rear garden of **The Alma** you can gaze out across open countryside as you savour your pint - the view is noted for its wonderful sunsets. Inside, the low-beamed ceilings and open fire have the authentic atmosphere of a traditional English pub. Your hosts at The Alma are Phillip and Sandra Godfrey-Cooke, a friendly and welcoming couple who provide quality ales and a good selection of wholesome food. During the season, hot and cold meals and snacks are available every lunchtime and evening and it's strongly recommended that you try one of Sandra's delicious home made meat & potato pies. Incidentally, The Alma takes its name from a British victory in the Crimean War

The Alma, 76 South Street, Mosborough, Sheffield S20 5DF Tel: 0114 248 4781

of the 1850s and a plaque outside the pub gives a brief account of that battle.

Set high up overlooking Mosborough, **The Wheel** is a stylish modern pub built in 1965. Mine hosts, Adrian and Jackie, can be quite sure about the date because it was Adrian's father who dug out and laid the foundations. Jackie is also a local girl so between them they have a comprehensive knowledge of the area. Although they only took over at The Wheel in 1999, both of them have wide experience in the hospitality business. The emphasis here is on serving well-maintained quality ales, amongst them Stones and Tetleys

The Wheel, Plumley Hall Road, Mosborough, Sheffield S20 5BL
Tel: 0114 248 4991

and a wide range of other brews. No food is served but you'll almost always find something going on. On Tuesdays, there's League Pool; Thursday is Singalong Night, with a regular duo; and on Fridays there's a general knowledge Quiz from 9pm. Then on Saturday live entertainment is provided and the week is rounded off on Sunday night with a Jackpot Quiz also starting at 9pm. This lively pub has a splendidly welcoming atmosphere and is well recommended.

RENISHAW

MAP 7 REF H13

9 miles SE of Sheffield on the A616

This sizeable village gives its name to **Renishaw Hall**, home of Sir Reresby and Lady Sitwell and located about a mile or so to the northwest. The beautiful formal Italian gardens and 300 acres of wooded park are open to visitors, along with a nature trail and a Sitwell family museum, an art gallery, a display of Fiori de Henriques sculptures in the Georgian stables, and a café. The Hall itself is open to group and connoisseur tours by special arrangement only.

Renishaw stands right on the Yorkshire-Derbyshire border and at the heart of the village is **The Masons Arms**, an attractive old pub whose origins go back some 300 years or more. Not surprisingly, it's very olde-worlde inside with lots of beams and interesting bygones scattered around the rooms. James and Diana Fothergill are mine hosts at this

The Masons Arms, Emmett Carr Lane, Renishaw S21 3UL
Tel: 01246 432687

welcoming hostelry where the well-kept beers include Stones and John Smiths. James and Diana always seem to have something going on to entertain their customers - and also to raise money for charity. On Monday evening, there's men's darts, crib and dominoes; on Tuesday, karaoke from 8.30pm; Wednesday is ladies' darts and dominoes night; Thursday is 'Play Your Cards Right' evening; on Friday there's another karaoke evening, and the week is rounded off with a disco on Saturday from 8.30pm. What on earth do the good people of Renishaw do on a Sunday evening one wonders! The Masons Arms is open every lunchtime and evening, Monday to Thursday, and all day on Friday, Saturday and Sunday.

WALES

MAP 7 REF H13

9 miles E of Sheffield on the B6059

A mile or so to the west of Wales the **Rother Valley Country Park** provides excellent facilities for water sports including sailing, windsurfing, canoeing and jet skiing, as well as a cable water ski tow. Visitors can hire equipment or use their own, and training courses from beginner to instructor level are available in various water sports. Other attractions include a lakeside golf course, a Craft Centre with craftspeople at work, cycle hire, gift shop and cafeteria.

Known to its regular patrons as The Wales Bar, **The Waleswood** is a spacious 1950s building in the heart of this village just a few minutes drive from junction 31 of the M1 and close to the Derbyshire border. Business partners Wayne Fletcher and Andy Burrows

took over here in the autumn of 1999, their first venture as tenants although both have experience in the licensed trade. As we go to press they are finalising plans to start offering good wholesome pub grub at reasonable prices by the spring of 2000. To begin with, food will be served only at the weekends. But the excellent, well-maintained ales are always available with a choice that includes Stones, Caffreys and John Smiths Smooth. Entertainment at The Waleswood includes Sky TV, a Pop Quiz on Thursday evenings, and on Friday and Saturday evenings there's either a lively disco or a karaoke night.

The Waleswood, 114 School Road, Wales, Sheffield S26 5QJ Tel: 01909 771623

About 3 miles northeast of Wales is the **Tropical Butterfly House, Falconry and Wildlife Centre**. Here you can, if you wish, hold a tarantula or fondle a snake. Children can cuddle a bunny or bottle feed a calf. The Centre includes a well-stocked tropical butterfly house, a Bird of Prey centre which has regular flying demonstrations, an Animal Nursery, Farmyard Corner, Nature Trail, children's play area and gift shop.

ROTHERHAM
Map 7 ref H12

7 miles NE of Sheffield on the A630/A631

The town's most striking building is undoubtedly the **Church of All Saints**. With its soaring tower, pinnacled buttresses and battlements, and imposing porch, it is one of the finest examples of Perpendicular architecture in Yorkshire. It dates mainly from the 15th century although there is evidence of an earlier Saxon church on the site. A church here was listed in the Domesday Book and in 1161 the monks of Rufford Abbey were granted the right to prospect for and to smelt iron, and to plant an orchard, and from that day industry has existed side by side with agriculture.

Seventy-five per cent of the Borough of Rotherham is actually rural but it was heavy industry that put the town on the map. From the mid-18th century, the Walker Company of Rotherham was famous for cannons, their products featuring to lethal effect in the American War of Independence and at the Battle of Trafalgar. They also built bridges, amongst them Southwark Bridge in London and the bridge at Sunderland. Another famous bridge builder was born here in 1901. Sir Donald Coleman Bailey invented the Bailey Bridge which proved to be of great military value, especially during World War II.

The town also had lighter manufactures. Rockingham Pottery, produced here in the late 18th and early 19th century, is now highly prized by collectors. There's a fine collection at the **Clifton Park Museum**, a stately building whose interior has changed little since it was built in 1783 for the Rotherham ironmaster, Joshua Walker. The most breathtaking piece is the spectacular Rhinoceros Vase which stands almost 4ft high. In addition, the museum houses a collection of other Yorkshire pottery, English glass, silver and British oil paintings and water-colours. The grounds around Clifton House form the largest urban park in the Borough which has 10 urban parks altogether, along with 3 country parks, 7 golf courses, 10 swimming pools and a leisure centre.

Another museum of interest is the **York and Lancaster Regimental Museum** in the Central Library. The regiment had strong ties with South Yorkshire, its recruits drawn mainly from Barnsley, Sheffield and Rotherham. The displays include historic uniforms, campaign relics and over 1000 medals, amongst them nine Victoria Cross groups. There are also sections on local militia, rifle volunteers and territorials.

The palatial 18th century mansion **Wentworth Woodhouse** boasts the longest frontage in England, some 600ft long. The house is not open to the public but is clearly visible from its Park. Also visible are a number of follies and monuments dating from the 1700s. The most curious of these is the Needle's Eye which consists of a tower with a stone urn on top and is pierced by a carriageway. Legend says it was built in response to a wager by the Marquis of Rockingham, owner of Wentworth Woodhouse, that he could drive

through the eye of a needle. One structure which *is* open, (on Sunday afternoons during the season), is the Wentworth Mausoleum which was built in 1788 in memory of the 2nd Marquis.

A little further afield, near the village of Maltby, are the dramatic ruins of **Roche Abbey** (English Heritage). The abbey dates from the 12th cen-

Roche Abbey

tury and takes its name from the rocky limestone of the riverside site. The majestic remains of this great abbey stand in a landscape fashioned by 'Capability' Brown in the 1770s as part of the grounds of Sandbeck Park, home of the Earls of Scarborough.

BARNSLEY

MAP 7 REF G11

10 miles N of Sheffield on the A61

The county town of South Yorkshire, Barnsley stands on the River Dearne and derived its Victorian prosperity from the rich seams of coal hereabouts. It has an appropriately imposing Town Hall although the building is comparatively recent, completed in 1933. Nearby, the **Cooper Gallery** is a lively centre for the arts which hosts a varied programme of exhibitions throughout the year as well as housing a fine permanent collection.

The town's most impressive museum is actually located a few miles to the west, in the village of Cawthorne. **Cannon Hall** is a magnificent 18th century country house set in formal gardens and historic parkland. It offers unique collections of pottery, furniture, glassware and paintings, along with the 'Charge Gallery' which documents the story of the 13th/18th Royal Hussars.

Cannon Hall, Barnsley

About a mile to the south of Barnsley is the **Worsbrough Mill and Country Park**. The Grade II listed mill dates from around 1625. A steam mill was added in the 19th century and both have been restored to full working order to form the centrepiece of an industrial museum. The mill is set within a beautiful 200-acre country park which also includes the Wigfield Farm rare breeds centre.

Another three miles to the southeast, situated in attractive South Yorkshire countryside just off the M1 (J36), the **Elsecar Heritage Centre** is an imaginative science and history centre which is fun and educational for all the family. Visitors can discover hands-on science in the Power House; nostalgic travel on the Elsecar Steam Railway; the history of South Yorkshire in the 'Elsecar People' exhibition; and

Elsecar Heritage Centre

interactive multi-media in the 'Newcomen Beam Engine Centre'. The centre is also the base for several working crafts people who make and sell their products here. Special events include a 'Friends of Thomas the Tank Engine' day.

SILKSTONE

MAP 7 REF G11

4 miles W of Barnsley off the A628

The travel writer Arthur Mee dubbed Silkstone's parish church 'The Minster of the Moors' and it is indeed a striking building. Parts of the church date back to Norman times but most of it was built during the golden age of English ecclesiastical architecture, the 15th century. Outside, there are graceful flying buttresses and wonderfully weird gargoyles. Inside, the ancient oak roofs sprout floral bosses on moulded beams, and old box-pews and lovely medieval screens all add to the charm.

The old stocks just outside **The Ring o' Bells** are another sign of the antiquity of this former mining village. The Ring o'Bells itself dates back to the 1700s and it was here, in 1842, that the first Mines Union meeting took place. Christine Pickering who, together with her husband Alan runs this charming old inn, is fascinated by the history of the pub and the surrounding area. She can point you in the direction of many old sites of interest,

like the old waggon way that runs past the back of the inn - one of the first railways in the area. Inside the Ring o'Bells there are many old prints and bygones and Christine's interest is strengthened by the fact that her great aunt and uncle used to run this very pub in the 1930s and 40s. This exceptionally welcoming inn serves lunches and

The Ring o'Bells, 78 High Street, Silkstone,
Barnsley S75 3LN Tel: 01226 790298

dinners daily, (except on Mondays), with High Teas also available between 5 and 7pm. During the season, the Ring o'Bells is open all day from 9am, (when breakfasts are served if ordered in advance), and only closes for an hour or so in the afternoon during the winter. At the time of writing the inn has one guest bedroom to let, a twin; by the time you read this a second twin room should also be available.

THURLSTONE
MAP 7 REF F11
9 miles SW of Barnsley off the A628

Thurlstone developed when the first settlers realised that the nearby moors provided extensive grazing for sheep and the lime-free waters of the River Don were ideal for the washing of wool. Today the village still has some fine examples of the weavers' cottages which sprang up during the early 19th century, the best of which can be seen on Tenter Hill. Here the finished cloth would have been dried and stretched on 'tenters' - large wooden frames placed outside on the street which gave the road its name.

The village's most famous son was Nicholas Saunderson, born in 1682, who was blinded by smallpox at the age of two. He taught himself to read by passing his fingers over the tombstones in Penistone churchyard - 150 years before the introduction of Braille. Nicholas went on to attend grammar school and rose to become Professor of Mathematics at Cambridge University.

Conveniently located on the main A628 Barnsley to Manchester road, **The Huntsman** is a must for anyone who appreciates Real Ales and wholesome, home-cooked food. The Huntsman has won CAMRA awards for the quality of its real ales. There are always 5 or 6 different brews on tap. Counting guest ales, as many as 100 different varieties are on offer here during the course of a single year. Ian Morris, who runs this friendly traditional hostelry with his wife Sheila, calculates that since he became landlord here his customers have had the chance to sample 344 different real ales. The Huntsman hosts two Beer

Festivals each year: one over the April Fools Day weekend and another at Halloween. On both occasions, customers will find more than 30 real ales to choose from. The food at The Huntsman is also a big draw with home made, home cooked meals, served with steamed fresh vegetables, available Thursday to Sunday

The Huntsman, 136 Manchester Road, Thurlstone, nr Penistone, South Yorkshire S36 9QW Tel: 01226 764892

from noon until 8pm. Booking ahead is recommended. This lively pub doesn't neglect its customers entertainment either - Tuesday and Thursday are Quiz Nights and there's live music on the first Friday of each month.

PENISTONE

MAP 7 REF F11

15 miles NW of Sheffield on the A628

Perched 700ft above sea level, Penistone forms a gateway to the Peak District National Park which extends for some 30 miles to the south of the town. Penistone's oldest building is the 15th century tower of its parish church which overlooks a graveyard in which ancestors of the poet William Wordsworth are buried. Later centuries added an elegant Dissenters' Chapel (in the 1600s) and a graceful Cloth Hall in the 1700s.

Situated in the heart of this popular market town **The Old Crown** is an attractive old building, parts of it dating back to the 17th century. "Mine hosts" at the Old Crown are Helen and Steve who offer their customers good food, well-maintained ales and comfortable accommodation. Traditional home made and freshly prepared meals and snacks are available at lunchtimes and in the evenings, and the choice of quality ales

The Old Crown, 6 Market Street, Penistone, Sheffield S36 6BZ Tel: 01226 762422

includes Tetley and Stones plus Caffreys, draught lager and cider. The second floor of the inn has recently been converted into six twin and single rooms, available at competitive rates, which are equipped with TV and tea/coffee-making facilities. A full English breakfast is included in the tariff and there are special rates for longer stays. This lively inn hosts a music and general knowledge Quiz on Wednesday nights; on Friday and Saturday evenings there's a disco (in a separate room); and once a month, on a Sunday, a live band provides entertainment.

Built as a farmhouse in 1720, **Cubley Hall** is an outstanding hotel, restaurant and Free House. Open all day every day, it is surrounded by its own magnificent grounds. Many original features remain in this splendid establishment. In 1983 the Hall, after many years of lying semi-derelict, was transformed sympathetically to complement and enhance the unique original architectural features, mosaic floors, stained glass, old oak panelling and ornate plaster ceilings, while incorporating the most modern facilities and amenities expected in a country house

Cubley Hall, Mortimer Road, Penistone, Sheffield, South Yorkshire S36 9DF Tel: 01226 766086 Fax: 01226 767335

hotel. In 1990 the massive oak beamed, hewn stone barn was converted into a characterful and impressive restaurant. The professional staff and team of talented chefs create modern cuisine to satisfy the most discerning diners. The 12 en suite guest bedrooms are top of the range for comfort, luxury and style. A relaxed and informal atmosphere ensures that guests feel at home. The pub offers traditional hand-pulled beers and a good range of wines and spirits.

OXSPRING

MAP 7 REF G11

6 miles SW of Barnsley on the B6462

The Waggon and Horses is a charming 18th century building which was once a farmhouse and smithy. When the railway arrived, the old barn was home to many of the navvies. The establishment became an inn in the early 1800s and it has remained so to this day. Samantha and Tony Brewis took over here in early 1999. Brimming with ideas and enthusiasm they have created a warm and welcoming hostelry which also boasts an outstanding menu based on fresh, good quality, home cooked food. With a table menu consisting of a large variety of starters and main courses along with a daily selection of home made sweets and snacks there is definitely something here for everyone. Quality ales and a short but perceptively selected wine list add to the dining pleasure. On Friday nights the regular menu is supplemented by Tea Time Specials and on Tuesday evening children under 12 eat free. Attached to the inn is a converted, self-contained, licensed barn which provides an ideal setting for all kinds of functions and celebrations. Tony and

The Waggon and Horses, Sheffield Road, Oxspring, nr Penistone, Sheffield S36 8YQ Tel: 01226 763259

Samantha's motto for the Waggon and Horses is "Small enough to care yet large enough to cater for your every need" - a credo that is definitely true of this picturesque pub.

DUNFORD BRIDGE   MAP 6 REF F11
15 miles SW of Barnsley off the A628

Located just inside the Peak National Park, **The Stanhope Arms** is very much a hidden place. The hamlet of Dunford Bridge is only shown on very large scale maps but if you are travelling westwards from Barnsley on the A628, after 13 miles or so you will see a sign for the pub off to the right. It's well worth seeking out this grand old inn, originally built in the 1800s as a shooting lodge for the Cannon Hall Estate. It stands beside the entrance to the Woodhead railway tunnel which runs beneath the moors for more than 3 miles. When the tunnel opened in 1852 it was twice as long as any other in the world. There's an interesting display of memorabilia regarding the tunnel and the camp built for the Tunnel Tigers, (the navvies who built it), in the snug of the Stanhope Arms. This inviting inn is owned and run by Christine and Les Tyas who offer their customers an extensive choice of appetising food rang-

The Stanhope Arms, Windle Edge Road, Dunford Bridge S36 4TF Tel/Fax: 01226 763104

ing from hearty main courses such as home made Steak, Mushroom and Ale Pie, or Tuna Steak in a hoi sin sauce, to well-filled sandwiches. Food is available every lunchtime and evening except Monday lunchtime (unless it's a Bank Holiday) and Monday evenings during the winter. Children are welcome, (there's a safe play area for them, too), and accommodation is also available all year round in 5 upstairs guest rooms, all of which are en suite.

CONISBROUGH
5 miles SW of Doncaster on the A630

MAP 7 REF H11

The town is best known for the 11th century **Conisbrough Castle** (English Heritage) which features prominently in one of the most dramatic scenes in Sir Walter Scott's novel

Ivanhoe. The most impressive medieval building in South Yorkshire, Conisbrough Castle boasts the oldest circular Keep in England. Rising some 90ft and more than 50ft wide, the Keep stands on a man-made hill raised in Saxon times. Six huge buttresses some

Conisbrough Castle

6ft thick support walls that in places are 15ft deep. Visitors can walk through the remains of several rooms, including the first floor chamber where the huge open fireplaces give one a fascinating insight into the lifestyle of Norman times. The castle also offers a visual presentation, a visitor centre and a tea room.

Not far from the famous castle and named in its honour, **The Castle Inn** is an interesting old building dating back to 1806. It was originally a bone mill, standing next to a brook and waterfall, but its waterwheel has long since gone and when Joanne and Kevin Smart took over here, early in 1999, the premises were in a sorry state. They undertook a comprehensive refur-

The Castle Inn, Minney Moor Hill, Burcroft, Conisbrough, Doncaster DN12 3EN Tel: 01709 862204

bishment and through sheer hard work have made the Castle a great success. During the summer, the inn is open all day, every day, and out of season it is open all day over the weekend; from 4pm during the week. The quality ales on offer include Stones, John Smith's and John Smith's Smooth, plus 3 draught lagers, cider, Guinness and Murphy's. By the time you read this the Castle will also be serving food at lunchtimes and evenings, with a Carvery on Sundays. Meals can be enjoyed either inside or on the patio overlooking the beer garden. There are Happy Hours, Monday to Thursday, from 4pm to 8pm, and on Saturday there's live entertainment from 8.30pm.

Just a short walk from the town centre, the **Lord Conyers Hotel** is a spacious 1930s building where you'll find excellent food, ales, accommodation and lots of atmosphere. Popular with both locals and visitors, the hotel serves food every lunchtime and evening, (except Monday lunchtimes, unless it's a Bank Holiday). There's an extensive menu and a Carvery is also available. The stylish restaurant seats about 95 but if you want to dine here at the weekend you should

**Lord Conyers Hotel, Old Road, Conisbrough,
Doncaster DN12 3LZ Tel: 01709 863254**

definitely make a booking. The quality ales on offer include two Real Ales - John Smith's and Barnsley Bitter, along with two keg ales, lagers, cider and Guinness. The hotel has 6 guest bedrooms, all of them en suite and varying in size from singles to family rooms. One is a bridal suite, complete with 4-poster bed. Entertainment at the Lord Conyers includes quizzes on Friday evenings from 9pm and on Sunday afternoons from 1pm, and karaoke nights on Wednesdays, Saturdays and Sundays from 8pm.

CADEBY

MAP 7 REF H11

4 miles SW of Doncaster off the A630

Listed in the Domesday Book as *Catebi*, this pleasant little village is surrounded on all sides by prime agricultural land. For centuries Cadeby had no church of its own but had to travel the two miles to the parish church in Sprotbrough. Then in 1856 the owners of the huge Sprotbrough estate, the Copley family, paid for a church to be built in Cadeby. It was designed by Sir George Gilbert Scott, the architect of St Pancras Station in London, and resembles a medieval estate barn with its steeply pitched roofs and lofty south porch. A century and a half later, Cadeby is again without a church since Sir George's attractive church has recently been declared redundant.

For more than 200 years **The Cadeby Inn** was a farmhouse on the Sprotbrough Estate. It became a pub in 1975 and all the old farmhouse features are still in place - three roaring open fires, beamed ceilings, lots of exposed brickwork and local bygones scattered

around the olde-worlde rooms. Run by Craig and Karen, the inn is a Free House so there's an excellent choice of ales, amongst them John Smiths, Tetleys and Sam Smiths real ales, plus a guest ale. The Cadeby Inn's food is highly recommended, especially the Carvery which enjoys an almost legendary reputation amongst local people. Food is available throughout the day and along with a comprehensive choice of meat, poultry and fish dishes

The Cadeby Inn, Main Street, Cadeby, Doncaster, South Yorkshire DN5 7SW Tel: 01709 864009

the menu also includes at least 7 vegetarian options. In good weather customers can enjoy their meals in the pleasantly secluded beer garden.

DONCASTER
18 miles NE of Sheffield on the A630

MAP 7 REF I11

The Romans named their riverside settlement beside the River Don, *Danum*, and a well-preserved stretch of the road they built here can be seen just west of Adwick le Street. The modern town boasts some impressive buildings, notably the **Mansion House** built in 1748 and designed by James Paine. The parish church was rebuilt in 1858 by Sir Giles Gilbert Scott and it's an outstanding example of Gothic revival architecture with its lofty tower, 170ft high and crowned with pinnacles. The lively shopping centre is enhanced by a stately **Corn Exchange** building and a market which takes place every Tuesday, Friday and Saturday. Doncaster was also one of the most important centres for the production of steam engines. Thousands were built here, including both the *Flying Scotsman* and the *Mallard*. The *Mallard* still holds the record for the fastest steam train in the world, achieving a top speed of 125mph in July 1938.

There is no-one connected with the racing fraternity who has not heard of the St Leger, one of the oldest classic races, which has been held at Doncaster since 1776. Doncaster, in the Yorkshire tradition, provides a magnet for all horse-racing enthusiasts and there are a total of 26 meetings each year.

On the racecourse side of town lies the Art Deco **Earl of Doncaster Hotel**. There has been an Earl of Doncaster hotel for more than 150 years but the present hotel was built in the 1930s although, because of World War II, it was not opened until the late 1940s. The current owners acquired the establishment in 1993 and have recreated the former grandeur of the 1930s. All 55 bedrooms have full en suite facilities and represent a step into times past in terms of style. The same style is also present in the public rooms and most strikingly in the magnificent ballroom with its half wood-panelled walls. The ballroom can cater for up to 250 people and is an ideal location for wedding receptions, dinner dances and business meetings or presentations. Throughout the hotel an elegant and relaxed atmosphere is combined with high standards of service, most notably in the Earl's Restaurant which offers a reasonably priced traditional table d'hôte menu. Excellent food is also available in the Earl's Bar every lunchtime and evening.

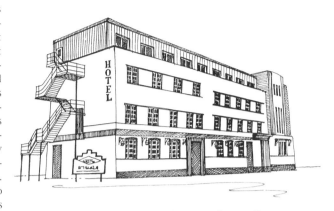

The Earl of Doncaster Hotel, Bennetthorpe, Doncaster DN2 6AD Tel: 01302 361371 Fax: 01302 321858 e-mail: theearl@freeserve.co.uk website: www.theearl.co.uk

On the northwestern outskirts of the town Cusworth Hall is home to the **Museum of South Yorkshire Life** (free). The Hall is a splendid Georgian mansion built in the 1740s and set in a landscaped park. The interior features varied displays on the social history, industry, agriculture and transport of the area.

Another 3 miles or so to the northwest of Doncaster, **Brodsworth Hall** (English Heritage) is a remarkable example of a Victorian mansion that has survived with much of its original furnishings and decorations intact. When Charles and Georgiana Thellusson, their 6 children and 15 servants moved into the new hall in 1863 the house must have seemed the last word in both grandeur and utility. A gasworks in the grounds supplied the lighting and no fewer than 8 water-closets were distributed around the house, although rather surprisingly only two bathrooms were installed.

More immediately impressive to visitors were the opulent furnishings, paintings, statuary and decoration. The sumptuous reception rooms have now a rather faded grandeur and English Heritage has deliberately left it so, preserving the

Brodsworth Hall, nr Doncaster

patina of time throughout the house to produce an interior that is both fascinating and evocative. A vanished way of life is also brought to life in the huge kitchen and the cluttered servants wing. The Hall stands in 15 acres of beautifully restored Victorian gardens complete with a summer house in the form of a classical temple, a Target Range where the family practised its archery, and a Pets Cemetery where the family dogs - and a prized parrot bearing the unimaginative name of 'Polly' - were buried between 1894 and 1988.

ASKERN
MAP 7 REF I10

7 miles N of Doncaster on the A19

Lots of atmosphere, regular entertainment, excellent ales and, by the time you read this,

quality food as well, are all available at **The Railway** just a couple of hundred yards off the A19. Brother and sister team Linda and Steve Shufflebotham run this spacious Victorian pub which was originally built as a hotel to serve the railway just across the road. Linda and Steve took over here early in 1999 and they have given the inn a new lease of life. There always seems to

The Railway, Moss Road, Askern, Doncaster DN6 0JS
Tel: 01302 700289

be something going on here - on Mondays there's Bingo with a £1000 lottery draw; on Fridays a disco; Saturday is karaoke night and on Sunday a disco begins at 3pm and continues until 11pm. This lively programme probably has something to do with the fact that their parents ran a club for 28 years and Linda used to run a disco at a holiday camp. At the time of writing Linda and Steve are preparing to start serving food every lunchtime and evening and they will also be introducing themed evenings from time to time.

NORTON
MAP 7 REF I10

8 miles N of Doncaster off the A19

This sizeable village is located close to the borders with North and West Yorkshire and was once busy with farming, mining and quarrying. Nowadays it's a peaceful place, a tranquil base for commuters to Doncaster and Pontefract. Its most impressive building is the ancient parish church of St Mary Magdalene whose splendid 14th century west tower is considered by many to be the finest in Yorkshire. Once there was also a priory here, standing beside the River Went, but now only a fragment of wall remains. However, the old water mill has survived.

STAINFORTH
MAP 7 REF I10
7 miles NE of Doncaster off the A18 or A614

Stainforth was once an important trading centre and inland port on the River Don. It also stands on the banks of the **Stainforth & Keadby Canal** which still has a well-preserved dry dock and a 19th century blacksmith's shop. This area of low, marshy ground was drained by Dutch engineers in the 1600s to produce rich, peaty farmland. The place has retained the air of a quiet backwater, a little-explored area of narrow lands and pretty hamlets, the fields drained by slow-moving dykes and canals. The rich peat resources are commercially exploited in part but also provide a congenial home for a great deal of natural wildlife.

A popular stopping place for boaters on the Stainforth to Keadby Canal, **The New Inn** occupies a splendid riverside position with moorings for up to 12 boats. In good weather customers can settle down at one of the picnic tables on the lawn and watch the boating world go by. There's also a good view of the river from the lounge area where patrons can enjoy the quality food served every lunchtime and evening (except Tuesday and Sunday nights). The extensive menu is supplemented by a host of blackboard specials, all served in generous portions and at extremely reasonable prices. At

The New Inn, Canal View, South Bank, Stainforth, Doncaster DN7 5AW Tel: 01302 841614

lunchtimes there are special meals for pensioners. Carol and Ralph Fletcher who run this popular pub lay on a karaoke night on Tuesdays and on Saturday there's live entertainment from 8.30pm. With its waterside setting the New Inn is a delightful place to stay - the Fletchers have 2 guest rooms available which can accommodate up to 6 people. Both of them are smartly furnished and decorated.

FISHLAKE
MAP 7 REF I10
10 miles NE of Doncaster off the A614

Set along the banks of the River Don, which is known here as the Dutch River, Fishlake is virtually an island since it is surrounded by rivers and canals and can only be entered by crossing a bridge. It's a charming village with a striking medieval church famous for its elaborately carved Norman doorway, an ancient windmill and a welcoming traditional inn.

THORNE
MAP 7 REF J10
10 miles NE of Doncaster on the A614

This ancient market town on the River Don has been a port since at least 1500 with ships sailing from here to York, Hull, London and Europe. The waterfront was busy with boat-builder's yards where vessels of up to 400 tons were built. In 1802, Thorne gained a second waterfront, on the newly constructed Stainforth & Keadby Canal which attracted most of the water traffic from the unpredictable River Don. As late as 1987 there were still boat building yards at work here but in that year they finally closed and the area is being carefully developed in a way that will commemorate the town's heritage.

You would have to be very hard to please if you couldn't find something to your taste in the extensive menu on offer at **The Gates Tea Room** located in the centre of Thorne. Some ten years ago June Jenkins fell in love with this appealing 18th century building which in its time has served as a stone-mason's, a cobbler's, an alehouse and a private

The Gates Tea Room, 29 King Street, Thorne, Doncaster DN8 5AU Tel: 01405 813634

dwelling. It's now a popular tea room with a main dining room, a pleasant conservatory and for fine weather days a patio at the rear overlooking the garden. June's menu ranges from hearty meals such as her home made Steak, Chicken or Cottage Pies, through large Yorkshire Puddings with a filling of your choice, omelettes and salads, to freshly cut sandwiches, jacket potatoes and tasty snacks like Fluffy Scrambled Eggs on Toast. Naturally, a traditional Cream Tea is available along with a wide choice of sweets and there's a special menu for children. The Gates Tea Room is open Monday to Saturday from 9am to 4pm and on Sunday mornings fishing fanatics can call in for breakfast between 7am and 9am!

FINNINGLEY
MAP 7 REF I11
7 miles SE of Doncaster on the A614

A unique feature of this pleasant village close to the Nottinghamshire border is its five village greens, the main one having a duck pond complete with weeping willows. Finningley is a living village with a well-used Village Hall, originally a barn but which later served as the village school. Finningley has a beautiful Norman church with a rectors' list dating back to 1293 and a post office which has been in the same family for 5 generations. Just before World War II, Finningley RAF airfield was built to the west of the village and although the airfield is no longer in regular use it provides the venue for an annual **Air Show** which includes some spectacular flying displays.

Originally built as a farmhouse **The Harvey Arms** stands facing one of the village greens, an inviting pub with an open fire and olde worlde Tap Room. It was converted into an inn during the mid-1800s, taking its name from the Lord of the Manor at that time and becoming, it's believed, the only pub with this name in the country. The Harvey Arms is very much a family concern with your hosts Janet and Roy Kettlewood assisted by their son Mark, an accomplished cook. The hospitality business seems to run in Janet's

The Harvey Arms, Old Bawtry Road, Finningley, Doncaster DN9 3BY
Tel: 01302 770200

family. Her own parents ran a pub and her two brothers have inns in Cambridgeshire. The Harvey Arms is well-known locally for the excellence of the food on offer. Only prime quality ingredients are used - nothing frozen here except for the ice cream and the peas. Every lunchtime there's a Carvery from noon until 2pm (Sundays until 3pm) and evening meals are served from 6.30pm until 9pm (9.30pm Thursday - Saturday). Meals can be taken either in the separate, non-smoking dining room or in the spacious lounge. Children are welcome up to 9pm.

BLAXTON   Map 7 ref J11
6 miles SE of Doncaster on the A614

Conveniently located at the A614/B1396 roundabout, **The Blue Bell** has an excellent reputation for the quality of the food on offer and its wide selection of prime ales. The pub has been owned and run since 1996 by Mark and Deborah Anderson, with Deborah and her mum Annice responsible for the outstanding cuisine. Their menu is impressively extensive - the house speciality, chicken, for example

The Blue Bell, Thorne Road, Blaxton, Doncaster DN9 3AL
Tel: 01302 770424

is offered in 18 different variations and there is definitely something for every palate. Meals can be enjoyed in the delightful conservatory or throughout the pub and are available every lunchtime and evening except Sunday evening and Monday lunchtime (unless it's a Bank Holiday). A popular attraction at The Blue Bell is its Happy Hours - 5pm to 7pm Monday to Friday, 2pm to 4pm on Saturday, and 4pm to 6pm on Sunday. And if you enjoy a good Pub Quiz make sure you're here on Wednesday evening at 9.30pm. As we go to press, plans are under way to provide accommodation at the Blue Bell - by the time you read this it may well be available.

BAWTRY
MAP 7 REF I12
9 miles SE of Doncaster on the A614

This pleasant little market town stands close to the Nottinghamshire border and in medieval times it was customary for the Sheriff of South Yorkshire to welcome visiting kings and queens here. In the mid-1500s the then Sheriff, Sir Robert Bowes, accompanied by 200 gentlemen dressed in velvet and 4000 yeomen on horseback, greeted Henry VIII and in the name of Yorkshire presented him with a purse containing the huge sum of £900 in gold.

At that time, Bawtry was a busy inland port which explains how **The Ship** gained its name. In those days the inn stood closer to the River Idle but in 1901 it was moved lock, stock and barrels of beer to its present position a couple of hundred yards from the centre of this attractive market town. Completely refurbished in 1998, The Ship is run by Trevor and Christine Reeve, a welcoming couple with more than 16 years experience in the hospitality business. Food is available every lunchtime from noon until 3pm with a choice that includes the regular menu along with a selection of daily specials. The Sunday Roast Lunch is especially popular. Children are welcome and meals can be enjoyed either in the spacious lounge or in the public bar which is full of atmosphere. The Ship has 3 quality bitters on offer, Mansfield Original, Smooth and a guest ale as well as a wide choice of other brews.

**The Ship, Gainsborough Road, Bawtry,
South Yorkshire DN10 6HT Tel: 01302 710275**

TOURIST INFORMATION CENTRES

Locations in **bold** type are open throughout the year

Aysgarth
Aysgarth Falls, Aysgarth, North Yorkshire DL8 3TH
Tel/Fax: 01969 663424

Barnsley
Central Library, Shamble Street, South Yorkshire S70 2JL
Tel/Fax: 01226 206757

Bedale
Bedale Hall, Bedale, North Yorkshire DL8 1AA
Tel: 01677 424604 fax:01677 427146

Bentham
8 Station Road, Bentham, via Lancaster, North Yorkshire
Tel: 01524 262549

Beverley
34 Butcher Row, Beverley, East Yorkshire HU17 OAB
Tel: 01482 884354 Fax:01482 885237

Boroughbridge
Fishergate, Boroughbridge, North Yorkshire YO5 1AL
Tel: 01423 323373

Bradford
Central Library, Prince's Way, Bradford, West Yorkshire BD1 1NN
Tel: 01274 753678 Fax: 01274 739067

Bridlington
25 Prince Street, Bridlington, East Yorkshire YO15 2NP
Tel: 01262 673474 / 606383 / 679626

Clapham

Clapham National Park Centre, Clapham, via Lancaster,
North Yorkshire LA2 8ED Tel: 015242 51419

Danby

The Moors Centre, Danby Lodge, Danby, North Yorkshire YO21 2NB
Tel: 01287 660654 Fax:01287 660308

Doncaster

Central Library, Waterdale, Doncaster, South Yorkshire DN1 3JE
Tel: 01302 734309 Fax: 01302 735385

Easingwold

Chapel Lane, Easingwold, North Yorkshire YO3 6AE
Tel: 01347 821530

Filey

John Street, Filey, North Yorkshire YO14 9DW
Tel: 01723 512204 Fax:01723 516893

Grassington

National Park Centre, Hebden Road, Grassington, North Yorkshire BD23 5LB
Tel: 01756 752774 Fax:01756 753358

Great Ayton

High Green Car Park, Great Ayton, North Yorkshire TS9 6BJ
Tel: 01642 722835 Fax: 01642 724960

Guisborough

Priory Grounds, Church Street, Guisborough, North Yorkshire TS14 6HG
Tel/Fax: 01287 633801

Halifax

Piece Hall, Halifax, West Yorkshire HX1 1RE
Tel: 01422 368725 fAX: 01422 354264

Harrogate

Royal Baths Assembly Rooms, Crescent Street, Harrogate,
North Yorkshire HG1 2RR Tel: 01423 537300 Fax: 01423 537305

Hawes

Dales Countryside Museum, Station Yard, Hawes, North Yorkshire DL8 3NT
Tel: 01969 667450 Fax:01969 667165

Haworth

2-4 West Lane, Haworth, West Yorkshire BD22 8EF
Tel: 01535 642329 Fax: 01535 647721

Hebden Bridge
1 Bridge Gate, Hebden Bridge, West Yorkshire HX7 8EX
Tel: 01422 843831 Fax: 01422 845266

Helmsley
The Market Place, Helmsley, North Yorkshire YO2 5BL
Tel: 01439 770173 Fax:01439 771881

Holme on Spalding Moor
68 High Street, Holme on Spalding Moor, East Yorkshire YO4 4AA
Tel: 01430 860479

Holmfirth
49-51 Huddersfield Road, Holmfirth, West Yorkshire HD7 1JP
Tel: 01484 222444 Fax: 01484 222445

Hornsea
75 Newbegin, Hornsea, East Yorkshire HU18 1PA
Tel/Fax: 01964 536404

Horton in Ribblesdale
Pen-y-ghent Café, Horton in Ribblesdale, North Yorkshire BD24 0HE
Tel/Fax: 01729 860333

Huddersfield
3-5 Albion Street, Huddersfield, West Yorkshire HD1 2NW
Tel/Fax: 01484 223200

Hull
Central Library, Albion Street, Hull, East Yorkshire HU1 3TF
Tel: 01482 223344 Fax: 01482 616896

1 Paragon Street, Kingston Upon Hill, East Yorkshire HU1 3RQ
Tel: 01482 223559 Fax:01482 613959

King George Dock, Hedon Road, Hull, East Yorkshire HU9 5PR
Tel: 01482 702118

Humber Bridge
North Bank Viewing Area, Ferriby Road, Hessle,
East Ridings Of Yorkshire HU13 0LN Tel/Fax: 01482 640852

Ilkley
Station Road, Ilkley, West Yorkshire LS29 8HA
Tel: 01943 602319 Fax: 01943 603795

Ingleton
Community Centre Car Park, Ingleton, North Yorkshire LA6 3HJ
Tel: 015242 41049 Fax:015242 41701

Knaresborough
9 Castle Court Yard, Market Place Knaresborough, North Yorkshire HG5 8AE
Tel/Fax: 01423 866886

Leeds
PO Box 244, Gateway Yorkshire, The Arcade, City Station, Leeds,
West Yorkshire LS1 1PL Tel: 0113 242 5242 Fax: 0113 246 8246

Leyburn
4 Central Chambers, Railway Street Leyburn, North Yorkshire DL8 5BB
Tel: 01969 623069 Fax: 01969 622833

Malham
Malham National Park Centre, Malham, Skipton, North Yorkshire BD23 4DA
Tel: 01729 830363

Malton
58 Market Place, Malton, North Yorkshire YO17 0LW
Tel: 01653 600048 Fax:01653 698374

Northallerton
Applegarth Car Park, Northallerton, North Yorkshire DL7 8LZ
Tel/Fax: 01609 776864

Pateley Bridge
18 High Street, Pateley Bridge, North Yorkshire HG3 5AW
Tel/Fax: 01423 711147

Pickering
The Ropery, Pickering, North Yorkshire YO18 8DY
Tel: 01751 473791 Fax:01751 473487

Reeth
The Literary Institute, The Green, Reeth, North Yorkshire DL11 6TE
Tel/Fax: 01748 884059

Richmond
Friary Gardens, Victoria Road, Richmond, North Yorkshire DL10 4AJ
Tel: 01748 850252 Fax: 01748 825994

Ripon
Minster Road, Ripon, North Yorkshire HG4 1QT
Tel/Fax: 01765 604625

Rotherham

Central Library, Walker Place, Rotherham, South Yorkshire S65 1JH
Tel: 01709 823611 Fax:01709 823650

Saltaire

2 Victoria Road, Saltaire, Shipley, West Yorkshire BD18 3LA
Tel: 01274 774993 Fax:01274 774464

Saltburn-by-the-Sea

3 Station Buildings, Station Square, Saltburn-by-the-Sea,
North Yorkshire TS12 1AQ Tel: 01287 622422 Fax:01287 625074

Scarborough

Unit 3, Pavillion House, Valley Bridge Road, Scarborough,
North Yorkshire YO11 1UZ Tel: 01723 373333 Fax:01723 363785

Selby

Park Street, Selby, North Yorkshire YO8 4AA
Tel: 01757 703263

Settle

Town Hall, Cheapside, Settle, North Yorkshire BD24 9EJ
Tel: 01729 825192 Fax:01729 824381

Sheffield

1 Tudor Square, Sheffield, South Yorkshire S1 2LA
Tel: 0114 201 1020/2 Fax: 0114 221 4225

Skipton

Cravern Court Shopping Centre, Skipton, North Yorkshire BD23 1DG
Tel: 01756 792809 Fax:01756 797528

Sutton Bank

Sutton Bank Visitor Centre, nr Thirsk, North Yorkshire YO7 2EH
Tel: 01845 597426

Thirsk

23 Kirkgate, Thirsk, North Yorkshire YO7 1PQ
Tel: 01845 522755 Fax:01845 526230

Todmorden

15 Burnley Road, Todmorden, West Yorkshire OL14 7BU
Tel/Fax: 01706 818181

Wakefield

Town Hall, Wood Street, Wakefield, West Yorkshire WF1 2HQ
Tel: 01924 305000/1 Fax: 01924 305775

Wetherby

Council Offices, 24 Westgate, Wetherby, West Yorkshire LS22 6NL
Tel: 0113 247 7251 Fax:0113 247 6617

Whitby

Langborne Road, Whitby, North Yorkshire YO21 1YN
Tel: 01947 602674 Fax: 01947 606137

Withernsea

Pier Towers, Withernsea, East Yorkshire HU19 2JS
Tel: 01964 615683

York

The De Grey Rooms, Exhibition Square, York, North Yorkshire YO1 2HB
Tel: 01904 621756 Fax: 01904 639986

York Railway Station, Station Road, York, North Yorkshire YO2 2AY
Tel: 01904 621756 Fax: 01904 639986

York Tourism Bureau, 20 George Hudson Street, York,
North Yorkshire YO1 6WR Tel: 01904 620557 Fax: 01904 620880

INDEX OF TOWNS, VILLAGES AND PLACES OF INTEREST

INDEX OF PLACES TO STAY, EAT, DRINK & SHOP

THE HIDDEN PLACES
ORDER FORM

To order any of our publications just fill in the payment details below and complete the order form *overleaf*. For orders of less than 4 copies please add £1 per book for postage and packing. Orders over 4 copies are P & P free.

Please Complete Either:

I enclose a cheque for £ .... made payable to Travel Publishing Ltd

Or:

Card No: ⬜⬜⬜⬜ ⬜⬜⬜⬜ ⬜⬜⬜⬜ ⬜⬜⬜⬜

Expiry Date: ⬜⬜ ⬜⬜

Signature: ....

NAME: ....

ADDRESS: ....

....

....

POSTCODE: ....

TEL NO: ....

Please send to: Travel Publishing Ltd
7a Apollo House
Calleva Park
Aldermaston
Berks, RG7 8TN

THE HIDDEN PLACES ORDER FORM

	Price	Quantity	Value
Regional Titles			
Cambridgeshire & Lincolnshire	£7.99	....	....
Channel Islands	£6.99	....	....
Cheshire	£7.99	....	....
Chilterns	£7.99	....	....
Cornwall	£7.99	....	....
Derbyshire	£7.99	....	....
Devon	£7.99	....	....
Dorset, Hants & Isle of Wight	£7.99	....	....
Essex	£7.99	....	....
Gloucestershire & Wiltshire	£7.99	....	....
Heart of England	£7.99	....	....
Hereford, Worcs & Shropshire	£7.99	....	....
Highlands & Islands	£7.99	....	....
Kent	£7.99	....	....
Lake District & Cumbria	£7.99	....	....
Lancashire	£7.99	....	....
Norfolk	£7.99	....	....
Northeast Yorkshire	£6.99	....	....
Northumberland & Durham	£6.99	....	....
North Wales	£7.99	....	....
Nottinghamshire	£6.99	....	....
Potteries	£6.99	....	....
Somerset	£6.99	....	....
South Wales	£7.99	....	....
Suffolk	£7.99	....	....
Surrey	£6.99	....	....
Sussex	£6.99	....	....
Thames Valley	£7.99	....	....
Warwickshire & West Midlands	£6.99	....	....
Yorkshire	£7.99	....	....
Set of any 5 Regional titles	**£25.00**	....	....
National Titles			
England	£9.99	....	....
Ireland	£9.99	....	....
Scotland	£9.99	....	....
Wales	£8.99	....	....
Set of all 4 National titles	**£28.00**	....	....
		_____	_____
		_____	_____

For orders of less than 4 copies please add £1 per book for postage & packing. Orders over 4 copies P & P free.

THE HIDDEN PLACES
READER COMMENT FORM

The *Hidden Places* research team would like to receive reader's comments on any visitor attractions or places reviewed in the book and also recommendations for suitable entries to be included in the next edition. This will help ensure that the *Hidden Places* series continues to provide its readers with useful information on the more interesting, unusual or unique features of each attraction or place ensuring that their stay in the local area is an enjoyable and stimulating experience.

To provide your comments or recommendations would you please complete the forms below and overleaf as indicated and send to: The Research Department, Travel Publishing Ltd., 7a Apollo House, Calleva Park, Aldermaston, Reading, RG7 8TN.

Your Name:

Your Address:

Your Telephone Number:

Please tick as appropriate: Comments ☐   Recommendation ☐

Name of *"Hidden Place"*:

Address:

Telephone Number:

Name of Contact:

THE HIDDEN PLACES
READER COMMENT FORM

Comment or Reason for Recommendation:

....

....

....

....

....

....

....

....

....

....

....

....

MAP SECTION

The following pages of maps encompass the main cities, towns and geographical features of Yorkshire, as well as many of the interesting places featured in the guide. Distances are indicated by the use of scale bars located below each of the maps

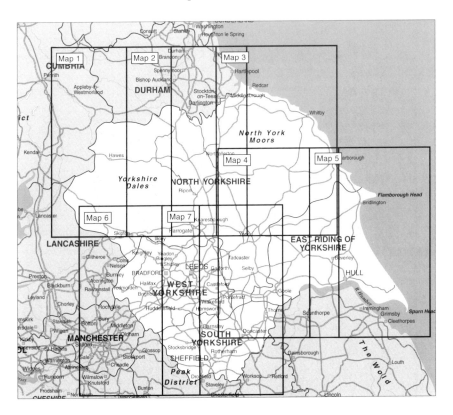

This page is left intentionally blank

Map 1

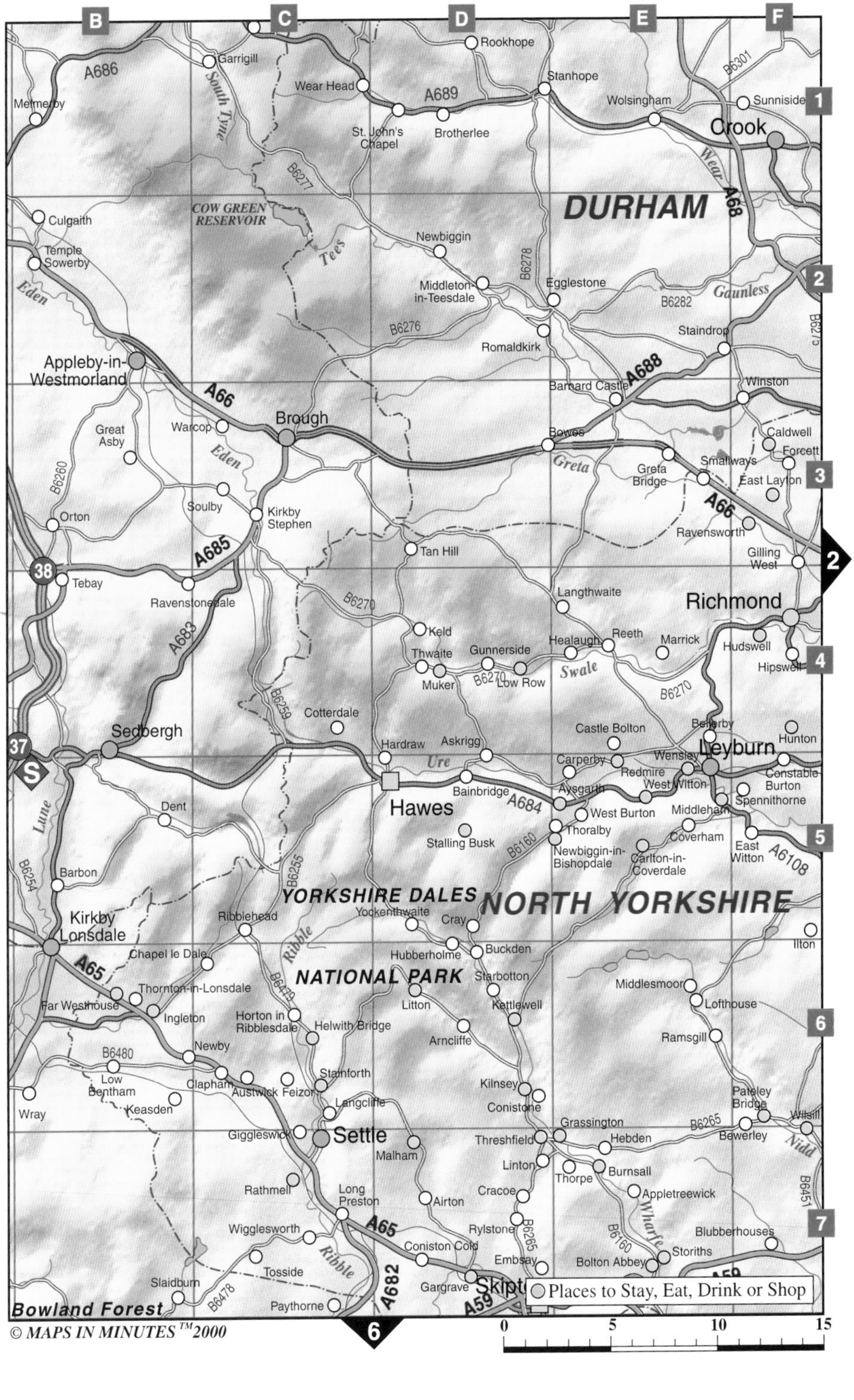

B   C   D   E   F

1

A686
Garrigill
Melmerby
Wear Head
A689
Rookhope
Stanhope
St. John's Chapel
Brotherlee
Wolsingham
Sunniside
Crook
B6301
Wear
A68

South Tyne
B6277

DURHAM

2

Culgaith
Temple Sowerby
COW GREEN RESERVOIR
Tees
Newbiggin
B6278
Middleton-in-Teesdale
Egglestone
B6282
Gaunless
Staindrop
Eden
B6276
Romaldkirk
B6279

Appleby-in-Westmorland
A66
Barnard Castle
A688
Winston

3

Great Asby
Warcop
Brough
Bowes
Greta
Greta Bridge
Smallways
Caldwell
Forcett
East Layton
B6260
Eden
Soulby
Kirkby Stephen
Ravensworth
A66
Gilling West

Orton
A685
Tan Hill
Langthwaite
Richmond

2

38
Tebay
B6270
Keld
Thwaite
Gunnerside
Healaugh
Reeth
Marrick
Hudswell
Hipswell

4

Ravenstonedale
A683
Muker
Low Row
B6270
Swale
B6270
Bellerby
Hunton

Cotterdale
Castle Bolton
Wensley
Leyburn
Constable Burton

37

Sedbergh
Ure
Hardraw
Askrigg
Carperby
Redmire
West Witton
Spennithorne
S
Bainbridge
A684
Aysgarth
Middleham
East Witton

Dent
Hawes
West Burton
Coverham
A6108

5

Lune
Barbon
Stalling Busk
B6160
Thoralby
Newbiggin-in-Bishopdale
Carlton-in-Coverdale
B6254

YORKSHIRE DALES
NORTH YORKSHIRE
Yockenthwaite
Cray
Ilton

Kirkby Lonsdale
Ribblehead
Hubberholme
Buckden
Middlesmoor
Lofthouse

6

Chapel le Dale
Starbotton
Kettlewell
Ramsgill
A65
NATIONAL PARK
Litton
Thornton-in-Lonsdale
Far Westhouse
Ingleton
Horton in Ribblesdale
Helwith Bridge
Arncliffe
B6480
Newby
Stainforth
Kilnsey
Pateley Bridge
Wilsill
Low Bentham
Clapham
Austwick Feizor
Langcliffe
Conistone
Grassington
B6265
Bewerley
Nidd

Wray
Keasden
Giggleswick
Threshfield
Hebden
Appletreewick
B6451

7

Rathmell
Settle
Malham
Linton
Thorpe
Burnsall
Blubberhouses
Wigglesworth
Long Preston
Airton
Cracoe
B6265
Storiths
Slaidburn
Tosside
Rylstone
Embsay
Bolton Abbey
A59
Paythorne
Ribble
A65
A682
Coniston Cold
Gargrave
Skipton
A59
Wharfe
B6160

Bowland Forest
B6478

○ Places to Stay, Eat, Drink or Shop

© MAPS IN MINUTES ™ 2000

6

0   5   10   15

Map 2

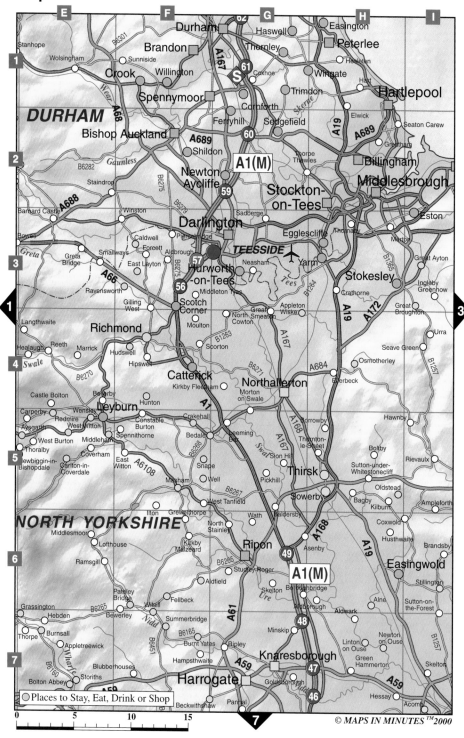

Places to Stay, Eat, Drink or Shop

© MAPS IN MINUTES ™ 2000

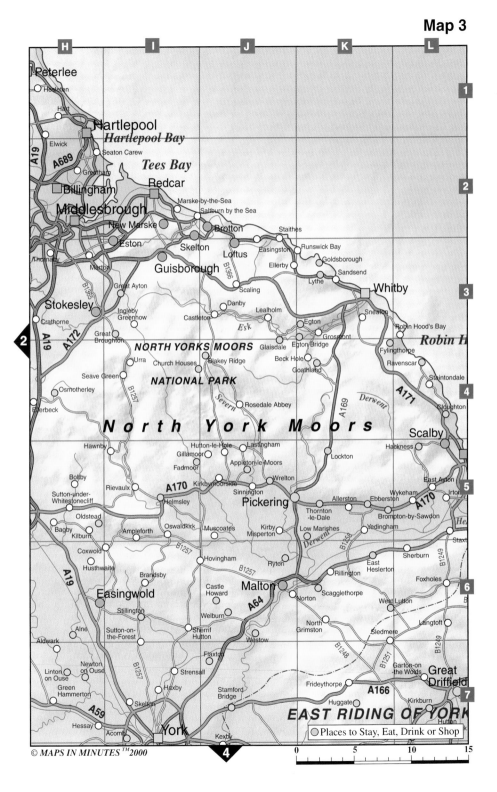

Map 3

Map 4

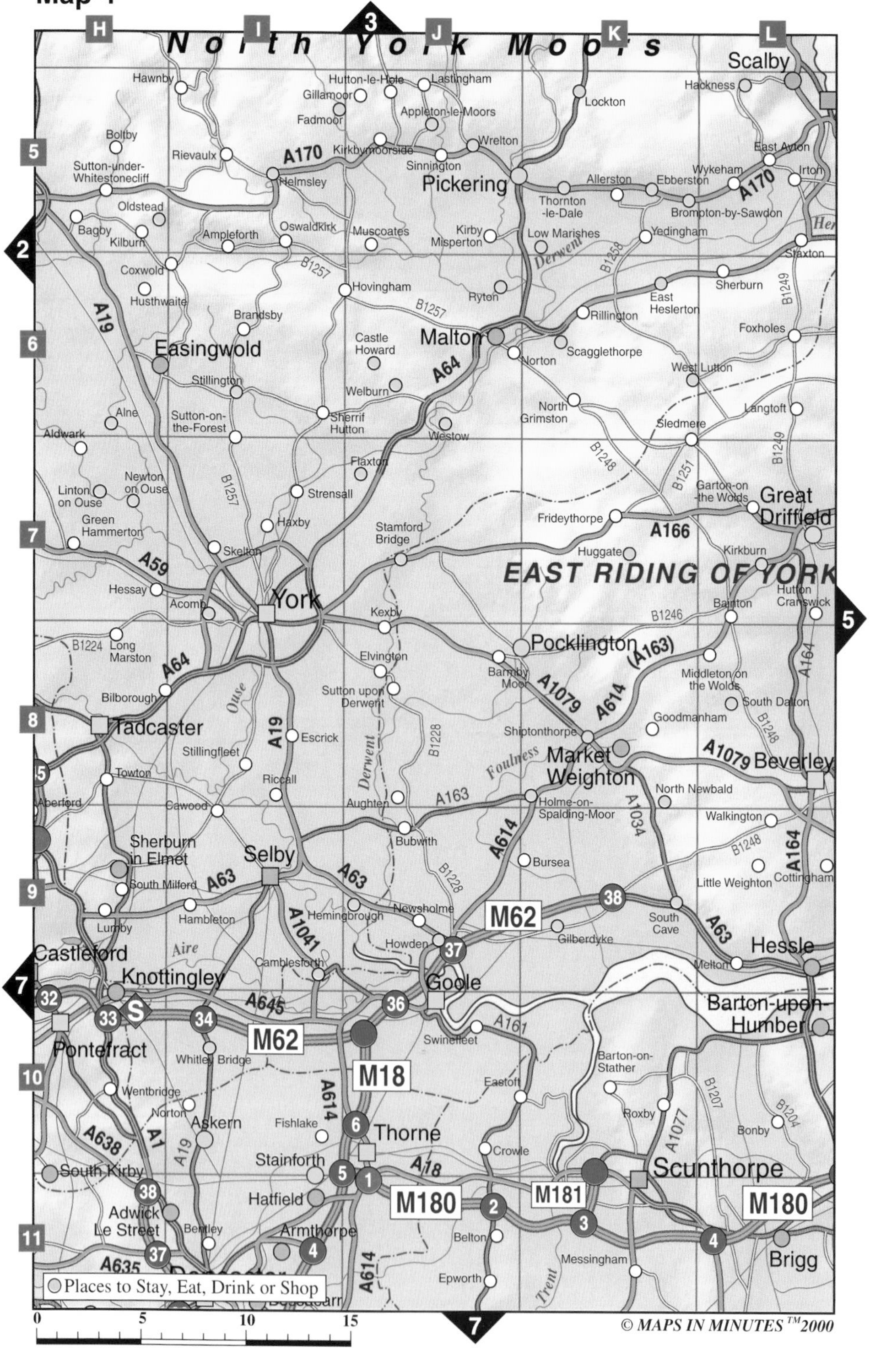

North York Moors

Hawnby
Hutton-le-Hole
Gillamoor
Lastingham
Lockton
Scalby
Hackness
Fadmoor
Appleton-le-Moors
Boltby
Rievaulx
Kirkbymoorside
Wrelton
East Ayton
Irton
Sutton-under-Whitestonecliff
A170
Helmsley
Sinnington
Pickering
Allerston
Ebberston
Wykeham
A170
Oldstead
Ampleforth
Oswaldkirk
Thornton-le-Dale
Brompton-by-Sawdon
Bagby
Kilburn
Muscoates
Kirby Misperton
Low Marishes
Yedingham
Staxton
Coxwold
B1257
Hovingham
B1257
Ryton
Derwent
B1258
East Heslerton
Sherburn
B1249
Husthwaite
Malton
Rillington
Foxholes
Brandsby
Castle Howard
Norton
Scagglethorpe
West Lutton
A19
Easingwold
A64
Welburn
North Grimston
Langtoft
Stillington
Sheriff Hutton
Westow
Sledmere
B1248
B1251
B1249
Alne
Sutton-on-the-Forest
Flaxton
Garton-on-the-Wolds
Great Driffield
Aldwark
Linton on Ouse
Newton on Ouse
Strensall
Fridaythorpe
A166
Kirkburn
Green Hammerton
B1257
Haxby
Stamford Bridge
Huggate
Balton
Hutton Cranswick
A59
Skelton
York
EAST RIDING OF YORK
Hessay
Acomb
Kexby
B1246
A164
Long Marston
B1224
Elvington
Pocklington
Bilborough
A64
Sutton upon Derwent
Barmby Moor
A1079
A614 (A163)
Middleton on the Wolds
South Dalton
A19
Escrick
Shiptonthorpe
Goodmanham
B1248
Tadcaster
Stillingfleet
Riccall
Foulness
Market Weighton
Beverley
A1079
Towton
Cawood
Aughton
A163
Holme-on-Spalding-Moor
North Newbald
Walkington
B1248
A164
Aberford
Sherburn in Elmet
Selby
A63
Bubwith
A614
Bursea
Little Weighton
Cottingham
South Milford
A63
B1228
Newsholme
M62
38
South Cave
A63
Hessle
Lumby
Hambleton
Hemingbrough
Howden
Gilberdyke
Melton
Castleford
Aire
Camblesforth
37
Goole
Barton-upon-Humber
Knottingley
A1041
36
A161
Barton-on-Stather
32
S
34
A645
M62
Swinefleet
B1207
33
Whitley Bridge
M18
Eastoft
Roxby
A1077
Bonby
B1204
Pontefract
Wentbridge
Norton
Fishlake
Thorne
Crowle
Scunthorpe
M180
Askern
6
Stainforth
A18
Belton
3
Brigg
South Kirby
A638
A1
A19
5
1
M180
2
M181
4
Adwick Le Street
38
Hatfield
Armthorpe
Messingham
Bentley
4
Epworth
Trent
37
A635

○ Places to Stay, Eat, Drink or Shop

0   5   10   15